Nourishment

A Philosophy of the Political Body

Corine Pelluchon

Translated by Justin E. H. Smith, and revised by François Cambien and Corine Pelluchon

BLOOMSBURY ACADEMIC
LONDON · NEW YORK · OXFORD · NEW DELHI · SYDNEY

BLOOMSBURY ACADEMIC
Bloomsbury Publishing Plc
50 Bedford Square, London, WC1B 3DP, UK
1385 Broadway, New York, NY 10018, USA

BLOOMSBURY, BLOOMSBURY ACADEMIC and the Diana logo are trademarks
of Bloomsbury Publishing Plc

First published in France, Les nourritures: philosophies du corps politique,
© Editions du Seuil, 2015

Copyright to the translation © Corine Pelluchon, 2019

Corine Pelluchon has asserted her right under the Copyright, Designs and
Patents Act, 1988, to be identified as Author of this work.

Cover design: Eleanor Rose
Cover image © Adam Burton/Nature Picture Library/Getty Images

A catalogue record for this book is available from the British Library.

A catalog record for this book is available from the Library of Congress.

ISBN: HB: 978-1-3500-7388-3
PB: 978-1-3500-7389-0
ePDF: 978-1-3500-7387-6
eBook: 978-1-3500-7390-6

Typeset by Deanta Global Publishing Services, Chennai, India
Printed and bound in Great Britain

To find out more about our authors and books visit www.bloomsbury.com
and sign up for our newsletters.

Contents

What is eating? How is this metonymy of introjection to be regulated? ... 'One must eat well' [il faut bien manger] does not mean above all taking in and grasping in itself, but learning and giving to eat, learning to-give-the-other-to-eat. One never eats entirely on one's own: this constitutes the rule underlying the statement, 'One must eat well.' It is a rule offering infinite hospitality. ... This evokes a law of need or desire ... orexis, hunger, and thirst ... respect for the other at the very moment when, in experience ... one must begin to identify with the other, who is to be assimilated, interiorized, understood ideally ... speak to him or her in words that also pass through the mouth, the ear, and sight, and respect the law that is at once a voice and a court. ... The sublime refinement involved in this respect for the other is also a way of 'Eating well,' in the sense of 'good eating' but also 'eating the Good' [le Bien manger]. The Good can also be eaten. And it, the good, must be eaten and eaten well.

Jacques Derrida, 'Il faut bien manger ou le calcul du sujet', Points de suspension.*

*Jacques Derrida, *Points ... Interviews, 1974–1994*, trans. P Kamuf et al., Stanford, Stanford University Press, 1995, pp. 282–3.

Introduction

'In the beginning was hunger', Levinas writes in his *Carnets de captivité*. Thus is the body the starting point of our experience. It beats back the pretension that consciousness is at the origin of all sense, and requires that we take into consideration the materiality of our existence. For the original and primitive character of hunger signifies that existence is not understood in its essence as 'project'. We are immersed in a sensible world, which is not only inhabited by human beings, nor even fashioned by them alone.

It is not the distinction between human beings and other living beings that is in question here. The notion of comportment, dear to Merleau-Ponty, is sufficient to inspire us to recall the efforts of contemporary philosophy, well known today, to confer to other species a moral status that is radically different from that of things, and to think of animals not simply as living beings, but as other existences.[1] Life no longer possesses the ontological poverty to which it was reduced by mechanism and by all the philosophies that conceived freedom as the absolute beginning and as a tearing-out from nature. This re-evaluation of life went together with the consideration of sensibility as susceptibility to pain and pleasure, and with the rehabilitation of the sensible, which is no longer assimilated to a confused representation. The idea of 'world' itself has been enriched by this phenomenology of the living, and by the work of ethologists who are shifting the boundaries between nature and culture, freedom and instinct.

These results constitute a theoretical attainment, although in practice we have not drawn out all the consequences, as testified by the violence that is still so present in our relationships with animals. However, there is a dimension of human freedom, and even of ethics, that has not yet been sufficiently examined. It concerns the fact that my liberty is exercised not only in a world and on nature, but that I am immersed in a milieu that is at once natural and artificial, and that I live – which is to say that I feed myself – from this milieu, from the air, the light, the foods, the work, the sights. Now, taking into consideration the corporeality of the subject who 'lives from' presupposes the fact that we insist on the conditions of existence that are at once biological, social, and environmental, ceasing to separate man from nature, and going beyond the dualism of nature and culture.

The corporeality of the subject

Environmental ethics, which first emerged in the 1970s, showed that every enterprise of domination of nature relies on a poor understanding of our dependence on it with respect to the conditions of our existences. Environmental ethics was opposed to the representation of human being that makes him into a being external to nature and an empire within an empire, exerting his action on an environment whose value and finality are relative to the usage that he makes of it. These philosophies however – if we think of English-language environmental ethics descending from Aldo Leopold, or Hans Jonas's ethics of the future – have not proposed an ontology capable of providing a conceptual basis for the social and political organization that the ecologists have called for.

To be the starting point of an 'imaginary creation … putting other significations at the center of human life than the expansion of production and consumption and positing different objectives of life, which could be recognized by human beings as worthwhile',[2] ecology should have been placed at the heart of a philosophy of existence. Now, even environmental philosophers, who today go beyond clichés about the opposition between anthropocentrism and ecocentrism, are not able to draw forth any significations or affects different from those that left us with the possession of material goods at the centre of our lives. This is why ecology remains, for individuals as for collectivities, a peripheral concern.

Ecology has not succeeded in improving our relationship to others, to work, to our bodies, and to ourselves, since it remains external to our lives. Moreover, the protection of the biosphere, the right of future generations to benefit from a healthy environment, and the interests of other species barely change our definition of politics, which continues to be conceived as a two-player game, exclusively concerned with actual people and with nations. Taking environmental considerations seriously has not really transformed democracy; it did not lead to revise the deliberative bodies, to reinforce the participation of citizens, and to change the manner the content and the argumentation of political programs are conceived. The terms of the social contract, which ecology compels us to reformulate, remain the same: the fact of doing harm to real people is the only constraint on my freedom.

Nowhere has it been possible to prevent the secondarization of ecology, whose transversal, global, and long-term dimensions cannot be taken into consideration within the context of atomistic politics, where a measure taken in one domain contradicts what is done in another. Finally, ecology has hardly been able to inspire a model of economic development that constitutes an alternative to capitalism.[3] This latter is in its nature as indifferent to the environment as it is disastrous for subjectivity and for human relations. Founded on the principle of overproduction, which does not take into account the external limits that nature places on all activity, it maintains, thanks to marketing and publicity, a true mystification, creating needs that are perpetually new and perpetually frustrated.[4]

Our inability to truly take ecology into consideration is not inevitable. It is explained by the fact that ecology has remained cut off from a philosophical investigation of existence. Philosophers of freedom, from contractualists to existentialists, have not sufficiently taken the measure of what it means, for us, to inhabit the earth. As for environmental ethics, its contribution is more critical than constructive: it has brought into question the foundations of morality and of law, but it has not penetrated into all domains of social and political life. It has been unable to change our behaviour because it has not articulated an ecology out of the human condition, and has addressed itself exclusively to reason.

The ambition for a philosophical reflection that thinks ecology *and* existence, and that conceives human freedom as being-in-the-world *and* being-in-nature, is to elaborate a different ontology than the one that is associated with the philosophers of freedom and with the existential analytic developed by Heidegger in *Being and Time*. The idea in this book is to identify structures of existence, or existentials, that translate the belonging of human beings to a reality which is both natural and cultural and from which they draw their nourishment. The emphasis here is no longer placed on what should or should not be done by the subject of responsibility in his or her relation to other human beings, to other species, and in his or her use of nature: we thus pass from a philosophy of the subject to an ontology, which follows from the description of the fundamental structures of the human existent in interaction with his or her milieu and with other existents. The things from which I draw life are not given as objects or as utensils, even when I make use of them, but rather trace a horizon where utility and production are not primitive. This is why they are called 'nourishment'.

The sense of human existence and the conception of freedom and of temporality are renewed from the moment we begin to consider the existentials that are connected with 'living from'. The latter are situated in the extension of the philosophy of corporeality elaborated by a number of contemporary phenomenologists, and sketched in my own earlier works, *L'autonomie brisée* and *Éléments pour une éthique de la vulnérabilité*.[5] To deepen this reflection on the corporeality of the subject leads to an integration of a dimension that has often been set aside by Western thinkers in their description of the human condition. Ecology will serve as the starting point for reckoning with this fundamental lacuna.

'Ecology' comes from *oikos*, which in Greek means 'home', 'hearth', and 'habitat', and *logos*, which denotes discourse, reason, and science. Ecology is the study of the milieus in which living beings live and reproduce. It is the science of the milieus and of the conditions of existence of living beings, which is to say of human beings and of animals, which are sentient beings in the sense that they experience pain; as well as of plants, which interact with their milieu; and of ecosystems, which are not organisms and are not irritable, but which develop and which have a capacity of resilience that can be threatened by the way in which we exploit it. Ecology goes together with the recognition that we act on these milieus and that we also depend on them and on other living beings. This field is at the intersection of several disciplines and of several sciences, which all have in common the interrogation of our conditions of existence and of the manner in which we inhabit the earth.[6]

The verb 'to inhabit' is by itself sufficient to challenge the dualism between nature and culture discussed above. It suggests that the world of human beings, despite its specificities, is not independent of the soil, of the elements, of ecosystems, and of the climate. The role of geography is equally central in a history that is not exclusively that of social groups or of social struggles. 'To inhabit' comes from the Latin *habitare*, which signifies dwelling, having this or that manner of being (*habituari*), this or that habit.[7] It is only after 1050 that the verb comes to denote the fact of staying somewhere and of occupying a dwelling. A habitat, which is part of the original vocabulary of botany and zoology, is the territory occupied by the plant in its natural state and, from 1881, the term has served to name the geographical milieu, the ecological niche of any animal or vegetal species. It is for the naturalists the 'ultimate expression of the form of life', and gives indications as much concerning the geographical milieu with respect to morphological characters and behaviour.[8] Finally, a habitation (*habitatio*) is the house, and also the habit that permits somebody to play their role. Prior to becoming a lodging or a home, it makes reference to the term *habitus*, which is to say the ensemble of frames that permit individuals to situate themselves autonomously in relation to them.

Thus the habitation is the 'process of configuring a place of sojourn', the 'product of a slow and unpredictable appropriation' by the individuals involved in this process; it relates to 'the complex ensemble of actions, of memories and of identities that are attached to it'.[9] It also implies that we reflect on our cohabitation with other species, which are our 'fellow voyagers … in the odyssey of evolution'.[10] Moreover, degradation of the urban and rural habitat raises the problem of the transmission of knowledge and of respect for the heritage left by our ancestors.

To speak of ecology and to take the *oikos*, the home of earthlings, seriously, thus leads us to go beyond the question of the responsible use we might make of resources. Certainly, this important problem is at the heart of any investigation of the environment conceived as a milieu from which human beings take the resources useful for their life and economic development. However, to think about the manner in which I inhabit the earth and in which I do or do not cohabit with other species, to speak not of resources but of nourishment, is to go further than any philosophy of the environment. It is to take a path that is assuredly not that of sustainable development.

Rather than declaring that it is a matter of reconciling economic growth, the protection of the biosphere, or the management of limited resources and social justice, philosophical reflection, when it is inspired by ecology, articulates all the dimensions of existence, from morality to aesthetics, passing through agriculture, education, economy, urbanization, and architecture. Ethics by itself is less of an interrogation of the moral status of different entities than it is a position within existence. It is indissociable from a reflection on the subject and on his/her relationship to the other. It is also a calling into question of his/her freedom through the existence of others, whom I must not deprive of access to nourishment, and on whom I must not impose a diminished life.

Inseparable as it is from a first philosophy exposing the fundamental structures of existence, ethics has to do essentially with the limits that I place on my freedom to act in the struggle for existence and in view of my development, which is an economic development as well. Ecology, far from being a simple field of specialized studies, on the contrary imposes a renewal of the philosophy that has served until now as the foundation of ethics and politics. It goes together with a complete reconfiguration of autonomy, which is 'true freedom ... that necessary self-limitation, not only with respect to the rules of social behavior but also in the rules we adopt in our behavior toward the environment'.[11] Finally, it opens up the path to a new social contract.

To make ecology into a philosophical question, to think about the *oikos*, is not to say that human beings are *like* the other species. Of course, animals experience empathy and are able to help one another, including animals that belong to different species. However, if the existence of certain animal and vegetal species may be threatened by the disappearance of other species, only human beings are able to deplore this disappearance. Moreover, our technological power is infinitely superior to animal industry. This power, in view of its scale and of the irreversible character of certain of its consequences, which today extend over several thousand years and affect an incalculable number of living beings, no longer has any common measure with the technology of our ancestors. But human beings also have the capacity to take care of other species and of future generations. This is the definition of responsibility that, in contrast with compassion, does not require the presence in flesh and in blood of those for whom I am responsible. Our responsibility even goes beyond our abilities of identification, indeed of representation, as when our actions have repercussions on thousands or even millions of people, or when they mortgage the conditions of life of individuals to come.

In leading us to truly take into consideration the conditions of our existence, and thus to think about that from which we live and which constitutes us as much as we fashion it, ecology leads us to no longer represent human beings as subjects and nature as an object. Our existence cannot be separated from that on which we depend; nature cannot be conceived by glossing over human beings and the manner in which they have transformed it over the course of centuries – as the landscapes teach us, which are the 'looks' at places. The objective of this book is not to present an ethics of the environment that is tied to the status conferred to the different entities and to the different legitimate uses that we make of it, but rather to propose a philosophy of existence that integrates what ecology teaches us about 'living from', and to deduce from this a political organization connected to the elaboration of a new social pact.

The latter is different from the one that we know today, to the extent that the protection of the biosphere, the interests of future generations, and respect for other living beings, in particular for animals, must be placed at the centre of politics. They thus determine the new duties of the state, and give a place not only to institutional innovations, but also to changes in the way we think about counter-powers, cultural politics, the relationship between those who govern and those who are governed, the content and the tenor of political programmes and debates, and the formation of citizens and of their representatives. Much more, in this political theory, which above all concerns, like Rousseau's *Social Contract*, the principles of political right, a phenomenology of nourishment that flows from a philosophy of corporeality and of 'living from' comes to play the role that the fiction of a state of nature played for the contractualists.

'Living from' is living as much from good food as from air and light, from cinema, from strolling, from work, love, sleep, the city and the country. Our milieu is essentially hybrid. Reflection on the conditions of existence and on 'living from', already present in all philosophy of corporeality that is attentive to what escapes our intentionality, finds in ecology the occasion for an unprecedented deepening, for one need not simply focus on the alteration of the body, which was at the centre of the ethics of vulnerability, that we have elaborated in our previous books. The latter stressed the tight connection between vulnerability as fragility, or need of the Other, and vulnerability as an openness towards the Other, or responsibility for the Other. Of course, I am responsible for the Other and touched by him, concerned by what happens to him, because I am a wounded subject, sensitive to pain, to ageing, who does not want to die alone or abandoned. But what happens when we integrate into our reflection not only fragility, alteration of the body, and the incompleteness of the psyche, but also pleasure, the fact that what we live from does not subjugate us, but makes us happy, like the dessert that I taste, the landscape whose beauty I admire, the water of the sea that relaxes me, the love of another, the presence of beings that are similar to me, such as that of animals, even the most untameable ones, the art that elevates me and the city I live in, even the work that is as carnal as it is intellectual, that is carnal even when it is intellectual?

A phenomenology of nourishment

'Nourishment' refers to that from which we live and of which we have need, the milieu in which we move, everything we procure for ourselves, the manner in which we procure it, our exchanges, the circuits of distribution, the techniques that condition our moving about, our habitations, our works, but also the ecosystems, constituted from biocenoses – that is, from living beings that exist there and of which we often do not have knowledge – and from biotopes, defined by their physical and chemical characteristics. To speak of nourishment goes beyond the dualism of nature and culture. It does not allow us to go on conceiving of nature as a resource that has no other value than an instrumental one.

Things, including technological objects, not only offer themselves to us as utensils, but are also the conditions of our existence. This reversal of the stance of representation was already present in the phenomenological conception of the world, notably in Merleau-Ponty, who exposed the reciprocity between consciousness of the self and consciousness of the world, and underlined their interlacing in every perception. However, in speaking of 'nourishment' we are making an additional step in the direction of a philosophy in which existence is 'a relation with an object and at the same time a relation with this relation which also nourishes and fills life'.[12]

There follows another way of conceiving the 'external' milieu, the alterity of nourishment, the forests, the lakes, and the plants, the seasons, the city, the roads, the foodstuffs. What is thought is my existence in and with these elements, which are not simple resources that I use, nor the not-I on which and against which I would exercise my will. Moreover, these conditions of my existence are also the conditions of the existence of others. They have been fabricated by time, which is as much that of evolution as that which the history and technology of human beings have transformed. Analysis of the corporeality of the subject, as we will see in particular in the case of birth, at once introduces us to intersubjectivity. We are bound to others through our relationship to nourishment which underlines, moreover, the interdependence of species.

What is more, that which I need in order to live constitutes me not only insofar as it permits me to subsist, but also, and above all, insofar as it gives value to my existence, or rather a taste, a savour. The value of life does not result from a judgement concerning the quality of the things of which I make use, nor concerning their energetic performance; it is in the taste that things have for me, in the manner in which, in incorporating them, I love life. Need and subsistence are only separated from this lived experience when I suffer from privation. To detach the use of things and their finality from this incorporation is to miss the relation that I maintain with them, which is above all a relation of enjoyment.

Life in the world of nourishment is enjoyment, since I take pleasure in living. Even before I knew myself and had started to take care of myself, before I projected myself in time by bringing into existence that which has value in my eyes, I love life. I am love of life before I am freedom. This love of life envelopes my freedom. It is expressed in the fact that the things from which I live delight me: 'The love of life does not resemble the care for being,'[13] but it is joy of being. Life is loved: it is its own end in itself. It is not a matter however of an existence riveted to its needs. It is when life is a life of poverty that privations impose need beyond pleasure. Hunger, cold, and forced labour explain that I throw myself onto foods without enjoying them but only because they help me recuperate an energy that will enable me to return to work.[14]

To say that life in a world of nourishment is the love of life is to say that a fundamental structure of the existence of this being, for which in its being the meaning of being is at stake, is the taste, the savour that things have for it, their beauty and everything in them that is pleasing. Rather than opposing enjoyment to ethics, it is thus a matter of thinking about the importance of this dimension that permits us to understand the manner in which human beings inhabit the earth. Enjoyment – distinct from certain pleasure in Epicurus's sense, one of the merits of which is to underline the connection between happiness and virtue – also refers in the present work to taste and to aesthetic pleasure, which not only is a distinct pleasure reserved for art, but also characterizes our manner of being in all domains of life.

In contrast to Levinas, we do not think that the passage from the relationship to the self to the relationship to the other and to others, from the place of enjoyment to that of ethics, constitutes a rupture.[15] Certainly, enjoyment is not morality. It is an egotistical quiver, as the popular wisdom in this adage conveys: 'A famished stomach has no ears.' What is more, it is the existence of the Other that calls into question my freedom. It is his or her needs that test what Levinas calls 'good right' or 'good consciousness of freedom', which is to say my right to do what I want to do and to consume what I desire.[16] Even the philosophy of human rights does not draw all the consequences of what the right of other human beings requires of me and of society. Supporting a negative conception of liberty, we are assuredly more inclined to recognize the rights to which we individually have access than our duties towards the other man and other human beings and other species as well, that are limitations placed on our greed.

Thus in speaking of the sensible world as that of nourishment, and in insisting on the vulnerability of the man who is hungry, Levinas is resolutely opposed to the philosophies that think of human beings first of all as freedom and define it as the capacity to make choices and to change them.[17] In these philosophies the care of the self is not disturbed by fear for the Other, nor by the question, without reply, of my right to be – this fear that 'my place in the sun' is 'a usurpation of places that belong to the other man, already oppressed by me or hungry'.[18] In this sense one cannot deny that the Other, who is mortal and who might not have access to nourishment, takes away my pleasure, or, as Levinas would say, 'instructs me'. Nonetheless, the objective of this work is to show that prior to the face-to-face encounter with the Other, as soon as I stand in relation to nourishment, I am already in the domain of ethics.

Even if I do not meet the other physically, the other and others are present in the milieu that is at once natural and artificial from which I nourish myself. My manner of consuming nourishment has consequences for the others. More fundamentally, my relationship to nourishment is itself a position in existence that arises out of ethics. If human beings nourish themselves from the elements within which they move, such as the air, then ethics cannot be limited to our relations with other human beings. It must take into consideration everything on which we depend, the beings that have fashioned the milieu from which we live today, and all those that maintain it or with which we share our nourishment. Ethics is *already* to be sought in our relationship to nourishment.

Ethics is the dimension of my relationship with others, human and non-human, established by my relationship with nourishment. In my manner of using resources and energy, of encouraging certain agricultural productions, of nourishing myself, I am already in relation with other men whose activity, and therefore also whose life, I support, or on whom my action has or will have an influence that is the more decisive in that it is the result of daily choices. As soon as I consume, as soon as I conduct myself in the world in a certain way in buying products, in getting around in my car, in throwing a cigarette butt on the ground, I am already in the domain of ethics. Prior to the face-to-face encounter with the Other who is in his exteriority the source of ethics – that is to say who introduces me to a way of being or to a dimension of human life that has nothing to do with knowledge or even with the contest of rival freedoms in quest of recognition – prior to the encounter with the face of the Other who designates me as responsible, there is the world of nourishment. My relation to nourishment is the original site of ethics.

This way of thinking about ethics does not take anything away from the fact that my relationship to the other is distinguished from my relationship to animals and to trees, and that it is governed by moral norms that I cannot always apply to other species. However, ethics not only is the dimension of my relationship to others; it also depends on my relationship to nourishment. Indeed, nourishment does not appear all on its own: it requires other people's work and poses the problem of sharing with other human beings and other species. Justice, the fact that our way of inhabiting the earth and of preserving its beauty pertains to ethics and politics, as well as the importance that nourishment has for us when we take pleasure in it – or when the destruction of it also harms us intimately, as if 'the world is one's body'[19] – implies that fields that are ordinarily separated, such as morality, politics, ecology, and aesthetics, are integrated within a philosophy of existence and with its underlying ontology.

To think about the world as nourishment is not to use a simple image in order to illustrate the manner in which the external becomes internal, as when I ingest food, digest it, and derive energy from it. The reference to alimentation reveals a philosophy that seeks to go beyond the dichotomy between the biological and the cultural, the intimate and the collective, the private sphere and social life, personal taste and family habits. Moreover, the affirmation of the centrality of hunger not only serves to underline the fragility of man and his susceptibility to pain, but also the fact that withholding nourishment has weakening and death as its consequence. It also radicalizes the reflection on our corporeality, which is 'a permanent contestation of the prerogative attributed to consciousness of "giving meaning" to each thing'.[20]

The emphasis is however not placed on passivity alone, as had been the case in the ethics of vulnerability. Pleasure, the pleasure of the eyes and of the palate, taste, and the need for novelty renew our comprehension of our dependence with respect to the conditions of our existence. They also renew our understanding of what it means, for us, to inhabit the earth, installing or reinstalling aesthetics at the centre of our ethics. Would we accept the degradation of ecosystems, the destruction of landscapes, and the abominable conditions of life that factory farming inflicts on animals if taste, rather than being one sense among others, or rather than signifying the belonging of individuals to a social class, were that which connected our senses to our heart and to our spirit, like *Gemüt* in Kant?[21]

Our dependence with respect to the conditions of our existence is also a dependence with respect to the Other, or, rather, a need that we have of the Other, of their body, work, knowledge, and know-how. We are never alone when we use the highway, when we cross a bridge, or when we read. Others before us, others at the same time as ourselves, bring it about that such actions are possible. However, this interdependence becomes evident in the act of eating, and it gives a paradigmatic character to this socionatural fact.

Eating is actually always eating with and through others, for the foodstuffs that I consume have been prepared by someone who has cooked them, whether I know them or not, or who has planted the tree from which I gather fruits. Our foodstuffs presuppose that we have produced and harvested wheat, and connect up with the systems of agriculture and distribution, and with the world economy which, as a function of yields and of reserves, determines the price of basic foods, like the grains that serve as food for human beings and cattle. Not only the culinary art, the culture, and generosity of those men and women who have taken the time to cook and to transmit their recipes from one generation to the next, but also what I eat, which is to say those whom I eat or whom I refuse to kill in order to feed myself, are implicated in this everyday act.

Our responsibility in relation to other human beings and to other living beings is engaged each time we eat, whether we are fully conscious of this or not. Eating connects us to other beings, human and non-human, to the circuits of production and of exchange, to the means of transportation. To eat is to dispute any separation between the disciplines, and to position oneself within existence, to be at once in the domains of ethics and of politics. The boundaries between the material and the spiritual evaporate, as in the religious rites in which prohibitions and precautions have always surrounded the act of eating, in particular when it came to eating the flesh of an animal. It is in this way, going beyond any hollow discourse of ethics and justice, that Levinas affirms that spirituality is the gesture of feeding 'a third world ravaged by hunger', and speaks in this connection of a 'sublime materialism'.[22]

When studied in light of a phenomenology of eating, the human being is not conceived as a being separate from other living beings who themselves are looking for food. However, the art of eating, the social dimension of food and conviviality, and the troubles that may be linked to our relationship with food, as seen in anorexia and obesity, all suggest the differences that exist between human beings and animals. To think that we live from soup, air, spectacles, work, ideas, sleep, as Levinas said, and to speak of all the links that we have with other human beings, be they past, present, or future, with all those who live far from us and with other species, leads us to a phenomenological description of the structures of our existence that has nothing to do with Heidegger's existential analytic.

Revising the existential analytic: Ontology and politics

Uncovering the corporeality of the subject is already a critique of Heidegger's ontology. But, in addition, the idea that existence is defined by care (*Sorge*) is undermined once we insist on the dimension of pleasure. We do not eat *in order to* live, except when we barely have enough to survive on: 'We breathe for the sake of breathing, eat and drink for the sake of eating and drinking, we take shelter for the sake of taking shelter, we study to satisfy our curiosity, we take a walk for the walk. All that is not for the sake of living, it is living. Life is a sincerity.'[23]

Nourishment can only be interpreted as a utensil or as a carburant in a world of exploitation, Levinas writes, after remarking that the utensil and utility mask, in Heidegger, the usage of things and their ultimate end, which is satisfaction or pleasure.[24] Finally, while speaking of nourishment, which connects us to other human beings and to other species, we articulate existence and ecology at a level that is not only that of ethics, but also that of ontology, the philosophy that we construct cannot be an abstract and egoistish philosophy (*une philosophie du pour soi*). Care for our own existence is enveloped in pleasure and satisfaction. Love of life precedes the project, which is to say that being-towards-death is not, in a phenomenology of nourishment, as fundamental or originary as it is in Heidegger. Moreover, the fact of eating things, and then the worry that these things might be absent, the work and the effort that I must undertake in order to bring about good conditions of existence, take me out of my solitude. From the start, I am even in a world that is not only a world of human beings. This milieu is not a simple springboard propelling me towards my freedom. It traces back to conscious and unconscious connections with other human beings and with other living beings, to the relations taken up with them, or to a way of exploiting them that is the product of a denial of these connections of dependence with them. This milieu also underlines the vulnerability of the human beings who are positioned at the extreme end of the food chain and who endure the consequences of the pollution that affects fish or the viruses that are contracted by birds and cattle.

In addition, our time is intertwined within a larger time frame, which is not only that of history, but also of nature, and even, for each of us, of the seasons and of the alternation of day and night.[25] Even those who live at night and who sleep during the day need to rest. They need this alternation like they need light, air, and water. The way in which Heidegger thinks of human temporality does not take this reality into consideration. He says that authentic temporality is the projection of the self in view of the possibility of the impossibility of one's existence: Doesn't this idea reveal a philosophy of freedom in which mortality, contingency, facticity, or the loss of the self in anonymity, which characterize human beings, are thought without paying attention to other conditions of our existence, such as nature, climate, milieu, and our interdependence with other living beings?

On a number of occasions Levinas writes that Heidegger's *Dasein* is never hungry.[26] A being that is hungry and thirsty and that experiences cold does not think of freedom as a conquest of self; for it, what counts is no longer suffering from privation, and experiencing pleasure, tasting life. Does not forgetfulness of this dimension go together with the manner in which Heidegger interprets existence, separating it from life and bringing almost exclusively to light its 'ek-static' dimension? What are we to think of the division it sets up between the beings that are present-at-hand or ready-at-hand, and that he defines in terms of the utility and the finality that we attribute to them, on the one hand, and on the other *Dasein*, which alone 'ek-sists' and, in existing, reveals the structure of the world and the sense of being?

After taking into consideration the vulnerability of man, which refers to a phenomenology of passivity that underlines not only the alteration of our body, and also openness to the Other and our responsibility for the Other (Levinas), after the deconstruction of the way in which philosophy has thought of the boundaries of morality and has instituted the sovereignty of the subject in opposing human being to animal and in excluding beasts from the moral community (Derrida), the phenomenology of nourishment enables us to examine in a new light the categories that continue to serve as the foundation of the philosophy of the subject, and even of Heidegger's existential analytic, and to elaborate another ontology.

This latter is not a doctrine of being in the sense in which one might speak of an essence of man. The end of metaphysics, understood as a doctrine spelling out what is specific to man, characterizing him as a rational animal or measuring his accomplishment in the light of a finalized conception of being – whether it is theological, as in Christianity, or cosmological, as in Aristotle – is a given. If human beings are engaged in activities that are at once biological and cultural, as we see in the act of eating, they have no nature in the sense of an immutable essence. This is why the phenomenology of nourishment is a philosophy of existence, and not an essentialism. Why, in this case, speak of ontology? Is it because the manners of being of human beings, their manners of existing, would make it possible to reveal the structures of being, to understand being, as in Heidegger?

The answer to this question is negative, for one does not exist in view of being. As in Levinas, we are concerned with the existent, and not with existence. The existent lives from nourishment and encounters the Other. He is neither primarily nor essentially understanding the world, but he is with the world, in contact with the world in sensation. Moreover, the phenomenology of passivity and of 'living from', developed by Levinas in his first works, breaks with the primacy of knowledge and with the posture of mastery that characterizes it. As we have seen, the insistence on the corporeality of the living and on the description of the epiphany of the face draws out significations that are radically different from those that prevailed in earlier philosophies, whether we are thinking of the primacy of knowledge over action, of contractualist theories that reconstruct ethics and politics on the basis of individuals who determine the rules that permit them to coexist and who base sociality on mutual advantage, or of Heidegger.

The latter describes the real by starting out from *pragmata*, those actions of man that are prior to scientific knowledge and that correspond to the manner in which, in his view, things offer themselves to us. The world of Heidegger is marked by technology, by work, by the care of *Dasein* for existence and by a sociality in which solicitude is not able to free anyone from the necessity of facing up, within an irreducible solitude, to his own death. For Levinas, the relation that the self maintains with itself, with the Other, and with others, is not an understanding of being, which justifies his rejection of ontology conceived as the doctrine of being, as well as his affirmation of ethics as first philosophy.

What is more, the phenomenology of passivity and of 'living from' is a philosophy of the sensible and of corporeality, which leads to an original conception of subjectivity. This philosophy, in which responsibility for the Other constitutes ipseity, and of which the ultimate end is the notion of substitution as elaborated in *Otherwise than Being*, is in one sense an ontology. It invites us to think about other possible foundations of political theory than those which characterize contractarianism in its present form, and even the interpretation of the human rights, which serves as the point of reference for international relations and for contemporary discussions of global warming and biodiversity.

Of course, it is not a matter here of developing an ousiology, nor of returning to metaphysics, since the singularity of the face and the transcendence of the Other imply that the Other eludes what I see or know of them, and any reduction to the same, whether this is to gender or to the concept of humanity. Nor is it a question of an ontology in the sense in which Heidegger understands this, or the significations that arise from the relationship of the existent to his or her body and to the Other are richer and less homogeneous than those that flow from an understanding of the world on the basis of intentionality or of the actions of human beings and of a *Dasein* that is essentially preoccupied with its own existence.

What makes Levinas's phenomenology interesting is that it is characterized by an ascent towards an original relationship of the self to the Other, in which the body is grasped through its materiality. The body is the site of responsibility, as we see in the description of maternity, but also in the phenomenology of passivity which culminates in *Otherwise than Being*, where subjectivity is defined as vulnerability. This philosophy of corporeality arises out of ontology.[27] It unveils a sense of existing that is different from the one at the heart of *Being and Time*, and even in the later works of Heidegger. Now, our ambition in this book is to elaborate a philosophy of existence that extends this effort of Levinas, who thought of 'living from' but did not draw the political consequences of his reflection on what he calls the 'elemental' and on the world as nourishment.[28] This is why this phenomenology of nourishment is, in a sense that is important to clarify, an ontology.

The description of existentials connected to 'living from' and to the world of nourishment can give rise to ethical, political, and legal innovations that are able to help us in facing up to the current environmental crisis. This not only is a crisis of resources; it also concerns our subjectivity, or relationship to our body and to work, and is connected to the possibility of the participation of individuals within a common world. Even if no fixed and immutable essence of man can serve as a point of reference for ethics and politics, we can still conceive a certain universalism which is distinct from the looming and substantial moralities that impose the moral or religious vision of a group.

This universalism, connected to the enrichment of the notion of world presupposed by a phenomenology of nourishment and by a meditation on the conditions of our existence, can provide some elements to help individuals consent to a transformation in their styles of life, necessary for containment of the environmental crisis and for the dawning of another model of development. The elaboration of an ontology that unveils a sense of existence that the various philosophies of freedom and of history have neglected goes further than a philosophy of the subject that requires our integrating, into the heart of our desire to live, a concern not to impose a diminished life on other human beings and on other species. It can be the introductory chapter of a vast field attending to the renewal of the ethical, legal, and political categories that we need in order to get out of the general impasse into which our model of development has led us.

Thus in the first part of this book, focused on ontology, we will integrate the reflection on the corporeality of the subject and the human condition into a phenomenology of 'living from' and of nourishment. The analysis of the manner in which human beings nourish themselves from the natural and artificial milieu in which they live will bring out significations that permit us to renew or to refresh what we most often speak of in terms of taste and aesthetics, to redefine the connection between agriculture and culture, and to think about the place of urbanism and architecture. Insisting on cohabitation with other living beings, which are at the heart of any reflection on the *oikos*, we will emphasize the place of the animal question within the moral transformation of the subject, which is indispensable, as Rousseau says, for strengthening the social contract.[29] For it is indeed in the hearts of people that the social bond is tied or untied, and that individuals acquire their sense of obligation.[30]

The second part of the book will be devoted to the formulation of the terms of the social pact: we will take up there the political problem as it presents itself to men and women who are conscious of the necessity of bringing ecology and the animal question into the republic. The concern will be to show that the idea of a social pact still has a sense, but that its point of departure is no longer the individual exiled into his own internal freedom, as in contractarianism as it is expressed from Hobbes to Rawls, for whom the social order is reconstructed on the basis of the interplay of egoisms. What rules might structure this social order, when it is founded on an individual who is not self-sufficient and who, in his relationship to himself and to nourishment, already relates to other human beings in the past, present, and future, as well as to other living beings? We will put forward proposals relating to the conditions of deliberation and of participations that might renew democracy, drawing out the consequences in the political realm of the phenomenology of nourishment developed in the first part. The concern will thus be to indicate what this change in the political culture requires in terms of the shaping of individuals and public opinion, and to clarify the sense that cosmopolitanism might have once we know that nature cannot play the role of a simple foundation, nor be considered as the mere decor of history.

Part One

A phenomenology of nourishment

We live from 'good soup', air, light, spectacles, work, ideas, sleep, etc. These are not objects of representations. We live from them. The things we live from are not tools, nor even implements, in the Heideggerian sense of the term. They are always ... objects of enjoyment, presenting themselves to 'taste', already adorned, embellished. ... The constituted ... here overflows its meaning, becomes within constitution the condition of the constituting, or, more exactly, the nourishment of the constituting. This overflowing of meaning can be fixed by the term alimentation. ... The world I live in is not simply the counterpart or the contemporary of thought and its constitutive freedom, but a conditioning and an antecedence. The world I constitute nourishes me and bathes me. It is aliment and 'medium' ['milieu'].[1]

EMMANUEL LEVINAS, *TOTALITY AND INFINITY*

Part One

A
phenomenology
of nourishment

1

Living from

Living is living from. The transitivity of this verb not only signifies that our existence is inseparable from materiality. It also designates the original character of sensing, which is our life in and with things, and cannot be confused with a faculty. To wrest sensation from the register of knowledge is not the same thing as rehabilitating it by refusing to make of it a confused idea and by recognizing in the sensible qualities – the colours of the sky, the smells of flowers, and the tastes of foods – their own value, which is to reveal the world in which we live and to reveal ourselves within it. To sense is fundamentally to be in contact with things and to feel, to enjoy in such a way that one lives the transformations of one's relationship to the world without being able to assimilate one's sensations, which are always particular to the events of one's consciousness or even to perceptions which, by definition, are connected to an object.[1] To sense is to be with the world, to enjoy it sympathetically.[2]

To describe the human condition while taking our corporeality seriously thus amounts to continuing on the path of contesting representation, which is the aim of phenomenology since Husserl.[3] However, the 'ruin of representation' and the end of the division that it imposes between subject and object, between consciousness and the world, are never so evident as when we envision the world as food: to affirm the nourishing character of the world is to say that it could not be reduced to a noeme, to a content constituted by the giving act of sense of a consciousness. The world is more generous than what my utilitarian appreciation suggests. More precisely it cannot be entirely constituted, since what there is that which cannot be constituted in it; what evades objectivization and science as much as it does perception is revealed by my sensations in what they have that is most particular and most gratuitous, in what is in no way subordinated in them to knowledge and does not connect up with a practical function as Heidegger's tool does, nor yet with a need, but with pleasure. Sensation, which is thus distinguished from perception, is in the order of enjoyment. Put another way, one does not content oneself with putting the body in the place of consciousness, though it is the register of the constitution that is found to be utterly called into question.

Enjoyment

Enjoyment testifies to this surplus of the reality of the world that explains that it cannot be entirely constituted and that one can speak of it as food. It awakens the elemental structure of the world: 'In enjoyment, the things revert to their elemental qualities',[4] without seeking to know whether the secondary qualities that constitute the frame of my sensations are faithful to objective reality, to a reality conceived as exterior to myself. Sensation does not target an object; it is not of the same register as knowledge and perception, which refer to a transcendent object. It has however its own truth, or rather, as Levinas says, its own sincerity, in its adherence to a content that makes me content. As in Descartes, whose philosophy of the sensible the author of *Totality and Infinity* welcomes, sensations allow me to orient myself in the world of knowledge and to know what is useful and convenient to me, what I love.[5] In sensation, there is no exteriority, since I move in a universe of qualities devoid of form, which Levinas calls 'the element', and since the anteriority of the sensible materiality of elements to the entire ambient world is that of an affective content:[6] sensibility bites into the element.

This 'sinking of one's teeth into things', which the act of eating illustrates in an exemplary manner, expresses the capacity of that which is constituted to revert into that which constitutes, the reversal of the constituted world into a condition of my existence.[7] Such is the specific contribution of the phenomenology of Levinas: distinguishing itself from Husserl, for whom intentionality still designates a univocal relationship that distinguishes the constituting subject from the constituted object, Levinas radically affirms the sensibility of the subject, underlining at once my dependence with respect to the world, and the generosity of this world that I constitute and in which I move.

Enjoyment, in expressing this surplus, also manifests a form of agreement or harmony between me and the world, as if it were easy to be happy, as if the happiness that we owe to it or that we have forgotten comes from it, were this easiness, this indulgence in the things that nourish us. There is pleasure because the contents that are the means of my subsistence are just as soon sought out as ends, and because 'the pursuit of this end becomes an end in its turn'.[8] The world is food, and the fact of eating testifies to an original relationship to things that is a relationship of enjoyment, in which it is not that I eat in order to live, but rather in which eating is living. Thus, I seek that which I need in order to live, and at the same time, since this fills me with life and satisfies me, I nourish myself on these activities that make me live. Happiness describes this independence in dependence which transforms into a sovereignty of the self, to the extent that the latter takes delight in the things that make it live: they are 'always more than the strictly necessary; they make up the grace of life'.[9]

Of course, this happiness is troubled, since food may not be available. These contents of life, which constitute its value or underline its indigence, are not my being. They are different from my substance and I must procure them or make them through work. My happiness can thus be fragile and my existence precarious, but it should not be thought of in an originary manner as thrownness or being thrown.[10] To designate the world as food and to think the alterity of nourishment is by contrast to affirm that 'life is already loved', and that my primary relationship to things is a relationship of enjoyment. There is a happiness attached to the simple fact of living.[11] The social conditions can make this happiness inaccessible or threaten it. However, the analytic of enjoyment that Levinas opposes in *Totality and Infinity* to the ontology of care refutes the manner in which Heidegger thinks of the primary or originary condition of a human being as tragic.

Far from denying the distress of the many billions of people suffering from hunger or malnutrition, this emphasis of the derivative or secondary character of thrownness indicts unjust social and economic organization. We will discuss this again when we turn to the global food crisis, which is not due to a shortage of resources or to a growth in population, but rather reflects the dysfunctions of our economy and underlines our political responsibility. For now, in elaborating a philosophy of corporeality that permits us to uncover those structures of existence that are often neglected by Western thinkers, it is a matter of insisting on the existential character of enjoyment.

That this should make 'the elemental essence of the world burst forth' testifies to the 'permanent truth of hedonist moralities: to not seek, behind the satisfaction of need, an order relative to which alone satisfaction would acquire a value'; rather, one must 'take satisfaction, which is the very meaning of pleasure, as a term'.[12] This truth of hedonism supposes that we do not consider the human being abstractly, cutting it off from the materiality of its existence, in order then to conceive its need as a limitation of its liberty that proves the tragic character of the human condition. When we truly take seriously the corporeality of the subject, we can no longer think about need as a simple privation, nor can we suppose that the limits placed on our power reflect our thrownness. The hedonism that flows from this philosophy of the sensible thus does not have as a background a thought that is haunted by death or by the regret that life is not such that we can enjoy it without encountering obstacles to our will.

To say that enjoying is touching the element, liberating the elemental structure of the world, is thus to introduce a hedonism that is distinct from that of Epicurus, which only obtains its sense from an obsession with the limits in which it is necessary to contain one's desires in order not to suffer. Contrary to the ancient philosopher who makes of hedonism a wisdom, there is no question here of working on one's representations. Nor is it a matter of sculpting one's life, or of cultivating the art of enjoyment in order to profit from the only good within one's reach, that is to say the present, and to offer to death 'a body that will have burned down to the last flames',[13] as in Michel Onfray, for whom the Hedonist Angel, who competes with Thanatos, maintains the aspect of challenge. The hedonism about which we are speaking is not an effort of the self, nor a morality. It designates the original relationship that we have with the world and with its contents, not what we should do in order to live well. Nevertheless, what it may have in common with the hedonism of Onfray holds to the manner in which the latter invites us to bring the human being back down into its body – and even into its stomach.

It is important to extract hedonism from any morality in order to describe the relationship of human beings with the world that is expressed in sensations, in particular in taste, which of all senses is the most distant from representation. In fact, when I bite into an apple, when a bit of food sits on my tongue, and when I ingest it and incorporate it, drawing from it an energy that reinvigorates me, I am installed within a relationship to things and to the milieu that expresses a truth about the world and about me.

In order to be able to extract this truth and to formulate it, let us thus cease to see a lack in need, as if we only ate in order to fill up a void. Not only is the body, which brings us enjoyment, not an enemy, but, moreover, the world is nourishment. Happiness, even if it is a respite, given that nourishment can be lacking, is in itself an accomplishment lived in the first person, an exaltation connected to the strangeness or alterity of the elements that agree with my taste, that restore my forces, and that increase my vitality. Human life is not represented as if it were primarily and essentially a desperate path towards death. To conceive it as the execution of a programme or of a destiny no more helps us to grasp the sense of existence than to bring out the fundamental structures that permit us to illuminate our being-in-the-world, which is a being-with-things and a habitation of the earth.

To think of enjoyment as an existential is to discover a gourmet ego, which is also a gourmet cogito, for which need is not primarily a care for existence, but a need of nourishment that includes at once the pleasure taken in nourishment, and then also the search for this pleasure and for that which can make it more intense or more subtle. We are thus the closest to our reality, to its concreteness – which etymologically designates that which makes us grow and which constitutes us.

This attachment to nourishment, which is an attachment to the world – of which we will also analyse the difficulties, notably where there is a question of anorexia or bulimia – resembles a game. It expresses the generosity of life and the energy that we place in living, beyond the battle against death. Watching young animals or young children play, Ricœur writes, we get the idea that life begins beyond danger, beyond balance, and that it is generous: 'Perhaps for the living being this is a manner of being which surpasses deathlessness'.[14] Our original relationship to the world is not characterized by negativity but by enjoyment, which is a sort of 'carefreeness with regard to existence'.[15] To live is to 'play, despite the finality and tension of instinct to live from something without this something having the sense of a goal, ... simply play or enjoyment of life'.[16]

Even if taste in the culinary arts and in gastronomy is educated in the search for refined pleasures that elevate us above our primary reality and our animality, it is important not to forget the connection between pleasure and happiness, between appetite and the desire to live. It is equally necessary to not misunderstand this sort of confidence in the nutritive character of the world, which we have from the beginning and which the fact of living originally designates. The sight of the newborn drinking the milk of its mother, concentrating on the breast or on the feeding bottle, and putting all of its being, all of its soul, into sucking, gives an idea of what the original confidence in life, which implies an adhesion to its contents, could be. This greedy character of the newborn, which we also find in animals, its imperious call telling of a hunger, and a thirst that must be appeased, as if it were imperative that the world satisfy them without delay, this hunger, and this thirst that go beyond the need to ingest a nutritive substance without which it would perish, this peace, finally, that it feels after having eaten, and that is more than the simple fact of having the stomach filled testify to our primordial relationship to the world. They illustrate the immersion of our sensibility in the element and the agreement that we expect to find at first glance between our needs and the world.

Enjoyment 'consists in sinking [my] teeth fully into the nutriments of the world, agreeing to [*agréer*] the world as wealth,'[17] knowing myself to be originally in the world that offers to me the contents from which I live. The suckling baby incarnates this life in the element that is sensibility. In enjoyment, I cause to burst forth the elemental essence of the world, its tastes that evade representation, concepts, and in general the register of constitution, and I know that life, whatever the obstacles it encounters and the dangers that stalk it, is love of life. Living is living from, and living from is enjoying.

The gourmet cogito

To think of a gourmet ego behind the thinking subject, more imperious than the *Dasein* with its care for existence, more immersed in the element, and more profoundly connected to the living world than permitted by the representation of the self as freedom, is not only to restore to sensorial certainty its truth. It is also to appreciate anew the place of each of the five senses. This gourmet ego, in view of the connection between the senses and the spirit, is at once a gourmet cogito. To the primacy accorded in the philosophical tradition to vision and to touch, we will oppose the fact of tasting the world. To taste and to smell we must add the description of what it means, for each of us, to breath, to feel the wind on our skin, to be cold or hot, and to be situated on earth.

This taking into consideration of our corporeality, grasped in its thickness and its materiality, in what Levinas calls its 'ontic charge', more nocturnal than any representation, than any constitution of a phenomenon appearing in full light in the external world, does not imply that we become our sensations. If the world is not relative to my representation, if it is not entirely constitutable and decipherable from the standpoint of the giving act of a consciousness that would cause it to appear as an object of knowledge, if it is not completely visible, but recedes from the implicit horizons that my sensations permit me to apprehend, this is because vision cannot be erected as a paradigm for all the senses.[18]

Vision is the model of knowledge and of a relationship of representation to the objectivization of the world: an accessible space is open that permits me to constitute things and objects, and to manipulate them. Vision thus invites the hand to exercise its grasp on things, which become objects, to comprehend them and to dress them with significations in the relationship that they have to other objects. Here we are in the world of Heidegger: a world of tools (*Zeuge*) and of objects that are ready-at-hand (*Zuhanden*), placed within a system of functionality (*Bewandtnis*) and of references (*Verweisungen*) to other objects. This ambient world is the one that shapes my action and that transforms technology. But we have shown that 'prior to being a system of tools, the world is an ensemble of nourishments'.[19]

However, in order to affirm the centrality of taste and to deepen the mystery of orality, that is to say of what goes through our mouth when we eat, speak, kiss, or laugh, it is important to understand why the privilege accorded to vision and to touch is inseparable from a philosophy that not only establishes a division between the constituting subject and the constituted object – the conscience and the world – but also conceives the latter as that which resists our will or cedes to our power. This conception of the relationship between man and the world is equally supportive of a certain manner of thinking sociality, the representation of subjects in competition with one another in their mastery or domination of the ambient world, which becomes the base from which contractual obligations are defined.

It is essential to uncover these representations that constitute the implicit and explicit foundations of ethics and of contemporary politics, if we wish to discuss them and to substitute for them another first philosophy that can serve as a basis for ecology. Our objective is to formulate the terms of a social pact on the basis of an ontology that will owe nothing to ideology or religion, but which will have its point of departure in the description of our original relationship to the world, that is to say in a phenomenology of nourishment. Indeed, in order to contest the philosophy of the subject and the ontology that serve today as the foundation of the social contract and that explain our difficulties in bringing ecology into our life and into politics, we must examine the place that has been accorded not only to vision, but also to touch, which designates the world as that which resists my effort. A brief detour through the philosophy of effort of Maine de Biran is necessary before we posit taste as an existential and before we bring out the gourmet cogito of the phenomenology of nourishment, which we will attempt to elaborate, step by step, throughout Part One of this book.

The fiction of a statue to which Condillac successively gives each of the five senses enabled the author of the *Traité des sensations* to prove that it is touch that confers to the individual the impression that he has a body. The sensation of solidity that the statue feels in placing the hand on a part of the body brings it to recognize the body as that which can respond to the pressure of the hand.[20] Thanks to this sensation of solidity that brings together two things that mutually exclude one another, two impenetrable bodies, the soul goes beyond itself. It discovers that there are other bodies when it touches a body without the soul itself being what responds to the sensation of solidity. Condillac, who asks how we know our body – which we cannot leave – judges that the hand is the organ that enables us to reach the real that is beyond us, and to localize the different parts of the body connected with the sensations that we feel. Without this organ, the human being would be a simple site of pure sensations, an impressional subjectivity reduced to olfactory sensations, and it would not have the capacity to designate the real within its exteriority. Being able, thanks to touch, to distinguish its own body from other bodies, the statue learns, according to the sensations of pleasure and of pain that are conferred to it by its experience of the world, to seek out certain foods that are pleasing to it and to avoid the substances that bring it disgust.[21]

Condillac however is not able to resolve this mystery: How does the hand move? What is the origin of our movements? Maine de Biran for his part seeks to go beyond this aporia. In his *Mémoire sur la décomposition de la pensée*, he explains movement through voluntary touch, that is to say through effort.[22] Distinguishing the way in which the hand knows itself by a sort of immediate experience of itself that is not an intentional relation, from the way in which it knows the bodies over which it moves voluntarily, he shows that the self is not the seat of purely passive sensations.

What is more, there is an originary corporeality, or, as Michel Henry will say, a sort of self-revelation of the original body, which places it in possession of itself and of each of its powers. Thus the body is a fundamental 'I can', of which I make constant use and which enables me to move around, to use the body that is mine from within. Henry will conclude from this that life is self-affection, that is to say that it does not first feel the world and its resistance, but rather presupposes this non-intentional relation to itself, the fact of feeling itself.[23] The origin of movements is thus not to be sought in the impressionability of the subject as in Condillac. If one is faithful to Biran's intuition, it will rather be necessary to think this immanence of all our powers in the flesh, an immanence which makes the flesh the site of an original memory.[24] This memory is deeper than the intentional memory we ordinarily speak of, for it reaches back both to the organic body, which continually resists the 'I can', and to the original corporeality that is the origin of this 'I can'.

Henry's philosophy of self-affection affirms that the impressions of our senses relate to our flesh and that the action of the flesh on its own body is the paradigm of all human action, that is to say of the primordial relationship of man to the universe. This relationship could not be an intentional or 'ek-static' one. While paying homage to Maine de Biran, whose phenomenology seems to him to be particularly radical to the extent that it draws out this immediate feeling of the self that is the original corporeality, Henry underlines that the world is not to be thought of as that which resists my effort. The description of the skin, where our sensations are interwoven, exchanged, and modified, provided a particularly interesting way of deepening this question.[25] However, Henry does not pursue it to the end.

The skin is a porous boundary between myself and the world. Because I feel well or badly in my skin, but cannot take it off as if it were a piece of clothing, the skin testifies to this primitive installation within ourselves that Henry calls our 'flesh'. This cannot be the fruit of an intentional constitution: it is given, and it is in it that we feel the world. It can however be regretted that the author of *Incarnation* does not insist further on the other aspect of what would be a phenomenology of the skin, namely, our susceptibility or our permeability to the world.

This aspect is particularly evident when we are cold and we have to find a shelter or put on warm clothing in order to protect ourselves from a glacial wind. Our sensibility testifies to this hypersensitive existence in which exterior things do not remain at a distance, do not simply glide over us, but touch us, as when we have goosebumps, or, when swimming, we experience well-being when we come into contact with the water. If 'it is in the sense of touch that the experience of "mine" is most compellingly effected', the skin that separates my body from others also places me in contact with them, thereby indicating that 'none of the senses entirely lacks the I-world relation'.[26] However, more than the skin that testifies to the fact that our senses are not 'devoid of pathic element', the act of eating illustrates this immersion in the world that distances us from any philosophy that erects a boundary between the constituting ego and the constituted world. Incorporation completely effaces this boundary.

It is surprising that there is almost nothing on hunger and eating in this work in which Henry masterfully sets himself off from the transcendental scheme that is still present in Husserl. For the act of eating by itself suffices to contest the presuppositions that the phenomenologists who have thought about the corporeality of the subject have sought to challenge, namely, the idea that my relationship to the world could be exclusively 'ek-static', that I might constitute the world or that it might be exhaustively constitutable, that I could constitute my flesh, and that my relationship to the world could be thought about in the light of a theory of action in which the real is that which resists my effort. In order to go beyond the sensualism of Condillac without supporting the philosophy of effort of Maine de Biran, it would have been necessary to descend into the entrails of beings, and to consider not effort but rather attention, which implies destitution before the thing.[27] Moreover, it would have been necessary to appreciate the sense of taste, which testifies to a relationship to the world that removes the pairs action/passion and effort/resistance from play.

Maine de Biran deserves credit for bringing self-affection to light but, in making the thing and the world a counterpart of my existence as force, he lacks what Erwin Straus and after him Henri Maldiney call the pathic moment, which involves what we have said up until now about sensing:[28] this is a sensing-with-things rather than a being-in-the-world, and it is at the same time a self-sensing, the presence of things, which are there for me, having this or that quality, as when 'the world resounds in the yellow' painted by Van Gogh.[29] The pathic moment is that 'interior dimension of sensing' by which 'we communicate with the hyletic data prior to any perceived object.'[30] It belongs to the state of that which is lived in the most originary sense, as we have seen in speaking of the enjoyment in which things return to their elemental structure, and thus it has nothing to do with the fact of experiencing the world as that which resists my effort.

When we confront the problem of our position on earth and of place, which are among the existentials in this phenomenology of nourishment, the question of landscape arises, which corresponds to the pathic moment and which is distinct from geography in the same way that sensing is different from perception. The reference to landscape opens towards a thought that makes aesthetics into an existential.[31] However, still more than attention to the landscape, taste teaches us of the depth of the sensible world and of the tie that binds our corporeality to a world that is not completely thematizable, since it is not reducible to mathematical objectivization or to technique, and since it is also not a simple springboard for our action. Moreover, the savour of foods, the fact that, in consuming them, all our senses are called forth, in particular the pleasure of the eyes and the smells, and the relation that exists between the desire to live, between gourmandize as an art of enjoying the good things on the one hand and aesthetics on the other: all these things invite us to affirm the centrality of taste.

Thus the phenomenology of nourishment, which underlines the nutritive character of the world, its generosity, and the pleasure it delivers to our eyes, our ears, our palate, and our hands, presupposes that we should describe the mouth, the organ thanks to which we taste and we celebrate the world in various ways. In order to measure the distance between a phenomenology of nourishment and a philosophy of effort, we may cite the passage of the *Mémoire sur la décomposition de la pensée* in which Maine de Biran imagines a hand that terminates in a single finger, endowed with a pointed nail that passes over external bodies.[32]

This organ would not sense the extension of bodies, nor would it experience solidity any the less. Maine de Biran affirms by this that the body does not define itself essentially through extension, and that the world is that which resists my effort. Biran's subject with the pointed finger 'cannot move continuously, but only by a series of repeated actions, and as if in leaping from one point to another on a solid plane.'[33] He is next granted the ability to slide over the object that he touches. Finally, he is enlarged in order to permit him to apply himself to solid surfaces without being able to withdraw into the bodies. In this way, he composes his ideas in diverse ways and manages to define the essence of existing reality as the force of resistance that bodies oppose to the action determined by our will.

To the configuration of the relationship between me and the world presupposed in this bit of philosophical bravura, the phenomenology of nourishment opposes a gourmet cogito, of which the emblem is less the stomach than the mouth. The latter has nothing to do with Biran's pointed figure. Nor is Henry's philosophy of self-donation the path that we shall choose in order to grasp the signification of orality. Of course, his philosophy of the flesh is sharply demarcated from the phenomenologies of appearance, for which all our senses throw us so to speak into the exterior. However, it is accomplished in a thinking about life that reaches back in the final analysis to the mystery of the *Incarnation*. In so doing it encroaches on religion and, above all, distinguishes itself from a thinking of the immanence in which the world and our relationship to the world are a point of departure.

The world is not only apprehended in its appearance, in the phenomena that take place in the light.[34] This is why we have begun to explore the nocturnal events that bear witness to an ontology that uncovers the sense of being-with-the-world. It is a matter here of introducing the dimension of intersubjectivity that characterizes the phenomenology of nourishment, for which the world is not a non-me, resistance to my action, but rather is the 'presence of the other'.[35] The mouth and orality are the emblem of this phenomenology. It calls back into question the register of the constitution, unveiling a different intentionality than the one that characterizes knowledge, perception, and action. It refers back to intersubjectivity, to culture, to traditions, and to the register of language and of the symbolic. The mouth thus separates us from the temptation, inherent to any hedonism, to fall back again into the sensualism of Condillac.

The mouth is barely an organ. The teeth, the lips, the tongue, and the associated mucous membranes exist, but the mouth is a cavity. It is however from here that centripetal and centrifugal movements begin.[36] I carry food to my mouth, it disappears, and I smoke a cigarette, kiss a friend, offer up words or cries, welcome my family by smiling to them, and react to the harmful statements of an adversary by pouting or grimacing under the impact of pain. Instead of thinking of the self as an effort and of the world as resistance, this radiant orality marks out a relationship to the world that places us at the heart of our existence, in activities in which the biological and the symbolic, the intimate and the social, the natural and the cultural, the material and the spiritual come together, as in cuisine, eroticism, and art.

Taste

The mouth is the entryway of a varied and dynamic network of relations and exchanges between the body and the world, the subject and society, me and the others, the individual and nature, human beings and animals. It cannot be tied to a single function, nor can the act of eating be reduced to nutritive intake, as if it were simply a matter of absorbing the food that enables us to grow, to 'preserve ourselves and repair the losses occasioned by small vital evaporations', as Jean Anthelme Brillat-Savarin put it.[37] More precisely, the fact of looking for foods that are suitable for our organism is in itself a complex phenomenon. In fact, if 'taste is the sense which communicates to us a knowledge of sapid bodies by means of the sensations which they excite',[38] then we cannot constrain this sense within the bounds of either consumption, or the seeking out or preparing of food.

Taste is, in the physical person, the 'apparatus by means of which he appreciates flavors'.[39] This definition, far from making of taste a sense that one could separate from the others, leads us right away to affirming the centrality of taste, and to underlining the connection that exists between its physiological and its cerebral dimensions, but also its intellectual, cultural, or artistic dimensions. All the senses are summoned in consuming, as is testified to not only by the importance of olfactive, retronasal, somatosensory, and visual impressions, but also by the texture of foods and even the sound that they make when they are bitten into and they are crunched between the teeth.

What is more, it is impossible to consider the physical aspect of taste without at once biting into its moral and cognitive aspects. Taste is, at the same time, that which invites us, through pleasure to preserve ourselves and which 'assists us to select from among the substances offered by nature, which are alimentary'.[40] Now, what excites our taste is of course hunger and thirst, but also the memory of the pleasure felt in consuming certain foods and the act of seeking out this pleasure, the effort that makes it more intense, more delicate, or that reinforces it through the decor, the setting, or the rites that mark the passage from the pleasure of eating to the pleasure of the table and to the meal.[41]

Thus it is difficult to think about appetite without also thinking about gourmandize. The appetite is the 'monitor', the 'first impression of the want of food' which declares itself before hunger begins eating into the individual 'by langor in the stomach, and a slight sensation of fatigue'.[42] However, the ordinary experience that is ours when we begin to be hungry and when we are just about to eat is that of desire. We do not simply want to fill our stomachs, nor to acquire the nutriments that are necessary for our organism, but rather we desire food that brings us pleasure. This is why Brillat-Savarin distinguishes gourmandize from gluttony or voracity.[43]

Whoever eats too fast, ingurgitates the food to the point of indigestion, and gets drunk, does not know how to eat or drink. She does not savour the foods; she swallows them. She does not take the time to savour them, to let their elemental essence burst forth, contemplating the roundness of the cherry, appreciating the robe of the wine, noticing the harmony of the colours that make up a culinary composition, and letting the flesh of the seitan melt after being chewed. She does not profit either from the atmosphere that is created around a meal, or from the ambience connected to the presence of guests who, by definition, are those with whom we eat. On the contrary, if there is a sense in elevating gourmandize into a virtue, it is that it associates the gustatory pleasure with conviviality.[44] The meal expresses this sharing of nourishment that is not only a sharing of goods, but a communion: women and men come together in the same place, around the same table, to experience with the others their relationship to the world in what it has that which is at once the most primary and the most sophisticated, this privileged moment being propitious for all manner of intrigue, business, and seduction.

Gourmandize, which cannot be confused with *gluttony*, *Lusternheit*, or *gula* and which, Brillat-Savarin boasts, seems, like coquettery, to be of French origin,[45] is an art of living and thus also an art of living with others. It is a 'passionate preference, well determined and satisfied, for objects that flatter the taste'.[46] We need to eat, but we also want to eat well, that is to say to give taste to our food. One must eat well, but the good and the bad are also eaten.[47] For it is important not to condemn other men and other living beings to a miserable life, as we see when we confront the political consequences that arise from our lifestyles and from our eating habits, and reveal the ethical sense that is inherent in the act of eating. Because ethics does not refer to an independent discipline, alongside daily life, over and above economy and culture to which it would add a supplement of soul or would serve as an alibi, to the extent that it is inscribed in the heart of an ontology which gets more precise as this phenomenology of nourishment develop, we begin to think of the taste of nourishment in opposing it to blandness.

Human beings, Claude Lévi-Strauss writes, had to overcome two great perils in their alimentary existence, 'the scarcity of food and its insipidity. For to eat one's fill is not enough. As a French proverb has shrewdly put it, one must not lose "the taste for bread".'[48] Cuisine is the art of composing entire dishes which bring our body what it needs, and which also cultivate our appetite, which is composed of pleasures that maintain and spark our desire to live. Thus it would not be an exaggeration to make of gastronomy a science, as Brillat-Savarin wished to do.[49]

The latter gives his masterpiece the eloquent subtitle *Meditations on Transcendental Gastronomy*, and considers Gasterea as the tenth muse.[50] In the same way, cuisine is at once a technique, a form of know-how, a science that is connected to bodies of knowledge related to chemistry as well as to dietetics, and an art that is connected to forms, to sensible qualities, to *aisthêsis*, from which the word 'aesthetics' is derived. The separation between the minor arts, among which we usually place cuisine, and the fine arts is not relevant once we have understood what taste is: going back to our sensations and calling forth our senses in their totality, it is in taste that the passage from the physiological to the mental occurs, from the biological to the social, from the egoistic need to preserve oneself to conviviality, or to Eros.

However, rather than continuing on the path of an elogy to cuisine and to its muse, gastronomy, who 'presides over the enjoyments of taste' and 'might pretend to domination of the universe' because 'the universe is nothing without life' and 'everything that lives eats', we would like to deepen the analysis of taste by insisting on the fact that it expresses lived experience in its globality.[51] This global character of taste, which also measures the narrow connection that exists between appetite and the desire to live, is manifest in our way of expressing ourselves: culinary metaphors come up when we admit that our life is bland, that we need to spice up a relationship, that the salt of life contains all its charm, or that a pleasure is acrid or a hardship is bitter.[52] We thus have a further reason to speak of cuisine as the culinary art.[53]

To eat well is to live well, and one needs art to succeed at this. This is what is called *savoir-vivre*. However, the arts of the table are not only connected to the art of *savoir-vivre*, which often rings of an elitist afterthought.[54] The latter is discriminatory towards those who have not mastered good manners, that is to say who do not have the manners of the dominant class, which establishes the criteria of taste. Alimentary behaviour, when we place this sociological consideration on the back burner in order to appreciate the relationship to the world of nourishment, to *aisthêsis*, which is the first, intimate, and archaic level to which our manners of eating are connected, no longer testifies (only) to a bipartition of social life between the bourgeoisie and the popular classes.

Of course, the search for quality, gastrosophy, and the aestheticization of existence, on the one hand, and the preference for substantial nourishment and concern about quantity, on the other hand, marks out a dividing line relative to which the intermediate classes, which are connected to the intellectual professions, and the diverse components of the middle classes, may position themselves.[55] As Pierre Bourdieu has shown, 'tastes in food cannot be considered in complete independence of the other dimensions of the relationship to the world, to others and to one's own body, through which the practical philosophy of each class is enacted'.[56] In the same way, dress, which is connected to table manners, to bodily care, to clothing, is a 'social product', shaping habits that are also connected to a sort of incorporation by which culture has become nature.[57] However, this in no way obviates the fact that, beneath this social level or through it, there is also a relationship expressed of each individual to life, or, better, to living.

Savoir-vivre means to have the desire to live, to know how to live, and to find the pleasure in living: one does not impede access to enjoyment either by indigence or by a sort of amputation of the senses that rivet them to the vital functions that assure survival or that subordinate them to the imperative of weight loss, work, or the multiple obligations of a life in which one never has enough time. Living well is, certainly, reflected in eating well.

Such an assertion does not only give credit to those who elevate cuisine to the rank of an art. Beyond the temptation of an elite hedonism in which one would abandon oneself, as Brillat-Savarin recommends, to 'gastronomical tests' in order to distinguish the *bons vivants*, whom one would like to have as friends, from the dull, the sad, and the skinny, this connection between appetite and the taste of living, between alimentary conduct and *savoir-faire* taken in the sense of knowing how to enjoy, invites us to ask about the place of taste in education and culture.[58] As in Bourdieu, we remain on social ground, prior to confronting the troubles of eating behaviour that are experienced in the first person, such as anorexia and bulimia. However, it is less social determinism than the relationship of human beings to their body, to others, and to the world, which we are seeking to describe when we analyse our eating behaviour. The objective is to understand the existential and ontological malaise that underlies the contemporary tendency to reduce eating to an intake of food.

No one will dispute that the fact of eating and of eating well, having good appetite and having the possibility to share a good meal with one's friends, without being worried by the fear of not having enough, nor haunted by the anxiety of gaining weight, is already the proof of a good life. The individual enjoys a balance and a state of health that are not widely shared, if we think of the nearly three billion human beings who suffer from hunger or malnutrition, and consider the increasing number of inhabitants of rich countries that are obese, constantly follow diets, or exhibit troubles in their eating behaviour. A serene relationship to alimentation is sufficiently rare that we might do well to inquire into the relationship to the self and to the world that eating disorders express.

Rather than asking about the psychological origin of these maladies, we may examine here the role that taste plays in our life. The questions remain the same as for the psychologist or the sociologist, but the method, and what is being asked after, in the perspective of the phenomenology of nourishment supposes that we should place the emphasis on the significance of taste in order to understand the relationship to the world and to the body that certain manners of being and eating imply. It is a matter of knowing why, in everyday life, cuisine looks so little like an art.

Why are lunch and dinner, with the exception of major occasions, going out to restaurants, or banquets at which we celebrate an event, so rarely anything other than a taking in of foodstuffs, as if one needed an exceptional event in order for the meal to be a feast, as if the meal should not be a feast in itself? Is not such a mutilation of the act of eating, snacking in front of the television or swallowing a sandwich at the office, the symptom of an amputation of taste, reduced to its physiological dimension alone?

Far from revealing the elemental essence of things, our sensations would themselves be turned from the register of enjoyment and reduced to the pure and simple satisfaction of a need that is experienced as an emptiness or as an absence to be filled. To eat would be to plug a hole, to fill a gap that is the larger, the more the satisfaction is without pleasure, without joy, and thus it becomes necessary to ingurgitate food continually in order to experience satiety. Or indeed, by treating food as an enemy, we would refrain from eating. Eating becomes a need to satisfy, but it causes us to lose time. It becomes a trap, a necessity that we deny in order to affirm the triumph of our will, which is capable of mastering the body in an extreme way, so that the body is no longer loved for itself, but rather is exhibited, emaciated, before the world, as a reproach and an advertisement. To eat would be to satisfy or to trick our hunger, without happiness and without the Other. In the rich countries, what have we lost in this difficult relationship that we maintain to nourishment?

To respond to this question by saying that we have lost the sense of taste presupposes that we recall what has been said concerning the centrality of taste and the fact that it expresses our lived experience in a global way. We have lost the sense of taste in daily activities because we have lost contact with the world as nourishment. We have forgotten that the world was nourishment because we have cut ourselves off from feeling and we represent the objects of the world to ourselves by manipulating them, by objectivizing them. We no longer have confidence in our sensation, but rather think that our head is the point of departure for our experience. Such is the signification of this amputation of the senses mentioned above.

It is not a matter of extolling unhindered enjoyment, perpetual ecstasy, but rather of descending into the body, to the point of contact between the 'I' and the world, in order to seize this being-with-things that is also, as we saw in speaking of the pathic moment of sensing, a being-with-others. This loss of the world is also a loss of the taste of the world and of the savour that existence can have here and now. It thrusts us outside of ourselves and procures a sentiment of thrownness that, by contrast, art and contemplation of a landscape attenuate. This does not mean that art is a consolation, but, by bringing us back to ourselves, in immanence, where we are able to liberate the elemental essence of the world and feel ourselves living, the work of art, when it expresses our being-with-the-world, returns something to us that we lack most of the time, although it concerns our deepest reality.

To speak in this way of art, while underlining the existential character of aesthetics – which does not refer to a discipline, as in Hegel, but to an exploration of the forms or sensible qualities on which our sensations nourish themselves – is not to make of it an activity that is cut off from life, reserved for the distractions of a Sunday and for exchanges marked by snobbism through which we test the cultural level of others. To speak in this way of art, pointing to its truth and to the place that it occupies in our existence, is also to suggest that there is no sharp separation between art and life, nor, a fortiori, one between the minor arts and the fine arts.

Not every painting is a work of art, for not every painting has the capacity, in communicating at the level of *aisthêsis*, to draw out a world that concerns others, or to reveal to them something essential. Conversely, it is not a matter of saying that painting is the same thing as cuisine. The idea is rather to affirm that painting, cuisine, and finery arise from art in what they communicate, in different ways and at the level of our primitive sensations, the presence of things whose appreciation designates less a movement that evades intentionality than a new form of intentionality.

In the same way that eating makes manifest the reversibility of intentionality, the transformation of the constituted into that which constitutes, so the work of art 'nourishes' me in such a way that the act of individuation by which I discover the painting and judge its beauty only operates through the play of forms. The latter address themselves to my feelings in what they contain that is at once the most personal, the most intimate, the most universal, making room for a communication and a sharing of the emotions that can be expressed in words, but that words cannot exhaust, which is to say giving way to a communion. This double reference, in taste, to the body and to the spirit, to the palate and to judgement, shows that we can speak of earthly and spiritual nourishment. Moreover, it justifies the assimilation of art and the table, which perhaps has never been so well thought out as in the tea ceremony.

The tea ceremony

The misinterpretation, when we speak of the 'way of tea' (*chado*) that is the subject of Okakura Kakuzô's work, *The Book of Tea*, consists in interpreting it as an aestheticization of existence. To be sure, the tea ceremony (*cha-no-yu*) is an art of being-in-the-world or rather of being-with-things and with-others. Moreover, by inviting us to recognize in the presence of the others the greatness of small things – that of which one cannot be convinced unless one feels within oneself the smallness of great things – the wisdom that is expressed in the tea ceremony leads us to relativize what Pascal called the greatnesses of the establishment.[59] It also strongly associates a true democratic spirit, connected to the affirmation of the equal capacity of its adepts to become aristocrats of taste, to the consideration of the value that is unique to each moment.

All of our acts, whether they are connected to those who are similar to us, to other living beings, or to the environment, are important. This is why the way of tea is indissociable from the promotion of three moral traits: sincerity, which extends to all of the domains of our life and to all of the actors we encounter there, the flowers, the trees, the animals; purity, which presupposes the purification of the place, but also that of the heart and of the spirit; and serenity, which permits each of us to find ourselves thanks to discipline and to the frame of the ceremony.

It would thus be wrong to consider the *cha-no-yu* as an index of an elitist lifestyle, as if refinement and the art of living were subordinated to the art of appearing and of comparing oneself to others in order to establish criteria of distinction. This way of presenting the 'way of tea' completely overlooks the philosophy of immanence that constitutes its spirit and that goes together with the affirmation of the equality of individuals, of the consciousness of our smallness, and of the teaching of humility.[60] Compassion, frugality, and modesty go together in a sort of thought that is not exclusively reserved to adepts of Taoism, but rather involves a universal dimension, even if the emphasis that it places on imperfection and asymmetry contrasts sharply with the manner in which Westerners conceive of progress and beauty.[61]

If the 'way of tea' promotes a democratic ideal attested by the equality that reigns in the tea room, this harmony does not signify that there is no rule, of which one is convinced when one notices the attention to the smallest details that structure this ceremony – from the opening of the entryway that requires of everyone, even the richest, to bow the head, to the choice and the disposition of the flowers that depend on the seasons, and also to the place that each participant occupies. The preparation of the tea itself follows very precise rules, which presuppose that one is concentrating on the present moment without giving evidence of any hurry or of any thought of anything other than what is happening here and now. Rituals determine a frame and a period of time for paying homage to what people recognize as being essential to life, namely, the present moment, harmony, and the attention that is conferred to all the gestures in the exchange. Thus the discipline and the order of the guests, carefully determined in advance, as are equally the respective place and role of the guest of honour and of the other guests, all offer us an 'authentic freedom – that of finding ourselves on a fully human plane and of leaving behind us the troubles of the world'.[62]

It is certainly difficult to import the tea ceremony into our part of the world. Moreover, exoticism is not the guarantee of a more respectful relationship to our body, to the things of the world, and to other people whom we might envy in other civilizations, including people who are considered primitive who never forget to honour the animals that they are preparing to consume.[63] Nonetheless, we can take advantage of this meditation on the path of tea, for it enables us to measure the gap between what an art of living-with-things and of living-with-others on the one hand, and our most current ways of being on the other hand, particularly in our eating behaviour, might be.

When we realize that children no longer know that vanilla is a pod plant, when they draw a square upon being asked to give the representation of a fish, we realize that they have lost something essential that is not connected either to their intellectual level or to their technical ability. In the same way, when we assess the future situation of the industrial production of food products, and we see all these ready-made dishes, all these fruits and vegetables filled with pesticides and herbicides, whose responsibility for the growth of certain cancers is now attested, the idea that we do not respect our body by not respecting the manner in which we eat appears self-evident.

Finally, the sufferings that we inflict on the animals that are called, in factory farming, 'production animals', and that are maintained throughout their short and miserable existence in abominable conditions, as well as the pressures exerted on farmers to produce ever more meat or milk at an ever lower price, are not only the symptom of a model of development that is both exhausted and counterproductive. They also testify to a total lack of respect towards animals and towards the people who produce these foods. To celebrate the new year by eating foie gras, which is unhealthy liver obtained after several weeks of force-feeding, is to incorporate this suffering and this torture. There is a striking contrast with the respect, compassion, and frugality, which constitute the spirit of the tea ceremony, and with the rites practised by the Tsimshian Indians in the aim of paying homage to the animal that they have killed and of avoiding the situation in which 'the "ashamed" [fish] would never come back again'.

It is not however in limiting ourselves to a denunciation of the aberrant conditions of factory farming, nor in blaming an agricultural system that has become a prisoner of companies that commercialize phytosanitary products, that we become conscious of the impasse at which we are operating. It is also a matter of saying that the crisis of our model of development – that the food crisis, as we see, reveals in a particularly sharp way – is a crisis of taste. We also connect this crisis to the amputation of the senses that make us incapable of understanding that hedonism can be something other than indecency.

Hedonism consists in tasting existence, and in communicating with others thanks to the most archaic and the most complex sensations. It is thus inseparable from the respect that we have for ourselves, for others, and for the environment. Like good humour, politeness, and all the other small virtues that make being-with-others and being-with-the-world more agreeable and more harmonious, hedonism is incomprehensible without consideration as Saint Bernard understood it. Consideration requires knowledge of 'what you are, who you are, and how you are', and begins with the self in order to go out towards the world – without forgetting that we arrived in the world entirely naked from the womb of our mother.[64] A humanity that has lost its sense of taste no longer sees the harm that it commits. It does not see the uglification of the world; it tolerates the destruction of landscapes and the disappearance of species, and encourages an exploitation of resources that is inseparable from the exploitation of people and that leads to famine and war. A humanity that cultivates the sense of taste, beginning by having respect for those who prepare food, for the peasants who work the soil, for the animals, and who teach children, from the youngest age, to cook and to receive guests, is a humanity in the process of placing itself back on its axis. Ethics and justice are unthinkable without this point of departure.

The terrestrial condition, the localization, and birth

To take seriously the corporeality of the subject is also to be led to think about the terrestrial position of *Dasein*. Prior to being-there, it is here, supported by the element. In the same way that position on earth is prior to any initiative of subjectivity, localization makes movement possible, that is to say motion towards an over-there. Moreover, the earth to which we hold is not a body and it is more than a planet. It has, Ricœur explains, an existential significance: 'It is the mythical name of our corporeal anchoring in the world.'[65] This is why Husserl was able to write that it does not move.[66]

This assertion does not contradict the truth of Galilean science, which refuted geocentrism and showed that the earth, far from being immobile, moves around the sun. The assertion, rather, describes the phenomenological origin of corporeality: far from being a planet like the others, the earth is the unchanging ark, the ground or even then the arch-home from which all movement takes place.[67] It is in relation to it that movement and rest come to have a sense. Even when I imagine that I am a bird in flight or the pilot of a spaceship that is taking off towards a distant planet, I do this by taking off from the ground. The movements of animals and of all beings only have their sense from my constitutive genesis, which is characterized by this 'earthly precedence':[68] 'It is certainly not so that [the earth] moves in space, although it could move, but rather, as we tried to show above, the earth is the ark which makes possible in the first place the sense of all motion and all rest as mode of one motion. But its rest is not a mode of motion.'[69]

We walk in a space in which the movement and rest of bodies relate back to a centre of reference that is our flesh. Similarly, the earth is the arch-home that is the condition of the origin of all givenness of things. In the primordial experience that we have, our flesh is neither in motion nor at rest, as we have already seen with Michel Henry, but rather, 'I stand still or go; thus my flesh is the center and the bodies at rest and moving are around me.'[70]

If Husserl can say that 'I have a ground without mobility', this is because this ground is not to be thought of as a body, but rather as the home of movement and of rest. The analogy between the earth as ground and my flesh, from which I constitute space, is justified, since they are both originary. This is why 'the Earth can no more lose its sense as "primordial homeland", as the ark of the world, than my flesh can lose its wholly unique ontic sense as primordial flesh from which every flesh derives a part of its ontic sense.'[71]

Finally, this primordial earth is the same for everybody and it is unique, as Husserl writes, 'There is only one humanity and one

Earth.'[72] In fact, phenomenology subtracts the earth and space from all physics and from all geometry, in order to describe its originary constitution on the basis of the modes of incarnation and of our earthly condition, or, as Husserl says, from our constituting life which is defined through this terrestrial precedence. If we return to the most originary layers of lived experience by opting for a radical phenomenology, as is the case for the author of this 1934 text, we understand that our terrestrial condition indicates nothing that could make us think that thrownness is originary, as if human beings were 'thrown-there' (*dahingeworfen*) or in exile. If, moreover, we are no longer speaking of our terrestrial condition, but of our terrestrial position, we see that each of us holds to an earth that carries us and that each of us weighs on a ground that is not only our object, but is also the foundation of our experience of the object, marking out 'the relation with my site [that] in this "stance" precedes thought'.[73]

In other words, if we consider the fact of being positioned on the earth as an existential, we understand that to exist means to assume the priority of a situation that one cannot overlook: 'Human being, because of his existence, is always already overwhelmed.'[74] The sense of being of the food or of the place could not have the structure of a noeme or of an object of representation. The food and the place are two existentials that illustrate, in a paradigmatic way, the world as nourishment.

Of course Heidegger, in speaking of being-in-the-world (*In-der-Welt-sein*), already enabled the contestation of the sovereignty of representation over existence. And yet, if *Sein und Zeit* is an essential step in the calling into crisis of representation, it is necessary to recognize that Heidegger's insistence on being thrown, as an ontological interpretation of thrownness, leads him at first to neglect a thinking of dwelling.[75] The *In-der-Welt-sein* of the 1927 work is not yet a reflection on what it is to inhabit the earth and to arrange a space.

Moreover, the gravity of the subject, as Levinas says, the weight that he has in positioning himself on earth, implies that thought, whose point of departure is material, connected to a 'here' that is his base but also his refuge, his retreat, has nothing to do with facticity. Far from expressing the absurdity of our condition, on which a limit would be imposed, position and localization, which give rise, in *Totality and Infinity*, to a meditation on the dwelling, constitute the possibility of finding a home and of being secure.[76] The origin is that over which I cannot exercise any control, and the milieu is that in which I move and which protects me. To deeply install the human being in his sensibility by uncovering the existential character of eating and of place does not lead us to interpret our inability to master the origin as a marker of something tragic in our condition.

In a text entitled *Pouvoirs et origine*, Levinas analyses the connection between the affirmation of the originary character of thrownness and the register of power that is evident in Heidegger.[77] Finitude indeed has, for him, a foundational character. Fighting it or denying it is a reaction of flight. However, the fact for *Dasein* of not being the foundation of his existence is a limit, an ontologically determined deficiency that underlines the absurd and the tragic in our condition. For the author of *Sein und Zeit*, the conditioning of existence, thought as facticity, can signify my loss, unless in projecting myself towards my death as my ownmost possibility, I choose to do something with my life and to express myself. Moreover, the fact of not having chosen my birth is the mark not only of my contingence, but also of my facticity, defined as that which limits my power. It is interpreted, Levinas writes, as a scandal, in view of the privilege enjoyed, in such a thought, by the notion of power and by the idea of freedom that underlies it.[78] This thought of existence is indeed a thought of finitude, but it lacks the signification of the world as nourishment, as well as that of birth, for it is connected to 'the obsession of power'.[79] On the contrary, the signification of birth does not testify to a limit imposed on our power, but rather inscribes intersubjectivity in the heart of subjectivity, within our corporeality, and opens up to the consideration of the connection between the generations. In the same way, the fact of forgetting that localization refers to a here, and to think about being-in-the-world as being-there, goes together with a focus on thrownness and the project. It is because he did not think existence in its materiality through to the end that Heidegger did not develop a thinking of the corporeality of the subject, and that existence is not, for him, immersed in sensibility. This explains why he conceived existence as *Sorge* (care).

We have seen that the philosophical tradition had the tendency to interpret sensing while not leaving any place to the living being. Either sensations lead back to perception, or they are reduced, as in Hume, to simple excitations. While sensations express the pleasure and the suffering of a being that orients itself in the world, experiences it and experiences itself in its corporeal existence, these conceptions do not take the living being into consideration.[80] Thus we are, as Erwin Straus writes, in the situation of the executioner who is surprised to no longer find attached to the body the head that he has just cut off.[81]

Similarly, a phenomenology that does not develop an authentic thinking of place, by beginning with an analysis of position on earth and of localization – which refers back to a here and now and even to the difference between sleep and wake – is truncated. Finally, a phenomenology that does not meditate on the signification of the being that is engendered can only think about existence in the light of the pairs thrownness/power and facticity/resolution. It leads to a philosophy of freedom that does not permit us to oppose, to the individual moral agent and to the conception of sociality that serves as the foundation of contemporary political theory, another thought that is able to bring nature, animals, and future generations into the social contract. On the contrary, if we elaborate a philosophy of corporeality by introducing new existentials and by liberating the significations that renew our relationship to ourselves, we will be able to reformulate the political problem.

The 'haecceity' of the subject – its 'here' – and the fact that it is engendered are two existentials that remove us from the register of power and open up new perspectives for the human in its individual and collective existence. In fact, the 'here', which is the position of the subject, is also its localization, the place that it occupies in space or the place that it inhabits and arranges: for 'I am with the others of my here'.[82] In other words, 'I can only be-with-the-Other in the place in which I find myself', and on the condition that I am in a state of wakefulness, that their presence is really felt.[83] To take sensing seriously is to take seriously the present and localization.

'In sensing, every thing is here for me', and every thing '*is*, at all, only as it is for me'.[84] It is not a matter of arriving at the in-itself of things or at the truth; rather, sensing unveils that which, for me, is real.[85] To see something implies that this something is a moment of my own being-in-the-world. The real thus does not designate what has happened in the world, but rather signifies what has happened to me. Sensorial certainty is connected to the distinction between sensing and perceiving, in which we are not exactly the same: 'Sensing is to knowing as a cry is to words', Erwin Straus writes.[86] While the word can have a sense in my absence, 'a cry reaches only him who hears it, here and now'.[87] In the same way, the landscape is distinguished from geographical space, which is divided up according to a system of coordinates and systematized, as we see in looking at a map: 'In a landscape we are enclosed by a horizon; no matter how far we go, the horizon constantly goes with us. ... The place in which we find ourselves never encompasses the totality'.[88] In other words, 'when I am in the presence of a landscape, I am not *in front of* it. ... But there is, behind me, the presence of all horizons. All the distances are integrated in my neighborhood.'[89]

On the contrary, when we ask someone for directions, or even use a map, then 'we establish our "here" as a place in a horizonless space'.[90] The point that serves me for orientation on the map is arbitrarily fixed, but once it is established as the point of departure, it is absolute: my position will always be determined, as I advance along my route, in relation to its situation in the system. It is different when we are in a landscape, in which my current position is always defined by the one that is nearest, by the fact that I can still continue to move. I cannot determine position in a panoramic ensemble. To be lost, in the literal as well as in the figurative sense, when one is struck with behavioural troubles or with hallucinations, is to have left the systematically ordered context of social space, to have no place sociologically, since geography cannot develop from the landscape. The route cannot be regained.

While in normal life we go beyond the horizon of our landscape and of the most subjective sensations, and while that which is individual is found in an objectively established context, just as we encounter the shared world or we 'attain to geography', psychosis designates a trouble in orientation and in the interpretation of lived experience, which modifies the landscape itself. Since 'the subject only attains to himself *in* sensing',[91] which is corporeal and which expresses being-in-the-world – that is to say that it is sympathetic – hallucinations are primary modifications of sensing, and not troubles of perception or judgement.

These are not pathological images within normal sensorial spheres, but rather 'pathological images in abnormally altered sensorial spheres'.[92] The sick person suffers from a trouble or a modification of a sympathetic mode of sensing: it is his communication with the world that is altered, as if he remained in the landscape and obtained within its horizon the geographical world that is on display in familiar language.[93] As Eugène Minkowski has shown, cited by Erwin Straus, psychotics

> live within the horizon of their landscape, slaves of the unmotivated and unfounded certitude of impressions which no longer can be adapted to the general order of the world of things and general meaning context of language ... When the illness progresses, the increasing looseness of thought, the total deterioration of language, point to the progressive loss of geographical space; the deadening of affect indicates the desolation of the landscape.[94]

In light of what has just been said concerning orientation in the world, which has a material sense and a social sense, and which expresses, at the level of sensing, the relationship of communication between the 'I' and the world, we see that position is an existential. The pair passivity/activity could not characterize this originary phenomenon which inscribes the subject in space as well as in time. The *et* of *hic et nunc* means that it is from a 'here' that one goes there, and that one orients oneself in the world, and that this here, which is also a now, is the point of departure of any projection into the future. This 'here' is not an exile in an originary manner, a thrownness, but the difficulties that we might have in finding our place in the world and the sentiment that certain individuals have of being completely lost go back to this primary relationship to the world that is defined by sensing, whose pathic moment has already been underlined a number of times.

Sensing testifies well to a contact between the 'I' and the world that is first experienced corporeally, before being formalized by articulate language, and before cutting a path within a general context or in the common world. Similarly, it is in taking account of the existential character of position on earth that one can understand habitation, which is the fact of having a roof, a dwelling, of being able to remove oneself from the sights and sounds of the world in order to have one's own intimacy, in order to be with oneself. The dwelling also brings it about that we possess that which makes us live and that which results from our work.[95] Finally, the home (*chez soi*) and the security that a dwelling offers also enable us to receive guests, hospitality being made possible by the material and moral (or spiritual) conditions of reverence.[96]

The reader will have recognized, in these last lines, the Levinasian analysis of dwelling. The author of *Totality and Infinity* establishes a connection between position on earth and fecundity, and declares that, far from inscribing itself in the register of power, our earthly condition and position are connected to the fact of being engendered. Rather than insisting, as Levinas does, on fecundity, which is a manner of thinking intersubjectivity straight from our corporeality in placing ourselves in the perspective of the person who engenders (the mother or the father), we choose here to describe birth in placing ourselves in the point of view of the person who is born.[97] Such an approach enables us to draw out the signification of birth in indicating everything that opposes it to the thoughts that are characterized by obsessions with power.

In *Freedom and Nature*, the pages that Ricœur devotes to birth show well what an analysis of the fact of being born brings to a philosophy of corporeality. Until now, we have drawn out some elements of a phenomenology of nourishment that is, in reality, a radical phenomenology of sensing. This will be completed in the following chapter, which concerns the place and the milieu, but also the space that is inhabited and arranged, all of which represent, with eating and enjoyment, the two constitutive dimensions of what we call 'nourishment'. However, in order for the description of the structures of existence to be complete, and to open the path to an eco-

phenomenology, it is necessary to deal with birth and death.[98] Beings
that eat and live on earth are alive, that is to say that they are born and
that they will die. Yet what reflection on birth brings to any ontology
is above all connected to the fact that, contrary to sensing, it is not an
experience that is made in the first person.[99] This aspect is rich with
implications for the meaning of my existence and the place accorded
to freedom; it also clarifies my relationship to Other people, present,
past, and to come.

It is not sufficient to say that we do not bring ourselves into the
world all by ourselves, and that we are not the ones behind our birth;
it is important to recognize that this capital event, in relation to which
we date all events in our life, is not a memory. Abandoning the plane
of lived experience, I must place myself as a spectator of this objective
event about which I know something only through the account that
is given to me of it by others. In a general sense, I always find myself
after my birth, for I was brought into the world before being able to
voluntarily carry out any act: 'I find myself in alive – I am already
born.'[100] Everything happens as if there were two beginnings, the one
of which would be that of my life, the other of which has to do with
my acts or with my freedom.[101]

Moreover, my dependence with regard to two lives is not simply
a dependence with regard to two freedoms. It cannot simply be said
that others *wanted* my existence for me: 'They did not exactly will
it, since I know very well that it is a monstrous collusion of chance,
instinct, and another's freedom cast me up on this shore.'[102] I received
my nature from my parents, that is to say the law of growth, a principle
of organization: 'To be born means to receive from the another the
capital of heredity.'[103]

My ancestors, who are like donors, bind me, in a sort of 'umbilical
connection of the living', to the scale of a lineage or even of the species.
Thus, 'I explain my filiation not as *my* ancestry, but as my ancestor's

posterity',[104] or rather of my ancestors. The explanation of my being is an alienation, since 'I leave myself in order to place myself in a being outside my control, the ancestor',[105] and from him I descend the chain of effects that 'has the remarkable quality that it is exactly what Cournot means by chance ... the encounter of independent causal series. Thus I appear to myself as an effect of chance.'[106]

My ancestors are the foundation of my existence; there is the trouble of multiple existences behind me. Of course, to exist is to be for oneself the centre of one's own existence, from which 'I illuminate what is behind me as well as what is ahead of me'.[107] People say I descend from Mr and Mrs So-and-So, rather than speaking of their ancestors as a cause. Consciousness of oneself is the act by which I integrate and assume what I am, that is to say also my character, which 'presses on me from so close by'. To live is thus to 'consent to be born', to consent to life with its fortunes and obstacles, as Ricœur says, while assuming the limit that is receding from me and that is that of my birth.[108]

My consciousness, which concerns what I do after my birth, my acts, always miss my first beginning, since I already began to live when I say 'I am'. This signifies that the cogito is essentially an engendered cogito. Yet this anteriority of my beginning relative to my own apperception is complicated or enriched by the fact that it is connected to these lives that are behind me, to these men and women whom I will never meet in flesh and blood (since they are not my contemporaries), whom I do not know (for they are too numerous), but who are in a certain respect in me. Although they are not all of the same family, they make up, as we go deeper into the past, one and the same family, which is the family of humanity.

The engendered cogito is thus not connected to Other people simply because it owes its life to Other persons or, as in Levinas, because it reveals itself in giving life to another, who is not the same as it but who constitutes its identity, making it into a mother or a father. Intersubjectivity and even the intergenerational link are inscribed at the heart of the engendered cogito, in its bosom, in its flesh, for it is connected by the ancestors to all human beings. Such is the lesson that we can draw from the analysis that Ricœur offers of birth.

Moreover, to not position oneself in existence, but to have been brought into the world, to be always already born before saying 'I am, I exist', is not to affirm that existence is tragic because it is opposed to power, but rather to say that we are never alone in the world. We are always older than ourselves, since we are already (born) before realizing anything at all, and because our birth precedes everything that we begin consciously. We are at the same time always younger than ourselves, in that our birth is a limit that escapes us, and that we can only integrate by consent – which leads Ricœur to say that 'the experience of my receding birth is rich in its poverty'.[109]

Thus it is not only the future that is important, nor even the fact of being able to engender another person in one's turn. The past also determines us. If all people from the past constitute us, racism is an absurdity, since present people are all ultimately the result of chance and the fact of a mixing that blurs the boundaries between peoples, nations, and races. What is more, the duties that we have towards the ones and the others are also duties that take into consideration what it is that we owe to our ancestors. In other words, if the cogito is essentially an engendered cogito, this means that the social contract cannot be structured exclusively by mutual advantage and by reciprocity with respect to our contemporaries.

We should not only bring, into the formulation of the political problem, a consideration of the interests of future generations. The respect that we owe our ancestors, through the simple fact of being born, and that we address to all human beings, who belong to one and the same great family, are part of our obligations and should be reflected, in one way or another, in laws. This does not signify that there will be deputies to represent our ancestors. However, in the same way that it is unjust to allow the burden of pollution and of a degraded environment to weigh on future generations, it is unjust to defend an agriculture or an architecture that deteriorates the natural and cultural heritage that has been passed down to us. It is not only in commemorating the past, in honouring the memory of those who have fought for freedom, and in ensuring that the victims of evil not be forgotten that we relate to history: it is present in our flesh and in the manner in which we make use of nourishment.

The final lesson that we can draw from this meditation on birth, which makes of being-born an existential and which enables us to speak of the engendered cogito, concerns the sense of death. The fact of engendering and, thus, of prolonging oneself beyond one's existence, beyond oneself, was always considered as a fundamental desire of human beings. If we think of Plato's *Phaedrus*, or of the manner in which Levinas insists on fecundity and filiation, or if we refer to ordinary experience, it is clear that the desire to have children seems to be the most common way in which human beings affirm that they are able to achieve a victory over death. However, it is not this reality that our approach invites us to emphasize. To place oneself in the position of the engendered being, and to describe birth, rather than fecundity, brings to the surface another meaning of mortality. In fact, to say that we need to engender in order to fight against our disappearance and to prolong ourselves supposes that being is being-towards-death. But it is not death that is primary in a phenomenology of nourishment, but life.

The fear of death and the desire to endure do not obsess the gourmet, engendered cogito. The desire to construct an inhabitable world, which others will come and shape in their fashion, is more important to this cogito. An engendered being is limited in time, and will die. But as soon as we understand that living is living from, that is to say feeling, being-with-the-world and being-with-others, and as soon as we recognize in our flesh the pulsing and the trouble of past lives, we also hope that our pleasure in living and our enjoyment do not bring with them the pain and misery of others. Hedonism is not indecency and is not the ethics that is necessary for life, but rather it is the life that is itself, straightaway, ethics. Existence is, in each gesture that we make here and now, an ethical position. The care of the engendered cogito is thus not to express itself nor to prolong itself through others, for its physical body dies and its achievements, most of the time, are forgotten. The subject of a phenomenology of nourishment wishes that the world remains inhabitable and that human beings to come, be they our children or our grandchildren, have the means to conduct themselves in an honourable way, constructing landscapes and cities that are beautiful and agreeable to live in, and being capable of promoting a culture that testifies to the fact that they have not lost the sense of taste.

2

Space, milieu, and other existents

Between human beings and the earth a concrete relationship is forged that testifies to what Éric Dardel has called the 'geographicity' of being. This expression not only designates the fact that we are localized, that we are always somewhere, but also expresses a 'geographical worry' that precedes and sustains objective science.[1] Whether we need to cross the country or seek to anchor ourselves somewhere, we must recognize that space is an essential dimension of our existence. This existence, Dardel continues, looks for a horizon, for directions, for existents to draw closer to itself, and offers paths to follow, whether clear or riddled with obstacles, whether sure or uncertain.

It is not by chance that we use so many spatial metaphors in order to describe our lived experience, as when we speak of a tortuous path, of a steep way, of the stages of life, of distractions and errancies, of deviations, of turning points, of a difficult slope, of social climbing, or of people who are close to us, or who keep a distance, or are inaccessible. These images prove that the earth is the concrete space towards which we move, through which we pass, and in which we take our bearings. To exist in this sense is to have one's feet on the earth.

Walking takes account of this spatial dimension of existence, which goes beyond mere localization and underlines the connection between the 'I' and the world. Human beings are fundamentally beings who walk: not only are they positioned on earth, but they also have need of exploring the world and of experiencing, in this discovery, a surprise that also enables them to become situated, to know where they are and where things stand with themselves and in their lives. To walk is to feel this presence of the soil underneath one's feet, and also to feel oneself in this contact with the soil – to encounter oneself in going across the country. This need to move shows that existence is extension prior to being projection. It is as much spatiality as it is temporality.

In the same way as diastole and systole are complementary in the beating of the heart, so too one must lift the foot and bring it down to earth in order to take a step. The need to move is also integral with that of dwelling (*oikon*), of having a dwelling (*oikos*), or, at least, of sojourning in a welcoming place. The spatial dimension of existence is not a synonym of placement (*Stelle*) in the sense of occupying an objective space, as the example of cars parked in a parking lot might perfectly illustrate. We require rather a location (*Ort*) that gives or accords us a site (*Stätte*), and that thus becomes a place (*Raum*), that is to say an inhabited space.[2]

The geographicity of being, the ecumene and mediance

Geographical space, in contrast with the abstract or homogeneous space of the geometer, is perceived as hospitable or hostile, near or far, because it is connected to spatialization, to beings that occupy the space, discover it, and discover themselves in it. This discovery of self implies that the space is not reduced to the localization, but rather signifies. It is essentially qualified in view of the manner in which we find ourselves there and in which we experience it. Thus, the human being and the place are grounded reciprocally, since, if the place participates in the identity of the individual, the individual in turn gives an existence to the place. From the place, we thus pass to the milieu, since it is not a matter of describing an elementary spatial unity, whose position could be determined in a system of coordinates, and would depend on relations with other places. Rather, it is a matter of thinking about the relation of humanity to terrestrial extension, which Augustin Berque calls the 'ecumene'.

The ecumene presupposes the biosphere but is not reduced to it, which means that the milieu cannot be identified with the physical or ecological environment. More precisely, the notion of ecumene, which Berque uses in the feminine, is not to be confused with the study of the ecological relationship between human beings and the inhabitable earth (*œkoumène*). Berque situates the reflection at an ontological level that underlines the character of reciprocal appropriation of a people and a country. The territory is thus not assimilated to the result of a process of production, which would include strategies of organization, of domination, and of exclusion. It is not only the projection of a system of intentions on a portion of the terrestrial surface. The physical and ecological dimension of milieus is not erased in favour of a conception of territories that would remain abstract in spite of its insistence on the games of power of which these milieus can be the object. Berque denounces 'metabasism', which is the illusion that culture and nature are independent, but it does not mean that he promotes a determinism that would presuppose that we represent in a simplistic way the influence that the soil and the climate can have on human beings and on ways of life.

Not only is there a certain contingency in the way in which human beings encounter their milieus, but moreover the reciprocal appropriation that defines the habitation is a co-institution. Our representations determine the landscape and develop our environment in relation to the way in which we conceive it. Conversely, we perceive it according to this development. This is why Berque maintains that this relation, which goes beyond the subject/object alternative, is essentially 'trajective':

> Japanese society, throughout its history, interprets nature according to its own predicates (its ways of feeling, of thinking, of speaking, and of acting), but these predicates are constructed from this base which is the island arc of Nippon.[3]

'Trajection' describes this historical process. The reality that results is neither arbitrary nor completely determined. It is essentially contingent, which means 'that it could be otherwise, but that it is what it is as a result of the history of the milieu'.[4]

It is thus as a landscape that we apprehend our environment, at the same time physical and phenomenal, ecological and symbolic. Thus the study of human milieus, or 'mesology', replaces the study of nature or of the environment, which still testifies to a certain dualism of nature/culture, object/subject. In mesology the emphasis is placed on the relationship uniting human beings to terrestrial extension. The term 'mesology' comes from the Greek *mesos*, 'milieu' (*medium* in Latin), and from *logos* ('discourse', 'science'). Though it was introduced in 1865 by Louis-Adolphe Bertillon, who was also a physician, a statistician, and an anthropologist, it had already been used on 7 June 1848, at the foundation of the *Société de Biologie*, with its inventor Charles-Philippe Robin giving to it a meaning close to what we today call 'social ecology'.[5]

This word translates well the fact that milieus are related at once to the physical characteristics of a country (wind, climate, hydrology) and to the social aspect of the environment, including the habits and customs, the mores and institutions. Better than the term 'ecology', which appeared one year later and which was more successful, 'mesology' suggests that it is 'the totality of the human being that is engaged in its milieu'.[6] Things bring together in their concreteness what makes us what we are. Opposed to any subject/object relation and describing the co-institution of man and of the milieu, their growing together (*cum-crescere*), this concreteness underlines the relational essence of the milieu. Moreover, it manifests the interaction between the symbolic dimension of our relationship to the world, techniques, and the ecological basis of human society.

The 'ecumene' describes an eco-techno-symbolic relationship, which necessarily presupposes the biosphere from which it has emerged. This ontological structure of the ecumene is determined in reference both to the works of Leroi-Gourhan and to the thought of the Japanese philosopher Watsuji Tetsurô. Leroi-Gourhan described, in *Le Geste et la Parole*, the process of hominization, of anthropization, and of humanization, a triple and mutual engendering that relates back to the animal body, to technology, and to the subjective transformation of things by means of symbols.[7] The ecumene emerged from the biosphere and was born from a process of hominization, anthropization, and humanization. This human work that is the ecumene has been articulated through its deployment in space, causing rice fields to appear, for example. These presuppose collective and cumulative developments, as we see in the hydraulic system from which the fertility of the soil depends. The rice field is thus heritage that implies collective management and cumulative social capital, which cannot be simply considered as a purely private good, but rather is essentially transmitted.[8]

Far from being separate from its concrete sense, that is to say from history and from the singular milieu in which people, things, and signs have 'grown up together', the place, in its ecumenical reality, possesses a double reality: it arises at once from the *topos*, from mapped space or from the environment, and from *chôra*, that is to say that it is existential.[9] This opposition between the *topos* and the *chôra*, which Berque borrows from Plato's *Timaeus*, does not exhaust the sense that the latter can have. Derrida writes it as *Khôra* and does not have it following a definite article, as if this matrix or receptacle that gives us a place and welcomes us, but is not itself in any place and blurs all genres, sensible and intelligible, resembled a proper noun, whether it is one of the unpronounceable names for the Jewish God, or of a place that cannot be found, that Socrates does not occupy, but from which he replies to his proper name.[10] The *chôra* or *Khôra* describes a matter that is always ready to receive an imprint, and refers to the original memory that conserves it or that makes a narrative of it possible, as in the *Timaeus*, in which each tale becomes in its turn the container or receptacle of another narrative.[11]

The landscape is the deployment of the ecumene, that is to say it refers to the *chôra*. Moreover, it could not be considered a simple place occupied by an individual or confiscated by a group that would exploit it with the sole aim of drawing benefits from it, without taking into account its ecumenical reality. This is particularly evident in the case of the rice field, as we saw above. However, the ecumenical character of the landscape can be transposed into other realities that not only are objects – that is to say goods possessed by one or several individuals who make use of them as means for their existence – but also pertain, in what is the juncture between our individual existence and our collective or medial existence, to a heritage that is transmitted throughout history.

Reflection on the milieu, or more precisely on the mediance that translates the two halves of our reality, the one individual, the Other constituted by the eco-techno-symbolic structure of the ecumene, breaks with modern Western thought and with the ontology elaborated by Heidegger in *Being and Time*. The reaction that this work triggered in Watsuji, who read it already in the summer of 1927 when he was staying in Berlin, led him to write *Fûdo*. Watsuji reproaches Heidegger for not granting sufficient importance to spatiality and for apprehending existence as being solely individual.

Not only are we not able to abstract away from space and from this inscription in a space that relies on a historical process – which Berque calls trajection – but, in addition, our individual body is not assimilated to an individual person, as in the *Habeas Corpus* of 1679. Our body itself must be thought both as an animal or individual body, which lives and dies with the person, and as a medial body, which transcends the mortality of each individual. It is because he has considered neither spatiality nor the dual character of human existence that Heidegger, in *Being and Time*, does not make historicity, which is inseparable from mediance, appear concretely.[12]

Our medial body overlaps with what Leroi-Gourhan called the social body, which is collective and constituted by the technical and symbolic systems that have exteriorized and deployed certain functions of the animal body. He also makes reference to the ecological foundation of our existence. Our mediance, a translation of the term '*fûdosei*', about which Watsuji writes in the preamble to his work that it is the 'structural moment of existence', expresses this dynamical and sense-generating relation between the two halves (*medietates*, from which 'mediance' is derived) which make up the human being.[13]

Contrary to modern ontology, which is characterized by the thought of a self-instituting subject, and which holds that everything is extinguished when the individual dies, Watsuji's thought shows that the environment is part of the human and that the medial body survives after the animal body. Thus, instead of thinking *Dasein* as being-towards-death, mediance is inseparable from what Watsuji calls a 'being-towards-life'.[14]

In mediance, the extra-individual part of being does not die with the individual. It is perhaps even that which confers a sense to our ephemeral passage on the earth. The point of departure of thought, and of the apprehension of the sense of existence is not only an individual (*hito*), but the study of the human milieu. The fact of thinking mediance as a structural moment of existence implies that we take into account the 'connection between' (*aida*), that is to say the relation of a human being with his milieu, his inscription in his eco-techno-symbolic environment, and his relations with other persons (*aidagara*). Ethics does not concern only the relationship of individuals among themselves, but has to do with the human (*ningen*), which presupposes a taking into consideration of this dual character of existence.[15]

When we grasp human existence at once individually and socially, or rather medially, temporality and spatiality correspond, Watsuji declares, 'With the elucidation of the space- and time-nature of human existence, the structure of human association also appears in its true light'.[16] The affirmation of the dual character, finite/infinite, of human existence reveals the diverse forms of community and of union, which human beings construct as systems of dynamic movements, not as static structures of society.

The meaning of ethics and of politics is likewise clarified in a new way once these no longer concern an association of individuals, but rather have to do with space (*kin, aida*), which is between individuals (*nin, hito*), which is to say the social world (*yo no naka*) and that which is public (*seken*).[17] The meaning of the world, which is one of the major problems of contemporary philosophy, is thought differently than in Heideggerian ontology and in the modern and contemporary theories that serve as a foundation to the social contract in its current form. The study of the genesis and of the meaning of the word *'ningen'*, which designates the human or humanity, and not only the human being as an individual, helps us to understand what 'being-in-the-world' means by causing us to exit the frame of thought that is exclusively centred on the existence of the individual and on his or her freedom.

Indeed, the human being is not simply the *Man* or the *Mensch* of anthropology. As is evident in the ideographical aspect of *ningen* (人間), which literally signifies the 'space between people', this word was constantly used, in the Buddhist writings that the Japanese received from China, in the sense of 'world', or to designate 'the public'. Afterwards it came to signify 'the person'. Indeed in the poems, sentences, and proverbs transmitted to the Japanese by China, the human being (*ningen*) always has the sense of 'world'. What is more, 'what was said about *yo no naka* ["the world"] always held good for the persons *who lived within it*'.[18]

In other words, the human being is apprehended at once as a part and in his totality, which has to do with his belonging to the world. It is the same with the word 'company' (*nakama*) which designates the group, but which also serves to express the presence of a single person. A whole series of Japanese words, such as 'domestics', 'friends', 'soldiers', and 'adolescents', are in the same case. '*Rôdô*', for example, serves to describe domesticity and the individuals who belong to this group. The way in which, in Japanese, one utilizes these expressions shows that 'in human existence, the whole exists in the parts and the parts exist in the whole'.[19]

One should thus not be surprised that *'ningen'*, which means 'world', today also designates the person who lives within this world. This does not mean that the first sense has been forgotten; on the contrary, if we take into account the origin of this word, we understand that the human being is at once the world and the person. This dual signification of the word '*ningen*' refers ultimately to the community that exists from person to person and to the social life. The individual person is fundamentally different from the society and, nonetheless, is part of this society. The human being lives from this dialectic, from this union of opposites, Watsuji contends.[20]

The word '*ningen*', designating at once the person and the social world or the community, is distinguished from '*anthrôpos*' and presupposes that the sense of being-in-the-world is not to be thought in the way Heidegger does in *Being and Time*. If Heidegger is right to transpose the structure of intentionality into the heart of existence in order to describe being-in-the-world, he is wrong, according to Watsuji, to interpret it as something that concerns our interaction with tools. In such a phenomenological ontology 'the between-ness between man and man is hidden in the shadow of the relationship between man and tools'.[21]

On the contrary, Heidegger's successors will seek, like Karl Löwith, to oppose to this ontology an anthropology that treats the relationship of human beings among themselves, understanding being-in-the-world as the fact of being with or in the company of other persons, as the fact of mutual encounter. This perspective opens the path to ethics, since 'to exist' signifies 'adopting an attitude of mutual encounter', and since this attitude includes 'man's fundamental attitude, man's *fundamental morality*, i.e., man's *Êthos*'.[22] The world is the world of interhuman relations, of social or community existence.

In the same way, when Watsuji analyses the meaning of the word 'world' (*yo no naka*), he is not content to draw attention to the fact that *yo* also has the sense of 'society' and of 'epoch', suggesting the idea of a temporal transition and of a spatial reality, of something from which one distances oneself, or that one traverses while walking; he adds that the translation in Japanese of *In-der-Welt*, being-in-the-world, requires the joining of *yo* to words such as *aida* (between) and *naka* (within). Indeed these words 'differ from the German "*in*"... [they] do not express merely a spatial meaning, nor as in Heidegger merely a relationship of involvement with tools, but in addition they clearly express human relationship'.[23]

These words reveal the dynamic character of human relations, which are not objective relations emerging from within the subject, like the relations of one thing to another:

> They are behavioral bonds of association between persons, such as in *majiwari* [communication] and *kōtsū* [association], where one finds *subjective*, mutual related-ness. ...Unless they behave as subjects men cannot exist in any 'between' (*aida*) or relation (*naka*) at all, but at the same time they cannot behave or act except in some 'between' or a 'relation'.[24]

This is why the relation (the between) must be thought as 'a living dynamic relationship that is a subjective behavioral association'.[25]

Considering our attempt to elaborate a phenomenology of nourishment that implies a relational conception of the subject who is in contact, in his daily acts, with other human beings, past, present, and future, and with other living beings, this concept of world and of public (*seken, yo yo naka*) shows the advantage of maintaining the spatiotemporal signification, which has a tendency to disappear from our usages of the word *Welt* or 'world', often taken as if it were reduced to the totality of things in objective nature. But the words '*seken*' and '*yo na naka*' preserve the signification of something that is subjectively extended and that is constantly in transformation; we find in them reference to history, as well as to the social and environmental dimension of the human being. 'In other words, *seken* and *yo no naka* are human existence which is historical, climatic, and societal'.[26]

Existence (*sonzai*) also does not coincide with the words *Sein*, *einai*, or *esse*: 'being'. For *son* is the active preservation of the self, the act of maintaining oneself in life, which is opposed to loss and to forgetting. A being that maintains itself in an active and subjective way becomes an identifiable entity, existing through itself and able to return into loss. *Zai* expresses 'that *a subject exists in some place*'.[27] This word is opposed to the notion of departure, to the fact of leaving on one's own from a place, in order to move towards another, and designates the capacity to sojourn in a place that is, each time, a social place. *Son* signifies the grasping of a subject through himself, and *zai*, the fact of finding oneself at the centre of human relations. Thus, *sonzai* 'is *self-maintaining of the subject as between-ness*, i.e. the fact of "human being" preserving its own self … it is the "behavioral relationships of human beings"'.[28]

Existence thus expresses the structure of the human being that is at once subjective, practical, and dynamic, and refers to an active network where history and the social and environmental dimensions of our lives combine. To exist is not only to move outside of oneself in order to go towards the world, whether it is a world of tools, the social world, or the environment defined as a simple launching point towards freedom. Of course, the subject is always already turned towards something, but one would be wrong to conceive this something as an intentional object at which consciousness takes aim. The example of the cold enables us to understand the way in which we can think being-in-the-world without falling back into the subject/object scheme, without identifying the world with a noeme, but rather in underlining the combination of the natural and the social that is designated by mediance.[29]

When we are cold, this impression is not a point of departure from which a relation with cold air could be established. The sensation of cold is already in itself relational. It is in this relation that the cold is discovered. It is not a simple event of my consciousness, but rather a moment of my experience, as a subject, of my existence. I am cold; this means not that I remain in my sensations or that I target the cold, but that the cold air seizes me. The question of knowing how the sensation of cold is in relation with the coldness of the exterior air is poorly framed, for it testifies to a disregard for the relation between the 'I' and the world that is designated by the word 'to exist'. When I am cold, I already inhabit the coldness of the exterior air. I have to do with the cold, that is to say that what I see in the cold is myself. Moreover, I do not only encounter myself, but also join up with the 'we'.

We understand ourselves within phenomena such as cold, rain, storms, and wind. It is not *Dasein* that, in existing or in its manners of being, understands (*versteht*) being; we discover ourselves within the milieu (*jiko hakkensei*), contracting our bodies when we are cold and putting on warm clothes or opening an umbrella.[30] Having-to-do with the cold, the suitable arrangement that we have in the milieu, engages us individually and socially in all sorts of means of warding off the cold. We make ours an accumulation of long-standing arrangements that go back to our ancestors, as is testified by our types of habitation, which fix the way in which we construct our homes and which show that this way is never established without having-to-do with the milieu.

There is no more a milieu that is separate from history than there is a history separate from its milieu, Watsuji writes, adding that this can only be made explicit from the land-based structure of existence, from mediance. The tool is 'a thing for', like the hammer that serves to fabricate the shoes that we use in our societies. However, the tool is always in the process of indicating a 'what for', and this linking emanates from the human.[31] The milieu objectivizes human existence. Human beings extend themselves; they discover themselves within the milieu, as when one wakes up fresh and well-disposed in the morning and says to those around, 'Isn't it a lovely morning?'[32] This reviving freshness is neither a thing nor the nature of a thing (of the morning, for example), but rather a way of existing (*arikata*), that is to say of extending oneself and of exchanging, within our 'interconnection', as when we go out together into the fresh air of the morning and we have there a certain way of existing, or when in the spring the Japanese students stroll or organize parties under the blossoming cherry trees.

We are charged with a history and with a milieu and 'the climatic character is the character of subjective human existence'.[33] Concrete human existence always implies a way of doing things that is peculiar to a given epoch and within a given territory. This does not mean that we endorse a thinking of rootedness, as is evident when we recall what was said about the essentially contingent connection between the human being and the milieu, and when we understand that existence is an active, subjective, and above all dynamic network. This manner of thinking the relation between the human being and the world, that is to say of thinking about the milieu whose eco-techno-symbolic structure has already been underlined, is not connected to anything static. Just as any determinist interpretation – which would make of manners of existing, of the forms of conduct, and of the mores of human beings, the simple results of the climate or of the soil – is a misinterpretation, so too does the confusion of mediance with any thinking of rootedness fail to hold up to analysis.

It is important not to freeze in time Watsuji's phenomenology, which one could reproach for a certain nationalism. Thus one could refer to the lovely passage of *Fûdo* in which he writes that the summer is not connected only or essentially to a rise in the temperature and to the force of the sunshine. In fact, when the weather is nice in autumn or winter, this is not sufficient to make us feel that we are in the summer. In order for there to be summer, the 'humour of summer' is required. One must be able to hear the insects rustle cheerfully in the luxuriant verdure, or see the birds flying from tree to tree and stealing the fruits of the fields and of kitchen gardens. A season is not defined by the weather outside; it is an existential mode of the human: 'Without the humor of the summer, there is no summer.'[34] The human being possesses an existential mode that is the summer. Thus when we take an airplane to a hot country, if we become aware of this humour of summer all around us, with its sounds and its colours, we immediately feel ourselves to be in the summer, even if it is the 31st of December. The first thing we do in getting to our hotel is thus to change into light and thin clothing.

Dwelling, building, cultivating

If we wish to deepen our reflection on the existential character of spatialization, we should equally describe habitation. For the individual is not situated in a space that is given in advance, but rather inhabits the space. Not only does he need a shelter against the elements, as if he could be lodged in any place and in any way. The place is a base, because the subject, in his corporeality, is position and localization, as we see particularly well in sleep:

> Sleep reestablishes a relationship with a place qua base. In lying down, in curling up in a corner to sleep, we abandon ourselves to a place; qua base it becomes our refuge. … Sleep is like entering into contact with the protective forces of a place.[35]

The habitation not only is connected to the residence, to the home, but rather also implies a manner of arranging a place, which organizes the space, that is to say my being-with-others-and-with-things. To inhabit is always in a certain way to cohabit with human beings and with animals, to trace the boundaries between them and us; it is always to build, to arrange, as Heidegger says, our sojourn among things, in building houses and cities, or in building up the places that delimit our residence and our being on earth.

What is more, the habitation presupposes that we think about that which is between beings and things, and that we apprehend the relation that exists between the outside and the inside, between the fence (or the enclosure) and the opening, between nature and culture, the country and the city, rest (or withdrawal) and work (or going out). Indeed, if the fact of living somewhere enables me to gather my thoughts, it is also necessary that I be able to leave, instead of being locked in my home as in a prison. In the same way, if it is necessary to have a residence in order to be able to welcome the Other and others, I do not really live in my home when the lack of privacy that I am experiencing makes intimacy and hospitality at once impossible. Finally, to live somewhere is to be capable of opening up to other cultures, to other universes, while having the possibility to return to oneself, and while celebrating, as well, the moment of return.

Thus it is impossible to speak of the habitation without speaking at the same time of the manner in which we arrange places in order to make of them milieus, whether they are the landscapes or the cities in which we reside, work, and nourish our bodies and spirits, and in which we move. Yet this arrangement of space that is the edification of places occurs, as Heidegger has shown, in building. When, in *Building, Dwelling, Thinking*, he writes that it is necessary to build in order to inhabit, and that building is already inhabiting, he does not want to say that just any construction would be a habitation, but rather that habitation reveals the manner in which we are on earth: '*Bauen* originally means to dwell. ... *Bauen, buan, bhu, beo* are our word *bin* [am].'[36] This reference to Old German recalls what has been said of the Latin etymology of habitation (*habitatio*) and of its relationship with habit and with posture. The manner in which we are on earth is the habitation which, in Heidegger, also presupposes a way of residing before the gods, of being on earth as mortals, under the heavens, as we see in his notion of the 'Fourfold' (the earth, the heavens, the gods, the mortals).[37] To inhabit is to build, in the sense of enclosing and taking care, of cultivating the land, and of building up the places. These places, by definition, make a place for the fourfold, and are not to be conceived as units of geometric extension, nor as simple territories that issue from economic, social, or cultural practices.

The examination of spatiality thus orients the phenomenology of nourishment towards a phenomenology of habitation. This means that the rupture between agriculture and culture, as well as that between urban space and the country, is no longer really relevant. The thought of habitation leads us to consider the city as a biotope and to insert or to reinsert architecture into a context determined by the actors who inhabit the buildings, but also by the environment and the climate, which characterize the place in which we construct a shopping centre, a retirement home, a recreation space, or a school. Conversely, to live somewhere is not only to be lodged, to have a ceiling above one's head; it is to be an inhabitant, a resident who is concerned with the decisions relating to the place he lives and who, when he is also a citizen, participates in these decisions, whether they are related to the city, to the village, or to the country of which he is a part.

The political dimension of the reflection on habitation is evident when we think of the social consequences of urbanization, of territorial inequality, of gated communities,[38] or of the relegation of certain populations to ghettos. It has, moreover, an original sense: to inhabit is to have the right to be somewhere, to be someone who has a

right to being located, to a place that is for him. It is to be a protected
person whose imprescriptible rights are recognized and who is at the
same time inserted into a social context. The city, in the sixteenth
century, designates at the same time the ensemble of ramparts and
buildings (*urbs*) and the political community defined by the type
of association that is realized between its inhabitants (*civitas*).[39] In
the same way, the inhabitant is someone who, materially, resides
somewhere, but also, beyond his existence as a subject of rights and
of duties, someone whose identity is connected to the place where he
is found and to the milieu, which is necessarily larger, within which
the place is defined, that is to say to the social context.

To build buildings so that citizens will have a residence, so that
they will inhabit it (*wohnen*), thus presupposes to resist to a way of
thinking according to which the city, the buildings, and the agriculture
are conceived independently of the actors who live there and of their
milieu or of their mediance. This soilless thought completely bypasses
the sense of habitation that Heidegger, in his 1954 text, began to
elucidate. For if, for him, to inhabit is to build, he also adds that 'only
if we are capable of dwelling, only then can we build. ... To build is to
cause to inhabit.'[40]

It is necessary to deepen our analysis of habitation, if we wish
to understand the transformations of cities and of the countryside
since the beginning of what is being called 'the third globalization'.
This globalization is characterized by the fact that 50 per cent of
humanity lives in cities today, by the emergence of megacities and of
a globalized economy, which goes together with the weakening of the
role of states, and by the emergence of new technologies that make a
new space out of the virtual, and that modify our access to the real.[41]
The present philosophical work aims equally to take the measure
of the aberrations that are connected to a completely industrialized
agricultural production, to a soilless system of feeding and raising

animals, and envisions a reconquest of the meaning of agriculture, which plays an important role in the way in which landscapes have been fashioned.

Finally, this approach helps us to take a certain distance from any thought of the arrangement of territories and of the management of space, and to articulate the social, cultural, environmental, and existential dimensions that should be part of any politics of the city, as of any reflection on the becoming of the countryside. Instead of speaking of urbanization or of combatting, through programmes of development, the desertification of the countryside and the poverty of peasants, phenomenology describes, as we see in Henri Maldiney, the connection between inhabiting and building. The French philosopher shows that to inhabit is to build a world in which we have a place to be and in which we cohabit, in which the outside and the inside, private and public, interior and exterior come into harmony.[42] This idea is precious, since it implies maintaining together the political and ontological wings of the interrogation of habitation, inscribing it in the heart of a philosophy of corporeality and of 'living from', and renewing the manner in which we are able to think the common, the public space.

We can already say that, for the phenomenology of nourishment, of which we have already identified certain characteristics, the point of departure of any political reflection on what can constitute a common space is the body. Not only is inhabiting a corporeal experience connected to localization, but in addition the experience that we make of space, of a city, of transportation, or of landscapes is in the first instance lived carnally. We can also think of the feeling of suffocation that we experience in a crowded subway. The privation of freedom is a corporeal privation, prior to becoming a sentiment of alienation and causing annoyance or anger. Conversely, the excitement that many Europeans feel when they discover or rediscover New York, walking for hours in this engulfing city in which everything leads to a shore and where the traffic, the chaos, and the racket, rather than being crushing, give the feeling or the illusion of living more fully, is in the first instance a physical sensation. A city is first of all a rhythm, which traverses the body and connects to the pathic moment of sensation, by which we feel our being-*with*-the-world:[43] 'The experience of rhythm – in which we encounter it *here* and as it *takes place* – is the order of sensing (and of communication in sensing). ... Rhythm is the truth of *aisthêsis*.'[44]

This sensation of freedom or of closing-in also depends on our use of technology. For certain tools are not convivial, and bring about forms of counterproductivity.[45] Ivan Illich refers by this term to the 'perversion of the tool becoming its own end'. Its effects, beyond a certain level, become contrary to those that it is supposed to produce, as we see when cars, which were supposed to increase the mobility of individuals, slow them down by making them the prisoners of traffic jams. The counterproductivity of tools and of institutions, which goes together with the creation of monopolies and with the appearance of what Illich calls the mutilating classes that designate the experts and specialists, leads to 'the great closing in'. To this perversion of the tool that compromises the autonomy of individuals, he opposes 'conviviality'.

This, for Illich, qualifies first of all the objects and the institutions that do not generate counterproductivity. However, if it does not designate human beings, nor does it entirely lose the first meaning that it had in Brillat-Savarin, which associated it with the pleasure of sharing a meal in good company. This relationship between the use of the tools of conviviality, of autonomy, and the sharing of experience, which is first of all the sharing of space, can be illustrated by the example of a bicycle ride.

Indeed, the bicycle, which does not produce the opposite of what it is supposed to provide, since it does not obstruct traffic and does not pollute, also makes it possible to appropriate the space traversed. While, in a car, or a fortiori in a plane, we traverse landscapes by suppressing space; on a bicycle we cross infinitely less distance, but we forge an intimate and corporeal relationship with the space. Our lived space is smaller, because we cannot travel as many kilometres as in a car or airplane in the same length of time, but our inhabited space enlarges. The art of inhabiting, whether we are dealing with our own house, or with the way of being in a space, consists in 'inhabit[ing] one's own traces', letting 'daily life write the webs and knots of one's biography in the landscape'.[46] Even if I am only passing through somewhere, I can inhabit the place and nourish myself from it.

In the same way, the transformation of the place into a homogeneous, isotropic space, saturated with objects of consumption, that is to say into an anti-place and into material, where a human being experiences the loss of the common sense and the disappearance of his or her vernacular knowledge, woven out of habits in a determinate place and at a determinate moment, is a corporeal experience. The feeling of absurdity flows from our sensations, which are immediately diverted, blocked by the objects. We no longer have access to the real through our sensations, since the sensible qualities that express our carnal belonging to the world are immediately recuperated by a flux of images, advertising spots, and noises that turn us away from ourselves. On the contrary, a convivial city is a sensual and hedonistic city – hedonism being taken not in the sense of the absence of limits to our desires, but in the sense of confidence in the senses, in the elemental structure of the world, felt carnally and not represented.

It is a result of having insufficiently meditated on this sensuality of our relationship to places that numerous architects and urbanists have elaborated, mostly since the 1960s, projects and plans that have not met the anticipated success. When a building celebrates the ingeniousness or the virtuosity of the architect, and we forget that it is destined to be inhabited by people, when architecture becomes an intellectual operation and not an art of edifying places, which presupposes that one takes into consideration the actors and the environmental conditions of the space to be inhabited, and which makes reference to the ecumene, there is a significant chance that the building will degrade, and that it will be necessary to destroy it after a few years. In general, a construction project that seeks to house people, instead of thinking of habitation as an art and as a way of being, is destined to fail, since individuals will not tolerate for long being in what Illich called a 'human garage'.

This is what happened in Barcelona, with the social housing of Can Tunis that was built in 1978-9 and intended for the Roma.[47] The project, which obtained the prestigious FAD Awards in 1979, envisioned an ensemble of aligned housing units with a simple construction and with exterior spaces. But ten years after their construction the buildings were in a state of total ruin: garbage was piled up in the yards, and drug traffic plunged the neighbourhood into delinquency. The reasons for this failure appear evident when we learn that Can Tunis was built on vacant lots belonging to the Corporation of the Autonomous Port of Barcelona.

These were residual parcels of land that resulted from the cutting through of the highway that had been built for the 1992 Olympic Games. The area was located between the foot of Montjuïc – where there is a magnificent cemetery, offering a beautiful view of the Mediterranean Sea – and the industrial installations of the city's port. Thus Can Tunis was adjacent to the port enclosure, surrounded by vacant lots, separated from Montjuïc and from the cemetery by the highway. At the entry of the neighbourhood there was a tunnel, and it was only after having crossed these boundaries and gone through this tunnel, and after having zigzagged through the traffic, that one could arrive in the city, the nearest inhabited urban network lying at a distance of 600 metres. The range of standard housing options established in a nowhere land was not well suited to a mobile population that is organized into tribes. Thus it is not surprising that Can Tunis was entirely destroyed by bulldozers in 2004.

With respect to the transformations of great metropolises, it could be said that urban enterprise is for the city what the 'human garage' is for the art of inhabiting. This is not only the replacement of places by the fluxes that characterizes the contemporary city and that bring with them, with the disappearance of limits, discontinuity, and social fragmentation. Claude Lévi-Strauss, in describing Karachi in *Tristes Tropiques*, had remarked in the 1950s that the city became the realm of non-relation and of indifference when its limits were pushed ad infinitum.[48] This is why urban sprawl, which is one of the specificities of contemporary cities, goes together with social exclusivity and the gentrification of neighbourhoods. As in Paris, social mixing tends to disappear, and we witness the emergence of true territories of segregation, which condemn the inhabitants of certain suburban areas to immobility.

The divorce of the *urbs* and the *civitas* is also evident in the decline of urbanity, which associates the manner of putting oneself into relation or of feeling at one with the common space of the city on the one hand, and civility on the other.[49] It is also explained by what Illich has called, in the final part of his work, the passage from the technical era, in which we are confronted by the counterproductivity of tools and institutions, to the era of systems. These integrate the user into processes. It is no longer the individual, but the system, that has needs. We act and react according to the needs of this system, advised by experts who determine our behaviours and our choices, which are thus not autonomous, but rather defined in view of the techno-economical order that dictates the imperatives of growth, of urban concentration, and of consumption.[50]

Analysing the effects of technologies on our lived bodies, Illich depicted the city as a paradoxical place of encounter and of alienation, in which consumer goods replace living vernacular connections. Even if he does not express it in this way, his analyses help us to think about what an urban Nemesis could be.[51] It is not only a question of a sort of vengeance of the city against urbanization, which began in the nineteenth century and is a product of the industrial revolution and of the industrial mode of thinking, of planning, of regulation, of the parcelling out of spaces in accordance with zoning rules.[52] In describing a confined human being, who lives 'the great closing-in', Illich describes a situation that corresponds to what certain inhabitants of the megalopolises might experience.[53] This does not exclude the possibility that there is in addition an urban and industrial beauty that is accessible to the person who, like Baudelaire's wanderer, has the time to stroll, and does not endure the closing-in within constraints, in a residence and a routine.

This closing-in goes together with a sentiment of no longer being able to breath, and of constantly being under pressure, serving big machines whose initial objective was to educate and to organize teaching, research, medicine, and culture. It does not decrease with the possibilities promised by the networked city, nor with their multiplication ad infinitum by means of the virtual. This closing-in is not only or essentially due to the absence of prospects. It follows rather from a loss of meanings, from the fact that it is no longer by our senses that we are connected to ourselves, to others, and to the world.[54]

The loss of meanings is one of the manifestations of what Illich calls the era of systems. Possibilities exist, but they are, so to speak, already engaged in a series of signs and cogs, of networks. They more closely resemble the bad infinite of which Hegel speaks, the unlimited and the indefinite repetition of the same, than they do a singular, unexpected event, whose significance would ravish us and transport us somewhere else. Possibilities are not really possibilities, since they are not lived as surprises. Nor do we experience our existence, for in order to be happy to exist, we must be able to encounter that which we did not expect, beyond all envisionable possibilities.[55] This is what Maldiney calls 'transpassibility', a fundamental structure of existence that implies not only the possibility of surprise, beyond what is expected and even sought after, but also the capacity to be moved, that is to say touched both by one's own senses and straight to the heart, prior to representing anything or to taking any decision.[56]

In the same way, Illich writes that 'one demonstration of the destruction of the commons is the degree to which our world has become *uninhabitable*'.[57] 'The commons' designated the lands for which customary law guaranteed that all villagers could make use of them, not in order to produce market goods, but rather in order to ensure their subsistence, which imposed particular forms of communitarian respect. In this way Illich establishes a connection between disincarnation, the rupture of transmission and of common sense, the loss of vernacular knowledge, and dissolution in anti-places, which are homogeneous spaces of consumer goods and recreation areas reflecting the non-space of networks and fluxes. Constant delegation, the profusion of norms, and the 'reign of the show' cause dependence and heteronomy to grow, and with them the feeling of closing-in, which is a dispossession and a withdrawal into oneself.[58]

The transposition to the city of what Illich said of the medical Nemesis, and of its iatrogenic effects, enables us in turn to imagine what a convivial city could be, a city characterized by proportionality, to what is appropriate and suitable at a given time and in a certain region. Everything happens as if we had been deprived of our capacity to develop our good sense and our *phronêsis*, in the sense in which Aristotle speaks of this in Book II of the *Nicomachean*

Ethics to designate the virtue of deliberation that characterizes the prudent man, who aims in all cases for the golden mean. We become prudent through experience and through the imitation of prudent men, but also in experiencing pleasure in beautiful and virtuous actions, where the pleasure crowns the effort of a being that has brought to accomplishment a disposition that, without being innate, is also not contrary to its nature. The return to limits and to the re-appropriation by human beings of their capacities of thinking and of acting go together.

Conviviality also comes through the confidence that human beings have in their senses, which are the most certain clarifiers of our relationship to a place. It is in this way that a crisis can have liberating virtues, to the extent that, conscious of the cage in which we are enclosed and of the possibility of living differently, we are able to rely on experiences undertaken here and there. While the loss of limits and the great closing-in that it brings with it rest on a humiliated perception, the rediscovery of a thought that is no longer soilless is accompanied by a direction, an order, informed by tradition, connected to a place, and qualified by the choices of its inhabitants.

This does not only mean that it is salutary to rely on the diversity of experiences. These, assuredly, testify to the capacity of beings to organize the common space and to live there in the best way possible. They are a possible inspiration, but there is no model of the convivial city nor a collection of recipes to apply. It is not a question, for example, of motivating all the inhabitants of the megalopolises to start gardening on the roofs of their buildings, as is done today in Brooklyn. In this New York neighbourhood, the cultivating of the earth and of fruits and vegetables, far from covering all the alimentary needs of those who engage in it, makes it possible above all for individuals to create social connections in practising an activity in which they see what they achieve, in which the work, should one be attentive and should one acquire the knowledge required for the management of the soil, is gratifying. The path towards a convivial manner of constructing and inhabiting passes in general through the appropriation of what is already there. It is in this way that one can refer to the knowledge and to the practices that have been recognized as good within a culture and that enrich the memory of a place, and one can rediscover the virtues that, being expressed in work, in craft, in the art of inhabiting, of dressing, of nourishing oneself, are not practised on an abstract planet, but rather on a particular and common soil that these actions have enriched with their traces.[59]

The social housing constructed in France in the 1960s and 1970s illustrates what Illich called the 'human garage', with its host of problems such as isolation, depression, delinquency, the feeling of abandonment and degradation, to which it is in vain to respond with repression, or by imagining that sports is sufficient to fill up a life. On the contrary, an experiment conducted on the Boulevard du Bois-le-Prêtre, near the Porte de Saint-Ouen in Paris, makes it possible to establish some criteria that help to transform a social housing tower into a place of life.[60] Reinforcement of the relationship to nature and the creation of private exterior spaces, through the addition of terraces or of collective gardens, completely modifies the space that is ordinarily dedicated, in cities, to vehicles. The placing of value on communal spaces also makes it possible to reinforce social connections. Finally, the employment of concierges and of people charged with the upkeep of the buildings humanizes the relationships and contributes to the creation of a community. Lacaton and Vassal and Frédéric Druot, following collective meetings with the residents, made similar proposals in the neighbourhood of La Chesnaie in Saint-Nazaire, and the results are encouraging.[61] Everything that makes it possible for human beings to feel the proximity of nature, and even to derive benefit from the gracious presence of other living beings, the contemplation of which is a source of surprise, creates interesting new paths, opening up new possibilities and creating a connection, thus drawing individuals out of their closing-in.

As we see, there is no question of creation out of nothing. Those who seek to 'maintain, continue, and repair our "world" so that we can live in it as well as possible',[62] whether they are architects, urbanists, or landscapers, adopt a narrative and contextualizing approach in identifying the specific needs of the different actors. In addition, this approach is opposed to a soilless way of thinking for an additional reason: it implies not only the consideration of the social and environmental milieu that is itself the fruit of a history, but also the reintegration of the city into its territory. In doing this, it effaces the separation between the countryside and the city, which has led to the industrialization of the countryside, to its transformation into vacation villages, and to contempt for the work of the peasants who, throughout the centuries, have composed the landscapes *pagus* by *pagus*, in the way that a writer writes a book page by page, and labours it into regular furrows.[63]

No notion is more apt for helping to move beyond the dualism of nature and culture, of interior and exterior, of countryside and city, than that of landscape. This writing on the surface of the earth that is the product, not always conscious or voluntary, of human activities, is rooted in the verb *pango*. This word arises in Latin from agrarian terminology and means 'to plant or to drive in posts', and then, by extension, 'to limit'. The word 'country' (*pays*) originally designated the inhabitant of a *pagus*, that is to say of a village or a canton, prior to referring to a space that is delimited and organized by human beings. The landscape (*paysage*) is formed by the inhabitants of a country (*pays*), in particular by the peasants (*paysans*) who have dug, tilled, excavated, burrowed, and traced durable shapes on a foundation that is more or less resistant, giving them various appearances as a whole (expressed in the suffix *-age* of *paysage*).

It cannot be said that a landscape exists in itself, outside the eye and the work of human beings. However, it would be futile to settle for a purely subjective definition, as if the outside that the window transforms into a landscape had no reality or thickness, as if we could think about a place without also referring to the soil. Of course, modern painting has transmitted to us the idea that a landscape is what we see from a given perspective that spreads a horizon behind nearby objects, but to reduce it to its pictorial aspect or to overestimate the subjective dimension is to forget the soil, the territory, and the living milieu in which it is integrated, and to neglect its climatic characteristics.

In order to grasp the richness contained in the notion of landscape, we can apprehend it according to five perspectives, which are also five points of entry.[64] Of interest at once to the landscaper, the architect, the gardener, the sociologist, the geographer, the ecologist, the painter, and the philosopher, the landscape is perceived as a cultural representation, in which the subjective dimension, connected to the regard of the subject and to the art of painting that educated it, is brought into relief. It is also an inhabited territory, grasped in its relation with the sum of practices and of habits that a group has developed in this place. It can designate a systemic complex in which the organization of urban and rural space is placed within a morphological and climatic ensemble, or it can refer to a space of sensible experiences that are resistant to diverse forms of objectivization. Finally, it can be a site or the context of a project. These five perspectives mingle several rationalities together: aesthetic, instrumental, moral, political, and dialogical (or related to the symbolic framework in which the principles of the communal life are constructed). They presuppose that, instead of separating the urban space from the rural space that surrounds it, we are able to think about the city in a way that sets out from its integration with and in the territory, the soil, and the living milieu.

In promoting a thought in context that weaves together the relations between the city and its territory, one opposes abstract planning and an urbanization that is born in the heads of specialists who are ignorant of the milieu they are seeking to shape, which is both social and natural, urban and environmental. The creation is connected to something that is already there. As Jean-Marc Besse writes, 'it is a matter of fabricating, of elaborating what is already present and what one does not see'. Just as the philosopher discovers his thought in writing, and recognizes it through the efforts he makes to express it, so 'the landscaper must construct in order to see what is there, in order to discover what is. One must trace in order to know what one desires and what one wishes to draw.'[65] The project also invents the territory in representing and describing it. However, 'what is invented is at the same time present in the territory, but as something that is not seen or not known until that time'.[66]

This manner, for the landscaper, of conducting a project by transforming the resistances of a site into possibilities, and in this way extending nature, joined to what has been said about habitation, might inspire a philosophy of architecture. This domain presupposes that we understand the logic of the project as one of suitability, not of truth, since there are no true or false projects, but rather some projects that are ill-adapted and others that are relevant.[67] The principal criterion could not be that of performance alone. The person who creates is not alone and it addresses people who are going to inhabit these places. Moreover, it has to work with a natural milieu.

Thus the despotic posture, that of the demiurge pretending to remodel nature or to dominate matter from the outside, is replaced by another paradigm, that of piloting and accompanying, or of a thought of non-action. The human being accompanies and extends or imitates nature, as we will see in the case of agroecology. Thus a phenomenology of inhabitation, which is at the same time a reflection on cohabitation and on the relations that exist between the without and the within, the interior and the exterior, the countryside and the city, leads us necessarily to inquire into the relationship of the human being to nature, that is to say into agriculture and the place that it occupies within culture.

If, as we have seen, to build is also to cultivate the earth, agriculture, conversely, is also part of culture. The Latin *colere*, which designates the act of cultivating the earth and which is also present in the word 'culture', as well as the analogy between agriculture and writing that the etymology of *paysage* authorizes us to take up, blur the artificial distinction between agriculture on the one hand and spiritual or artistic activities on the other. Not only is a philosophy of corporeality and of 'living from', such as the one we are attempting to elaborate, unable to do without a reflection on agriculture, which is connected to the foundations of human life, to eating, and to landscapes, but moreover examination of the meaning of inhabitation, which is an essential chapter of our phenomenology of nourishment, also invites us, against any thought of urban planning and of the reductionism that characterizes it, to reintroduce the city into an ecological cycle.

Cities are linked to the rejection, beyond their walls, of the power of nature, on which they have nourished themselves from the era of Mesopotamian agriculture to the exploitation of carbon resources, passing through the manpower of the proletariat. But if we think of a mode of planning of the ecumene, we are led to underline the connection between urbanism and agriculture. This connection is tight, though it has often been neglected. It is explained not only in terms of alimentary dependence, nor by the fact that cities tend to externalize their waste products and to relocate industrial production in the surrounding countryside. The attractiveness of the cities should not be minimized either, as they offer spectacles, services, and goods that are difficult to enjoy in the countryside, where, moreover, isolation can lead people, particularly the elderly, to desperation. The interest of a reflection that challenges the break, actually very recent, between agriculture and culture, nature and society, is to underline the relations that any ecosystem maintains with other human activities. This goes for the countryside as well as for the city.

Such is the deep meaning of 'permaculture', which does not only designate a permanent or durable agriculture, guaranteeing alimentary self-sufficiency and seeking to develop tools for durable prosperity and happiness: its ambition is also to promote a cultural model that is different from the soilless model. This project, which may include a diversity of currents, was born at the end of the 1970s in reaction to the crisis of an industrial system that was exhausting its resources, polluting, and creating ever more social segregation, both within cities and between the city and the country.

The epistemological foundations of urbanism, associated with thermodynamic energy and a reductionist approach that separates the city from what encircles it – including those cases, such as Paris, where the city was constructed in a very rich agricultural basin – are crumbling. Permaculture is opposed both to the presuppositions of the model of industrial development, which is a soilless model, and to intensive agriculture, which requires that we drain the earth of all life, in order to cultivate large fields of grains on a substratum provided by the petrochemical industry, and to impose a monoculture. It encourages another type of agriculture, as well as another type of city, where the habitat must include not only the simple fact of being accommodated, but also the possibility of nourishing oneself within a certain socially shared *well-living*.[68]

Agriculture in the city is thus a clue for constructing a convivial city, which will not be like an empire of concrete implanted just anywhere or on any soil whatever. However, it is in looking more closely at the manner in which the inspirers of permaculture think about culture and nature that we understand the meaning of this project which, in certain respects, is able to vindicate Fukuoka Masanobu when he speaks of a 'revolution from a single piece of straw'.[69] The defenders of permaculture distinguish themselves from those who prefer agroecology, which implies a piloting of the living world. There are differences between, on the one hand, Albert Howard, Rudolf Steiner, and Hans Peter Rush, and, on the other hand, Fukuoka, who advocates non-action and even rejects composting. However, these approaches arise from one and the same spirit, and they authorize us to speak of a philosophy of agriculture.[70]

Envisioned as a component of human wisdom and referring to the culture of the world that is, if we recall the etymology of the word '*mundus*', the woman's ornament, the dressing, and refers to the idea of the order and beauty present in the cosmos, agriculture is considered as the just production of food and the promotion of a just, that is to say healthy, food, both with respect to its provenance and because it is suitable for human beings. Agriculture is also inseparable from consciousness of the soils that condition the fertility of the earth and are essential to the life of human beings.

These types of agriculture, whether it is a matter of organic agriculture or of Fukuoka's natural agriculture, place the emphasis on the fertility of soils, the humus, and the forest cycle. Whatever the manner in which human beings imitate the cycles of nature, using compost, cultivating different grains at the same time, or engaging in agroforestry, the approach to nature is always dynamic, agriculture being conceived as a relation with the living. Indeed if living beings, such as plants, need nutrients, it is out of the question to administer them chemical fertilizers: the point of departure of this management of the earth will be to conserve or to restore its fertility. This fertility being connected to the cycle of organic matters, it will be necessary to supply it with waste organic products, or, as in Fukuoka's more radical approach, to not intervene.

Thus agriculture is the culture of nature, in the double sense of the term, in the sense that it maintains it and in the sense that it knows it, and that this knowledge, which begins in attention to the soils, is also a knowledge of oneself, a reminder of the fact that existing is positioning oneself on a soil. Humility comes from humus (soil). This is why agriculture is a part of wisdom. There can be no wisdom without taking agriculture into consideration. The end of cultures is at the horizon of the end of agriculture.[71] Conversely, the renewal of philosophy, as well as its effort to go beyond the dualism of nature and culture and to truly take seriously the corporeality of the subject and of 'living from', implies a growing interest in agriculture.

Finally, a phenomenology of inhabitation that places agriculture at the heart of a philosophy of 'living from', aiming to articulate ecology and existence, would be incomplete if it were not extended by a reflection on the animals with which we cohabit, either because we have domesticated them for breeding, or because they keep us company, or because they occupy a space that we should take into consideration in our activities when we exploit a forest, construct cities, or build buildings. Our relations with animals, and the manner in which we cohabit with them – often ignoring the fact that the space that we occupy is neither virgin, nor reserved for human beings alone, and forgetting the responsibilities that domestication conferred to us – must be examined. This will enable us to clarify the practices of breeding, of hunting, of fishing, and all other forms of exploitation of animals, and to ask ourselves what a political project would be that ensures more justice for all the members of the mixed community that we form with other living beings.

After having attempted to define the forms that can be taken by respect and justice towards animals, which are connected to us in diverse ways, and after having elaborated a relational theory of rights and of justice, we will be able to ask whether it is legitimate or not to kill an animal in order to eat it. Considering what motivates those who decide to abstain from consuming animal products presupposes that we confront the death of animals. This implies taking into account the current conditions of raising and of slaughter that most often follow the industrial model, but also of interrogating the meaning of carnal food, and of the division that it institutes between those beings whose flesh we consume and whose skin we use, on the one hand, and on the other those that we bury and do not eat.

Empathy, communication with animals, and sharing of the common world

'It is in the world of sensing that we encounter animals; this is the world shared by man and animal. In it, we understand the animal and, even more important, the animal understands us.'[72] The community that we form with animals is rooted in this communication that arises on the plane of sensing. The encounter with these beings that have a subjectivity, a lived experience, and a good that they experience in the first person, without needing their certainty of the world and their access to the real to be reflected or represented, does not only prohibit us from assimilating them to machines. It also proves that they are not simple moral patients towards whom we might have duties but who would be considered as if they were incapable of knowing what they need and of making us understand their needs and preferences.

Animals are individualized beings endowed with a non-representational subjectivity, and some of them communicate with us by means of sensing. In order to be a subject having interests and to communicate them to the Other, in order to have, as Husserl says, the power to make appear, it is not necessary to self-represent the world, nor to accompany the expression of the self with an 'I think'.[73] Nor is it necessary to be the observer of one's own life, to be conscious of one's place in the series of generations, and to espouse what Husserl, in the *Ideen II*, calls a vocation for being a self and for having a life, including a life in a community. Moreover, that an animal cannot say 'I' does not prevent it from having the structure of a self (*Ichstruktur*).[74] It addresses itself to us and can ask us something, as when my cat meows in a certain way for me to give her something to eat and in another way for me to open the door. That she is an *ego*, without being an *ego cogito*, changes nothing for the fact that she can look at me, that is to say return my gaze to me, thereby signifying that she exists not only for me, but that I also exist for her and that, if I have already *seen myself being seen* by her, as Derrida said, she knows when I am looking at her.[75]

Thus, animals exist, which is to say that they constitute their milieu. To live, for them as for us, 'is to radiate, it is to organize the milieu from and around a center of reference, which cannot itself be referred to without losing its original meaning.'[76] Animals do not see the world as we see it, but they are themselves the centre of their surrounding world and they communicate with other living beings. Not only is there only one world, the common world (*Mitwelt*), which is the world of life, but moreover we have 'the task of understanding the psychic life of the beasts, to lead it to a more and more complete experience.'[77] If we fail to recognize and to know the psychic life of animals, even when it is far from our own, will our world not have, Husserl asks, 'essential indeterminations'?[78]

This knowledge passes through the analysis of the notion of behaviour. This is the projection beyond the organism of a possibility that is interior to it; each living being takes, in its unique way within the milieu, what enables it to thrive. Thus, there is a plurality of milieus or of surrounding worlds (*Umwelte*), adjusted to the plurality of living beings, which thus divides the world according to their perceptual organs (*Merkwelt*) and their action (*Wirkwelt*).[79] Jakob von Uexküll distinguishes the notion of *Umwelt* from that of *Umgebung*, showing that the *Umwelt* is a circle of significativeness (*Bedeutungskreis*) in which a perceptual trait can only penetrate if it also finds a corresponding active trait. If we wish to understand the ambient world that matters for an animal, we must only bring into consideration that which has significance for this animal. Our ambient world is not the only world and, at the same time, we cannot say that every world is a surrounding world among others.

The world is thus a world that is shared with the animals, which does not mean that we can always understand them (well), nor that we have access to their psychic life in a direct way. As we will see in the definition of empathy, we can only interpret the comportment of the animal from our own perspective and from what we experience. Nevertheless, the world, as soon as there are living beings, ceases to be matter full of juxtaposed parts. As Merleau-Ponty says, the world 'opens up at the place where behavior appears'.[80] This normativity of the living being, which makes it possible to come up with new responses to new situations, and this individual global creation, which implies that the animal grasps in an affective or pathic way whether something is suitable for it or not, cannot be adequately expressed by the Pavlovian theory that reduces animal action to an ensemble of reflexes conditioned by excitation.

Whoever lives with an animal knows that there is someone behind the fur or the feathers, and that the manner of existing of our dogs or cats is significant. Each animal is a centre around which a comportment, charged with freedom, is organized. Like us, the animal is essentially curious, turned towards the world that it explores, and oriented towards an end. Therefore, it is not the category of causality, but rather that of signification, that enables us to understand the behaviour of animals. Although they do not say 'I

think' (*ego cogito*), they are still incarnated psychical egos that relate
to the world in a certain way. This is why Merleau-Ponty speaks about
them as Other individualized existences.[81] It is why in the relationship
with a companion animal, as well as with a pig, a cow, or a chicken,
something happens between them and with us.

This communication is facilitated when we have access to a
'kinesthetic system' (sensations and movements) that is not foreign
to our own. This explains why the affective exchanges that we have
with a dog, whose expressive eyes and bodily motions betray certain
emotions, can be intense. On the contrary, it is difficult to be touched
by insects, since we have trouble understanding them, in view of the
exceedingly large difference between their corporeality and ambient
world and ours.

As Husserl writes in a text of 1921, 'Normality and Animal Species',
the community of communication (*Mitteilungsgemeinschaft*) is
connected to a community of empathy (*Einfühlungsgemeinschaft*).[82]
A minimal capacity for feeling-with or for be-affected-by (*re-sentir*)
is necessary in order to communicate. This is why, even if we do
not express our emotions in the same way our dogs do, we can feel
with them and, likewise, they can know that we are sad.[83] However
certain animals sometimes have facial expressions that are similar
to our own, though this resemblance is the source of numerous
misunderstandings. This is what happens with the great apes. They
give us the impression of smiling in a friendly way when they expose
their teeth, the corners of the mouth extended back and downwards,
when what they are expressing by this grimace is their fear and
their submission.

Thus, even if I can understand the Other, whether it is a matter of
a human being or an animal, and can establish, to different degrees,
communication with them, I am nevertheless unable to enter into
their mind. Empathy does not imply fusion. On the contrary, it marks

the distance that separates me from the Other, whether this is a human being or an animal. This distance, as Husserl showed in the fifth of his *Cartesian Meditations*, is the very condition of possibility of empathy. Empathy occurs on the plane of sensing, but remains related to comprehension, since the capacity to grasp the emotion of the Other from within (*Einfühlung, empatheia*) enables me to gather information about them, to know what they are doing that is good or bad, or to imagine what I can do to ameliorate their situation (sympathy). The help that I can offer them presupposes that I understand that what is suitable for me is not necessarily well adapted to a different organism.[84] Emotional identification is at work in empathy and its neutralization, engendered in human beings, as in great apes, by situations of rivalry is an aspect of dehumanization.[85] However, empathy designates a modality of understanding, while pity is a modality of affectivity.

In other words, empathy presupposes at the same time distance as well as a certain resemblance between me and the Other, because, in order for it to be possible, I must recognize that the Other is a subjectivity. Empathy consists in attributing to the body that one sees, by empathetic transfer, a form of consciousness, and to consider that one is dealing with a flesh, an animate body (*Leib*), and not with an inanimate body (*Körper*). I thus confer to it the capacity to feel itself (*Leiblichkeit*).

Husserl, in this same text, as well as in 'Normality and Animal Species', confronts the question whether the animal is a form of alterity by proceeding, in conformity with his method of imaginary variation, to the analysis of diverse situations drawn from limit cases. I attribute a consciousness to a being from signs that permit me to think that it possesses an intentionality similar to my own. The Other, even if it is phenomenally strange, indeed 'monstrous', 'abnormal', is recognized nevertheless as being a consciousness, because I can ascribe to it a mobile 'point of view' on the world.

The examples that Husserl uses in the 1921 text (a man who has only a torso, a blind person, a mammal) show that it is always my flesh that constitutes the axis from which I ascribe a form of alterity and a consciousness to a being: it is the 'original apperception' and the 'necessary norm'.[86] It is in modifying my own body in my imagination that I can understand what is felt by the human torso, that I represent the modification of the perceptual system of the blind person, and that, taking note of a certain mobility in the animal, I am able to empathetically transfer an intentionality to it. The problem posed by this understanding of normal and abnormal modifications of my flesh resides in the fact that Husserl presupposes that my body is *the* norm, while in fact there exist several norms.

This difficulty, which he articulates in section 55 of the *Cartesian Meditations*, saying that 'the constituting of abnormality is possible only on the basis of an intrinsically antecedent normality' testifies to the intellectualist and egological character of Husserl's phenomenology.[87] We can ask ourselves whether this approach, which makes animality into a handicapped humanity, has only an epistemological meaning, or whether it also has, as certain passages in Husserl suggest, an ontological meaning. In this case, it would echo a sort of scale of beings, at the summit of which would be the human being, who would be a sort of recapitulation of the creation to the extent that he has several psychical layers (*Seelenschichten*) and possesses simultaneously a vegetative life, mobility, and rationality – it would be in starting out from him that I could understand the other living beings, by removing certain of the layers.

The question whether Husserl has a privative conception of the animal is however less interesting for clarifying the phenomenon of empathy than the idea that, as Merleau-Ponty also recognizes, 'we cannot think about the animal except from the foundation that we ourselves always are'.[88] Indeed, if we understand animals on the basis of our understanding of human beings, and we recognize the beasts as part of our world thanks to empathy, which is an 'assimilating modification of empathy between human beings', is this not in the first place because of our own limits, and because of the finitude of our power of knowing?

Of course, if Husserl thinks that animals are *really* 'abnormal variants of my humanity', this means that he is missing their alterity and condemning himself to conceiving of animals as inferior beings. Only seeing in them what they are 'missing', instead of recognizing that they have a different access to the real, he thus falls under the famous critique of Derrida, who, in *L'Animal que donc je suis*,[89] analyses the discourse of philosophers who have thought of animals as *alogon*, as that which does not speak, which reacts instead of responding, and so forth. However, it could be that instead of hurrying to accuse Husserl of anthropocentrism and even of anthropomorphism, one must consider the light that his approach throws on the notion of empathy, and on the condition of the encounter with animals, that is to say the subjectivities of different species.

We propose to define the type of community that we form with animals and, above all, to specify the form of empathy that characterizes our grasp of an animal. Indeed, on this subject it is important to note that, for Husserl, animals are not foreign human beings, but rather they exist as singular creatures that are so-and-so, and that are situated in particular relations with us. Moreover, what the philosopher brings, beyond the critiques that one can level at it – making of the animal 'a disfigured man', only considering the 'higher animals' – is to speak of degrees of empathy. We do not have the same capacity of feeling-with for a dog, a mosquito, or a louse (independently of the fact that these latter are, for us, undesirable guests). If our capacity to enter into a relation with certain animals and not with others does not prejudge their moral value, it is clear that the familiar animals, and those with which we share a corporeality and an ambient milieu that are not radically different from ours, give us the possibility to encounter these subjectivities of other species, and even to maintain relations that are not exempt from reciprocity, as we see with our domestic animals.

This question of degrees of empathy is at the heart of the analysis conducted by Max Scheler in *The Nature and Forms of Sympathy*.[90] It is different from an intellectualist conception that is in continuity with the Aristotelian *continuum* that leads to placing human beings who are capable of thinking high on the scale, while the insane and animals are lower. Scheler describes empathy as an immediate affective grasp. Feeling-with an animal is not putting oneself in its place in order to learn how it feels, but rather encountering it in its manifestations. Just as we read anger in a gesture without needing to recall or to imitate anger, so too we are able to understand the joy of a dog in seeing it bark and wag its tail, without needing to make these gestures ourselves. It is in this sense that Scheler postulates an elementary base that reflects a common affective life, a unity of pre-individual affectivity.

If this affective sensibility gives rise to a community of communication that is only possible between human beings and certain animals, this does not mean that insects, with which our affective exchange is non-existent, are either not endowed with sensibility or that they are not able to communicate between themselves. If it is important to liberate empathy from the intellectualist schema in which Husserl confined it, we must nevertheless not confuse it with pity, which is a pre-reflexive identification and the original condition of empathy, as we will see. Pity, although its roots extend into a more primitive affective state, remains a modality of understanding. In order to interact with another living being, notably in order to care for it, it is necessary to understand and to feel with it. In this situation, the act of understanding and the be-affected-by (*re-sentir*) are conjoint and not disjoint.

This is what we see with veterinarians: they are responsible for patients that, like newborns, do not speak our articulate language and that express their affects and their pain in a different way than our own. In observing the behaviour of animals, veterinarians must be able to read in it anger, distress, fear, and weariness. Without this empathy, care is impossible. However this faculty of feeling-with and of understanding the Other, above all when the Other does not possess our language, does not require us to put ourselves in the place of the Other, asking ourselves what it is like to have a broken paw, for example. In order to understand what empathy is, it is necessary to stop believing that it is possible for a human being to feel the fear of a beast being led to the slaughterhouse. The other pitfall is reductionism, which consists in denying the suffering of the animal, pretexting that it does not express it in the same way we do. Thus, empathy presupposes that we recognize that the animal in front of us has its own way of experiencing the world, and that we find ways to approach it, in order to grasp what it needs, for the language that we use is a way, starting from ourselves, to understand others.

In fact, I cannot suffer in the body of another, nor can I feel its pain and its suffering, in particular when I have no experience of this pain and of this suffering, and when I belong to another species. However, I can know that the Other suffers, by paying attention not only to its manifestations, but also to the words that I use in order to translate them. Thus do ordinary words open up to us a non-reductionist perspective on the animal, for the grammar of language, which in this sense breaks down the species barrier, reveals to us that, when we say that this animal that is in front of us suffers, these words have meaning. The question is not one of imagining what it is like to have a broken paw, but rather to ask ourselves at what moment we use this or that word to describe the real ('suffer', 'being conscious', etc.). This examination of the use of words and this philosophy of ordinary language open up a path for an approach to the animal that enables us to speak for it, to know when it has pain, and thus to better interact with it in order to relieve it, to practice this or that intervention, or even to stop an experiment.

This analysis of empathy removes nothing of the importance of pity, which plays a major role in our relationship with others. However, while empathy proceeds from feeling and from understanding, and while it presupposes a certain distance between me and the Other, pity is situated only on the plane of the pathic, and it is originary. It is a pre-reflexive identification, prior to any other identification, including that which, in enabling us to recognize ourselves as members of the human species or of this or that social category, distinguishes ourselves from other living beings.[91] This innate repugnance at seeing any other living being suffer unnecessarily, and the fact of suffering from its suffering, strike at the very heart of our shared vulnerability.

Pity precedes the separation between the 'I' and the 'not-I'; this separation makes understanding and targeted assistance possible, but it also accounts for the cleavage that is expressed in the suspension of our affective investment towards certain beings. Like the neutralization of pity, this defence mechanism is generated by the conditions of factory farming. It is also one of the means used by farmers and consumers to accept killing an animal and eating its flesh. Before reviewing the philosophical questions that arise in connection with eating flesh, it is important to show that factory farming is characterized by the rupture of the connection and of the symbiotic understanding that exists between human beings and animals, and by the burying of pity.

This symbiotic understanding is defined by pursuing and fleeing. The first stage of sensorial experience is that of separation and union, for the sensing being is destined to unite itself with certain other parties or to separate from them. In other words, sensing is an experience of empathy, a sensing-with-things, 'directed to the physiognomic characteristics of the alluring and the frightening'.[92] In the same way, this polarity that unfolds in the reciprocal movement of approach and distancing is essential in our relations with animals. Symbiotic understanding can only occur if this double possibility – fleeing or pursuing – is on offer. The act of pursuing only makes sense if the animal is able to flee: 'Any external curtailment of these polar relationships prevents or destroys symbiotic understanding'.[93]

The privation of freedom is thus the mutilation of this polar relationship. Animals in a cage have no possibility of shying away when they are approached and they are unable to understand the friendly attitude of human beings. The closing-in of the gestating sow in an impoverished environment in which nothing happens is a mutilation of its body, which is the place of the immediate relation of the animal with the world and with time. This hindered body also illustrates the mutilation of sensing that is imposed on it, since the world that it endures is deprived of any signification other than to eat and to drink. The sow lives this non-expression of its senses in its body. It must undertake an immense task of acceptance in order to bear this lack of power and this absence of signification.

Finally, in factory farming, any relation of animals among themselves and with the human beings who raise them is destroyed. The stereotyped behaviours, like the fact that sows bite incessantly at the bars of their cages, attest to the erasure of their free behaviours. Condemned to experience a time that does not pass, this is how they react.[94] The behaviours of the animals attest to a breach of their integrity and of their capacity to act on their environment. They do not reveal their madness – since they are indeed within the real – but rather the illegitimacy of the system of factory farming that destroys beings, prohibits any relation between them, and, in reducing animals to tools of production, dehumanizes us, and severs us from the meaning that raising animals has had since the Neolithic.

For what our relationship with animals teaches us, in particular with the animals that we have domesticated, that we have invited into the home (*domus*), and that live with us, is that these other subjectivities are not only subjects of their surrounding world, nor even subjects of a common world that we form with them. The recognition of their intentionality and of their individuality, which familiarity ties make irrefutable, also opens up to a veritable encounter with them.

The domestic animal leaves a specific mark on us, as does every human being we encounter. It shares with animals of the same species a certain number of common traits, connected to its ethological needs, and it is unjust not to respect these needs when we raise animals. Moreover, each animal has a personality, a unique way of treating the world, of relating to us, and a biography. Animals humanize us in the sense that, in contact with them, we become reconnected to our emotions, we communicate on the plane of sensing, and we experience the truth of an empathic encounter and of a 'communication with the world more ancient than thought'.[95] They also connect us to the history and to the space that our predecessors transmitted to us and that they constructed with animals and, in part, thanks to them.

Rather than defending an abolitionist perspective, pushing for the disappearance of domestic species in order to end our domination on farm animals and pets, we think that respect and justice for them presuppose that we assume the responsibilities that are related to the situation of dependence in which they find themselves with regard to us, as well as to the vulnerability that is the consequence of this dependence. This implies being grateful for everything they bring to us by providing to them the care they need and by ensuring that their freedom is not excessively limited – a freedom that is necessarily hampered in the case of the domestic animal, as we see with our cats and dogs that are sterilized and that we walk on leashes and only let out while under surveillance. Through our affection and our efforts to procure for our pets an environment that permits them to thrive, we are able to compensate in a morally acceptable way for the privation of their liberty that domestication entails.

Gratitude also makes sense when considering animals that are raised to produce food or wool. Indeed, factory farming is characterized precisely by a total absence of reciprocity: animals must produce more and more in a minimum of time and at ever lower cost for the people who exploit them. Their most elementary needs are not satisfied and they are locked in for life, without their freedom of movement, their desire to explore the world, and their need for contact ever having the possibility to be expressed.

When we consider the being of animals and the possibility of establishing communication with them, we place ourselves at the level of sensing, at which we encounter them as members of a moral community that merits our consideration. Not respecting their needs and their desire to live, preventing them from expressing the joy to exist, which is, as we have seen, originary, and which animals communicate as soon as they are in an appropriate environment, is to make the common world in which we encounter them into an alien world, where it is unlikely that we experience happiness. For animals are not other existences alongside our own: their existence is mingled with ours, whether we have forged bonds of affection with them, as for our pets, or whether we consider the attachment of farmers, in extensive farming, for the cows that they know and that they have seen being born. The fact the farmer leads them to death raises questions, but this does not diminish the force of his sentiment of attachment to his animals, which is indissociable from his vocation and which explains why he feels justified in his work when he knows his cows are happy.[96]

On the contrary, in factory farming animals are reduced to a single function, in conformity with intensive labour. They are not individualized, as in traditional farming, wherein each cow has a name, and anyway they are too numerous for the needs of each of them to be attended to. Specialized labour forbids farmers to spend time with their animals, and the living conditions of these animals do not permit them to communicate in any other way than in reacting by cries or by panicked movements, as seen in factory farms where cows are permanently stabled and the farmer provokes a reaction of fear whenever he enters the building. The cage, the darkness, the iron bars, and the overpopulation make up their surrounding world. It is a world that closes them in and from which they cannot escape. However, whatever means are used by a system that has changed the meaning of domestication by constructing buildings in which animals are parked, and thus remain invisible to the inhabitants of the farm as well as to visitors, the life of animals remains intimately mingled with our own.

In fact, farmers earn their living from this work that makes use of animals, and this activity nourishes them in the sense that they construct themselves through it, whether it makes them happy or not, whether they are satisfied by it (because they could reach their objective of profitability and of performance, which are still socially valued), or whether they are ashamed of the conditions of life that they inflict on these sensitive beings. Individuals invent all sorts of strategies in order to not suffer (excessively) from the suffering of animals, but the majority of them remain haunted by traumatizing images, as the employees of industrial slaughterhouses confess, which give them nightmares in which living animals are pursuing them.[97] We are not able to mistreat sensitive beings without being profoundly harmed by what we do to them. This is true also when farming and slaughtering destroy all communication between human beings and animals, because the number, the objective of profitability, and the rate of production prohibit any relationship, and force farmers and slaughterhouse employees to harden themselves, or because the conditions in which the animals are held and killed reify the animal that, when it falls ill or panics, is killed or beaten in order not to slow down production or to interrupt the chain.

We know today that factory farming, which emerged after the Second World War but which is related to a project of industrialization of all spheres of production that was born in the nineteenth century, is an untenable model. The environmental cost of factory farming was known by the 1990s, and the economic and social disaster to which this system leads is apparent today in an irrefutable way. Of course, it was clear from the beginning that the objective of profitability that led the transformation of farming into an industry could only lead to failure: the farmers were required to constantly expand in order to produce more for less, and they were forced to take on debt. They became more and more dependent on companies selling foods and drugs for cattle, as well as on technicians controlling the rations that were given, the productivity of their enterprise, and the moment at which it is appropriate to declare a cow or a sow unfit. The farmers are themselves also the victims of a system deriving from an economic model that cannot take into consideration the value of the human and non-human beings involved, since its sole objective is profit.

Such a system, which crushes workers, also exploits consumers by manipulating them, since it is only viable if outlets exist to which the products may be exported. It is thus maintained by a vast marketing campaign using health-related arguments and relying on the complicity of public authorities, as we see in public health campaigns that promote the daily consumption of meat and animal products and that prohibit vegetarian meals from being offered in school cafeterias.[98]

Not everybody is aware that consuming meat daily is an imperative dictated by the agroalimentary industry, and not the result of taking into consideration our nutritional needs and our health. On the other hand everyone knows today, thanks to videos circulating on the internet, the toll this system takes on animals and on the human beings who raise and slaughter them. In the same way, no one ignores that the slaughterhouses, which since the nineteenth century are found on the outskirts of cities, are places where an extreme violence takes place. The number of animals that, after a long and distressing journey, wait for hours without water or food to be killed, and the infernal rate of the chain of production, which requires from employees that they perform repetitive gestures as fast as possible, rendering impossible the accompaniment of the animal that is going to die, and sometimes making the compulsory stunning of animals before slaughter impossible to apply, are not a secret. In addition to the muscle and bone pains brought about by the repetition of the same gestures, which wears down the body prematurely, the employees of industrial slaughterhouses are daily witnesses of a mass murder.

This suffering and this injustice towards human beings and animals, submitted to constraints that go against their subjectivity, hit them on the plane of sensing and of empathetic communication, which implies that they are affected at the heart of their most immediate relationship to the world. This does not however motivate consumers to reduce their demand for meat and for animal products, though these lifestyle changes could have a considerable impact on the agroalimentary industry, for this only operates as a result of demand and, for this reason, it creates ever new needs that serve as outlets for the flow of products, whatever the waste that is occasioned by this overproduction.

Such a remark is not meant as an accusation against consumers, but rather as a way to expose the community of misery that unites animals and human beings, in particular those who produce foods and those to whom the task of killing animals is delegated. It also underlines our individual responsibility. Human beings today are not guilty: they no more speak elogiously of factory farming than they take responsibility for the creation of capitalism. However, as a result of their history that is also, since the Neolithic, the history of domestication, they are responsible for the animals that our ancestors, 10,000 years ago, brought into the home, made dependent on us, and modified through selection, so that they would acquire traits suitable to us. These animals are not among us, they are with us, whether we encounter them or not, whether we consume their flesh or not. Our political community is also a 'zoopolitical' community: we have a duty of justice towards animals, in particular towards those that live with us.

Thus is history not only human history; it is also important to write it taking into consideration 'the animal point of view', as Éric Baratay writes.[99] Our history is a history of co-constitution, for we would not be what we are without cows, horses, donkeys, or sheep. It is important to recall that the objective of domestication – which only works with animals capable of communicating and living with us, and that are relatively agreeable and affectionate – was not initially exclusively to feed on their flesh. The raising of sheep for wool, the use of animals for ploughing, the role of pasturage in the design of landscapes, and the presence of animals in war, horses and mules, as well as cats, pigeons, and rats, testify to the multiple functions of domestication and of the common work of human beings and animals. However, this does not mean that it is legitimate, when we speak of the world that is common to humans and domestic animals, to speak of a tacit domestic contract.[100]

The social contract presupposes consent. This is why it is impossible, as Hobbes writes in chapter 16 of *Leviathan*, to make contracts with gods and animals. Moreover, it requires symmetry between all the beings who find some benefit in it. The exchange should guarantee an equality and a reciprocity, and should realize the rule of quid pro quo, for if human beings provide food and a home to the animals that they raise, they also lead them to death and often do not allow them to attain an age that would permit them to enjoy their existence. They maintain them moreover in a relation of dependence that the animals are not able to terminate. Not only are the great majority of them, as a result of the traits that have been selected, unable to live in the wild, but moreover they do not have the freedom to get out from this situation. To argue that this natural contract is tacit is to forget that domestication, even when it is characterized by a certain respect for animals, was accomplished in the interest of human beings, and not that of animals. The animals cannot break the contract, since domestication is irreversible. It is thus illegitimate to speak of the domestic contract.

These remarks do not preclude the fact that the interests of animals should be taken into consideration in the formulation of the duties of the state and of the principles of political rights, which constitutes the social contract elaborated in the present work. This contract takes effect between human beings, but the interests of domestic animals, which form a moral and political community with us, are included in the definition of the common good. In the same way, we cannot act as if the orangutans, whose habitat has been destroyed by palm oil plantations, did not exist, and as if we had the right to exterminate them. The animals are there: their simple presence obligates us. As for the domestic animals, they belong to our world.

Two additional reasons explain why it is necessary to do away with the notion of a natural or domestic contract: it legitimizes violence towards animals and masks the fact that they are raised in order to be killed. It is important to face this truth, even when farmers offer their animals good living conditions. The transformation of farming into the production of animals has not led to a rupture of the domestic contract, since there never was a contract between human beings and animals, but it has indeed brought about a rupture of the bond between human beings and the animals they have domesticated. Now that these animals are here, with us, in our world, they impose on us duties and recognition of their rights. These rights flow from their status as sensitive beings, but also from their capacity to be moral agents, having their own good and being able to communicate it.

The interest of a relational theory of rights, which goes further than the affirmation of the inviolability of sensitive beings endowed with universal negative rights, protecting them from torture, bad treatment, confinement, is that it is inserted within a larger project. It is a matter of thinking about justice towards all of the members of a mixed community, without confusing the duties that we have towards our human brothers and sisters, and those we have towards the various animals.

Either humans and animals live together in the same space, as is the case with the domestic animals that can no longer return to the wild, or humans and animals occupy separate spaces, as we see with the animals that do not wish to live with us, or, still, humans are confronted with a group of animals – such as foxes, dormice, or pigeons – that are called liminal because, without being domesticated, they settle in the proximity of our dwellings and find conditions there that are favourable to their development. The fact that we treat them as intruders by exterminating or removing them does not imply that they do not have the right to exist. This shows simply that we have difficulty coexisting with other species and granting a right of residence to those that have an intermediate status.

Zoopolis and justice towards animals

To speak of 'zoopolis' is to take seriously the fact that we are not the only species on earth.[101] The interests of animals must also enter into the definition of the common good. Of course, the political community that we form has its rules and we cannot accord citizenship to everyone, but this community is not exclusively human. This becomes clear when we recall that the foundation of the political theory that we are seeking to elaborate is a radical phenomenology of sensing and a philosophy of corporeality and of 'living from'.

To limit the political community to the community of human beings alone is only meaningful if we judge that the intellect of human beings authorizes us to subjugate all other living beings. Such a declaration is nowhere to be found. We do not find it in the biblical texts.[102] Nor can we pass our time blaming Descartes for his theory of the animal-machine, let alone accuse him of being the leader of anthropocentrism.[103] In fact, for him, only God is a final cause, and it is presumptuous to think that the world was made for us, since 'instead of discovering the perfections that are truly within us, we will attribute to other creatures imperfections which they do not possess, so as to raise ourselves above them'.[104]

The despotic position of human beings in relation to nature is thus relatively recent, since it dates from the beginnings of the Industrial Revolution and culminates in the second half of the twentieth century. It is delegitimated as a result of its disastrous ecological, social, and economic consequences, and because it goes together with a mutilated conception of the human being, the materiality of whose existence and whose medial dimension are not taken seriously. A third reason authorizes us to reject the premises of this despotic position, which has also served to maintain an economy that is blind to the outer limit of all production and indifferent to the meaning of the various goods that are exchanged and to the real needs of beings. This reason is founded on the phenomenology of habitation and of cohabitation, which flows from the updated description of existentials in the philosophy of 'living from'.

Indeed, to live is to 'live from' and to 'live with'. Yet, if we live from landscapes, if we nourish ourselves on plants, it is clear that animals, in virtue of their sensibility or of their vulnerable self, but also of their capacity to reveal the world and of the empathic communication that exists between them and us, are not only that from which we live, nor those with whom we cohabit. They also form with us a moral and political community. What is needed now is to clarify what this moral and political community implies in terms of rights and duties.

In order to do this, the theory of justice defended by Sue Donaldson and Will Kymlicka is very helpful. They integrate the approach that has classically been adopted by those who think that animals have rights. However, they do not limit themselves to establishing the list of negative rights that protect the basic interests of animals, asserting their inviolability, that is to say the fact that these interests cannot be sacrificed for the greater good of others. They also specify what their positive rights are, adopting a relational and differentiated approach to rights and thus concretely indicating the obligations of human beings. Moreover, in grounding the affirmation according to which animals possess inviolable rights on the fact that they are subjects who have a subjective experience of life and of the world, they reinforce this juridical theory, which is classical in the animalist literature and has considerable practical implications, since it implies removing animals from confinement, slavery, vivisection, and butchering.

In *Taking Rights Seriously*, Ronald Dworkin showed that a right is, as in a card game, a sort of trump.[105] It protects those individuals to which these rights are conferred by preserving them from situations that would be harmful to them, and by being enforceable. Indeed, if we apply, as Donaldson and Kymlicka do, this definition of the rights of animals, any utilitarian approach that argues for the well-foundedness of the sacrifice of some animal lives for the happiness of a greater number of human lives, will be pushed aside. Utilitarian calculi will not be admitted, nor those theories that propose a threshold of tolerance that permits certain uses of animals, and establishes criteria of acceptability in the exploitation of animals.[106] Thus, when it is declared that animals are the bearers of universal inviolable rights, it is necessary, to speak with Locke, to put up a 'protective barrier' around them in order to guarantee respect for their basic rights. This position presupposes an egalitarianism that confers basic rights to all members of a political community. We can no longer adopt 'Kantianism for human beings and utilitarianism for animals', to take up the expression used by Robert Nozick in *Anarchy, State, and Utopia*.[107]

To think that inviolability applies to all sensitive beings does not however mean that animals have the same rights as humans, as if it were a matter of extending the rights of human beings to animals and basing these negative and positive rights onto those that have meaning for human beings. More precisely, in a relational theory of justice, domestic animals and wild animals are not the bearers of the same positive rights, since they are not entitled to claim the same things. However, all have the right to be protected from treatment that violates their basic interests. For the principle of inviolability flows from their quality as subjects, even if their lived experience and the life they experience in the first person are not reflected upon and do not become the object of a representation which they would be able to debate, as in the deliberative model of Rawls or Habermas.

Such an affirmation not only coheres with the argument that takes marginal cases into consideration, notably human beings who suffer from severe mental disabilities and who are incapable of formulating their vision of the world or of philosophizing about their own interests, even though we consider them as subjects bearing inviolable rights. Instead of simply denouncing the speciesism that leads to granting rights to all human beings whatever their cognitive capacities, and thus to preserving them from certain painful experiments, and accepting at the same time that these same experiments are conducted on animals, Donaldson and Kymlicka judiciously place the emphasis on the meaning and the origin of inviolability.

The fact that an individual possesses a moral status and has the right to juridical protection limiting the right of others to exploit him does not flow from his capacity to engage in complex reasoning. The affirmation of the inviolability of a being derives rather from the recognition of its subjectivity. As soon as there is someone behind the fur, the skin, or the feathers, this individual has inviolable rights. It is not necessary to subordinate negative rights to the possession of personality, which is traditionally attached to certain intellectual faculties or to the capacity to universalize one's maxims. Subjectivity, the fact of being a vulnerable self who is the subject of one's own life, suffices to be a bearer of rights. The interest of this approach is not only that it permits us to take into account the dependence in which we all find ourselves at one moment or another of our existence, without thereby becoming people of a secondary rank. It also shows that inviolability is the fruit of an intersubjective recognition, making from our relations the point of departure of the understanding of rights.

That the theory according negative rights to animals is difficult to accept, in view of the consequences it entails, namely the suppression of a number of practices that violate their basic rights, does not preclude the fact that, at a theoretical level, we are able, even if we are coming from different moral and religious traditions, to arrive at overlapping consensus.[108] In fact, recognition that all vulnerable beings have the right to protection of their basic rights is accessible to everyone, whatever our beliefs and whatever these sources of morality to which we have recourse.

This is what is at issue as well in our philosophy of corporeality, which insists on vulnerability and rests on a phenomenology of feeling, whose pathic dimension has been affirmed several times, not least when we showed that it is here that human beings and animals communicate. Everyone is able to admit that a being that is a subjectivity demands different protection from what is required in the case of ecosystems, of plants, and of everything that constitutes nature. This does not mean that the plant is nothing, nor that sensitivity does not pertain to it, although, in this case, it is important to make a distinction between the sensitivity of plants, which interact with their milieus, and that of animals, who experience pain and suffering.

The harm that plants and ecosystems can undergo as a result of our behaviour imposes limits on our right to exploit them as we please. These limits testify to the fact that human beings are not authorized to mortgage the future of other human beings and of other species by destroying the planet so as to gain personal enrichment. They thus connect human beings to their responsibility in the way in which they inhabit the earth they have inherited. Even if we accord a non-instrumental value to plants, which are not only there for us and were not created for us, we will speak of them in terms of respect, and not of justice, the latter term being reserved for beings of flesh, human and non-human, who inhabit or will inhabit the earth. As soon as we are dealing with animals, it is no longer only a question of harm inflicted, but of injustice.

This injustice not only concerns the relationship between the human species and other species; it has a meaning for each human being and each animal taken individually. Individuality, the insistence on vulnerability as susceptibility to pain and suffering, as well as the fact of existing by ever considering the world in a unique way, implies not only that animals have inviolable basic rights, which must be guaranteed, but that moreover they possess positive rights, which the analysis of our relations with them enables us to uncover.

It is in this sense that there is a call of the animal. It speaks to us and, whatever our culture, we are able to understand this call. Animals count: they enter into ethics and justice. As a result of our habits and of our narratives and fables, to which we still make reference in justifying our eating habits and our leisure activities, we struggle to derive the consequences of this truth. Nevertheless, in our depths, when we situate ourselves on the plane of sensing, we know perfectly well that it is irrefutable.

Recognition of animals as vulnerable subjects presupposes recognition of the inviolable rights of which they are the bearers. It is thus unjust to kill an animal, to torture it, or to confine it, except when we cannot do differently. This restriction is connected to what Rawls calls, in §22 of *A Theory of Justice*, the 'circumstances of justice'.[109] It suggests that universal rights are not absolute, although this has nothing to do with the theory of thresholds of acceptability of animal exploitation, or with the arguments that see in experimentation a necessary evil. That inviolability depends on the circumstances of justice implies only that I do not have the right to kill an animal, except when this is the only way to save my life or when it is necessary to hunt in order to eat.

It is important to recall that in so-called primitive societies, to kill an animal in order to eat was so far from being taken for granted that it was taboo to do so without offering some of it to the gods. This offering could not be assimilated, except by an abuse of language, to ritual sacrifice, in which a sheep is slaughtered without first being stunned in order to please a God who is thought to appreciate the spilling of blood and who, in exchange, will protect his child or his goods.[110] The sacrificed meat of so-called primitive peoples does not signify that it was legitimate to kill an animal because the death of the animal enabled human beings to obtain the favours of God. On the contrary, the offering meant that the act by which one takes a life is not neutral, and that it is only acceptable if it is necessary. In our societies, in which we have fruits and grains in abundance, and in which it is possible, if we take the trouble to cook, to nourish ourselves adequately without causing the blood of animals to flow, we have the duty to promote the circumstances of justice that enable us to respect the inviolable rights of animals, and that bring it about that their killing is an exception.

If the notion of inviolability attached to all vulnerable subjects, as well as the notion of negative rights, can be universally accepted, it remains evident that the way we think about the rights of animals is often insufficient. Most of the time it boils down to denouncing the illegitimacy of practices, or of demanding the abolition of any form of animal exploitation. This approach has practical as well as theoretical limitations. It leads us to associate the recognition of the rights of animals with abolitionism, or to affirm that detention of a companion animal is illegitimate, that it is necessary to cease domestication, and no longer raise cows, pigs, cats, and dogs. Now if the theory that confers inviolable rights to animals has demanding practical implications, it is not necessarily opposed to domestication. Moreover, this approach, which restrains the question of justice towards animals to a declaration that simply puts forward their negative rights, does not enable us to know what relational obligations we have towards them. Such a lacuna, which explains why in practice the classical theory of animal rights has never led to a substantial amelioration of the condition of animals, also testifies to a misunderstanding of rights.

In fact, rights are not essentially intended to express the being of beings; they have above all a functional role. They orchestrate relations between human beings and, in the case of interest to us, between human beings and animals. They indicate what will happen to us if we do not respect this or that rule. Thus, instead of deriving obligations from the moral and juridical status of different beings, as is done in animal ethics, it is more judicious to determine rights on the basis of the relations that exist between the concerned parties. This is particularly important when we are seeking to elaborate the rules that give a positive content to laws and that make obligations explicit.

It is because it starts from our relations with different animals, in order to determine their positive rights and to think about our obligations towards them, that Donaldson and Kymlicka's theory strikes us as relevant. It presupposes that we distinguish between domestic, wild, and liminal animals. It would be a misinterpretation to think that these categories serve to grant a different moral or juridical status to each of these groups of animals, or to establish a hierarchy among them. It is rather a matter of understanding what they may expect from us. Even if our politics is a zoopolitics, as we interfere with animals, all of them are not living with us. However, all are affected by our activities, including wild animals and migratory animals that pass through our territories. It is thus appropriate to ask which interests each category of animals seeks to preserve, in order to know how we might respect them.

Donaldson and Kymlicka draw inspiration from the distinction between citizens, members of sovereign communities, and residents, in order to determine the content of the rights conferred to the three groups of animals mentioned above and to think about our obligations towards them. Domestic animals are thought of as our fellow citizens, who have the right to live with us and whose interests should be taken into consideration in the definition of the common good. The theory of citizenship, enriched by works that for the past few decades have attempted to bring disabled people out of the social and political invisibility in which they were long confined, enables us to think concretely about the rights of domestic animals by conceiving them as moral agents that not only have rights, but must also factor into political decisions and be represented. This tour de force, which presupposes that animals have positive rights and not only negative ones, requires a reconfiguration of the categories of autonomy and participation.

In order to recognize that beings that have their own good and are capable of communicating have the rights attached to citizenship – such as the right to inhabit our territory, to benefit from measures of care and from decent conditions of life, but also to participate in collective decisions – it is necessary to free ourselves from an intellectualist conception of autonomy. The dependent-agent model that is used to maintain the autonomy of people in a situation of disability is, in this respect, particularly interesting for proving that one can be autonomous, even when one is deprived of the cognitive and linguistic ability to make one's voice heard in a public context.[111]

People with severe cognitive deficits have desires and values, which means that they attach a sentiment of self-esteem to the realization of certain activities, and confer a moral importance to certain choices. They have, moreover, interests to assert. A just state must undertake to defend these interests by protecting vulnerable people against the abuses to which they can easily fall victim. However, they often have difficulty in translating their desires and their values into acts; they must thus be represented by people who are capable not of deciding in their place, but of deciphering their will and of proposing to them solutions that suit *them*.

Not only does autonomy, thought of in this way as a double capacity (to be an axiomatic subject and to be able to translate one's values into acts), remain relevant even in beings that do not speak or that are not endowed with representational subjectivity, but moreover we see clearly that it is sufficient to enter into a symbiotic communication with them in order to represent them, which is to say to speak in their name while respecting their will. In order to be a citizen, it is thus not necessary to have a philosophy of life that makes it possible to formulate the metaphysical foundations of one's positions or to make arguments. In the same way, recognition of the political status of domestic animals, which are individualized agents and possess a moral status even if they are not deliberative agents, presupposes that we authorize them to express themselves and to communicate with us, instead of confining them within a world that mutilates and that destroys any interaction between them and with us.

We can add to what Donaldson and Kymlicka write, that the interests of domestic animals, which should be taken into account in agriculture negotiations and in the organizational aspects of raising animals, could be defended by those who know them well. Former farmers or ethologists could thus be in a sense the 'representatives' of animals in new deliberative bodies, as we will see below in the chapter on the renewal of democracy. Even if it is very unlikely that we witness in our lifetime the disappearance of animal exploitation that leads to their death, it is certain that a relational theory of justice towards domestic animals, accompanied by institutional modifications that are necessary in order to bring them into the republic, would lead to an improvement in their condition. Enclosure, deprivation of social bonds, castration without anaesthetics, debeaking, early weaning, and all the practices that testify to the greatest iniquity towards animals would cease: they would be considered as vulnerable subjects that do not count for nothing and are members of the political community, even if they are not assimilable to our fellow humans and cannot vote. The fact that animals do not have a memory of the decades of horror that we have inflicted on them and that we alone are responsible for their future underlines even more our injustice towards them.

With respect to wild animals, justice, according to Donaldson and Kymlicka, consists in respecting their right to live independently of us. We must guarantee the conditions for the exercise of their sovereignty. This does not necessarily imply, as it does in Hobbes, the establishment of an authority, such as the state, that is opposed to society and that is capable of exercising absolute power over it. In reality wild animals form sovereign communities, for, even if they do not have a state, the great apes or the wolves live in societies that are organized according to strict rules. They do not manifest any desire to live with us, and our presence, if we encroach on their territory, disturbs them. Recognition of the sovereignty of wild animals means that it is our duty to respect their legitimate right to maintain their social organization on their territory. What obligations, now, flow from this affirmation?

To capture wild animals in order to make them work in circuses, where their life might be longer, but where we allow ourselves to isolate them from other members of their species and to remove them from their environmental and social milieu, is unjust. As for their detention in zoos, it is only acceptable when it concerns endangered species, and when they have enough space and a rich environment. Recognition of the sovereignty of wild animals also requires that we limit the noise pollution that can disturb their organization and degrade their environment. Moreover, their existence requires us to recognize that the forest that we exploit is not empty, and that our right of occupation of land is not absolute. When we invade their territory and we destroy their habitat, we act towards them like the colonists acted towards the Native Americans.

Finally, if sovereignty is connected to territory, it is clear that each territory is home to several communities of animals. All sovereignty is shared sovereignty, as we see in particular with birds and fish. A respectful cohabitation with sovereign animal communities would justify that, during the period of bird migration, the lights in skyscrapers be turned off at midnight. This is what is done in New York to prevent the birds that use the moon and stars at night as points of reference from becoming disoriented by the artificial light of the buildings and crashing as a result.

In the case of natural catastrophes, as well as when their living conditions are threatened by the pollution that we have created, our responsibility goes beyond the duty of non-interference that enjoins us to let animals live their life. The creation of sanctuaries, where their living conditions might be acceptable, but which serve above all to give us a good conscience, is insufficient to express these duties of care and of assistance. Parks and sanctuaries are created in order to prevent the animals whose habitats we have destroyed or divided from dying of hunger, or to keep them from being killed by humans who have monopolized their space and reduced them to feed on their plantations, as is the case with elephants. They do not demonstrate that we have succeeded in establishing relations of justice with these wild animals. Respect for their sovereignty prohibits invasion, colonization, and exploitation, and is opposed to a paternalist management of their life, since this respect goes together with the recognition of their capacity to maintain their social organization on their territory and to regulate their population.

These remarks bring us to the last group of animals that Kymlicka and Donaldson invite us to consider in the light of the rights that are conferred to residents. Liminal animals, which do not manifest the desire to interact with us but live close to our habitations and sometimes in our houses and gardens, such as rodents and squirrels, are not considered as citizens forming a mixed political community with us. This does not mean that they do not have the right to be there, nor that we should treat them as intruders that must be removed or exterminated. This is however what happens most of the time, liminal animals having an intermediate status that leaves them particularly exposed to human cruelty, while also explaining their proliferation, which is related to the abundance of food available to them in cities and villages. How can we think about relations of justice towards liminal animals, and in what sense can reflection on the status of residents, whether it concerns immigrants or refugees, help us to understand our obligations towards these beings?

These animals are diverse, since we find at the same time species that have adapted to our habitat, such as squirrels and foxes, as well as exotic animals that have been introduced into a milieu, or that, deprived of their predator, have significantly increased, such as the river rat in France. There can also be individuals whose ancestors were domesticated, as is the case with certain cats, but also pigs and horses. Most of the time, liminal animals are perceived as invaders. In most cases they do not allow themselves to be approached, and they cannot be domesticated. However, it is not because they cannot be treated as our fellow citizens that they must be despised. We did not invite them into our homes, even if sometimes our imprudence or lack of hygiene makes us responsible for their proliferation. The problem is that the response to their presence, often experienced as an inconvenience, is extermination by poison or by gun, or removal. Yet it is appropriate, Kymlicka and Donaldson write, to respect the basic rights of these individuals who are our co-residents while also controlling their population.

Their status as co-residents means that their interests are not included in the definition of the common good in the same way as domestic animals. We do not have the duty to accept them, but, once they are there, we ought to coexist with them rather than deny their right to existence. The task is not necessarily easy, for example, when dealing with rodents. It is likely that we sometimes find ourselves placed in circumstances in which the only solution is to kill them. However, it is our duty to promote those circumstances of justice that make peaceful coexistence with these animals possible, by managing our trash with caution and by constructing barriers that prevent them from coming in and proliferating. Finally, the simple fact of respecting their right to exist instead of stigmatizing them enables us to measure the gap that exists between the discourses that, for the pleasure of hunters, categorize certain species among the harmful ones, and the reality that often shows that these animals provide important ecological services, such as the fox that eats rodents. Moreover, whoever has a bit of critical spirit will understand that these animal populations are self-regulating in relation to their ecosystems and to the available food, on the condition nevertheless that other individuals are not introduced in order to satisfy the desire of the hunters, and that a situation is not created in which their overpopulation makes necessary the brutal intervention of human beings.

This politicization of the animal question is thus connected to a complete theory of justice, founded on the affirmation of inviolable rights that derive from their non-representational subjectivity (selfhood) and from the fact that they are existents that have interests to preserve and that are capable of communicating these interests. It has the merit of integrating the importance of sensibility, as susceptibility to pain and suffering, while allowing us to derive our obligations from the relations of dependence, of interaction, of cooperation, or of sovereignty that are woven between them and us. It offers, moreover, useful tools for a subsequent evolution of rights and of practices.

Even if the French civil code, which made the domestic animal into a movable good and the wild animal into a *res nullius*, has evolved, it is not certain that our relationship to animals will change radically in the years to come. Meat consumption remains elevated, and even if Europeans were to become more restrained, the demand for animal products coming from emerging countries will continue to feed the meat industry for a long time, and to impose immense suffering on farm animals. On the other hand, it is highly probable that industrial farming will collapse, as a result of the ecological, social, and economic impasse that it entails. Degradation of the environment and the problem of world hunger will also force individuals to reduce their consumption of animal flesh. At that point, it will be important to have at our disposition a certain number of written documents explaining what would characterize a state that takes into consideration the condition of animals and works to improve it. Kymlicka and Donaldson's relational theory of justice is an interesting path to follow, provided we recall that the animal question does not amount to an island of preoccupations alongside medical ethics and social justice, but rather is inserted in a broader project whose ambition is the elaboration of a new social pact and the promotion of a renewed humanism.

Finally, it is clear that the practical implications of the theory elaborated above are considerable. Before examining those implications that could be the object of a democratic consensus in the short term, it is appropriate to pose a question located at the limits of politics and that concerns our existence in the most intimate way: who are we, who accept the spilling of the blood of animals in order to feed ourselves, when we have vegetables, grains, and fruits in abundance? Is it legitimate to speak, in reference to meat foods, of a civilization founded on the sacrifice of animals?

Eating meat and the love of animals

To speak of eating meat is to face the death of the animal that was raised for its flesh, and the killing of which was planned from its birth. To eat meat is to accept that we are killing a being whose life is as important for it as our own is for us. It is to know that the animal is afraid when we lead it to the slaughterhouse, that the smell of the blood of fellow members of its species tells it that something terrible is taking place, that it knows anguish, and that, to the end, it resists, because it wants to live and because the impossibility of fleeing causes it to panic.

Certain farmers, in the past, brought in a professional to kill the pig at the farm. (This has happened from time to time still today.) Those who chose to kill it with a firearm, so as to take responsibility for this fact that is part of raising animals, while subsequently delegating to a specialist the task of bleeding the animal and cutting it up, knew perfectly well that their animals which were, like the majority of animals, sociable and agreeable, would have been able to live for a longer time. The killing of animals, often when they are very young, as for lambs, and calves, but also pigs destined for *charcuterie*, which are killed when they are six months old, is an act of extreme violence. Whether the task of killing these animals is delegated to industrial slaughterhouses, or we try to provide them a decent death by entrusting the killing to professionals who come to the farm, does not make any difference with regard to the violence of this act of killing.[112]

Farmers who are concerned about the animal's conditions of life and death would also like to control the manner in which they are killed. It is for this reason that, today, some of them reject industrial butchering, which values profitability over respect for the animals and the labour conditions of wage workers. The distress of animals raised on factory farms and the sordid death that they endure are sufficient motivation to incite people of good will to invent forms of resistance to a system that is iniquitous from start to finish.

Vegetarianism too is a form of resistance. It is frequently triggered by the trauma that follows from revelation of industrial methods of raising and butchering animals. The current system of production and of killing explains why certain people refuse to eat meat and fish. They are not ignorant of the arguments of those who say that it is contradictory to demand that humans abstain from meat while at the same time accepting that foxes nourish themselves on rodents. However, once we understand that vegetarianism can be motivated by the refusal to be complicit in a system that imposes a life of torture on billions of animals, there is no longer any contradiction between the vegetarianism or veganism of human beings on the one hand, and on the other hand the carnivorous diet of certain animals or their status as predators.

Alongside this protest vegetarianism, which depends on the current context, there is also a philosophical vegetarianism that is a consequence of the refusal to kill an animal in order to eat. To make sense of philosophical vegetarianism and veganism, which call culinary traditions into question and oppose the domination of animals by human beings, does not mean that one must be mistaken about who one's adversary is in levelling accusations at farmers. They are also the victims of the industrial model, engendered by a type of economy that must be escaped. Accusing farmers and meat consumers is also to adopt a haughty position, considering oneself to be innocent once one refuses to consume animal products. But vegetarians who consume milk and cheese cannot forget that dairy production presupposes the premature separation of calves from their mothers, and the killing of the former. Moreover, by analysing the profound meaning of vegetarianism one discovers the intimate wound by which, becoming hostages to the animal question, we open up ourselves to a common world in which we share the suffering of animals and of human beings.

The cleavage that enables us to convince ourselves that the killing of an animal is justified, either because it is the final product of breeding or because it differs from murder, is not possible for a person who is concerned, in the strong sense of the term, by the condition of animals. Suffering from the suffering of animals, this person is situated exactly at the pathic moment that is pity. This does not designate a self-affection and, in contrast to empathy, it does not begin from oneself. It is not a mode of understanding of the Other's suffering that leads to feeling the Other's unhappiness. The experience of pity and the sadness that characterizes it are anterior to the 'I am', and they come from the Other. Thus I do not feel sorry for the Other when it suffers evils that could affect me, but the Other, who is not understood relative to myself, is encountered in its naked presence, in its vulnerability. This is why pity is at once the experience of the alterity of the Other and the experience of an alterity in oneself.

To experience pity is to be disturbed in one's flesh by someone else and to be dispossessed of oneself. This movement is prior to any representation. When experiencing pity I do not say 'I', for I am not a spectator external to the world.[113] It is why those who suffer from the suffering of animals also suffer, at the same time, from the fact that human beings do so much harm. They do not accuse their fellow human beings, but for them, all reasoning, all justification, all cleavage, and the separation between the 'I' and the 'non-I' do not succeed in burying the initial identification with the suffering other. Moreover, they feel that the violence towards animals exercised by their fellow humans weighs on their own innocence.

Pity is not ethics, but rather its pathic moment and its condition. It is 'consent to the call of an alterity that forces me to be there where I act'.[114] Without pity there is no ethics, because it alone enables us to get out of ourselves, to be truly concerned with the Other, instead of bringing everything back to ourselves. The experience of pity, in which I do not start from and come back to myself as a separate individual, opens us up to the shared world and, as Emmanuel Housset says, causes a community of misery to emerge. Indissociable from a movement in which we feel ourselves to be part of a community with other beings, pity is an identification that precedes other identifications, including those by which we establish a hierarchy between living beings and by which we classify species. This community therefore encompasses all beings that are vulnerable, in the sense that they suffer when we do not respect their interests, and when this suffering, as distinct from the damages caused to plants and to ecosystems, possesses a face. Pity, understood ontologically, and not as 'a simple secondary psychic phenomenon which would ontically deliver morality to sentiment',[115] causes us to descend again to the pathic moment that conditions all our moral engagement.

It compels us to cross over the boundaries between myself and the Other, between the human being and the animal, which is not to say that we are unaware that the being that we are killing is a pig and not a human being. Pity is an existential possibility of the affection of *Dasein*. It is distinguished not only from empathy, but also from egoistic altruism, which means that human beings and animals are sometimes able to come to the rescue of others in order to avoid having to endure their suffering and hear them screaming. Thus pity enables us to communicate on the plane of sensing, reaching a truth that is older than thought, and to which the sciences, at least since Darwin and the beginning of research on animal ethology, confer their legitimacy. To accept pity is to accept being exposed without restraint to what happens. And this acceptance, a condition of our receptivity to the Other in its singularity, reveals our own responsibility to us. The suffering of the Other alters me, not because I could also know the misfortune that has struck it, but because it 'excites in me an alterity that I must receive in order to remain faithful to myself .... . The naked being, in its misery, receives the other in its misery.'[116]

It is perhaps because animal existence is naked that animal suffering has such a strong impact on those who experience what Zola called 'the love of beasts.'[117] This love, which differs from what we feel for our human brothers and sisters and which is not compensatory, but rather seems to feed off the knowledge of past injustices and on history, certainly comes from the fact that the beasts do not speak. They communicate, but they cannot defend themselves all alone. Their suffering is even more unbearable for us that they are locked in it, as we have seen with the gestating sows, whose stereotypical behaviours do not indicate madness or the loss of a relationship to the real, but rather the fact that they live in a mutilating milieu, deprived of meaning. They are condemned to the non-expression of their senses and, moreover, they do not have, in contrast with the human prisoner, the language to escape it, nor the hope that one day the progress of history will bring it about that the tortures that they endure will be abolished. This is why the love of beasts is not only connected to the fact that animals count, and that they enter into the sphere of our moral consideration; it 'moves in us the ground of our humanity'. Therefore I have, 'deep down in my memory, great sadnesses that reawakens sometimes, of dogs without masters that I encountered ten years ago. ... And that remained in me like the suffering of the poor being who cannot speak and who, even in our cities, cannot be nourished by his labour.'[118]

This love of beasts thus has an intimate relation with the love of justice – with that which, in justice, is related to pity as its condition.

The love of beasts and pity can only be expressed if we agree to place them on the plane of sensing. This love and this pity are not learned and do not flow from reading or from reflections. It can however happen that an individual, having experienced dehumanization and being unburdened of the representations that maintain the self in the certainty of belonging to a particular world or of being someone privileged, is better able to go to the Other while being exposed and sensitive to its misery.[119] Pity arises, as Rousseau said, from what is innate. It can however be suppressed. Becoming insensitive as a result of its neutralization can even be encouraged by speciesist arguments, which erase the community of misery that exists between human beings and animals and make us believe that the latter are there to serve us, or that we have all rights over them.

One could go as far as to say, shifting Levinasian category that underlines responsibility for the Other to the point of our own substitution of ourselves for them, that we are hostage to the animal question.[120] The person who feels responsible to such an extent for what happens to animals also feels guilty because they place themselves neither above other human beings, nor outside of the industrial system that has degraded the condition of animals. Moreover, for them, the killing of a pig, a cow, or a chicken, even when it is carried out in decent conditions, is a murder. This does not mean that the murder of a human being and the murder of an animal have the same meaning, as one convinces oneself when not considering them from the perspective of the victim, for whom the anguish and the result are the same, but from the perspective of the assassin.

When Levinas writes in *Totality and Infinity* that killing is 'not dominating, but annihilating', he wants to say that the hatred of the assassin, which is different from the hatred of the thief, is addressed to the face of the victim, to his alterity, which he would like to suppress by ensuring that the individual had never existed. It is in this sense that murder is a 'renunciation of understanding', because the assassin does not want to feel responsible for the person he kills, in any case he does not feel himself to be his brother's keeper.[121] The murder of an animal does not have the same meaning as the murder of a human being, because it is unlikely that envy could be the motive of violence towards a beast. Envy, which is the sadness brought about by the happiness or success of others, is the opposite of pity. Usually, this passion is only experienced towards another human being, in particular towards an individual who elicits admiration. On the other hand, what has destroyed pity in our relations with farm animals is not envy, but insensitivity.

We massacre animals in following a process that has legitimized the analogy between slaughterhouses and concentration camps. However, there is a fundamental difference between the massacre of animals and the genocide of the Jews, for our objective is not to exterminate every last pig, in order to erase their name and their culture, but, on the contrary, to produce them indefinitely in order to consume their flesh indefinitely. In order to do this, we suffocate the pity that is in us, by saying that they are only animals or that they were born for this. We persuade ourselves that their life is not important, distinguishing artificially between slaughtering and murder.

It is inappropriate, if we wish to delimit more closely what happens each time we kill an animal, to confuse the massacre of animals and the Shoah. There is no need to speak of genocide in order to take the measure of the transgression that characterizes the killing of animals, in particular in industrial slaughterhouses, nor in order to exit from the violence of social and political invisibility that we inflict on them. Moreover, such a confusion misses the precise meaning of genocide, which is not synonymous of every war, however abominable, since it consists in denying to a part of humanity the right to take part in it.[122]

Animals, as we have seen, form a single moral community with us, and our political community is also a zoopolitical one, which requires that we be just towards them, even though they are not our human brothers. The love that we have for them is not the same as the one we have for human beings, for example towards a child. Moreover, objectivization and reification of animals, evidenced in industrial farming and slaughterhouses, do not reflect the same type of violence as the murder of human beings: In the first case beings are annihilated, considered straightaway as nothing, because this enables us to treat them as meat on legs and to exploit them without mercy; in the other case, the explicit will to deny the Other, to exercise one's domination over him, is excited by the resistance of the victim, as is also evident in rape.[123]

Those who opt for a philosophical vegetarianism seek to bring to light the transgression involved in the killing of an animal. To opt for philosophical vegetarianism or veganism is to refuse the separation, instilled by tradition, between the beings that one cannot kill with impunity and those for which slaughtering is justified. The reason for this justification, in primitive societies, was that human beings could not nourish themselves without hunting from time to time. In our society, in which we have the possibility of cultivating cereals and of replacing animal proteins by vegetable proteins, such as seitan or tofu, carnal eating is not necessary.

Hunting is a leisure activity in our societies, where it only rarely serves to regulate animal populations. The raising of pheasants or boars destined to be killed by hunters generates a disequilibrium that is harmful to farmers. The latter often support hunters, without necessarily knowing that the animals that invade their fields would be less numerous if they had not been artificially introduced by human beings. As for the argument that invokes an instinct of predation in human beings, it would only be convincing if humans were devouring animals with their bare teeth and eating raw flesh. We are also led to recognize, with Plutarch, that carnal eating is neither natural nor necessary in our society and, thus, that the violence that it imposes on animals is unjust and disproportionate.[124]

In other words, the fact that we continue to kill animals for their flesh, although we could nourish ourselves without shedding blood, proves that we refuse to recognize that these sentient beings are part of our moral community and that we have relations of justice towards them. Philosophical vegetarianism not only calls into question the culinary traditions that themselves come from a distant past at a time when men hunted, and that were constructed once the habit of consuming meat and fish had already been adopted, as well as the habit of conferring to the products issuing from animal farming and from fishing a certain prestige indicating the prosperity of a country and its inhabitants. It also questions the foundations of a society that is built on a distinction between animals and human beings, killing and eating the former being allowed, while the latter must never be the object of any sacrifice.

The mention of sacrifice does not mean that we subscribe completely to the thesis, however seductive, of Derrida, who speaks of the 'carnophallogocentrism' of our society, suggesting that the sacrifice of the animal serves to delimit the boundaries between humanity and animality.[125] Of course, this carnophallogocentrist logic consists in denying to the killing of the animal any character of a criminal killing. Moreover, it conceals the violence that characterizes the destruction of the animal life, because animals, since the Grammont Law of 1850, are no longer slaughtered in French cities in the public's view, and in supermarkets consumers who buy meat no longer think, in looking at the packaged product, of the animal from which it comes. The consumption of meat presupposes this denial, which echoes the cleavage mentioned above between farmers and those to whom they delegate the task of killing their animals. It is likely that human beings traced out moral boundaries in distinguishing the beings that they are allowed to kill and eat from those that say to them, 'Thou shalt not kill'. But can one say that carnivorous sacrifice is still the condition of possibility of the institution of the human subject?

If we rely on the history of intellectual representations, whether in philosophy or in religions, we can appreciate that, in order to feed the discourse on what is proper to man, it was necessary to oppose the essence of humanity to that of animality, and to think about animals not only by erasing their extraordinary diversity, but also by defining them in a privative way. However, this reading, inspired by Derrida, should not make us forget the singular voices of Condillac or Montaigne. Above all, it is not sufficient to explain the violence that we currently inflict on animals. Humanity, in the twenty-first century, no longer needs to affirm the indignity of animals in order to defend its own dignity. Undoubtedly the complexity and the richness of the psychical and social life of animals are still largely unknown, but it must be admitted that injustices towards animals do not come from the fact that we consider them incapable of experiencing pain and suffering. The animal, today, no longer serves as the absolute counter-model of the human being, which means that even if we do not read enough Darwin, we have nonetheless assimilated certain of his teachings.

It is not the sacrificial structure of our civilization that explains that human beings still eat meat. Nevertheless this declaration does nothing to remove the fact that the dividing line between animals and human beings has a symbolic meaning that we find in religious rites, in particular when human sacrifice has been suppressed. In the Bible it is not Isaac who is sacrificed, but a lamb that God has sent to Abraham after having tested the solidity of his faith. In the same way, religions are connected to dietary prohibitions and can even prescribe certain manners of killing animals, as we see in Judaism and Islam.

If however fasting and the particular manner of eating permit the faithful to inscribe their faith into daily life and to mark their belonging to a community bound by traditions and customs, it is necessary to recall that the Quran stresses on several occasions the importance of pity towards animals. Similarly, in Judaism the rule of *tzaʿar baʿalei chayim* prohibits inflicting any gratuitous pain on an animal, as well as killing an animal and its offspring on the same day.[126] It is thus not clear that the cruel practices of ritual slaughter are really justified by these religions.

Wouldn't vegetarianism be the diet most suitable to the Jewish tradition, which prohibits the consumption of the blood of animals? As for halal slaughtering, stunning the animal immediately after bleeding would be in better conformity with the respect for animals promoted by Islam, in particular in the case of bovines that, in contrast with sheep, do not lose consciousness in a matter of seconds, but rather in ten or fifteen minutes, and are thus bled while they are still conscious. Finally, we must wonder whether it is the spirit or the letter that takes precedence in the respect to a religious denomination, especially if we recall that religions are connected to a history and to a context. Sacred texts, including the Quran, which is considered as uncreated, offer several levels of reading and interpretation, requiring us to take into consideration authors, or at least intended readers, as we know since Uriel da Costa or Spinoza, if not since Maimonides, and as biblical science has definitively established.

This progress, which is that of the Enlightenment and which is not opposed to revelation, but only to the literal interpretation of texts, is at the horizon of our critique of the abusive use of the term 'sacrifice' when it serves to justify violence against animals and the fact that, in the name of tradition and of community belonging, certain individuals remain blind to this truth, reflected in our pity towards animals, that is universal and prior to any thought. However, we wish to go further and affirm that the notion of sacrifice is unable to explain our relation to carnal eating.

In fact it is unlikely that the consumer who buys his meat at the supermarket or at the butcher's shop has, like the members of so-called 'primitive' groups of which Lévi-Strauss spoke, the feeling of owing something to the animal that has been killed. There is thus no offering and no sacrifice. Moreover, the idea that our civilization rests on the distinction between human beings and animals and that it therefore has a sacrificial structure is no longer tenable once the majority of human beings know, as they do today, that they do not belong to a species that is external to evolution. Finally, the fact that there are so many people who live with a companion animal, to which we accord as much attention as if it were a member of our family, shows that the boundaries drawn by human beings between those who are part of our moral community and the Others are not determined by criteria that depend on species. It is rather the relationship that we have established with beings, human and non-human, that explains whether we integrate them into the sphere of our moral consideration or whether we exclude them from it.

This manner of making the value of a being depend on our judgement, without any axiological principle that is external to our point of view, has nothing to do with the relational theory of rights outlined above, which implied first of all recognition of the inviolability of the basic rights of sensitive beings. In a sense, this idea, that someone has value only if I recognize this of him, also explains the extreme violence that human beings today are ready to commit as soon as they are dealing with a stranger, that is to say an individual, human or animal, that they do not bring into the sphere of their affection. This affective community is more fragile than any moral or political community founded on universal principles and on the affirmation of one's own responsibility. For this responsibility, resting on the recognition of the inviolability of beings that experience their life in the first person, asserts an exigency of justice that can be universally accepted, and to which the experience of pity gives an original foundation. The difficulty that we have today in rising to universal principles also shows our difficulty in getting out of ourselves. It is in this way that in their affections as in their indifference or rejection, human beings today are particularly inclined to divide themselves into groups, expressing warmth to the persons who belong to their affective community, and being completely insensitive when the being that is being tortured is not of their family or of their clan.

This is why individuals, nearly all of whom today know that the meat that they are eating comes from an animal that was never respected, do not change their eating habits. They do not hate animals, but they are not concerned by what happens to these sensitive beings. They continue to eat foie gras and to buy coats with fur collars. Such a situation prohibits the use of the word 'sacrifice', which implies an awareness that a being has paid with its life *for* another, and that this death, the tragic aspect of which is not erased, was necessary. The fur industry and the system of meat production presuppose that we can kill certain beings for the good of other beings. However, the death of animals is not necessary, and nobody is benefitted by the massacre of raccoons or of foxes. To speak of sacrifice is, in the case of fur and even of meat, illegitimate. This is only to justify the unjustifiable, which it is more honest to accept as such.

We have inherited from our ancestors certain practices and certain eating habits that are expressed in our usages and customs, and that testify to the boundaries between human beings and animals, which can shift, but cannot be totally eliminated, since we are not with the animals as we are with other human beings. Nevertheless, it is not only a matter of throwing off the yoke of traditions in order to denounce certain practices that testify to unbearable violence towards animals, but to encourage or promote those that testify to more consideration for them.

If we wish to develop other culinary habits, it is necessary that individuals who do not know how to replace meat learn that there are vegetarian dishes they can enjoy, and that these dishes be offered to them as early and often as possible. In the same way it is important to encourage a fashion that implies respect for animals and for human beings who are manufacturing the fabrics, and is ecologically sustainable and economically responsible. The battle against the delocalization of businesses makes it possible to win on all three fronts. These initiatives – as will be made more clear in the second half of this work – are inscribed in the heritage of the Enlightenment, as is testified by the role that is assigned to thinking and to the sciences, and by the affirmation of the centrality of taste.

At the end of this analysis, it is possible to briefly indicate the practices whose abolition might be the object of overlapping consensus, even in the near future. Support for farmers who are concerned about the conditions of life and death of their animals, and the reduction of daily consumption of animal products, seem to be measures that are accepted, at least on a theoretical level, by the majority of our fellow citizens. Public support policies for organic livestock and farming would be welcome, especially if these objectives are addressed transversally by implicating economy, culture, education, and communication. No animal should be killed without being stunned in the correct way.

Some products, like foie gras, cannot be made compatible with the well-being of animals, other than by an abuse of language. Fishing could be better organized in order to avoid the exhaustion of resources, but also the massacre of turtles, dolphins, and whales that are taken in the nets of fishermen. Hunting with hounds, which is connected to an aristocratic ideal and makes it permissible to kill a deer that has come to take refuge in the garden of a private individual who is not a hunter, was abolished in many countries of Europe, and this is an example that we could follow in France. Finally, it is contrary to the democratic organization of society in which hunters, brought together in powerful lobbies, dictate laws to representatives, as we see with the powerful departmental federations of hunters to which, in France, the protection of wild animals is entrusted.[127]

Finally, the *corrida*, even if it has vastly fewer victims than factory farming, gives rise to several serious problems.[128] This tradition transmits an erroneous image of bulls, which are herbivores, that are not inclined to attack, but rather to flee. The art of the *toreros* loses its aura once we have understood that this animal, that enjoys a wide panoramic field of vision thanks to the widely separated eyes on the sides of its head, has a reduced binocular front view, which results in perceiving vague images lacking detail and a poor ability to evaluate distances.[129] Its ocular apparatus is not made for concentrating its attention on a precise object, but rather for discerning forms and movements. The *torero* thus plays with the characteristics of the animal, as when he waves his cape while moving himself to the side, since he knows that the bull only charges at what is in movement. When the bull charges, because it is panicked by the vague images that it distinguishes in the arena and through the movements that disorient it, it lowers its head in order to place its horns in front of it, then it raises its head in order to observe the situation. The game of the *torero* consists in killing it slowly, according to the procedures emerging from the slaughterhouses, where the *corrida* was invented in the eighteenth century. It is thus a matter of forcing it to keep its head down by cutting the dorsal muscles by blows of the spear, making it weaker in order to limit its responses at the moment of killing, 'bleeding it by cutting the large vessels of the neck, not with a knife from underneath, but with a sword, noble and martial'.[130] In addition, the bulls frequently undergo mutilations before entering the arena, such as the *afeitage* of the horns. There is another reason pushing us to insist on the prohibition, in the near future, of this unequal combat between a tortured animal and a man who is armed to the teeth.

The *corrida*, often presented as a religious inheritance of Mithra, coming from Iran and imported into Rome, is associated with rites and, above all, with the idea that the animal is being sacrificed. Aficionados consider themselves the friends of animals, and affirm that their passion goes together with the admiration that they have for the bull, in particular for the 'brave' (*bravo*) bull. According to them, the *corrida* is a way for a man to take his measure against an animal that symbolizes force and bravery; in taking its life, in killing it with art, they believe they are not only confronting death and respecting animality, but also interrupting the violence of society, as if the blood and the torture of the bull had an expiatory value. However, to speak of sacrifice, in suggesting that there is here an exchange and a gift, that the animal dies (as certain Muslims also say, who justify ritual sacrifice with these same words[131]) to help us to extirpate our own violence, is little credible in the case of the *corrida*.

When faithful Muslims watch the ritual slaughter of the sheep that they have brought to make an offering, they often cry, as we see in *Adak* by Amandine Faynot. Their faces betray the turmoil of those who, far from rejoicing when they kill an animal, are perfectly conscious of what their offering, and their desire to be pleasing to God or to solicit his help, cost this animal. Now what is morally more problematic in the *corrida* is the applause of the crowd that enjoys the spectacle of a tortured animal. There is no room for pity. These spectators adore the vision of the domination of the animal by the man. Is it coherent to tolerate this spectacle, when at the same time we intend to encourage an ongoing evolution, that testifies to the fact that more and more humans are ready to integrate animals into the sphere of their moral consideration?

3

Eating disorders

The problems of hunger and malnutrition and the economic and environmental consequences of the demand for animal products in Western, and even in emerging countries, depict ethics and justice as positions in existence in an exemplary manner. A philosophy that takes the fact that we 'live from' seriously, on ontological and political grounds, must begin with the Other's experience of hunger, with the deprivations that they endure. Only this starting point allows us to move beyond abstraction. In fact the compelling nature of hunger wrenches us from the contentions of philosophies of freedom, which favour formal rights and lead to a theory of distributive justice that is certainly useful in rich countries to distribute goods among properly nourished individuals, but that is much less relevant in situations of extreme poverty. Therefore, if we want to understand the obligations that hunger imposes on human beings as individuals, societies, and international organizations, we must describe the absolute deprivation that characterizes hunger.

Hunger as the starting point of ethics

Aharon Appelfeld's narrative of his years spent in Ukrainian forests, following his escape from a concentration camp when he was about ten years old, states that 'starvation reverts us to our instincts, to a kind of language that precedes speech'.[1] The individual who feels the bite of hunger experiences life in its nudity, openly, because they have refuge nowhere else, except in dreams or hallucinations.[2] Similarly, they immediately know, while they are rummaging through garbage or begging, what can soothe them and who is willing to help. This knowledge of the senses precedes thought.

Hunger has eyes, because an individual who endures it will anticipate when the Other is going to give them something to eat or when, on the contrary, they will leave them in this state, but also because there is a look of hunger. This look is a call for help. Anyone who has crossed paths with a starving individual cannot help but be struck by this look that says, 'Give me something to eat.' The source of ethics is the Other's body, their needs, and their existence in its materiality. It is therefore not surprising that Levinas, who broke from the philosophies of freedom, mentions hunger so often in his works. The Other does not primarily appeal to me through freedom or conscience, as if the relationship with others were essentially a rivalry or competition in which recognition is the first challenge; their hunger puts me into question.

A starving individual's look, that direct look that comes from the bowels and testifies to an obsession, accuses me in that it prevents me from acting as if I had not seen anything and that it was not my problem. It also makes me wonder about the state of prosperity in which I live, since I have access to the food that I need. This is what Levinas suggests when he speaks of removing the bread from one's mouth in order to give it to the Other, we must understand it like this. Being responsible for others is passing on our subsistence to nourish others. From the beginning, the existence of others in their materiality installs itself in me, at the heart of my *conatus*. The Other's hunger immediately interrupts the monologue of consciousness. In questioning my place in the sun, it forbids me from being duped by morality.

Considering hunger as the starting point of ethics and justice renews the meaning of these notions. Not only is the community of destiny between human beings and animals highlighted by such a beginning, but with it we also come to understand that ethics cannot be confined to relationships between human beings or even to relationships between humans and other living beings. Our relationship with nourishment qualifies our existence and makes it, primarily, ethical. Similarly, justice, before referring to the equitable distribution of resources, has meaning as soon as I eat, because, by doing so, I indicate the place that I give (or not) to others and, on the other hand, the food that I eat encourages the type of production and distribution.

Therefore, we cannot employ the terms of ethics and justice lightly in a world where one person out of eight is undernourished. However, we must not make the wrong diagnosis. Indeed, if hunger and malnutrition are a technical problem due to shortages, then the solutions are also technical: they consist in increasing agricultural production and delivering food supplies to starving individuals. The productivist discourse, the use of agricultural methods that succeeded in increasing agricultural productivity following the Second World War, and the widespread use of GMOs will be remedies. If, on the contrary, hunger and malnutrition are consequences of poverty and essentially pose a problem of justice, it is necessary to point out the responsible factors of this situation: this would imply the denunciation of the international economic system and of the rules of the global market.

Furthermore, it is essential to analyse the type of goods that we have to deal with when talking about food, in order to ask whether or not it is legitimate to sell cereals as if we were selling televisions.

It is important to say why agriculture, one of the functions of which is to feed human beings, should not be viewed as any other industry. Finally, we cannot forget the role played by our eating habits, whose impact on the production, distribution, and sharing of food proves that ethics and justice have a meaning as soon as I sit down at the table. These three questions constitute the specific contribution of a phenomenology of nourishment to the global food crisis debate, the denunciation of the total liberalization of the global agricultural market being based not only on the description of the social damages that it generates, but also on the specific goods that food designates and on the examination of the meaning of agriculture.

Reminding ourselves of certain facts will help us to understand the magnitude of the global food crisis. According to an FAO report dated 9 October 2012, 868 million people are suffering from hunger. Of them, 852 million live in developing countries, where they represent 14.8 per cent of the population – in sub-Saharan Africa, notably in the Congo and in Ethiopia, but also in Nicaragua, Peru, Haiti, in the Middle East, in Afghanistan and Bangladesh, in Indonesia and North Korea, as well as in certain regions of India.[3] The vast majority of these individuals are rural, specifically farmers who cannot afford buying food. Yet food is available in their countries, either because they produce and export food, or because poultry and cereals from the United States and Europe are available on local markets.

Hunger and malnutrition, which kill one child under ten years of age every five seconds, do not result from shortages. They mostly occur due to the fact that certain individuals are deprived of food entitlement, because of their low purchasing power and a global market that facilitates the export of products from countries that subsidize their agriculture. Small-scale African farmers are unable to sell what they produce and are ruined. Pushed into rural exodus, they are crammed into slums where, 'persecuted by hunger', they feed themselves by rummaging through garbage.[4]

This diet, undiversified and low in proteins and micronutrients, vitamins, and mineral salts, leads to physical and mental underperformance in children and causes blindness, anaemia, beriberi, scurvy, or kwashiorkor.[5] It weakens their bodies, which become vulnerable to the slightest infections.[6] To the individuals who die of starvation or diseases linked to under-nutrition after weeks of agony, two billion people, suffering from malnutrition or what the United Nations calls 'hidden hunger',[7] need to be added.

The lack of drinking water, hygiene, and health care further deteriorates the general state of these individuals, who do not have 'regular, permanent, and free access to quantitatively and qualitatively adequate and sufficient food, whether directly, or through monetary purchases, corresponding to the cultural traditions of the people', to which they belong, and which 'ensure a physical and mental life, individual and collective, free of [fear], fulfilling and dignified'.[8] Thus, for three billion out of the seven and half billion people who inhabit our planet, the right to food is only a right on paper. This right, recognized by Article 25.1 of the Universal Declaration of Human Rights of 10 December 1948, and by the International Covenant on Economic, Social, and Cultural Rights, which entered into force in 1976 and was ratified by most countries, is denied.

Furthermore, conflicts and natural disasters, such as floods or drought, exacerbate the situation. By themselves, these events do not cause famine, as the latter designates an exceptional situation that can last in time, but is neither constant nor regular, unlike malnutrition and 'hidden hunger'. Famine is characterized by acute malnutrition, affecting more than 30 per cent of the population in some communities during a given period, and by a strong increase in mortality. Famines can occur in the absence of wars or conflicts; however, political organization plays a key role in their materialization or prevention, as famines primarily affect countries with totalitarian regimes.[9] Finally, to dispel false evidence associating hunger with food shortages, it may be added that famines can occur even when countries have strong agricultural production and export grains, as in Bengal in 1943.[10]

A problem of justice, not of shortage: The capabilities approach

To understand famines, it is imperative to abandon the classical approach that emphasizes food availability and, following Malthus,[11] draws attention to the imbalance between resources (supply) and population growth (demand). Food availability decline does not allow famines to be understood in their true variety. A more general approach, analysing the causes of famines by positioning ourselves on the victims' side and reviewing the entitlement to food of various populations, is more likely to reveal the mechanisms responsible for this disaster that does not affect all members of a community. As Amartya Sen writes,

> For the elimination of hunger in the modern world, it is crucial to understand the causation of famines in an adequately broad way, and not just in terms of some mechanical balance between food and population. What is crucial in analyzing hunger is the substantive freedom of the individual and the family to establish ownership over an adequate amount of food, which can be done either by growing the food oneself (as peasants do), or by buying it in the market (as the nongrowers of food do). A person may be forced into starvation even when there is plenty of food around if he loses his ability to buy food in the market, through a loss of income.[12]

This microeconomic approach to famine in terms of food-entitlement decline is not limited to the interpretation of the food crisis as a purchasing power crisis following a decline in revenue. It involves the careful articulation of three key concepts.

The first is that of endowments, the pooling of resources legally owned by individuals, such as land, equipment, and animals, but also the labour force and human capital. Second is the concept of entitlements includes all of the possible combinations of commodities that an individual can legally obtain by using their endowments. Finally, entitlement mapping illuminates the relationship between endowments and entitlements, helping us to understand at what rate resources can be converted into commodities that are included in entitlements.

These conversion processes are done through production, which is an exchange with nature, but also through salaries or even transfers or inheritances. An individual's entitlement mapping varies depending on the legal, political, social, and economic characteristics of the society and the individual's position in society. Their entitlements diminish when they suffer a loss of endowments (loss of land, destruction of fields or herds, health problems), when there is greater competition on the labour market, or when their trading conditions have changed according to the market rules. They may then experience deprivation.

This is how famine struck Bangladesh in 1974, following an employment crisis in the agricultural sector after flooding. Certain social groups, such as rural artisans and agricultural workers, were more affected than others, notably city dwellers. The analysis of mechanisms that could lead to a famine assumes that the problem of production and distribution of food is integrated within a network of relationships. The latter determines a person's capacity to procure a sufficient quantity of food, since the availability of food is one aspect, among others, that affects a person's entitlements. Integrating analyses focused on the decline of food availability, the entitlements approach provides a general framework allowing famines to be analysed, each within their specificity. The social dimensions of famines and their link to poverty are clearly highlighted.

Nevertheless, the question remains whether this poverty is related to situational factors, such as the employment crisis and the loss of endowments, or whether it is due to structural factors resulting from political and economic conditions created by human beings and the total liberalization of the market. This is why, if we want to discuss the mechanisms that could lead to the chronic malnutrition and famines that affect certain countries and even certain social groups, we must not only consider the victim's point of view, but also analyse the dynamic of the power relationships between the victims and the beneficiaries.

This enlargement of the entitlements approach also allows us to emphasize the behaviour of individuals whose coping strategies for managing risks or for reduction of their vulnerability to risks also follow customary law, which is particularly important in developing countries. Donations, inter-family and intra-family transfers, and recourse to informal credit are not taken into account with an exclusively legalist approach to entitlements.

This criticism of Sen led him, at the end of the 1980s, to expand the notion of entitlements to include more informal rules that are expressed at household and family scales, but also within ethnic groups and communities. Free access to resources falls under common ownership, which means that communal lands are owned by the state, as in Namibia, controlled at a community level by leaders, and used by farmers. The latter therefore depend on the community for their access to land, and the community fixes the price to be paid for use of the land. To access natural resources, informal rights are thus crucial.

If the individual and collective responsibility of Westerners in this drama that is neither a natural disaster nor inevitable is attested, then one of the possible solutions would be to rearrange the global market and make sure that investments serve local agriculture, in order to nourish the local population. The objective would not so much be food security as food sovereignty. The question is not to send large amounts of food to starving populations without worrying about the manner in which we send it, but to promote each country's right to self-sufficiency in food production. This requires radical changes, both on the agricultural and global commercial fronts, and a questioning of how basic commodities, such as grains, are subject to the play of supply and demand.

We cannot resolve the global food crisis by simply increasing production, contrary to what has been argued in numerous reports, including the FAO. Many authors of prospective proposals on food security still consider that a 70 per cent increase in agricultural production is the solution to feeding the anticipated world population of nine billion people by 2050. They recommend the use in poor countries of machinery and fertilizers that made the success of the Green Revolution following the Second World War in developed countries, and they believe that the use of GMOs is a panacea. However, these agricultural methods have shown their limits, causing pollution and salinization of soils, by making farmers vulnerable to the volatility of fuel prices and subjecting them to transnational firms that own the seeds that are used.

In addition, a consequence of these remedies is to neglect the multiple reasons that explain why farmers in developing countries suffer from hunger and malnutrition. They also force us to ignore the necessary innovations required to cease this crisis. Instead, thinking of world hunger as a justice problem and analysing the various mechanisms that play a role in maintaining this situation – which, if we do not undertake radical changes, could be worsened by global warming, whose consequences are already present in sub-Saharan Africa – impose a different approach both in terms of the method and objectives.

In the productivist approach, the global market rules and the problem of nutritional patterns, especially increased meat consumption, which explains why a significant portion of the grains produced in the world are used to feed cattle, are not mentioned. The fact that rich countries use farm land available in Africa to develop agriculture intended for export, instead of encouraging investments in subsistence crops, is not mentioned either. Finally, the fact that developing countries lose millions of dollars each year because of foreign assets held in tax havens is not mentioned. Yet these phenomena are obstacles to development. The productivist discourse only deals with the symptoms of poverty.

Conversely, speaking of the right to food is not only to affirm that millions of starving individuals deserve more than our charity, but it is also to ask what the Other's right to have enough to eat requires of me. Therefore, in thinking of food as a right, an equal emphasis must be placed on both the changes that we need to make in order to stop being complicit in this drama and on the entitlements of starving individuals. The contribution of philosophy to this debate on hunger is to articulate these economic and political dimensions that refer to the root causes of poverty, as well as to a questioning of the meaning that we attach to the act of feeding ourselves.

Food ethics and policy

The politicization of the problem of hunger and malnutrition, as well as the discussion of a right to nourishment, leads to the promotion of a horizontal and multidisciplinary approach.[13] Instead of clinging to the recommended technical solutions of the productivist approach, we should focus on agricultural systems, investments, and subsidies such as the CAP in Europe. Lifestyles, governance, and the fight against discrimination towards women, who are widely represented in the agricultural sector in developing countries, must also be taken into account both in diagnosis and in coming up with solutions. To this we must also add an international trading system that is disadvantageous to poor countries, and their external debt, which amounts to $500 billion and is inconsistent with the pursuit of development goals.

With this approach, we are no longer standing on the side of the victims, but on the side of the system that maintains poverty and opposes development. That is why we will connect the food crisis to the debt that deprives poor countries of the opportunity to invest necessary funds in the development of agricultural, social, transport, and service infrastructures that would allow them to fight against floods, obtain better agricultural productivity, and achieve food autonomy, at least for staple foods.[14]

In this regard, we may note that these countries' debts continue to increase, because they import industrial goods whose prices have been multiplied threefold while the price of food has remained stable. The price of agricultural products depends on the market, on the law of supply and demand, but also on speculation, as we saw in 2008 and 2011 with the hunger riots. The latter were caused by the spike in grain prices, due to the panic that gripped the market following the announcement of a bad harvest, and the producing countries' refusal to sell their stocks. However, the opposite is also true: the national and international economic system depends on the price of food products.[15]

Finally, only a few African states attain food self-sufficiency, which means that other countries, even in the absence of drought or conflicts, must purchase goods from the global market. Their harvest is not sufficient to close the hunger gap, a term used for a shorter or longer period that separates the exhaustion of available food between the most recent harvest and the next one. Not only does the lack of investment in subsistence farming render most poor countries completely dependent on the global market for their population's food, but, in addition, there is no regulation that allows them to protect their markets and regulate their prices by stocks.

All in all, this lack of regulation is fairly recent. During the Cold War, to prevent peasants being driven by hunger towards communism, agreements were made between producers and buyers to avoid brutal drops in prices. Now the World Trade Organization prohibits states from purchasing when there are spikes in prices to support the producers' incomes. They also no longer have the right to sell their stocks during periods of high prices in order to support food entitlement to the poorest consumers. Thus the rules of international trade, and the debt that requires poor countries to produce for export (cotton, for example) in order to have currency for repayment, make the development of a local agriculture that could ensure food autonomy difficult.

In addition, arable land, plentiful in Africa and very coveted due to the low cost of labour, is used by OECD countries that heavily invest in production for export. But the concessions made to them by states explain why these projects, which benefit the international market and not the local one, have no fallout for these host countries.[16] The reorganization of production and of the international market must therefore go hand in hand with political changes favouring the population's participation in this great project of innovation that is the only way to allow poor countries to leave a system that condemns them to poverty.

Thus, when analysing the rules of the global market, it is clear that food is not considered a human right, except on paper or abstractly. World hunger will not fade until these rules are modified. Indeed, the global price of grains is determined by the lowest cost price. However, to access the global market, European farmers receive grants from the European Union, so that 'Norman or Picard wheat (or Ukrainian or Midwestern wheat) arrives in Dakar or Lagos, at prices of eight to ten dollars per quintal. The Senegalese and Nigerian productions are then squashed.'[17]

Rather than seeing the world hunger problem as inevitable, the first track to consider in order to provide a response for this tragedy is to question the organization of exchanges within the simple game of supply and demand, in a market where productivity gaps regarding staple foods are considerable. This productivity gap, which also explains why farmers from the Central African Republic or Cambodia produce at higher cost than the farmers of Champagne, and therefore sell their products at higher and less competitive prices, implies that a completely free market, where access to certain goods is not regulated, is not equitable. Taking the right to food seriously means ensuring that prices of staple foods are determined in order to allow everyone to get its supplies, avoiding soaring prices, such as in Mexico in 2007, where the price of tortilla doubled. Similarly, speculation on basic grains must be avoided. Finally, the right to food and food sovereignty in each country requires redefining the boundaries of the market.

Food can be exchanged, but not just in any way, since it consists in basic necessities, essential to survival, and reflect the original relationship between human beings and their environment and other beings. Buying or selling food requires appreciating its value, which is not only related to its price, but also to culture, to human beings living in an environment, to their heritage, and agriculture. The idea is that the way in which we produce, process, distribute, and consume food within a country or in international trade should be consistent with the type of goods that they represent, instead of treating them as mere commodities.

Capitalism, which has nothing to do with Locke's or even Adam Smith's liberalism and which, today, is related to financial speculation, ignores the different types of goods exchanged and the meaning of activities, and takes place in parallel with a homogenization of taste. On the other hand, by emphasizing the value of life and the meaning of food and agriculture, and declaring that justice requires an organization of production and trade, and thus of the economy, that takes into account the meaning of the activities and the individuals involved, the phenomenology of nourishment refutes the foundation of capitalism. Ecology, when it is linked to a philosophy of existence, deeply questions the capitalist economy, since it contests the roots of its ontology. It goes without saying that food should be exempt from the ruthless rule of a market that we dare to call free, but that is, in reality, deregulated, since it does not reflect the value of the goods exchanged, nor of the individuals who live from it.

Indeed, subordinating food products to the market's ruthless laws not only closes our eyes to the work that was necessary to cultivate them and the suffering caused to the animals that we exploit for meat or milk. It also ignores the importance of agriculture in the eyes of those who exercise this profession, which requires an exchange with nature, a knowledge of soils, and an adaptation to geographical characteristics and to the climate. It also equates food to tools or fuels, accepting the loss of meaning that accompanies eating behaviours, and encouraging the degradation of taste and all activities that contribute to its education and that demonstrate its centrality. Finally, it is not allowing to put a stop to the industrialization of food production, especially of meat, since from such premises it is impossible to find a real counterweight to profit seeking.

Common sense and justice require that certain goods therefore be exempt from the laws of competition and of supply and demand. In 1981, the French government fixed a single price for books, thus allowing bookstores to maintain an essential advisory role for the promotion of a quality literature. Similarly, with regard to the staple foods that correspond to vital needs, it is necessary to implement regulations that will reduce competition when market prices constitute a threat to the population.

Thus, staple foods, as well as common goods, such as climate, water, or the environment, can become the object of international, specific, and adapted protection, avoiding a situation in which the law of the market reigns alone, and ensuring everyone a right to a minimum of these goods.[18] Human rights designate everyone's right to enjoy nourishment, and not only resources. They therefore assume that the individual moral agent's right to consume arrives at its limit when it inflicts a diminished life on other human beings and living beings. This is the meaning of a justice designed for the sharing of nourishment, and placed at the heart of the social pact and of global justice, which is to say relationships between countries, especially between the north and the south.

In this regard, it should be noted that asymmetry between civil and social rights, which do not benefit from the same protection while their universality and inviolability have been repeatedly affirmed, is problematic. Political freedom, such as the freedom to vote or freedom of expression, has no meaning for a person who suffers from malnutrition or who does not have access to basic health care.[19] However, though a person subjected to torture in their country can go before international tribunals, there is no court to bring justice to those who die of starvation. Yet the right to food is a fundamental right, not only because food deprivation and malnutrition threaten the lives of individuals, but also because hunger is an affront to their dignity. Letting an individual be without food is a crime that no circumstances can attenuate.[20] The right to food and food policy, necessarily cross-sectional and multidisciplinary, as well as a phenomenology of nourishment, change the social contract by changing the terms by which we usually define the political problem. They also involve innovations with respect to international institutions, enforcing this right everywhere in the world, and punishing states that starve their people as well as those who use food as a weapon to weaken the country with which they are in conflict.

By subsidizing fruits and vegetables, and helping farmers who adopt sustainable agriculture as well as those who take steps towards organic farming, Europe, for its part, can encourage consumption of seasonal products and short food channels. Moreover, European directives – such as the 'Nitrate Directive', which recommends not exceeding 170 kilograms of nitrogen per hectare, the PMPOA, the Farming Pollution Management Program, and the 'Habitat' and 'Bird' directive (Natura 2000) – suggest a change in the perception of the profession of farmers. They are no longer seen as polluters and poisoners who, to produce more, must dominate nature and subjugate it to machinery and, especially, to chemistry (pesticides). An evolution is occurring for the promotion of a type of agriculture relying on knowledge of ecosystems, and which, to reduce or suppress agricultural inputs and to produce more and better with less chemistry and energy mimics nature and reproduces, at the scale of the field, what the latter accomplishes in its cycles.

The phenomenology of nourishment and agriculture

Resorting to GMOs and to factory farming in the productivist approach assumes that we consider food and land as simple resources. Agriculture is thought of as an industry, the plants and animals as factories: we fertilize plants and nourish animals with food rations (inputs). They turn them into products (outputs) whose quantity and quality we evaluate based on certain standards. Agriculture is the mastery of these processes, which are conceived on the basis of the production model of manufactured items, in which we press steel to make bolts. This lack of consideration for living beings and the suppression of the human being's relationship with them, which constitutes the meaning of agriculture and cattle rearing, make it impossible to take the condition of animals into account. From the beginning of their lives until their deaths, animals are treated as things and, in the productivist approach, this model is presented as a necessity in order to feed the planet. As in *Tintin in America*, cows enter the slaughterhouse on a conveyor belt and exit on another conveyor belt as corned beef in tin cans.

The use of GMOs is a logical continuation of this vision of things that makes of agriculture not a relationship, but rather an enterprise. Farmers are not even in charge of this enterprise, and they are losing their autonomy, because their work consists of following recommendations that require them to use certain products from private firms. Finally, farmers are necessarily obliged to increase the doses of pesticides, in view of the plants' resistance to them. This is because living organisms adapt – their essence is change – and so the successes of GMOs used in agriculture are necessarily short-term successes.

By contrast, the phenomenology of nourishment unveils the presuppositions that underpin the different solutions proposed for the food crisis, whether it is the extension of the industrial model of agriculture or the fact that we exchange food like cars on a fully liberalized market. Speaking of nourishment is not only refusing to think that certain goods are commodities like any other, but also affirming that plants, animals, and land are not simple resources and that agriculture and cattle rearing are not industrial processes.

Agroecology can illustrate this phenomenology of agriculture. It does not represent a step backwards, but rather involves working with ecosystems, which further explains why it requires very specific knowledge. For instance, legumes that fix nitrogen in the soil are combined with other crops. Instead of using chemicals to kill small animals which, like worms, are true engineers of the soil, they are used to fertilize it. Waste, such as compost and manure, replaces chemical fertilizers, and hedgerows promote the return of birds that feed on insects. Instead of pesticides, one takes advantage of animals such as ladybugs that feed on insects that threaten plants. Similarly, the push-and-pull technique keeps insects away from cultivated surfaces by introducing certain plants in the field that repel them, and other plants outside the field that attract them. Finally, agroforestry, which restores the land destroyed by deforestation, yields excellent results, as can be seen in Mozambique.

This type of agriculture, which is not exclusive, is particularly well suited to the current circumstances, characterized by the high price of oil, the exhaustion of fossil fuels, and global warming. It protects farmers from high prices of agricultural inputs and prepares for a transition towards an agriculture that is more resistant to climatic variations and more sustainable, avoiding the problems of soil erosion, degradation of biodiversity, and pollution, caused by the industrial model. This agriculture is undoubtedly one of the major elements of the attainment by developing countries of food self-sufficiency and of autonomy in general.

Agroecology makes farmers independent from machinery and from the chemistry provided by rich countries, and it prevents takeover by transcontinental firms. In addition, by relying on knowledge of soils and biological processes that agronomy can help to understand, the meaning of agriculture, which is to monitor the living world, to cultivate it, and not to act from the outside, is restored. This type of agriculture makes farmers the main actors in recapturing their cultural identity. They no longer apply rules dictated by firms: they take care of their land, grow crops, and raise their cattle.

Nourishing the soil and feeding cattle are once again gestures that are full of meaning. The profession of a farmer becomes again a profession that men and women can live from, because they can make a living from this flourishing activity. The pride of being able to freely cultivate one's land and to live from one's work, expressed by farmers in Africa who have adopted this type of agriculture, contrasts with the feeling of shame and humiliation that they felt when they couldn't feed their children, and with the despair linked to the vicious cycle of poverty and debt. Finally, this type of agriculture makes them artisans of a genuine redefinition of the relationship with nature – they are pioneers.

The idea is to make quality become a discriminating criterion in our world, and that it replaces the obsession with quantity, which is also a legacy of past wars, especially the Second World War. The quality of the food is nutritive, but also related to the way in which it was produced. This is because the absence of agricultural inputs and the time allowed for fruits and vegetables to grow have repercussions on their taste. To demand quality food is also to get to know what we eat and to appreciate the work that was necessary in the production of these foods. Trust and recognition become an element of exchange between the consumer and the producer. Similarly, there are foods that are inappropriate to consume because they are not in season, because disproportionate energy was used to produce them, because their environmental cost is too high, or because they impose an intolerable suffering on sentient beings.

Thus, when we speak of food, everything is connected: the consideration of the hunger problem in the world as a justice problem; the fact that the global food crisis is the result of a perverse system; the criticism of the full liberalization of the market that extends to products of the highest necessity and to common goods; the role played by the education of farmers; the fight against discrimination of the many women exercising this profession, especially in developing countries; the transition to sustainable agriculture, which promotes food sovereignty in poor countries and grounds agriculture in culture; and the condition of animals. There is, however, a last element to consider: lifestyles and the meaning of food when we consider it from the eater's point of view.

A food policy, which is necessarily transversal, requires a concerted education in sobriety. This policy is pursued through a reduction of meat consumption for environmental reasons and reasons of justice towards humans and animals that have already been mentioned, but also because of the ethical meaning of eating. Food is a feature of self-respect and also expresses respect for others, past, present, and future, human and non-human. We are not what we eat, since if we were, we would become our food. But what we eat and how we eat, in concerning ourselves with where our food comes from and what was needed to produce it, reflect what we are, what we feel, what we are entitled to do, and what we prohibit ourselves from doing. Some believe that their right to be is absolute. In a phenomenology of nourishment, this right is limited by the existence of others and by the concern not to impose a diminished life on them.

Eating is therefore an economic, moral, and political act. This is especially clear when it comes to meat foods. If I eat meat every day, I consider myself to be a privileged individual, holding special rights, since I know perfectly well that this lifestyle cannot be extended to all human beings. I accept that due to the demand for meat in the West and in developing countries, grains produced in poor countries will be exported to feed the cattle of Europe. The social and environmental consequences of this meat production, and the generalization of factory farming, which would be the only way to respond to the demand for animal products from seven billion and half people, underline the non-transferable responsibility of the individual, although stereotypes about globalization make us believe that we cannot change the course of events.

Therefore, when I eat I reveal who I am and indicate the place that I give to myself and others. I say whether, in my opinion, others, human and non-human, have the right to exist and whether or not I assign limits to my right. Eating is speaking (*un dire*). In eating, I speak the law, the need, the desire, the respect of others, and justice. Moreover, the Other's right is part of my *conatus*. Even if I do not want to hear about it, other human beings, present and future, and other living beings, are present when I eat – they invite themselves to my table. These are the invisible guests that a phenomenology of nourishment makes visible.

So ethics is not only or mainly a discipline used to define the just and unjust, good and evil; it is mostly a position in existence that reveals who I am. It assigns limits to my right to use all that is good for my conservation in the name of the right of others to access their own nourishment. Existence is this ethical position in itself. As soon as I eat, I am in ethics: I say whether other human beings (present, past, and future) and animals have a place in my life and in the system of values that constitute my identity.

Justice, too, is already present in this daily act. Even if I eat my meals alone, I am in a relationship with others with respect to food. Like ethics, justice does not start with meeting the face of the Other, whether it be a human or an animal, but the way in which I consume and inhabit the earth raises problems of justice in itself. Its basic meaning is the sharing of nourishment. Justice is not only nor mainly the distribution of nourishment to those who are deprived of it, but the sharing of nourishment that occurs as soon as I nourish myself. This is why sobriety is not a slogan that would derive from the credo of de-growth considered ideologically, but rather a moral trait or virtue to develop so as to assume responsibilities towards others and to live in accordance with the ideal of justice that results from the phenomenology of nourishment.

At this point it is appropriate to consider those disorders of eating behaviour that reveal other dimensions of the act of feeding, dimensions that are connected to its relational character but that also go beyond ethics and justice.

Anorexia, bulimia, and obesity: A painful orality

Anorexia, bulimia, binge eating, obesity, and the difficulties encountered by people who follow diet after diet but never feel well in their bodies show that eating is not limited to its nutritional function and that it cannot be separated from its emotional, social, and symbolic dimensions. The suffering that people experience, in which food becomes an obsession that invades their psyche and 'devours' them, is connected to their personal history. Every generalization about the causes of anorexia and bulimia is unsatisfactory, since each case is unique and each story is complex.[21]

Hunger reflects a primitive necessity that emphasizes our essential dependency, which is biological, but is also related to another being and to all those who, from our birth, were present to support our most basic needs. Therefore, our relationship with food is always linked to our relationship with others. It is built from our first relationship with our mother, especially when she has breastfed or bottle-fed us. This act is also an act of love, the first response to the newborn's call or cry, to its original desire to be recognized. This is why, if this act is emptied of its meaning, as when the interaction between mother and child is frozen in gestures only destined to ensure the body's survival, a lack of symbolization can explain the baby's anorexia or produce symptoms revealing a painful relationship to the body and to orality in a subject who does not feel as though he or she is being recognized.[22]

Our relationship with food also expresses the manner in which we perceive our body, what happens in it, what it stores, what fills it, and what it evacuates. A dialectic between the inside and the outside, the full and the empty, and a gamut of images related to incorporation, is involved in the pleasures or afflictions linked to food. Therefore, instead of using the medical or psychiatric terminology that describes eating disorders, we will talk about painful orality. Orality refers to the mouth, but it also pertains to organs and viscera, such as the anus, guts, and especially the stomach.

The latter is often conceived as a lair retaining food that people who are suffering from anorexia or bulimia are afraid to fill, or that they immediately seek to empty by vomiting.[23]

Anorexics, who have fantasies of having the body of an angel, evanescent, transparent, and prepubescent, often conceive their body as a tube. This image, which makes the body a place of passage and disposal, is also present in bulimics who similarly have difficulties understanding the transformation processes involved in the assimilation of the food that is required for our energy and life. The body is rigid; the stomach is a sac in which fat-producing food piles up. The Otherness of food is threatening, since it is perceived only as calories, rather than as being good for the body and providing energy.

Why is food that is essential to our survival considered by some as a poison or an enemy? Is it because it symbolizes dependence on things – and thus on others – and because, for certain individuals, all dependencies are a threat? Is this why they seek to exercise maximum control over their bodies by depriving them of what they need? Their representation of the body, which is always symbolic, is a key to understanding the drama that always unfolds around food in people who suffer from anorexia. It is therefore important to analyse the body–mind relationship that has stereotypically been expressed through anorexia since the Middle Ages, when beauty norms did not yet impose a standard of thinness.[24] If we wish to understand how anorexia, bulimia, and disorders that reveal a painful orality are the consequence, beyond personal history, of a non-pacified relationship with food, which itself reveals how difficult it is to think the Otherness of food and the assimilation and transformation process that it implies, it is necessary to uncover and analyse the representations of the organs associated with food.

The objective of this phenomenological approach is not to explain the genesis of a disorder. This is the work of psychiatrists, psychologists, and psychoanalysts; this work is essential for untying psychical knots and for illuminating the history of a person who has had such a hard time affirming themselves as a subject that they used extreme thinness as a means of expressing their identity and opposing the commands of others. For bulimic individuals, or individuals whose anorexia is accompanied by binge eating, the result is a seeking of refuge in food. Binge eating, which is genuine acting out, allows them to temporarily calm down or escape from a conflict between their desires and the search for compliance with the standards that suffocate them.[25]

Analytical work is valuable, but it only makes sense in a relationship between a therapist and a person who accepts this relationship and trusts someone who helps them find their way to a certain liberation. In addition, in the case of a person affected by eating disorders, the liberation brought about by analytical treatment is not necessarily accompanied by a disappearance of the symptoms.[26] This does not mean however that behavioural approaches are more successful than psychoanalysis. It would seem, as observed in services that receive patients for temporary hospitalization or consultation, that a partnership between a psychoanalyst (or a psychiatrist) and a nutritionist is necessary[27] but not sufficient.

If anorexia and bulimia are not mainly eating disorders but the expression of a painful orality and even a way of being-in-the-world, being-with-the-world, and being-with-others, it may be interesting to adopt a phenomenological approach complementing the therapeutic one. This will involve a deconstruction of the relationship that the person has with their body and with food, but the specificity of this approach is that anorexia and bulimia will be conceived as lifestyles more than as pathologies.

In other words, for individuals with unbearable suffering and particularly severe symptoms, whether they be anorexic, bulimic, or obese, working with a psychoanalyst or even a psychiatrist is an obligation.[28] However, without examining what they know about alimentation, analytical work does not necessarily let a person improve their eating behaviour. Any person's relationship with food is linked to their emotional and family history, but it is also structured by cultural representations, by what they know about the process of eating, and by considering food within an affluent society, or, on the contrary, from the collective experience of deprivation. Thus the examination of a person's relationship with food is also a key to understanding the manner in which they conceive their intimate relationship with the world, and to seeing how they can express themselves and live while remaining true to themselves, without placing themselves in danger.

As is apparent in dialoguing with caregivers who have taken care of anorexic, bulimic, or obese patients, there are many failures and relapses. The medicalization of eating disorders faces limits both theoretically and practically. The medicalization and psychiatrization of these disorders are solutions that are even less suitable for adults who have already had a long experience in life and sometimes have spent years in psychoanalysis. However, this phenomenon is better understood once we know that the symptom – which, in the case of anorexia, is visible through emaciation – is part of a psychological construction, and that it is a way for the person to assert their identity or to have their difference recognized.

We already said that anorexia existed well before fashion imposed standards of thinness on our countries. The example of mystic anorexics, such as Catherine of Siena who died of cachexia in 1380, shows that the idea of the popularity of thin bodies as the cause for anorexia is short-sighted, even though it is undeniable that this plays a role in the idealized body image that is shared today by most Westerners. The extreme thinness of anorexics is not only explained by the desire to look like models. Deprivation, which is a rebellion against the laws of the body, is sought beyond the stage of thinness and brings enjoyment.

It is important to note that anorexia does not exist in countries where famine is present.[29] Similarly, it would seem that people of African descent do not have this disorder, even in families of African descent living in the West.[30] Is this to say that anorexia, beyond the reasons linked to the essential relationship between mother and child, is also a rebellion against the commandment that is made, in our societies, to respond to all our needs through their immediate satisfaction and through abundance? Whatever the answer may be to this question, we must admit that eating is the expression of orality in its biological, emotional, and erotic dimensions, but also in its social and cultural dimensions. In addition, regaining a serene and happy relationship with food can only be the result of a global and multidisciplinary approach.

It is difficult, if not impossible, to understand the fixation of anorexics and bulimics on food. Moreover, it is impossible to explain a given expression of eating behaviour, even by tracing a person's family history. On the other hand, the nutritionist, who focuses on the intake of nutrients that would allow a person to reach a 'healthy weight', often has to struggle to change the patient's relationship with food. Psychoanalysis helps people know themselves better, but it does not help them eat better.

If nutrition is only conceived in a quantitative manner, without being backed by a reflection that accounts for the multiple dimensions of eating by helping the person to gradually regain the meaning and taste of food, nutritional intervention can be counterproductive. This is a common observation in people whose obesity worsens over the years and with diets.[31] Might a phenomenology of eating, which works to deconstruct the representations associated with orality and the stomach, but also with the alimentary function and with metabolism, be able to help a person modify their relationship with food, and accept the change that requires them to stop clinging to their symptom?

The benefit of a phenomenological approach compared with a medical approach to these problems is that the former is not focused on the symptoms. It also puts into question the convergence, noted by many specialists of food disorders, between bulimia and anorexia, considered as two sides of the same pathology, that is, the addiction to food experienced either as deprivation or as excess. In fact as we will see, the analysis of the meaning of the two disorders, when they are envisaged as ways of being, as responses by individuals to an internal conflict between autonomy and dependence, requires them to be distinguished. In addition, it is important to maintain distance from the stereotypes that circulate about anorexia and bulimia, starting with those that are connected to their names.

The word 'anorexia', which etymologically means 'lack of appetite', is misleading, because it is not certain that the person has a lack of appetite, either literally or figuratively. Anorexics control or deny their hunger, but they do not lack vital energy, as evidenced by their hyperactivity. Their desire to live is clear, even if it takes paradoxical forms. Certainly, tiredness is a result of deprivation, but beyond the symptoms of a pathology that can lead to death, and whose severity is related to the fact that the person denies their condition, there is an expression of a fierce desire to assert oneself as a subject and to impose an autonomy that was difficult, if not impossible, to gain by ordinary ways. What occurs, now, in terms of caring for the person, and thus helping them, when we no longer use the vocabulary of pathology and we view an individual's behaviour as a way of existing, of being oneself (*Eigenwelt*), of being present in the world (*Umwelt*), and of being-with-others (*Mitwelt*)?[32]

If we use these forms of the *Daseinsanalyse* developed by Ludwig Binswanger, we must first ask ourselves how a person exists and experiences their relationship with their body, how they handle their presence with things and communicate with others.[33] Such an approach assumes that we consider that the different forms of expression of a painful orality pertain to a style, including the perspective that the person has on the world. This refers to an aesthetic, along with value judgements that are associated with it. These are expressed by the oppositions hard–soft, firm–flaccid, empty–full, and by the ideals of transparency, purity, self-control, and mastering of impulses that today's anorexics share with the mystics of the Middle Ages.

The style states the how, Maldiney writes. It reveals how we inhabit the world and our own body. Eating, which does not emphasize the exteriority of things, but rather our receptivity to them, is infinitely more than just a nutritional function: it is the 'how' for all of us.[34] That a subject can be affected in its receptivity shows that the notion of project cannot exhaust that of opening, and that the way we eat expresses our intimacy more deeply than our actions.

By thinking of anorexia as a style, we are not encouraging the anorexic persons to attach themselves to their symptom. Rather, this approach seeks to allow for a change in the expression of the self and, most importantly, to combat the anorexic's resistance to change. This is because one of the characteristics of anorexics is their tendency to lock themselves into habits and a constraining daily environment, with rituals that are reassuring to them but are also a manifestation of their fear of change. Change, which is the essence of life and which is at work in our body's nutrition, is unacceptable for the anorexic.[35] The body is fixed for them, as if change, beginning with the body's metabolism, were synonymous with losses that mark the subject's failure and powerlessness. Instead of counting the calories that the patient should ingest and treating only the symptoms, it is most important to listen to the patient.

It is not uncommon for someone who demonstrates painful orality to feel misunderstood by others. Anorexic persons often lack confidence in themselves and others: they will not trust enough to let anything enter their mouth; they are afraid to fill themselves, or else devour food to fill a void. This is why anorexics feel brutalized by anyone who enforces their obedience to a norm; this affirms their idea of the world, others, and themselves, and isolates them even more. Rather than asking an anorexic to gain weight and to respect an intake of 2,000 calories a day – to adhere to a norm to which they are averse – it seems more pertinent to focus on the obstacles to reducing weight loss.

As for bulimia, which is literally 'a hunger (limos) for beef (bous)', we see again that misnaming things adds to the misfortune of this world, as Camus said. It is not because the person is hungry that they start binge eating, and devour everything in the fridge without even taking the time to cook the food. It appears, rather, that anorexia is a rebellion and a drama of autonomy that is played out against a backdrop of a body–mind dualism in which the mind imposes its authority on the body until it causes it to disappear. Nevertheless, the severity of symptoms and their morbidity should not conceal the extraordinary desire of anorexics to live. It is necessary to rely on this appetite, to allow the person to express their desire to affirm their uniqueness in another way than through weight loss. Conversely, under the often normal appearance of bulimics, whose weight, because of vomiting, does not worry anyone, there lies a great suffering linked to the feeling of emptiness, the certainty of having no value, and the person's efforts to comply with existing standards and meet the desires of others. The shame caused by binge eating, which testifies to the inability of the subject to control themselves, and vomiting, all sharpen this lack of self-esteem.

Finally, the excess weight hides and aggravates the absence of self-confidence in people, and it may bury a family secret or even a trauma related to sexual abuse. The question for the phenomenologist is not, once again, to establish a genealogy of the disorders, but to conceive painful orality as a way of being in the world and of relating to oneself and others, the relationship with food being the expression on the plane of sensing of this way of being, and the sensing being considered in all its pathic dimension. How the person experiences their relationship with food and their body, especially their stomach, is the starting point of this way of being, which makes of orality a paradigm of both our vulnerability and our ability to enjoy and act, the difficulty for the subject being to accept both without (too much) guilt. Then the question is to know how we may eat better and live better, by working on the representations that we have of food that are today often stereotypical.

Kafka's *A Hunger Artist* allows us to better understand the multiple dimensions of anorexia that we have discussed than stories from people recounting their own disorders and hospitalizations.[36] In this story, it is evident that food deprivation provides satisfaction and that it is sought for itself, and not, as in religious or political fasting, for the purpose of obtaining the grace of God or to exert pressure on the people or those in power, as in Gandhi's case.

Because he must stay in a cage and starve himself for forty days, the hunger artist cannot do otherwise than to deprive himself of food. He transcends himself 'to the point of inconceivability because he feels no limits in his capacity to starve himself', and fails to bring himself to eat again at the end of the forty days. He is 'too fanatically obedient to hunger', and cannot make anyone understand the art of hunger. This is because his deprivation and his abnegation are an art and a vocation. He needs other humans to admire the spectacle of his emaciated body, emptied of its substance. The praise that he receives at the beginning of his career ravishes him and he suffers a feeling of injustice and despair when the crowd, abandoning him, runs towards other performances and forgets to notice the number of days that he has gone without eating, so that 'no one-not even the hunger artist himself – knows what he accomplished'.

Speaking of food deprivation as an art helps us to understand what the stakes are for the anorexic person. The restrictions do not only nor primarily allow them to be thin, as in the case of a regular diet. If anorexics all begin with a diet, not all dieting persons become anorexic. In anorexia, which distinguishes itself from bulimia in this respect, there is primarily a claim to originality, or even to superiority over others, in the affirmation of the anorexic's capacity to defy the laws of nature, biology, and death, and to conquer their urges. When we do not understand that anorexia, especially in its restrictive form, is a person's way of existing and a way of shaping one's life into a performance or an object of contemplation, we sidestep its philosophical significance.

The anorexic person, with their obsession for control and omnipotence, does not want to acknowledge that they are in danger of dying and that the complications to which they expose themselves will result in them encountering more and more obstacles to their projects. What started as a kind of freedom becomes a necessity that controls the hunger artist as forcefully as a drug addiction. There are no limits to this art, the mastery of which, Kafka writes, does not diminish as one ages. In this sense, the analogy with drug addiction is pertinent. It suggests that the anorexic person cannot escape this circle on their own. However, this analogy, which suggests that it would be as difficult for anorexics to stop depriving themselves of food as it is for drug addicts to stop using heroin, has two drawbacks.

The first is that it is silent on the fact that anorexia distinguishes itself from other addictions (drugs, alcohol, gambling, or sex) where the person is dependent on a product or an activity. Anorexia is certainly an addiction, but the anorexic is dependent on deprivation itself.[37] Moreover, the difference between anorexics and drug addicts, or people who drive themselves into ruin by gambling, is that the anorexic is proud of her addiction.[38] This is why she presents herself as an artist of hunger, and wants to be recognized in that way. In the same way that drug addicts can think only of getting their dose, the anorexic organizes their life around food. However, she resists food and will not succumb to anything that is served to her. Her obsession is to deprive herself. Very often, she will cook for others and worry about what they are eating. Her pride and identity are tied to deprivation. Not only does she have to demean herself to prevent herself from eating, in contrast with drug addicts who steal or prostitute themselves; she also derives satisfaction from her deprivation.

This characteristic distinguishes anorexics from bulimics, who can steal money to procure astronomical quantities of food in order to ingest it and, in certain cases, vomit it out. Bulimia presents a structure closer to drug addiction than does anorexia. The restrictive anorexic is a person who seeks to dominate their body in order to exist in the eyes of others. If there is a family drama behind this story that leads someone to abstain from almost all food in order to affirm themselves as a subject – a drama that has to do with identity and is tied to the struggle to feel recognized in her singularity – this is still not enough to explain the persistence of anorexic symptoms at least since the Middle Ages.

Anorexia is a pathology of control, attached to the violence felt by someone unable to attain self-acceptance. In the first place, they struggle to live up to expectations, and then have the feeling of losing themselves, of no longer knowing who they are. The model of the well-behaved child, of the good student who does everything that is expected of them and does well in school, is common among anorexics.[39] They have done everything to live up to what was expected of them, often without originality or passion, but then lose themselves and 'crack' by violently opposing the injunctions of their loved ones and society. The refusal to eat is an attack against parents and against their expectations, and is the expression of a will to live that cannot find a positive expression other than through a cry of pain or opposition. The emaciated appearance of the body is a way to manifest this opposition, and even to regain control on others who have sought to subjugate the anorexic or who have made her disappear under the weight of injunctions and norms.

Anorexia is a rebellion against a false self that the anorexic has assumed but that does not suit them. But it is also a revolt against those who did not listen to what they had to offer or say. This drama of autonomy and recognition includes the anorexic's reflecting back on their loved ones the guilt-inducing spectacle of their emaciated body as a violent form of revenge against the dependence that has suffocated them. They have suffered from being ignored; they have had the feeling of being silenced; and they found that they were good at that game, but have had enough: no food will enter their gagged mouth anymore.

This interpretation, which considers anorexia as an illness of control, is shared by many of the best specialists of this disorder. However, when an effort is made to look past the symptoms, and when the formidable will to live of these individuals is uncovered, it is clear that what is at stake philosophically in anorexia is autonomy. This is not to say that the anorexic subject is lacking autonomy or did not succeed in affirming their autonomy, but quite the opposite: they claim it. The anorexic is unwilling to abide by the standard of living that is presented to them as the norm. This refusal requires a great force, however dramatic its consequences are, to the extent that they put the patient's life in danger. If the fragility of anorexics consists of them not being aware of the severity of their state, it must be acknowledged that, in losing weight, they assert themselves as subjects.

Healing will not be sustainable if we don't recognize that an anorexic is beholden to a symptom that allows her to affirm herself as a subject. Instead of imposing a norm which will be interpreted by the anorexic as a rejection of her autonomy, the goal of support is to give her the means to affirm herself otherwise. The goal is not even 'healing', if we take this to mean attaining a normal weight, but to ensure that her life and freedom are not threatened by the consequences of under-nutrition.

The autonomy and obstinacy of anorexics is shared by mystic anorexics and those of today, who do not necessarily believe in God. The refusal of norms, which is expressed through the refusal to resemble others and to have a bodily figure, is also a refusal of functions assigned to women, such as maternity. This double refusal was found in Catherine of Siena. She fought against the bourgeois matrimonial strategy of the family of merchants she belonged to. Born frail, she was fed, whereas her twin sister Giovanna was put in a nursery and died shortly thereafter. Catherine was weaned shortly before the birth of her other sister, Nanna, who became (as her name suggests) the replacement for the deceased twin. In this way, 'Catherine found herself to be, from early childhood, in the position of someone who is quasi-deceased'.[40] She spends her entire life oscillating between life and death. She decides at the age of twelve never to get married and several years later, she attempts to escape the conjugal life imposed on her by her mother. She alters her femininity, refuses care when she contracts smallpox, and abstains from all cooked foods with the exception of bread until she loses half her weight.

These sorts of self-deprivation that led Catherine of Siena towards death are clearly related to crises in her family relations and to 'the claim to absolute self-conquest', as we see in her letter to Raymond of Capua, where she writes that her soul has become separated from her body which now can breathe. In this text, food metaphors abound, in particular when she discusses the relationship with God, which is a body-to-body relationship, the prototype of which is breastfeeding. Like Kafka's hunger artist, the anorexic's search for food deprivation becomes a way to affirm domination, purity, and abnegation, which expresses itself too in the desire for other foods: 'I could not find the food that was to my taste. If I had found it, believe me, I would not have caused a stir, and would have eaten my fill, like you and everybody else',[41] the hunger artist tells the inspector before he replaces him with a young panther to attract the attention of the spectators.

The hunger artist's response can be interpreted as a mark of his contempt for earthly food and as a testimony to his rejection of the body. The external domination exerted on his body reflects a dualist framework, as in the text written by another anorexic patient of Dr Lalau:

My brain, which should decode and express the signals emitted by my body through hunger and thirst, has inverted the process.

It is the authoritarian dictator of what my body needs without consulting it. As if it weren't a part of my body. This dictatorship ... gives it the illusion of controlling this body, even though in thinking this it has fallen into its own trap. ... The ideal, for me, would be to be a mind with no bodily container. I feel like a prisoner of this body, even though my prison is actually just my way of thinking. Even in knowing all of this, I feel divided. ... My brain seems invincible while my body becomes more and more fragile. ... As soon as my body fills itself with food, ... my brain immediately blames it and insults it.[42]

My mind is separated from my body and must take command over it, the patient says.[43] A dualism that makes the mind a tyrant and the body a burdensome hunk of matter also explains why food is the object of this sort of refusal: 'Combustion, which is a synonym of life, gives way to slow-burning self-destruction, little by little.'[44] This is because food is paradigmatic of what is substantial about the body. Food mixes itself into the body and this is repugnant for the patient who sees their body as an idealized and immaculate vessel. The anorexic could only psychically digest what food is by getting past the dualisms of body–mind, interior–exterior, and sensation–brain.

An anorexic's idealized image of an evanescent body, and their obsessive fear of storing food – that is for them, fat – is a natural companion to their refusal to accept change and the dynamic process by which metabolism transforms food into energy. The focus on food as the enemy comes from the rejection of a body made of fluids – a substantial body – that represents all that is dirty, limp, shameful. The body must obey the mind, which is the locus of identity. Mind–body dualism is not responsible for anorexia. However, conceptual frameworks that encourage rigid representations of eating reassure the anorexic person and feed their ambition: to make the body disappear in order to exist and to affirm their rebellion against the injunctions of others, especially the mother. This rebellion subjugates the body that their mother bore and connected to the basic functions of life to ensure their survival. Anorexia is a cry demanding a response to an originary call that was not heard.

Another way to interpret the hunger artist's claim that he cannot find any food to his liking is to move our focus away from his self-deprivation and the will to mastery and rebellion they express, and to focus instead on the secret aspirations they conceal. Here we return to the fact that anorexia is a style, linked to an aesthetic and to value judgements attached to representations. Everything limp, fat, or flabby reflects a lack of control, a vulgarity, a baseness to which the hunger artist opposes a lofty ideal made from asceticism and purity. The search for food that can satisfy the anorexic's ethos – particularly their hunger for beauty, elevation, and originality – can be a constructive way to support her.

Aside from responding by looking for foods that the hunger artist will like, it is imperative to further deconstruct the mistaken representations that lead him to think that foods are enemies. These mistaken representations can be corrected by information that can give anorexic people a better understanding of food and can give them – in keeping with the etymological origins that associate knowledge (savoir) with savour (saveur) – the taste for eating. The constructive and deconstructive components of the phenomenological approach, when they are linked to the work of psychiatrists and nutritionists, allow the anorexic person to relearn how to eat, that is, to stop fearing the Otherness of foods that are good for us and that we share with others. The idea here is to give the anorexic person the means to begin affirming their identity without asking them to be like everyone else by attaining a normal weight. That standard will always be too much for them, because what they see in the mirror is different from what we see.[45]

Thus, people suffering from restrictive anorexia are in a worse physical condition than bulimic and obese persons, but they have a very great living potential upon which it is important to rely if we want them to accept change and, hence, renounce deprivation or, at least, some deprivations. Everything happens as if the medical response to anorcxia, hospitalization, and enteral feeding could worsen the problem, especially in adults.

Conversely, the clinical manifestations of bulimics are not as alarming as those of anorexics, especially if they vomit and maintain a normal weight. However, this normal appearance, which also reflects their desire to look similar to others, to comply with standards and norms, and that markedly differs from the willingness of anorexics to assert their originality, masks a suffering that also demonstrates a misunderstanding of the process of eating. Bulimics have difficulties existing and asserting themselves; they despise or instrumentalize their bodies, which must be objects that will bring them success in the emotional, sexual, and social or professional domains, and not the place of their fulfilment. We are again dealing with a drama of autonomy on a backdrop of body–mind dualism, although this time the person is not in revolt but is submissive.

If we do not focus on symptoms but on the significance of the relationship with the self and others that characterizes painful orality, we see that bulimia is closer to obesity than anorexia. In addition, both bulimics and the obese never cease dieting or, at least, they have the feeling of being perpetually on a diet. Their relationship with food is never associated with pleasure, but with guilt. For them, norms, health, success, and happiness presuppose deprivation. Some foods are prohibited. The drama ongoing around food among bulimics who restrict themselves and then crack, and among the obese who eat badly and gain weight, is emblematic of the relationship that we have with food in societies that are characterized by a certain abundance.

In this regard, it is important to note that, unlike anorexia, bulimia only appeared recently.[46] Regarding obesity, it involves more than two billion people in the world and is a societal phenomenon, not only in the West, but also in emerging economies such as China. Bulimia and obesity are tragedies linked to food abundance, but also to the double injunction that weighs on individuals, whose senses are constantly solicited and who are encouraged to consume, but to whom it is recommended, at the same time, to stay thin if they want to be competitive and successful in their professional and emotional lives. The availability of food in our countries and these contradictory injunctions are manifested in the profusion of diets, and in the fact that numerous people spend their lives restricting themselves. The deprivations imposed by diets also trigger binge eating or snacking, thus initiating a vicious cycle.

Obesity and bulimia testify to a painful relationship with orality that is not found in individuals who intend to lose a few pounds at certain points in their lives, but are not addicted to food. Furthermore, the expression of painful orality is further increased when people who suffer from these disorders have difficulty finding the words that describe their relationship with their body and with food. We are no longer in the rigid framework of thought and behaviour of anorexics, but in an excess that eludes verbalization, at least at first.[47] These forms of painful orality, bulimia and obesity, are a way of being, but it is difficult to compare them to the aestheticization of suffering present in anorexics. Paradoxically, it is as if obese individuals tried to hide, to conceal their self. For their part, bulimics, who go through the trouble of living a confined life from which they free themselves in sudden and violent crises, not only have difficulties expressing themselves, but are also unaware that they have something to say. These expressions of a bullied orality, which have emerged recently, are symptoms of a relationship with food that is paradoxically encouraged by a consumer society and demonstrates a lack of consideration both for food and for those who ingest it.

Bulimics and the obese reflect, as in a mirror, the loss of meaning that characterizes a society that has reduced feeding to the intake of food. Diets and dietetics (which reduces food to its nutritional function) fit into this framework of thought that illustrates not only the obliteration of the social, emotional, cultural, and symbolic dimensions of food, but also the obliteration of taste. The body is considered as a means to reach happiness or, rather, as the instrument of the self: if we give it this or that ration, if we train or shape it in a certain manner, it will bring us success and accomplishment. The latter are not sought for themselves, like happiness or self-realization, but because they inflate the ego, flatter vanity, and are linked to representation.

Such a way of thinking remains dualistic. It is only hedonistic in appearance, because it ignores the fact that pleasure is the original dimension of our relationship with the world as a world of nourishment. Foods are considered on the basis of their nutritional value and the number of calories that they bring. The pleasure is quantified and is paid – in pounds or in deprivation – because it is thought of as essentially bad. Nourishment is no longer a relationship between the self and the world, in which food is our friend because it is good for us and the taste of things celebrates the pathic dimension of my existence, which is always both a being-with-things, emphasizing its carnal dimension, and a being-with-others, whether they are at my table or not. How, we wonder, can such a framework of thinking, which the radical phenomenology of sensing deployed in this philosophy of nourishment is intended to refute, offer individuals the means of establishing a serene and happy relationship with food, their bodies, and others who produce, prepare, sell, and distribute food?

Conviviality creates harmony, which is also, as shown by Fourier, praise of the diversity of tastes, flavours, and temperaments. It goes hand in hand with a happy sensuality.[48] On the contrary, the impoverishment of our relationship with nourishment generates not only suffering, but also ingratitude towards those who nourish us, whether it is our ancestors who bequeathed the world to us, our parents, farmers who produce food, the earth which gives its fruits, or animals. Who knows if people who suffer from a painful orality are not expressing the rejection of this impoverished world of which they are also the victims? To the contrary, the phenomenology of nourishment seeks to reconstruct the world, and even to establish a common world, by asserting the essential link between eating well and living well, between self-respect and the respect of others, humans and non-humans, present and future, enjoyment and justice.

Part Two

To institute a common world

I want to inquire whether, taking men as they are and laws as they can be made to be, it is possible to establish some just and reliable rule of administration in civil affairs. In this investigation I shall always strive to reconcile what right permits with what interest prescribes, so that justice and utility may not be at variance. I enter this inquiry without demonstrating the importance of my subject. I shall be asked whether I am a prince or a legislator that I write on politics. I reply that I am neither; and that it is for this very reason that I write about politics. If I were a prince or a legislator, I would not waste my time saying what ought to be done; I would do it or remain silent.[1]

JEAN-JACQUES ROUSSEAU, *THE SOCIAL CONTRACT*

4

A new social contract

It may seem paradoxical to refer to classical contract theories while the problems that we encounter today underline the limits of the conception of justice that prevails from Hobbes to Rawls, via Rousseau and Locke. Considering long-term global challenges that are linked to the environmental crisis, the protection of a fragile biosphere, whose resources are not infinite, and intergenerational and interspecific fairness requires a thorough reconsideration of justice. Moreover, considering the improvement of the condition of animals as a duty of the state, and asserting the centrality of hunger, which prohibits the exchange of staple foods as if they were automobiles, both require significant changes in our conception of the purpose of civil government and the principles that can guide public policies.

The political problem can no longer be exclusively defined by the desire to make the peaceful coexistence of individual liberties possible when, taking the materiality of existence seriously, we raise awareness of an eco-phenomenology and a philosophy of habitation and cohabitation, which shows that ethics and justice have meaning as soon as I nourish myself. The interests of future generations, other species, and individual animals must therefore shape our representation of the common good and determine our understanding of politics.

The impact of our consumption modes on human beings residing in other lands – as we have seen with the increase in demand for meat, which encourages the export of grains from poor countries – explains that we cannot achieve justice in our countries by ignoring the injustice that we generate on the other side of the world. Even if political organization is specific to each state, the manner in which we perceive the common good cannot leave us deaf to the interests of human beings who are far away, when we affect their living conditions through our consumption habits.

Finally, the social, health, and geopolitical consequences of global warming and pollution make us reflect on the responsibilities of each state, and the strategies that should be implemented at an international level. The awareness of irreversible and global risks related to contemporary technology had already abolished borders when the atomic bomb was dropped on Hiroshima and Nagasaki. The nuclear risk led to a totalization of the world and to a unity of humanity, and it shows that a common world must not only be preserved, but also be instituted.[1]

Accordingly we find ourselves in a very different context than that of the contractarianism theorists. Nonetheless, the social contract remains relevant, since the risks are major and we are, as Michel Serres said, in a 'world war', where we must reconsider our relationship with others and with the conditions of our existence.[2] The contract's artificialism is even more necessary when the common good to establish cannot be determined a priori and the human passions and interests at stake divide human beings and nations concerning the solutions to be adopted. Far from being natural or deriving, as for gregarious animals, from the place occupied by each member of their community, justice in human societies is only the result of a decision that aims to put an end to war or to avoid it.[3]

As with Epicurus and Lucretius, the contract is a response to a situation of violence, and its objective is common utility. The goal is to not reciprocally injure ourselves.[4] Utility involves individuals who find themselves in rivalries, similar to those of sovereign powers where nothing is binding before the imposition of laws. It also makes sense for a humanity in its entirety that must take charge of its destiny, so as not to suffer from unwanted consequences of the action that it now exercises as a geological agent. Indeed, the idea of the Anthropocene era is connected to the fact that we threaten, through our activities and the weight of our demographics, the resilience capacity of ecosystems by modifying the chemical composition of the atmosphere or the rainfall pattern.[5]

One thus rediscovers the link that the word '*foedus*' (pact) has with the military domain. As in Virgil's text, which Rousseau highlighted in his book on the principles of political law *The Social Contract*, the pact is a peace treaty, a mutual commitment undertaken by sovereign states at war who declare that they will stop fighting and protect themselves in case of attack: *Foederis aequas/Dicamus leges* ('State the terms of a fair agreement'), declared King Latinus, who expressed to his council the need to put an end to the war between the Trojans and the Latins and conclude a treaty with Aeneas.[6]

Environmental challenges and the phenomenology of nourishment developed in Part One of this book compel us to make the social contract evolve. Even if it is only existing human beings who get involved, and the earth or animals cannot be contracting members, the social pact can no longer be solely structured by mutual benefit. Moreover, existing human beings will not be the only beneficiaries: we must also think about future generations and guarantee them satisfactory living conditions. However, the notion that justice is the result of an agreement and that a social contract is necessary to ensure that people keep their promises makes sense in this context. Indeed, the challenge is to bring ecology and animal issues into politics and to integrate the interests of future generations, other species, and human beings who live far from us, into the definition of the common good. Yet, these are not issues that naturally apply to us. The philosophy of 'living from' that we have developed reveals that other human beings, past, present, and future, and other species are involved in our relationship with nourishment, that is in our daily acts, as when we eat. However, the eco-phenomenology discovered by phenomenological reduction does not imply that we are psychologically prepared to draw out its practical consequences.[7] Political artificialism is required for our promises to be valid.

Hobbes's artificialism, or the social contract as a response to violence

Justice, as demonstrated by Hobbes, cannot be conceived on the basis of well-understood interests. Individuals and peoples cannot put an end to the passions that oppose them in order to immediately accede to rules dictated by reason. In addition, they cannot be certain that they will keep their promises and that they will want tomorrow what they want today. Hobbes's absolutist solution must, of course, be avoided, by taking advantage of the teaching of his successors. Similarly, our ambition is to formulate the political problem in a new manner, by developing a social pact that will also be different from those of Locke, Rousseau, and Rawls. However, Hobbes's artificialism and the anthropology that underpins his political theory offer essential reference points for thinking about the common good.

Reference to Hobbes today, and to social-contract doctrines, does not mean that the consent of individuals is at the *origin* of society. As Hume wrote, there is a strong possibility that strength and usurpation are the true origins of societies.[8] This is not a voluntary act, but a habitual acquiescence that explains that individuals obey political power, which is often precarious, because most of them are not free to break from the social contract in order to settle elsewhere and obey other rules.[9] The idea of a primitive contract, constituting the genesis of civil association, is an abstraction and a decoy.

The relevance of contractarianism today therefore holds onto the fact that rules of justice, allowing for the establishment of the common good in a state and, as we will see, between states, are a result of an agreement. The social contract is not a fact, but a norm of political judgement, which nevertheless has its reality as a criterion in determining the legitimacy of laws, as seen particularly with Kant.[10] A foundation or re-foundation, allowing for the formulation of the principles of political law capable of responding to the political problem as it will be reformulated in the light of present-day challenges, is necessary, and this justifies our speaking of the social contract. We are therefore in the ideal order, and the transition from theory to practice is not the object of our concern: there is no question in this work of deciding on the ways of making the transition from one society to another, by either choosing the path of revolution or that of education.[11]

The social contract indeed has an inaugural character, since it is a voluntary act, a construction, and an artifice. In fact, the agreement of wills is not natural: it does not result from a balance of power, as with animals, and does not owe nature anything, unlike what happens with bees, when the queen immediately imposes herself on her congeners with her size. Human beings are naturally equal, because they can equally harm each other, regardless of their physical strengths, as well as because they all have the passion of inequality.[12] Inclined to compare themselves, to seek domination over others, and eager to acquire sustainable power, everybody is convinced of being more qualified than others to judge the affairs of state. Therefore, a well-understood interest cannot be the basis of the principles of justice.

Hobbes forcefully demonstrated that the unpredictability of human beings arises not only from rivalry between individuals and their propensity to feel superior to the rest of the world, which is to say vanity. Admittedly, this passion explains that the desire for things is also the desire to be valued in our own eyes and in the eyes of others, and that greed and appetite are also interpreted according to what possessions and positions represent in terms of prestige and honour. However, to this unpredictability that stems from the bellicose nature of human beings, another unpredictability is added that comes from our fickleness or from the fact that our desires change.

The specificity of human appetites explains that the life of human beings is marked by conflict and instability. Knowledge of the laws of nature, which order us to seek peace and be benevolent, cannot guarantee that future human beings will do what is in their best interest. Everyone, by examining others and examining themselves, knows that they cannot be certain that others will keep their promises. Promises, without the guarantee of the state connected to the sword, through the binding force of law, are just words.[13] They do not bind beings. In this general climate of mistrust, everyone, anticipating the Other's betrayal, starts by breaking their word. As a result, individuals enter into relationships where greed, vanity, the fear of injury by the hand of others, distrust, and other sad passions distract them from reciprocal usefulness.

The rule of common utility, applied to ecology, is clear in theory, but inefficient in practice. Everyone knows that they must change their habits and their modes of consumption to protect the environment and avoid the impoverishment of other human beings or the imposition of a miserable life on animals, but few are those who actually put these principles to use. An association founded on mutual benefit is not sustainable if it consists in a simple declaration of intent, but, moreover, sacrifices that everyone is ready to make are only fine words in the absence of a social contract.

This does not imply that people should be compelled to reduce their meat consumption and be sober. Such a solution would be contrary to political liberalism, founded on individuals' rights to choose their lifestyle and on consent. Our goal is not to advocate a tyranny of any sort, but to complement liberalism by modifying the philosophy of the subject upon which it is based – including also the conception of human beings and of sociality that characterizes it – and by proposing to transform some of its institutions.[14] This is also the reason why reference to the social contract as it was conceived by Locke, resting on individual consent and advocating a limited government, will serve as a model for the political framework that we will develop.

Nevertheless, even if we reject Hobbes's authoritarian solution, it is essential to go back to the author of *Leviathan* in order to understand our focus on the social contract. Reference to the contract means that individual and collective transformations that are required to take ecology and the animal condition seriously, as well as to make the right to food an effective right, cannot simply derive from ethics, from the awareness of individuals, or from a spiritual awakening. As with Hobbes, justice is a creation, and only a social contract will help ensure that compliance with living conditions of other human beings (present and future), ecology, and animal issues truly enter into politics.

If we do not want justice to be reduced to simple words, we need a written commitment that manifests the express intention of individuals and that engages them for the future. This commitment, according to Hobbes, must be a transfer of rights, meaning that everyone must undertake to renounce their right to all things.[15] All human beings may determine the resources that they need, and use them without any consideration except for that of their preservation and satisfaction. Since the spontaneous convergence of interests cannot be expected, as with gregarious animals, and because the concord is still threatened by our passion of inequality, the republic must invent itself. Not only is it artificial, but, moreover, the common good cannot be determined once and for all in its content, as if it reflected something objective: 'Where there is no common power, there is no law; where no law, no injustice.'[16] Only positive law declares that any particular thing is just: *Auctoritas non veritas facit legem*. Is this to say that justice has no existence beyond legality and that it is impossible to get along on a number of universal norms worthy of being held as valid by everyone who accepts the rules of discourse ethics?

This positivist interpretation of law, as found in Hobbes, is excessive in that it invalidates the possibility of collectively determining in an a posteriori way the norms destined to orient our public policies. In addition, the English philosopher supported the idea that representatives give a unity to the people that is, before this act of authority, only a multitude. In *Leviathan*, Hobbes refers to the Latin meaning of 'person', which signifies 'mask'. He 'desubstantializes' this notion that does not refer to any interiority, while stressing disguise, external appearance, and highlights the power of manifestation, the visibility of representatives.[17]

Individuals have reached a reciprocal agreement. However, this contract is established in favour of a third party that is neither a contractor nor someone who promises them anything. Through the authorization pact introduced in *Leviathan*, individuals entrust all their power to one human being or one assembly that will carry their person: 'Every one to own and acknowledge himself to be author of whatsoever he that so beareth their person shall act, or cause to be acted, in those things which concern the common peace and safety.'[18] Decisions or acts as depicted in *Leviathan* are attributable to the people who are responsible for what the representative does in their name. It is in allowing human beings or assemblies to act in the name of all individuals that the multitude, according to Hobbes, is unified.[19] The unity of the representative, who is depicted as the actor playing the roles written by the author in *Leviathan*, founds the unity of the people, which means that there is no a priori unity of the people.

Such is the absolutist solution to the political problem, which is to ensure the safety of individuals, allowing them to 'nourish themselves and live contentedly'.[20] It derives from the elements of politics that Hobbes analysed, namely the faculties of human beings, their passions, and the impossibility of reaching a stable agreement or lasting peace in the absence of a 'common power to keep us in awe', and forces us to fulfil our promises and to comply with natural laws.[21]

This absolutism is not equivalent to totalitarian power, insofar as individuals do possess individual rights, such as those regarding their relationship to their bodies and even their right to save their lives, even if it means disobeying an order given by the sovereign.[22] To be sure, this authoritarian solution cannot correspond to the transformations that make it possible to think and promote the common good in a democracy. As we shall see in the next chapter, the present-day ecological crisis requires not less, but more democracy. This declaration ceases to be a mere pleasant formula once we have understood that the environmental crisis is not limited to a resource crisis, but that it requires a rethinking of subjectivity, work, and trade, as well as of relationships with others and of the sharing of power.

Our relationship with nourishment is at stake, and constitutes the starting point of ethics and justice, so we will have to establish the social pact on the basis of the consent of individuals to change their consumption habits. The legal form of the contract that involves submission to laws will prevail, but the laws, rather than being dictated from outside by transcendent human beings or assemblies, will be decided, either directly or indirectly, by the sovereign people. Moreover, citizens will have to regard them as expressions of the common interest. So why must we refer to Hobbes's representation theory, before continuing with Locke and Rousseau and proposing a redefinition of the political problem that cannot be exclusively thought of in terms of freedom, equality, and security? The answer to this question requires us to draw all the consequences from Hobbes's advocacy of the social contract's artificialism.

Indeed, this artificialism keeps us free from certain illusions. In particular, the idea that the common good can be thought of a priori, as if there were common overarching values that all of the members of a community would recognize as constituting an *ethos* and that could serve as a basis for public policies, is demolished by Hobbes. Reading *Leviathan* convinces us to abandon the fantasy of a political community woven by habits or customs, linking its different members together by bonds of friendship and serving as a basis for the definition of a national identity.

This does not mean that the different sources of morality, which are expressed in religious and philosophical traditions, customs, and all that Hegel called *Sittlichkeit* or effective morality, can never be used as elements for the development of the common good. The very idea of a community, in the way that Hegel considers it, as *Gemeinschaft*, linked to a common *ethos* to which one would need to get back to establish laws that are adapted to mores and to a country's practices, keeps all of its meaning, as we will see with Rousseau, who spoke of the fourth kind of laws that the legislator deals with in secret, and which 'preserves a people in the spirit of their institutions'.[23] However, this common good can only be defined a posteriori.

In addition, the identity of a community refers to a narrative identity, open to different influences related to individuals from other places, and to all the exchanges that we can have with other societies, to all the loans that we make and that constitute us. The representation of a people considered as an a priori unity is a dangerous fiction. This is not to say that only a transcending power that sparks terror or awe, such as the mortal God that Hobbes spoke of, is able to unify individuals.

In a philosophy of freedom, where the problem is one of ensuring the survival of individuals and their peaceful coexistence, it is conceivable that fear is the reason for the union, and what discourages individuals from entering into constant conflicts. The depletion of resources will even make fear, if we maintain this conceptual scheme, the essential element of social life, as well as of political decisions and international negotiations. By contrast, when the starting point of political thought is no longer the individual considered individually and abstractly, as the subject of a right over all things and as freedom, but rather perceived in the materiality of his or her existence, as a being that is hungry and linked by the use of nourishment to other human beings (past, present, and future), to other nations, and to other species, then the political problem is different. It is no longer only a matter of ensuring security by limiting the greed of individuals and by preventing their passions from pitting them against each other; conviviality must be organized and instituted, and this cannot be done by fear, nor in an authoritarian or absolutist manner.

Conviviality must be instituted, because individuals, like nations, do not naturally think about their duties towards future generations, other peoples, and other species. A phenomenological reduction was needed to describe the existentials that inscribe the relationship with other human beings and animals at the heart of the subject in his corporeality, and to thus renew the meaning of ethics and justice.

However, these existentials are not universal moral values. Sociality and the common good, and even the common world to be instituted, cannot be established from conceptions of the good life that would be presented as emblematic of a culture or civilization. The universalism of values is a false universalism. It is the mask behind which those people hide who want to possess the truth and even impose it on others under the name of the morality or intellectual superiority that they attribute to themselves. Artificialism keeps us from the illusions and lies of this false universalism, without prohibiting us from resorting to a nucleus of truths uncovered by a philosophy of 'living from' that takes the corporeality of the subject, their spatiality, and the fact that they eat and cohabit with other species seriously.

Other elements of contractarianism should be modified, as we have already suggested when we mentioned the fact that mutual benefit is the bedrock of political theories from Hobbes to Rawls. The conceptual scheme that we propose is no longer based on the symmetry of persons, mutual benefit, or mutual retaliation, which is one of the classical characteristics of contractarianism. Indeed, the contractors will have to integrate the interests of other moral agents who are not deliberative agents, such as individuals with mental disabilities and dependencies, as well as animals. However, it is necessary to return to the first theorists of the social contract. By borrowing a number of concepts from each of them, we are progressively led to the development of a theory of justice as the sharing of nourishment.

Locke's moderate liberalism: Autonomy without waste or expropriation

Locke's promotion of individual autonomy, as a key concept of political liberalism, is particularly interesting for those who are attempting to redefine political problems in the light of environmental issues, because it allows them to articulate ecology and existence. Rather than deducing political principles from ecological norms, such as respect for biodiversity and reduction of the birth rate, as Arne Næss advocated, our aim is to protect nature and other species by starting with human beings.[24] The link that nourishment and taste establishes between nature and culture, intellect and emotion, ethics and aesthetics, helps us to imagine a theory of justice that excludes the dualisms of nature and culture, body and mind. The social contract that might result will point to purposes other than safety and the protection of freedoms and individual goods, but it will definitely be based on the consent of people. Now the foundation of this social contract on the consent of all individuals is what is original in Locke's political theory.

Not only is this consent not final, contrary to what Hobbes said, but, moreover, it goes hand in hand with Locke's idea of a very precise design of the limits, scope, and purposes of civil government. The latter is limited, meaning that it cannot be extended to all areas. It must not intrude into bedrooms, nor interfere with the sovereignty of the subject, who is free to experience happiness as he or she sees fit, provided that he or she does not violate the two pre-political norms, the natural laws directing me to conserve myself and the species.[25] When the state violates these limits, power does not respect the person and their property, that is their life, freedom, and goods, and becomes authoritarian and absolute. Instead of defending individuals and aiming for the public good, it is arbitrary. Such a power is illegitimate, because the legitimacy of civil government arises from the reason for which individuals have consented to the political body.[26]

The state of nature is not, according to Locke, a state of war, and humans are sociable, contrary to what Hobbes and Rousseau thought. In the state of nature, they weave emotional bonds and exchange with one another. However, this state has disadvantages: it does not allow humans to keep the promises attached to their nature because, in the absence of an impartial judge recognized by everyone, individuals are unable to settle their disputes in a satisfactory manner for all.[27] The origin of the civil government and its reason for being, which is associated with this legal function, both explain why citizens cannot be subjugated. How could they consent to an absolute and arbitrary power that presents no advantage for them and strips them of their freedom?

The social pact, which is therefore not a pact of subjugation for Locke, comes from the consent of individuals who undertake to obey magistrates, to whom they entrust the power of developing laws in their place and in their name, and to ensure the implementation of these laws.[28] In addition, these magistrates who are in charge of the public good take care of international relations. Legislative power, which belongs to the people, but which the latter exercises indirectly or through representatives; executive power, whose prerogative could not lead to a domination of the people; and federal power are organized so that the public good is administered justly.[29] The objective of civil government is the freedom of individuals and the protection of their properties, not their confiscation for the benefit of a particular caste.

Saying that the social pact is based on individual consent means that the mandate given to magistrates is a mandate of trust. Citizens, under the social pact and their consent to the civil order, commit themselves to obeying the laws enacted in their names by those who represent the will of the people, or who ensure the impartial application of laws. However, if these representatives are guilty of corruption, abuse of power, or various faults that are harmful to individuals and the public good, they lose their legitimacy.[30] Government, by violating the trust of the people, dissolves itself and the people are no longer required to obey the laws, which are only arbitrary decrees.[31] This is the meaning of the right of resistance with which the *Second Treatise of Government* ends.

Far from consisting in an apology of individual rebellion, the right to resistance that Locke spoke of comes from the fact that government, with its incompetence and corruption, has broken the trust pact that its legitimacy was based on. The starting point of the revolution is therefore the dissolution of government, not the discontent of the population. This is not the revolt of a few individuals, nor a violent uprising of the populace: the right to resistance is only meaningful when the majority of the population recognizes the government's dissolution, or the fact that the latter is at war with the people and causes damages.[32] The right to resistance is therefore the logical consequence of a theory based on the freedom of individuals, as well as their responsibility.

These comments illuminate the meaning of Locke's notion of autonomy. This is not only everyone's right to dispose of their person and goods, as long as they do not violate the natural law requiring them not to do anything that may endanger their conservation and that of the species. Autonomy also designates the individual ability to be responsible citizens on the political level. Legislative power, which belongs to the people who exercise it indirectly, is the most important power in this doctrine that goes hand in hand with the affirmation of the people's capacity for self-determination. The people, as individuals who have reached adulthood and know what their own good is, are no longer minors. They no longer need a father or a shepherd dominating and subjugating them 'for their own good'.[33]

This foundation of the social pact on individual consent, which goes together with the promotion of autonomy and political responsibility, and which necessarily assigns limits to power, is an achievement, as we shall see in the next chapter, focused on the cultural transformations that a non-violent response to the ecological crisis may require. This does not mean that we will strictly follow Locke, who still relies on an anthropocentric conception of ethics that does not include the duty to protect the interests and lives of other species in the natural law. Moreover, by resolutely opting for a democratic and not only a liberal theory, we must make reference to more recent deliberative theories, in order to see which modifications of institutions could give a voice to future generations, other species, and even individual animals. Important transformations of representative democracy, connected to a reflection on changes in the political culture capable of ensuring better participation of citizens in collective decisions, are also required, so that the political challenges arising from the phenomenology of nourishment can find an effective translation in reality.

However, it must be acknowledged that the originality of Locke's social contract, based on individual consent, and his insistence on the mandate of trust, which empowers governors and the governed, are useful reference points today, especially when we measure the challenges that individuals and peoples face, as well as our difficulty in resolving them, in meeting our commitments, and even in believing in the legitimacy of the elite and the justice of institutions. This responsibility and this trust are fundamental in establishing the conditions of possibility for a better functioning of institutions, and in promoting counter-powers that are able to contain what Locke, followed by Rousseau, called factions or partial societies, which we see today in various influence networks and lobbies.

Finally, the division that 'the sage Locke', as Voltaire called him, established between private and public lives is all the more interesting as ethical and pre-political norms, which he called natural laws, distinguish his moral liberalism from John Stuart Mill's refusal of paternalism. The latter allows for private vices, provided that they do not inflict any damage to others, and, unlike Locke, who distinguished freedom from licence and underlined the obligations that we have towards ourselves and the species, Mill rejected the notion of duty towards oneself. The pre-political norms to which Locke refers, which instruct me to preserve myself and to preserve the human species, have the merit of containing the greed of human beings within certain limits. These norms make his liberalism incompatible with that of libertarians, who do not place limits on the right of ownership and expropriation of land, the ransacking of nature, and the exploitation of resources, animals, and human beings in the name of profit and the right of entrepreneurship. These points will have to be clarified when the time comes to formulate the principles of a theory of justice conceived as a sharing of nourishment. However, two other characteristics of Locke's political doctrine must be examined now in order to understand in which sense he will help us further develop contractarianism.

The first concerns Locke's conception of human beings described in the *Second Treatise of Government*. Humans in the state of nature are neither alone nor defined by the freedom that is conceived in abstract terms, as if the ability to make choices and to change, which is the will, were sufficient to describe the human condition. Locke stressed the centrality of hunger and insisted on the need to eat and to take from nature what we need to survive.[34] Human beings who pick fruits from trees become their owners, because they add through their work, that is through their pain and industry, something that did not exist in nature.[35] They even have the right to pick more fruits than they can consume, and to amass wealth by selling these fruits. For Locke, it is legitimate to enrich ourselves, and no one should be obliged to confine their efforts so as not to exceed others, or to meet an ideal of equality of riches and situations. However, we must not prevent other human beings from accessing these resources, which must be sufficient in quantity and of good quality. Waste that, in a way, deprives the Other of resources that would have remained available is blameworthy.[36] 'God gave the world to human beings in common', meaning that 'the same law of nature, that does by this means give us property, does also bound that property too'.[37]

For Locke, land is a common heritage of humanity and it was given 'for the greatest conveniences of life they were capable to draw from it'.[38] We must discuss this instrumental conception of nature and this anthropocentrism of Locke's ethics. However, the fact of considering the conservation of the species before any positive law, meaning the respect for other human beings, present and future, who must also enjoy the fruits of the earth, implies a philosophy of freedom that would not justify the ransacking of resources, nor tolerate the destruction of other cultures and their environment. The manner in which Locke referred to an axiological axis external to the individual moral agent and contains the right of the latter to enrich him or herself within the 'limits of moderation' is sufficient to radically distinguish his liberalism from that of his successors.

Libertarians take up the right of the first occupant, which had been thematized by Locke, but consider that the earth does not belong to anyone and that the one who takes ownership of it and can draw benefits from it has all rights over it. Locke's clause, invoked by Nozick, is supposed to restrict this right, insofar as acquisition must leave enough resources to others for survival, and the entrepreneur must then offer a salary to the natives whom he expropriates, allowing them to work in his enterprise by preventing them from being completely disadvantaged.[39] However, this clause does not take account of the earth's non-instrumental value. It postulates that the loss of land and the destruction of a lifestyle can be appraised and offset by a salary, as if individuals did not nourish themselves from activities from which they live, and as if their living spaces did not constitute them.

The manner in which Nozick refers to Locke and founds the right of the first occupant on the idea that the earth belongs to nobody was in this sense a betrayal of the spirit of the *Second Treatise of Government*.[40] This libertarian frame of thought is also incompatible with the phenomenology of nourishment that has the potential to serve as the bedrock of a new social contract. Finally, the doctrine of the minimal state and the notion that the redistribution of riches is a charity problem, not a justice one, make libertarian liberalism, which is hostile by nature to the notion of the social pact and only thinks in terms of one-off contracts, is a foil for us. Locke's liberalism is moderate, since unlike the libertarian theories that adhere to abstract freedom and the subject, it is embodied: it takes into account not only other human beings with whom we trade and human species, but also what we need to survive and what nourishes, such as food and property.

What distinguishes Locke's thought from that of other philosophies of freedom at the basis of contractarianism, especially that of Hobbes as well as that of Rawls, is that, for the author of the *Second Treatise of Government*, freedom does not designate an abstract faculty by which we separate ourselves from nature. On the contrary, it is closely linked to the material conditions of our existence, to the fact that we eat and live from food, and that, through our work, we appropriate them. This is essential when seeking to define the principles of justice conceived as the sharing of nourishment, since it requires an approach that truly takes into consideration primary goods, such as food, water, air, or space, which are necessary for survival and health, as well as for happiness.

In other words, starting with a more material and incarnate conception of the subject than that of Hobbes or Rawls, we go beyond a purely distributive conception of justice, such as the one found in *A Theory of Justice*. Rawls focused on rights and freedoms, on the fight against discrimination, and on the fair redistribution of resources so as to reduce inequalities and to benefit the most disadvantaged. This gives a philosophical basis to the welfare state and includes social rights among human rights. However, Rawls is relatively silent on some primary goods such as health, nourishment, the right to a pleasant environment, and the conditions allowing for enjoyment of life. This is why his theory of justice, despite its pertinence, especially in our liberal democracies, is not useful to think about extreme poverty.

In building an ideal theory of justice as fairness, which is necessarily limited, as it requires 'circumstances of justice' and therefore a minimum of economic development and abundance of resources, as well as a pre-existing social fabric, Rawls did not sufficiently develop the notion of basic needs. His philosophy of freedom is only meaningful in rich and democratically organized countries, and, even in these countries, it is focused on freedoms and resources to be redistributed. It therefore cannot enlighten the relationship between enjoyment and justice, happiness and freedom. Yet, if living is not only surviving but 'living from' and enjoying, then we cannot develop a theory of justice that avoids carrying out a reflection on primary goods and fundamental needs, and even on the thresholds below which life is both precarious, or threatened, and meaningless.

There is another reason for our interest in Locke's theory of property. It has to do with the fact that human beings need to have homes in order to exist, for the appropriation of the fruits of the earth cannot be explained by our needs alone. If this had been the case, it would have sufficed for Locke to speak of possession. Yet, he spoke of property and made a natural right of property. Human beings need lands to exploit because this allows them to make a living, as well as because they live from them in the sense that being the owner of land nourishes or fills their lives. The right to property and even enrichment, far from being blameworthy in itself or in the name of an ideal that seeks to equalize conditions, is legitimate because individuals are free to search for fulfilment as they wish, and work and property are ways to exercise their freedom and express their identity. This is why the right to property is among the natural rights and is imprescriptible for Locke. Living is also having a home, being the owner of a place in which one lives and even, ideally, of the land where one grows a garden in order to obtain the food necessary for living and to beautify our existence.

Thus, natural law, which requires us not to endanger the survival of the species, contains human greed within limits beyond which development is ecologically unsustainable and socially unfair. The rights of the individual moral agent are clearly linked to the protection of their property, meaning their life, freedom, and goods: what makes them live. But these rights are not absolute, since they encounter a limit when they threaten the survival of humanity and result in waste.

The conception of a human being that serves as the basis for Locke's political theory is not an isolated being, deaf by nature to what goes on around it and completely independent from others. As soon as they pick fruits for consumption or exchange them, they enter into a relationship with others, since their right to property meets a natural limit which stems from the existence of other human beings, present and future. Moreover, in the state of nature, human beings who exchange and trade are sociable and experience mutual affections. Their main motivations are not vanity or representation, meaning the desire for power and the need to dominate the Others. Primitive passions are linked, for Locke, to the economic nature of human beings, to the fact that they are hungry, that they are obliged to work, and that they must ensure their conservation and that of the species. The utility that is the basis of the social pact is therefore not only individual: it is a common utility.

A project, a technique that would jeopardize humanity, would be rejected as illegitimate in this political theory. The latter opens an important space of freedom to individuals, to whom the state only ensures the conditions of life and self-development. This political theory is not paternalistic, since the state does not dictate lifestyles to individuals, although they do not have the right to suicide, nor to do anything opposing their conservation – which distinguished Locke from Mill. However, the role of the state is not only to protect individuals from prejudices caused by others and to deter them from causing damages to others. The civil government must also respect and enforce a natural law that is a pre-political norm showing how ethics can limit politics. This law does not command us to live in a certain way. It only indicates that endangering the survival of the species makes the action illegitimate, whether it be individual or collective.

Human rights are not absolute; they are anchored to the material existence of the individual, who is neither perfect nor alone, nor a disembodied subject, but a free human being, equal to others by nature or dignity, needing to express his or her autonomy and creativity in a singular way. This way of thinking is showing the path of a foundation of politics and of the social contract on beings that are not exclusively defined by freedom, but that 'live from'. Considering humanity as a point of reference that includes the use of resources, the appropriation of land, and, today, the use of technology, all within limits beyond which they become illegitimate, provides criteria that may be used to reject certain practices and certain technological applications.

Moreover, once human rights no longer rest on the right of the individual moral agent to use all that is good for its conservation, and once an ethical norm linked to the preservation of the species and the respect of its life circumscribes them and specifies their meaning, the political problem is no longer to restrict this natural right *from the outside.* There is no longer a need, as with Hobbes, to consider a legal form characterized by the absolute and reciprocal transfer of one's rights, nor to imagine that only a unified and transcendent power will be able to lead human beings to meet their commitments and renounce their natural right.

For Locke, respect for humanity and one's own life not only restricts the rights of everyone; it also underlines the meaning of these rights, which cannot be contrary to the law of preservation of the self and the species. The objective of civil laws and political authority is not to deter individuals by force from using their natural right, and to restrict the latter, conceived from the outside as everyone's right to all things. Rather, the *internal* limits of the individual right must be recalled, and institutions must reflect this concern for the preservation of the species by inscribing it as a duty of the state and by ensuring that this natural law is respected in all public policies. Hobbes's absolutist solution is therefore not necessary, and we can take advantage of the liberal framework established by Locke, who based the social pact on consent and raised autonomy and political responsibility to the rank of principles.

It also suggests the possibility that the protection of the biosphere and natural resources essential to other human beings and other cultures be included at the heart of the social pact. Finally, its emphasis on the imperative consisting of letting other human beings have sufficient access in quantity and quality to food and land establishes the respect for local cultures and landscapes, and the preservation of the common inheritance, as new duties of the state, in addition to safety, protection of freedoms, and the reduction of unfair inequalities.

The path is thus open to a radical reform of the social pact that includes the preservation of the species at the heart of the subject who is hungry and who 'lives from'. However, whereas Locke, unlike the utilitarian John Stuart Mill, did not say a word about the right of animals to use resources and inhabit the earth, we envision to abandon the anthropocentric framework of his ethics by considering as a duty the protection of the species that share the *oikos* with us. Moreover, animals that are individualized agents with interests to preserve, and that are able to communicate these interests, cannot be deprived of access to food in quantity and quality, nor of the possibility of expressing their happiness to be alive and to search for their fulfilment according to the norms of their species.

Justice as the sharing of nourishment therefore assumes that the social pact, which is based on individual consent and trust, takes other species, animal and plant, to which we can do harm and whose values are not only related to our uses, into consideration. This pact is also integral to the promotion of justice towards animals, whose ethological needs limit our right to use them as we wish, and impose specific obligations upon us, as we have seen in the chapter devoted to the politicization of animal issues.

If what we have said of zoopolitics makes sense, then individual animals, and not only species, are causing the social contract to evolve. We have to envisage what changes of representative democracy would allow the inclusion of their interests within the definition of the common good, instead of condemning them to a diminished life where any relationship between them and us and any pathic communication are impossible. However, before indicating the innovations that can bring us closer to this objective, it is essential to lift the veil on a major difficulty of contractarianism.

Indeed, if an agreement is needed to establish justice and to ensure that individuals will truly keep their promises and obey civil laws, the whole edifice of the social contract continues to be nonetheless based on individual consent, meaning their ability to recognize that the laws to which they agree to comply are not simple constraints, but express the public good, which is their good. As soon as we abandon Hobbes's absolutist solution, it is important to understand what establishes the sense of obligation in individuals and causes them to hear the voice of the general will. This question is at the heart of Rousseau's thoughts.

Rousseau's general will and the sense of obligation

Like other contractarian theorists, Rousseau reflected on the manner in which a community is formed and develops its laws. In formulating the political problem, which is to reconcile individual freedom and the necessary subordination of everyone to a collective regulatory order, he did not only insist on the legal form of the contract.[41] His contribution to political philosophy is not reduced to the affirmation of the circularity of laws, which implies the rejection of any political representation and any delegation of the will of the people. Certainly, the laws are, according to him, what prevent us from having masters, and they become the core of the republic. However, his originality is primarily determined by the manner in which he makes obligation the condition of possibility of the social link.

With Rousseau, there is an inaugural act establishing the community, a return to a first convention that refers to an original social pact, constitutive of the social contract and of the laws establishing obligations among the subjects of law. Citing Hume's critique, we have already expressed reservations about this idea of a primitive contract that would allow us to reflect on the genesis of civil association, and to derive it from the will. As Rawls said, we do not voluntarily enter a given political society, but we find ourselves there at a given time.[42] Nonetheless, even if political society cannot be considered as a voluntary association and the social contract is a norm and not a fact, the rules to which we submit ourselves should be freely determined.[43] The three constitutive elements of contractarianism that are found with Rousseau – the fact that the social contract is based on the free will of individuals, that it engages them and therefore brings about obligations, and that it takes place under an authority that guarantees it and sanctions the respect of obligation – will therefore be used to establish the principles of justice and elaborate the laws. Not only do these principles and laws give a people its identity, but moreover their determination and acceptance refer to a reflexive movement by which a people is a people.

This act of self-foundation consists in making explicit the values that are important in our eyes, and in designating the kind of society in which we want to live. It can give rise to a new development of the social contract or to the construction of a new social contract. This will be considered, in line with Rousseau, as a remedy for the malfunctions and inequities that characterize a society. It will also help us, in a more constructive manner, to respond to the challenges that we wish to include at the heart of politics and that are today related to environmental and biotechnical issues, food, and the improvement of the animal condition. Referring to Rousseau, when the current economic, social, and ecological crisis is experienced in a climate of widespread distrust, leads us to think that this act of self-foundation can be beneficial, and that the philosopher's task is to indicate which tools can be used to construct this new social contract. It is in this sense that we can conserve the idea, dear to the citizen of Geneva, of a social contract, and of an originary self-founded moment that introduces the social pact and sets the rules to which citizens submit themselves.

As with Locke, this social contract cannot subjugate individuals, because it expresses the freedom of individuals and acts in their best interest. Mutual benefit, which structures the social pact, is a last resort built upon the idea that life is our primary good: nobody can obey an order that opposes the cardinal principle of self-love or freedom. However, Rousseau added a fundamental element to this construction, which is quite close to that of Locke, other than his refusal of representation and denunciation of inequalities caused by the appropriation of land.

Indeed, the originality of *The Social Contract*'s author was to demonstrate that, if the social pact is the advent of general will and the right reflects the alliance of interest (or utility) and of justice, individuals should nevertheless be willing to hear the voice of the general will. Instead of simply asserting that a new self is born along with the social pact, Rousseau underlined the difficulty inherent in any political doctrine that bases justice on the free will of individuals. This difficulty is connected to a type of circularity, because the formation of a political community depends on the production of an effect that only it can generate.[44] The political body's life is entirely linked to the condition that the general will speaks above all to the heart of each citizen.[45]

Before expressing and to be able to express itself, general will must be formed. Yet, it does not denote a will that is transcendent or external to citizens. It does not even exist among citizens and is not formed by the overlapping of individual opinions that would allow a consensus to be formed. It is rather the expression of the general interest within each citizen. Therefore, the subject must make political decisions 'in the silence of passions', and must discard influences originating from partial associations, which tend to defend special interests and to stifle the voice of the general will.[46]

Auditory metaphors abound in the writings of Rousseau, who considers that the general will never disappears, but that it can be mute.[47] Similarly, the political art, which characterizes the legislator, consists not in proposing reforms based on a priori abstract principles, but in making the voice of the people heard and revealing it to him, while also allowing him to formulate what is already present inside of him. Yet, even if self-preservation is the true foundation of the social order and the general would reject what might lead it to ruin or loss, it must be recognized that individuals do not always see their own good. Blinded by their individual interests and insensitive to the fact that the common interest is also their interest, they can only give their points of view that, when juxtaposed, constitute the will of all, not the general will.

For this to emerge, individuals must listen to the voice of the universal in them or the voice of reason, and therefore they must already be citizens. Instead of just voting by considering their particular interests, they must think of themselves as a part of the whole and consider the common good as their own good. Rousseau masterfully summed up the difficulty that the social contract faces:

> In order that a newly formed nature might approve sound maxims of politics and observe the fundamental rules of state-policy, it would be necessary that the effect should become the cause; that the social spirit, which should be the product of the institution, should preside over the institution itself, and that men should be, prior to the laws, what they ought to become by means of them.[48]

If we want to assess the political problem as conceived by Rousseau, it is essential to recognize that the social link is first destroyed in our hearts as soon as we reach the situation when 'the State, on the verge of ruin, no longer subsists except in a meaningless and illusory form', and 'the basest interest shelters itself impudently under the sacred name of the public welfare'.[49] The state weakens, smaller societies flood into larger ones, and the common interest is altered or opposed when individuals fail to integrate their special interest to general interest. It is then that 'the general will becomes mute' and that 'under the name of laws, they deceptively pass unjust decrees that have only private interest as their aim.'[50]

This dissolution of the social link, which starts in the hearts of individuals, is also manifested in the opinion that forms the third intermediate instance between general will and public power and bears characteristics of both. The political problem is to reconcile individual freedoms and general interest so that, by submitting to the law, 'we gain the equivalent of all that we lose, and more power to preserve what we have.'[51] Nonetheless, Rousseau's social contract is not uniquely structured by mutual benefit in the sense that it would allow everyone to tend to their personal activities and to lead a peaceful life, free from fear and relatively comfortable. The real difficulty, in a republic that emphasizes the importance of autonomy, is to ensure that the general will is kept awake in the hearts of citizens so that it can 'speak'. Without this formation of opinion that designates the real political cement, without this transformation of individuals who make the social pact, collective decisions would not only be useless and iniquitous, but also be harmful.

The arrangement of Rousseau's work, which explicitly focuses on the principles of political right, testifies to the importance of this problem. The link between the end of Book II, which deals with a fourth kind of law that the legislator secretly takes care of and that has to do with mores, customs, and opinion, and Book IV, which is dedicated to the means by which it is possible to shape this opinion and to strengthen the feeling in individuals of belonging to a whole, shows that Rousseau was aware of the fact that he was facing a conundrum. What is the source of mutual obligation? How will individuals manage to see the general interest and accept that their immediate advantage is not a criterion for the institution of the common good? The answers that Rousseau brought to this problem, notably civic religion and the appeal of the legislator to imagination, and not only to reason, matter less than the discovery of this difficulty.

It is all the more essential to tackle this problem when we wish to develop a social contract that incorporates the interests of future generations and other species into the definition of the common good while avoiding Hobbes's authoritarian solution. If citizens are mature enough to decide the rules to which they will comply, and the republic assumes that they are interested in the public good, then they must also be capable of separating themselves from their special interests and personal situations, in order to understand what the common good is. They must also have the desire to reflect on the common good, and to believe that this approach makes sense. A minimum of confidence in institutions and others is required for them to agree on this effort and to come up with universal norms that can be valid for the community, instead of remaining with a position that reflects their private interests and personal beliefs. If everyone doubts the goodwill of others and their disposition to abide to the common good, if everyone is convinced that the ministers of the sovereign responsible for the application of laws are not impartial, individuals will only listen to their personal interests. Their passions and their anger will smother the voice of the general will that is inside them.

This transformation of human nature, which the social pact presupposes and generates at the same time, is at stake when we address environmental issues in the hope that they will receive an adequate treatment, instead of being reduced to a set of minor issues that current economic and social difficulties constantly relegate to the periphery of the public debate. The specificity of ecological questions is that they necessarily imply changes in consumption habits, in the system of production, and in exchanges. These changes are often experienced as sacrifices. This is the case when individuals, who know perfectly well what they would need to do to reduce their ecological footprint, are not inclined to change their lifestyles because they consider that others will neither reduce their meat and energy consumptions nor conceive or feel simplicity as a duty.

Similarly, if it is relatively easy to understand that we must make an effort so that the future of our children and grandchildren is not jeopardized, it is more difficult for most individuals to admit that other species have the right to live a good life, whether these be wild animals, liminal animals, or species that we have domesticated. What can give a sense of obligation to people and incline them to make the voice of the general interest be heard, as in Rousseau's republic, as well as to integrate into this general interest the interests of future generations, human beings who live far away, and other species, especially animals considered as individualized agents, feeling pleasure and pain, and able to express both?

Rousseau's question thus retains all its currency; it is even more urgent today, since common utility, even in the short term, must take environmental issues seriously. Moreover, many global warming experts believe that we have reached a point of no return and, thus, that we must devote more energy and money to preserving the biosphere and avoiding a disaster – which means that sacrifices required of individuals and populations will be even more important in the future. One might think that only a collapse or a series of collapses will lead politicians to make ecology a priority, and that they will convince people of the need to change their lifestyles and consumption habits. However, even in this case it would be impossible to avoid a reflection on the changes in values that are required so that the threats imposed on humanity do not lead to chaos.

The manner in which human beings treat both the land that they live on and other forms of life therefore needs to undergo a reassessment, and we must distance ourselves from the anthropology that serves as the bedrock for the philosophies of freedom and classical political theories. In addition, the present era is characterized by the fact that deterioration of the environment is added to an economic and social, if not spiritual, crisis that is particularly serious. Social inequalities and political tensions mingle with conflicts arising from the diversity of lifestyles and from the denunciation of certain practices, placing social groups in the same country at odds with one another, contributing to the formation of publics beyond national borders, and bringing together individuals affected by the indirect consequences of certain technologies or who are involved in a cause, such as nanotechnologies or the condition of animals.[52]

It is often said that our era is that of an inward focus, but social groups that gather around a topic of concern exceeding their private interests, and that exchange information and experiences on the internet, show that reality cannot be described in such a simplistic way, as if individualism and materialism were sufficient to make sense of it. The social bond has not completely disappeared, and persons devoting their time and energy to others, to the protection of the environment and of animals, to the elderly, and to individuals in a situation of dependency or vulnerability are not rare. However, there is, as John Dewey said, an eclipse of the public: publics do not constitute a single public or do not integrate into a whole.[53] Not only do individuals and groups live on ethical islets, but, moreover, these scattered publics cannot really weigh in on politics and modify the social contract.

The interpretation of a philosophy of 'living from' that is proposed in this book is intended to provide a number of criteria that can be used to unify human beings, without advocating a world order based on a single vision of life. The proposed existentials have a meaning for all human beings. The phenomenology of nourishment, which is a philosophy of corporeality and which leads to a phenomenology of habitation and to an eco-phenomenology, involves a universalizing dimension. We all have a body, we live from what we eat and do, and we need air, water, and light; our earthly condition, like our birth, is a structure of our existence and, even if we are nomads, we need to stop somewhere, at least for sleep. However, this is not a set of common values whose recognition would be a prerequisite for membership in a political community.

As Rawls said, the assumption of a 'continuing shared adherence to one comprehensive doctrine' can only be carried out through the oppressive use of state power, with its procession of crimes and its inevitable brutality.[54] Basing politics on values or on a uniting doctrine is contrary to democratic pluralism, which is linked to the affirmation of the moral equality of individuals. A group's vision cannot prevail over that of another one, and the diversity of beings, social milieus, and religious beliefs, as well as the division of labour, make moral pluralism unavoidable. Thus, we do not go from morality to politics without endangering freedom – without which the social contract is a contract of subjugation. However, we can move from ontology to politics, to the extent that this ontology, which everyone can follow due to the phenomenological reduction that requires individual preferences and socio-cultural determinations to be placed in parentheses, reveals structures of existence. These underline the body and the earthly condition of living beings, even their community of destiny, which has nothing to do with moral values, which is to say judgements or norms.

We have deduced an ethics from this ontology, since the phenomenology of habitation and nourishment implies that individuals cannot exploit the environment and animals as if they were simple resources and goods. However, a misinterpretation would be to believe that politics rests on morality. The principles of justice that are conceived in the light of a phenomenology of 'living from' are certainly more substantial than those arising from Rawls's theory, which is mainly limited to the promotion of individual freedoms, the fight against discrimination, and the reduction of economic inequalities between human beings. However, the lesson of the American philosopher, who modernized contractarianism in the context of a pluralistic democracy, which is still the context in which we find ourselves, is an achievement. It is especially important given that times of crisis are moments where problems can spark intellectual creativity, as well as the temptation of reaction or the return to a repressive moral order.

The phenomenology of nourishment, which exceeds the dualism of nature and culture, and of inside and outside, and underlines the paradigmatic value of nourishment, plays for the social contract that we are pursuing the role played by the theoretical fiction of the state of nature for the modern contractarian philosophers such as Hobbes, Locke, and Rousseau. The latter have resorted to this fiction to release individuals' primitive passions, in order to solve the political problem that the nature of human beings imposes. On the contrary, the phenomenology of nourishment does not present itself as a hypothesis allowing an anthropology to be inferred. It is already a phenomenological anthropology. The existentials uncovered by describing the human condition change the conception of human beings and of subjects that characterizes the philosophies of freedom. Our condition is not apprehended only in the light of freedom and temporality, but is also connected to the materiality of existence. A radical phenomenology of sensing, affirming the centrality of taste, the existential character of enjoyment, and the importance of spatiality, allows for ecology and existence to be articulated, and to situate human beings in close proximity to other humans and animals with whom we maintain relationships of justice.

However, this first philosophy led us to re-evaluate our values, as we have seen in the first part, especially in the chapter devoted to animals and the organization of space. In the phenomenology of nourishment, agriculture, soil, the inhabited earth, the space shared with other human beings and animals no longer have the meaning that they had in the philosophies of freedom, for which the earth was a springboard for human projects, and other beings were resources to exploit for our benefit. Not only are the most common acts, such as eating, immediately ethical and political, but, in addition, justice no longer has the meaning that it had with Hobbes or Rawls, since it does not serve to guarantee the safety of individuals, to protect their freedoms, or even to reduce unfair inequalities.

We will draw consequences from this phenomenology of nourishment in terms of the principles of political right and justice, to provide to this first philosophy with an appropriate theory of justice, and to indicate which political institutions could help it keep its promises for a new republican social contract, incorporating the interests of animals and the protection of the biosphere within it. However, at this stage of the analysis, and after having taken the measure of the difficulty raised by Rousseau, it is important to indicate that the philosophy of 'living from' that we have developed alters not only the image of human beings and the sociality that is at the basis of contractarianism, but also the subject that contracts or exchanges from inside. This is a subject that 'lives from' and that incorporates the existence of other human beings, present and future, and other species, whether it wants to or not, at the heart of its *conatus*.

It is impossible to reveal these structures of existence while accepting that animals are considered as a simple means. Similarly, this first philosophy leads to the refusal to assimilate agriculture to industry and to exchange foodstuffs like we exchange cell phones on the national or global market. However, what is specific to this foundation of political theory on a phenomenological anthropology is that it does not address social passions. Therefore, it does not entail the risk of being accused of partiality, while Hobbes's anthropology, for example, may be considered as the reflection of a pessimistic vision of human beings that reflects the point of view of its author. Moreover, the interest of the phenomenological method is that it is more efficient than the fiction of the state of nature, in that it reveals the existentials, which, while having a universalizing dimension, can be interpreted and contextualized by each culture.

Unlike Rousseau, we do not believe that it is the role of religion to cement the social link. If the description of the structures of existence can contribute to the transformation of the values of human beings, and if it has repercussions for the manner in which each person sees themselves in the world and with others and feels their existence, it is nevertheless necessary to go from theory to practice, to touch the hearts of individuals, and to ensure that the universal is universal in context. The ethical categories proposed by environmental ethics are sophisticated tools that have renewed philosophy, but environmental ethics is unable to change the behaviour of individuals, as seen in bio-centrist and eco-centrist ethics, as in the work of J. Baird Callicott, as well as Arne Næss.[55] It is important as well to touch on the affects and emotions of individuals if we want them to agree to a change in their lifestyles and to become available for what the necessarily hyperbolic principle of responsibility requires of them.[56]

In addition to a political theory, it is therefore necessary to promote a virtue ethics specifying which moral traits should be encouraged and developed, so that the protection of the environment, as well as the interests of future generations, human beings living far away from us, and other species, can be integrated into the common good and affect individuals, touching their hearts and making them work for them.[57] It is also essential to feed collective imagination with narratives that put other meanings than profit and competition at the centre of human life. If we think that a phenomenology of nourishment has a universalizing dimension, it is important, as Ricœur said, to look for the 'reflective equilibrium that we are seeking between universality and historicity'.[58]

This universality in context can bring about the transition of the phenomenology of nourishment to politics, because we would not be able to move from an ontology to politics without leaving to each community the task of formulating the meaning that this anchoring of the existing human in the materiality of the body and of the earth, which is always an inhabited earth, can have. Hermeneutics is therefore what allows us to interpret the meaning of this eco-phenomenology through a set of mediations linked to symbols, language, traditions, and even myths. By doing this, we are avoiding the confusion of a first philosophy, which allows structures of existence to be revealed, with a set of values. The latter can be recognized as valid in a given context, but only existentials have a universalizing dimension. Moreover, by underlining the importance of hermeneutics in the elaboration of national public policies, we avoid thinking that it is possible to simply apply a theory to practice, without passing through the mediation of language and culture.

Rawls's original position and the new social contract

The social contract does not require that individuals renounce their interests, but is rather an act of affirmation of these interests in a form that is compatible with the common life. Moreover, as soon as the protection of the biosphere, the living conditions of future generations, and animals enter into the definition of the common good, the meaning of the word 'interest' changes. We cannot imagine that present-day human beings, who are the only contractors, will accept to make sacrifices for future generations and other species without the slightest benefit. However, instead of achieving an alliance between utility and justice, the new social contract associates happiness with the definition of the public good.

This must not lead to the justification of a paternalistic state imposing certain behaviours on individuals. However, personal interest is not only thought of in the light of satisfaction. Similarly, the promotion of individual freedom, understood as the capacity of individuals to make choices (and to change them) and the hope of actually being able to realize a part of their life plan, is not enough to define a just society. Prior to clarifying in which sense the new social contract is based on happiness and justice, it is important to indicate that changes made to the classical liberal scheme are added to those required for the realization of a well-ordered society, in which 'social cooperation makes possible a better life for all than any would have if each were to try to live solely by his own efforts'.[59]

In other words, the social contract as Rawls conceived it, by defining the principles of justice as fairness, maintains all of its currency at an initial level. The two basic principles set out in his *Theory of Justice* and subsequently reformulated allow for a form of political liberalism that can be used as a criterion to conceive relationships among human beings living now.[60] The first principle is that 'each person has an equal claim to a fully adequate scheme of equal basic rights and liberties, which scheme is compatible with the same scheme for all; and in this scheme the equal political liberties, and only those liberties, are to be guaranteed their fair value'. In addition, 'Social and economic inequalities are to satisfy two conditions: they are to be attached to positions and offices open to all under conditions of fair equality of opportunity; and, they are to be to the greatest benefit of the least advantaged members of society (the difference principle)'.[61]

These two principles, referring to what Rawls called the nature of the basic structure of society, involve the way in which institutions distribute rights and fundamental duties. They also determine the distribution of the benefits of mutual cooperation. The 'original position' is the rational method or the heuristic principle that Rawls imagined in order to define these principles in an unbiased manner. Everyone must stand behind a 'veil of ignorance', concealing all of their non-deserved possessions, such as their social and economic status, ethnicity, gender, as well as their natural strengths, talents, and even their conception of the good.[62] To avoid choosing principles of justice that benefit us individually, we must imagine that we do not have these properties and ask ourselves which principles we would like to see adopted. This is how, by adopting a strategy minimizing risk, we choose the difference principle that would, if we were among the most disadvantaged, allow us to be in a better situation than if society were organized independently from this principle. Finally, a 'reflective equilibrium' must be found between the principles determined behind the veil of ignorance and the intuitive argument related to the equality of opportunity that is part of the common conception of justice.[63]

Rawls had to respond to the criticisms that were addressed to him, especially by feminists. The latter have revealed the invisible dominations suffered by minorities that the theory of justice as equality, supposedly neutral with respect to gender, was not able to appreciate. Rawls's successors promoted fair equality of opportunity that corrects the defects of formal equality of opportunity. It is important to take the analyses of Amartya Sen into account, who criticized Rawls for only thinking in terms of income or resources. Not only does the promotion of justice require equalization of 'capabilities', which designates what a person can actually do, but, in addition, it is necessary to organize public services and institutions by considering what it is that prevents some individuals, in view of their precarious situation, their age, or their handicap, 'from converting primary goods into the capacity to function'.[64] Instead of only enjoying rights on paper and having formal freedom, individuals, to whom it is not enough to give a package of primary goods, must be able to enjoy genuine freedom, which must be thought of in terms of rights of access.

These critics, who have enriched liberalism, are now well known. The manner in which Martha Nussbaum took up the capabilities approach to complete Rawls's liberalism and direct justice towards people in situations of dependency deserves to be mentioned, as she contributed to the modification of Rawls's social contract in a decisive manner.[65] She did this by insisting on two major aspects.

The first stems from the fact that disabled individuals, such as those who suffer from severe cognitive deficits, must participate in the world in one way or another. It is unfair that, due to their disabilities, they are deprived of their right to participate in public life, as if they were second-class citizens to whom the rules of common life would apply, but who would be unable to decide. Political liberalism, as has already been suggested in the chapter devoted to justice towards animals and in *Éléments pour une éthique de la vulnérabilité*, has evolved thanks to a reflection on justice towards disabled persons. These persons are not only subjects of our concern: it is important to promote their abilities to act and their citizenship thanks to a system of guardianship that is capable of flexibility.[66]

In other words, the new social contract no longer requires equality of power between individuals. The abandonment of this criterion, which was considered as a condition of the social contract by Rawls and is part of the circumstances of justice, is the abandonment of a Hobbesian premise still present in his theory. Equality of the members of the social contract, who are capable of mutually helping or harming each other, goes hand in hand, in Hobbes, with the fact that the social contract is founded on mutual benefit and that justice is rationally determined based on everyone's personal egoistic interests. Yet if we take the intuition of the moral equality of individuals seriously, which Rawls said cannot be separated from his theory of the original position, and which is connected to the Kantian inspiration in his thought, it appears that it is no longer necessary that those who determine the principles of justice and those to whom the principles apply have equal power, or even that they are deliberative moral agents.[67] The consequences of this thesis concerning the inclusion of people with disabilities and animals in the theory of justice are considerable.

This first amendment of the social contract assumes that the alliance between justice and utility is not only intended as a symmetrical exchange of good practices between people. The second point that confirms this modification of Rawls's social contract is related to the consideration of the vulnerability of the contracting subject. We are not disembodied moral agents; rather, the events and accidents of life, which put us all in a situation of dependence at one point in our existence, lead to the integration of asymmetry and even dissymmetry at the heart of the social contract. The latter is therefore structured not only by equality and freedom, but also and especially by responsibility.

In addition, the principles of justice revealed by the original position take the interests of animals into consideration, because the sense of belonging to a species, the degree of rationality, and the power that we have over others are part of the non-deserved and arbitrary possessions that must be placed in parentheses or behind a veil of ignorance if we wish to regard the rules organizing society as impartial.[68]

Rather than focusing on the results that Rawls attained by developing his theory of justice as fairness, it is important to emphasize his method. It is particularly fertile, even when trying to elaborate a social contract from different elements than those referred to by Rawls. It is often said that animals are excluded from Rawls's theory of justice as fairness, because they are not moral agents with a conception of life or an ability to deliberate, they are not in a situation of equality of power with us, and they do not have a sense of justice. Certain statements made by Rawls appear to move in this direction.[69] However, if we draw the consequences of the method by which he determines justice, we must also place behind the veil of ignorance our own belonging to the human species and our degree of rationality, which are among the non-deserved and arbitrary possessions that cannot justify that individuals who have them enjoy privileges.

Of course, the original position is a process used to describe the conditions of deliberation, and animals cannot deliberate. However, the exclusion of animals and all non-deliberative agents from justice, including people suffering from severe cognitive deficits, is a bias that leads to the selection of principles that do not take their interests into account or subordinate their interests to ours. Speciesism is a lack of impartiality and, therefore, is an injustice. This manner of asking oneself which principles must organize a society, by imagining that we do not know whether we are human beings or animals, founds the universality of the principle on the equal consideration of individuals, human and non-human. This is not to say that animals count as much as human beings, and to imagine that they will hold the same functions as we do, but only to realize that Rawls's social contract, if we remove the Hobbesian premise mentioned previously, leads to an attribution of direct rights to animals.[70]

As Mark Rowlands has said, we are all similar to a soul before its reincarnation when placed in the original position. God does not instruct it which body to choose for reincarnation, but rather which principles must organize the society in which it will live. There are strong chances that it will choose principles of justice that protect all sentient beings from treatments that violate their subjective interests and impose a suffering on them that nobody wants to experience.[71] This fiction, which does not require belief in God or in metempsychosis, is, like the veil of ignorance, a heuristic method that demonstrates that animals enter into justice. It also gives a supplementary force to the argument that sensitivity as susceptibility to pleasure and pain and as vulnerability is a criterion for becoming a subject of justice.

This does not mean that plants are devoid of sensitivity, or that it is allowed, in a just society, to do absolutely anything with ecosystems or even stones. Nature is the object of our responsibility and justice. However, it is not a subject of law. Thus, a neo-Rawlsian social contract does not allow for the extension of justice beyond animals, because individuals in the original position who would be ignorant of the species to which they belong could not be led to choose a principle protecting the inviolability of stones and preventing their barbaric treatment, as this principle has no meaning for these entities.

The protection of ecosystems and the respect for plants, which have interests to preserve and to which our actions and negligence do real damage, do not require them to be holders of direct rights. But stones and ecosystems can become the subject of indirect rights, because their destruction and degradation are unworthy of us and can represent an injustice towards other human beings and other species that cannot or will not be able to enjoy them. On the other hand, animals have direct rights that the social contract, of which they are not contracting members, can reveal. These vulnerable beings must be protected, for themselves and individually, against abuses violating their interests and causing them suffering. The damage that we can inflict upon them is an injustice towards them, and not only disrespect, as is the case for plants.

Is this to say that a neo-Rawlsian framework of thought is sufficient to develop a theory of justice as the sharing of nourishment? This would seem paradoxical, since the philosophy that must serve as the bedrock for this new social contract is a phenomenology of nourishment, which implies an alliance between happiness and interest that reveals a eudemonism foreign to Rawls's thought. This philosophy may imply a transgression of Rawls's principle, according to which one has to place a veil of ignorance over one's conception of good in order to determine the basic structure of the society.

It should be recalled that the phenomenology of nourishment is not akin to a theory proposing a substantial conception of good, even if the existentials that are described assume that certain behaviours are more just than others and that new principles of justice can be inferred beyond what a philosophy of freedom, like that of Rawls, can accept. To develop a new social contract, the philosophy of the subject that serves as the basis for Rawls's theory of justice is modified at its base. However, the method that consists in defining justice in an unbiased manner, thanks to the original position, remains an achievement. Moreover, because the phenomenology of nourishment does not reveal values but rather existentials, the original position that allows the rules of justice as sharing of nourishment supposes that individuals pondering the principles of society know that they 'live from', that they are hungry and thirsty. They are also aware that they have subjective interests to preserve, even if they do not know which ones. The subject of the original position is a bare subject, but an incarnate one: the subject is born, hungry, lives in a place that is a milieu, cohabits with other beings, is vulnerable, and 'lives from' or enjoys.

The emphasis on vulnerability leads to the establishment of responsibility at the heart of moral and political life, and to a renovation of the conception of human beings and sociality upon which Hobbes's and Rawls's social contracts rest. The equality of power and symmetry, which accounts for the fact that mutual benefit and give-and-take are constitutive elements of the social bond, is no longer required in order to see one's interests represented politically. The phenomenology of nourishment helps us, however, to go a step further towards a theory of justice in which happiness and conviviality are included in the definition of utility.

This first philosophy, which insists on enjoyment, and not only on passivity, which was the central principle of our ethics of vulnerability, reveals existentials related to spatiality, habitation, and the need for housing. It underlines the paradigmatic value of nourishment described through its multiple dimensions – nutritive, social, symbolic, intimate, and cultural – and it is integral to the affirmation of the centrality of taste that emphasizes the essential link between ethics and aesthetics. This manner of describing the structures of existence renews our understanding of ethics and justice, which are no longer conceived as external dimensions of our lives, imposing themselves in a binding way.

Responsibility, which is more original than obligation and modifies the subject from the inside, means that the relationship with others constitutes personal identity, since my response to the needs of others and the fact that I am concerned with what happens to them are, as seen in Levinas, the basis of selfhood, which is no longer self-referential. The moral and political thoughts that derive from the phenomenology of nourishment differ from those that relate to the philosophies of freedom, for which the major problem is to guarantee individual safety and satisfaction. The insistence on enjoyment and the link between habitation and cohabitation (which characterizes this phenomenology of 'living from') imply that certain primary goods give rise to rights that must orient public policies and national and international exchanges, as we have seen with the right to food. Every being has a right to food that ensures their living, including animals that feed themselves by hunting their prey. Leaving living beings without food is a crime that no exceptional circumstances can justify. At the same time, this phenomenology of nourishment gives a more joyful tone to responsibility than the ethics of vulnerability. It is not only responsibility towards other human beings (past, present, and future), other nations, and other beings that structures the social contract. Happiness and conviviality also bring a new angle to politics.

An unprecedented alliance thus arises between enjoyment and justice. This is not only explained by the fact that, as soon as I eat, I am connected to other human beings and other living entities and, therefore, that an ethical imperative commands me to limit my consumption and modify my lifestyle. Placed behind a veil of ignorance that makes him question the principles of justice without defining them in terms of his own economic and social situations, the subject that views the principles of justice as the sharing of nourishment cannot want a world where food is bad, landscapes are degraded, air is polluted, and cultures destroyed by the homogenization of taste. The rules governing society must ensure that living beings can enjoy life, not merely survive it.

Furthermore, the fact that I feel my existence in its materiality as being, firstly, an ethical position, modifies profoundly, on the level of sensing, my relationship with myself, other beings (human and non-human), and nourishment. My happiness and joy are inseparable from the taste of food: their savour, beauty, and also the fact that they are not produced or exchanged in just any way. Simple satisfaction appears as a truncated convenience, as when individuals only consider their immediate well-being and the individual dimension of their existence. On the contrary, the fulfilment of their individual and social self transforms the pleasure into joy. Therefore, the limits that we impose on our greed and egoism provide a sense of fullness, as if the acceptance of our own finiteness and the bounds of moderation went together with self-achievement and possibly with the certitude of prolonging, even in a modest way, our individual existence by opting for the love of life.

In the original position, the subject viewing the principles of justice as the sharing of nourishment considers the possibility of promoting this accomplishment, which requires knowing and accepting that we exist, both as individuals and as social selves, in every human being. We do not know what it means, concretely, to think about the principles that make the realization of this accomplishment possible, because we are also ignorant of its cultural aspect. However, it is necessary to include 'living from' as well-being and as conviviality in justice. It is here that the juncture between a theory of justice occurs, inspired by a contractarian model that is still liberal, and a eudaimonist motif, which will enrich liberalism by replacing the philosophy of freedom, which is the basis of Rawls's thought, with a philosophy for which the individual self is not the beginning and the end of all action and creation.

We thus recover the meaning of ethics as a relationship, and the conception of human beings as individuals and collectively, which was discussed in the pages devoted to the phenomenology of Watsuji Tetsurô. We also revive Aristotle, for whom virtue does not designate a moral strength that consists in combatting our selfish inclinations and our vices, but rather a way of being. The latter is not innate, although also not contrary to our nature, and it is linked to pleasure, as the virtuous human being is happy to do good. Similarly, human beings described in the phenomenology of nourishment, both presupposed and shaped by the social contract, do not have the feeling of living less because they consume in a different way and respect other human beings and living beings. On the contrary, by behaving like this, they feel that their lives are enriched. Nevertheless, this alliance between enjoyment and justice that is expressed in simplicity is not immediate. Like virtues in Aristotle, simplicity must be cultivated. It will be encouraged by a just society: if the social contract has to accept human beings as they are and laws as they might be by pursuing, as

Rousseau said, utility and justice, it also needs to change the nature of human beings, or at least to modify it.

With respect to conviviality, pleasure has meaning only when shared. Similarly, personal interest is inseparable from the preservation of an inhabitable world and even its institution, which calls for the creativity of individuals, their ability to act and to react to new situations, and their ability to transmit knowledge and know-how. The latter will allow future generations to assert themselves in a world that they have inherited, without exclusively devoting their efforts to the reparation of the damage caused by their predecessors.

The focus on vulnerability led to an ethics and politics marked by the concern not to impose a diminished life on other human beings and other living beings. The subject of the ethics of vulnerability, who asked whether his or her own right should exist or not, could not repress a sense of guilt, linked to the fear that 'my "place in the sun", or my home [is] a usurpation of places that belong to the other man, already oppressed by me or hungry'.[72] On the contrary, in the phenomenology of nourishment, the subject experiences joy. Happiness is not a simple satisfaction, but the fulfilment of the bodily, terrestrial, and social condition, and this fulfilment or joy of existing cannot be felt individually, while the milieus are degraded and other human and living beings are condemned to a life of deprivation and misery.

In a theory of justice conceived as the sharing of nourishment, happiness is therefore integrated into interests and constitutes them. We depart from the primacy of freedom, which is emblematic of Rawls's theory and gives a certain tone to this thought, characterized by the fact that everyone attempts in their existence to realize their life plans by making concessions that are generally offset by benefits obtained from social cooperation. Of course, a well-ordered society is a society that develops a sense of justice in all of its members.[73]

However, when reading Rawls's works one is struck by the focus of the American philosopher on freedom and equality, which primarily structure the relationship to oneself and others, and which are cardinal notions of his theory of justice.

Such a starting point, which determines the formulation of the political problem, misses other dimensions of existence that attest to its materiality – to the fact that to be free and to achieve our life projects, we need food and clothing. These dimensions of existence shed light on the meaning of our habitation of the earth, which is not a simple springboard for our freedom nor an indifferent space, but a milieu that is both natural and cultural, which has been transmitted to us, and which is inhabited. The latter has an emotional and aesthetic value and puts us in the presence of animals that live with us, traverse the places that we occupy, or live in spaces that we control. It is for all of these reasons that a phenomenology of 'living from' cannot rest content with a theory of justice centred on individual freedom and equality between human beings living now.

Furthermore, in Rawls, primary goods are conceived as resources to distribute. Yet the substitution of nourishment for resources, which is the starting point of the phenomenology of 'living from', prohibits the belief that goods are homogeneous. The existentials described in Part One of this book lead to the affirmation that activities must be organized based on their meaning and on the goods to be exchanged, as we have seen with breeding cattle and with agriculture that assume relationships with living beings and cannot be mistaken for an industry. Similarly, the production of food and its commercialization cannot obey the same rules as do the production and sale of manufactured goods. Finally, it is important to situate agriculture in culture, by valuing the role of farmers in the maintenance of landscapes and in the production of quality goods, which are beneficial to the body and have good taste. In other words, the manner in which Rawls envisaged the redistribution of wealth and resources does not provide sufficient guidance to ensure justice as the sharing of nourishment between human beings belonging to the same generation or between different species. It is also insufficient to ensure fairness between generations.

Indeed, the application of the difference principle, also called the 'maximin' principle, to intergenerational justice faces several difficulties. The first relates to the fact that it is impossible for later generations to help underprivileged individuals from previous generations. The difference principle cannot apply to intergenerational justice because the condition of reciprocity has no meaning in this case.[74] Rawls believed that we can only ensure that future human beings possess conditions of political autonomy, which may justify the obligation of just investment, and requires that we transmit liberal or decent institutions to subsequent generations, thereby ensuring their basic needs.

This response completely ignores the unprecedented situation in which we find ourselves with respect to future generations. Their living and survival conditions will be affected by our current choices on a level that has never been met by our forefathers, since our technological power, as we see with waste from the nuclear industry, produces global consequences that last for thousands of years. Consideration of the changes in our ability to act due to our technological power requires us to take the measure of an essential asymmetry between our generation and the following ones, as shown by Hans Jonas in *The Imperative of Responsibility*. We have received free institutions and a technical capital from our ancestors that increase our freedom of choice and improve our daily lives, while subsequent generations will have more difficult living conditions than ours due to global warming and to the pollution caused by our activities. Reciprocity is not relevant for the elaboration of a social contract that takes the current environmental challenges into account. The interests of future generations who can neither help us nor harm us must be integrated into the definition of the common good, since our activities will have a considerable impact on their living conditions.

Rawls's response to the question whether or not to transfer the same quantity of goods to future generations that we received from our ancestors is equally inadequate to the present environmental crisis. During a period of accumulation, he says, it is important to transfer more to the subsequent generation than we have inherited from the previous one. But once this stage of development is completed, we enter a stable phase during which we may transfer less to our successors than we have received.[75] This sufficientarian theory is blind to the political, geopolitical, social, and economic consequences that arise from the degradation of ecosystems and from climate change and pollution.

Finally, if we nevertheless apply the difference principle to intergenerational justice in order to choose between two policies, the maximin principle requires that their consequences be compared from the point of view of the more disadvantaged individuals in each of the worlds that arise from these policies. Now the difficulty is knowing who is the most disadvantaged. In theory, we would choose the world in which the most disadvantaged individuals are in better situations than the more disadvantaged individuals in the alternative world. However, it is difficult, in practice, to know if current human beings who experience unemployment and have low purchasing power, but who benefit from the exploitation of shale gas that allows them to get a job while reducing their energy bills, are more disadvantaged than future generations, who will inherit a degraded environment due to this exploitation and the massive energy usage that it encourages. Can we help the more disadvantaged individuals of the present generation without considering future generations? The sufficientarian theory that Rawls developed does not help to answer this question because its premises are those of a philosophy of freedom that, in addition, considers goods as resources, without accounting for the fact that the environment has a non-instrumental value and without integrating future generations and other species into justice.

On the contrary, by reworking the principle of primary goods and by considering the materiality of existence of the contracting subject, we are able to delineate the principles of justice as the sharing of nourishment. Before describing these principles and displaying in which way we need to both strengthen the liberal framework proposed by Rawls to protect individual existence and change it in a radical way by introducing a eudaimonistic argument, the political problem as it is derived from the phenomenology of nourishment must be formulated.

The political problem to which the social contract must be able to provide a solution is the following: *to imagine a form of association that protects the person, the goods, and the privacy of each partner, and promotes conviviality and justice conceived as the sharing of nourishment.* Everyone is connected, in their lives and through their use of food, to other human beings (past, present, and future) and to other living beings. The concern not to degrade the environment and not to impose a diminished life on other human beings, human and non-human, is at the heart of their desire to live, therefore limiting from the *inside* their right to sustainability. The contracting subjects entrust to representatives the responsibility of ensuring the promotion of the public good, which implies respecting the right of all human beings to physical, emotional, and social conditions that allow them to enjoy life, and requires a consideration of the interests of future generations and other species.

The alliance between happiness and interest, enjoyment and justice, is expressed in simplicity. The protection of the environment, conceived as a set of finite resources and also apprehended in its aesthetic, cultural, and emotional dimensions, and consideration of the condition of animals become duties of the state and are added to the purposes ordinarily attributed to political authority, which include the defence of life, goods, and the freedom of all partners. However, the political problem is not formulated as if the bedrock of the social contract was the individual, or as if the constitutive elements of the civil association were human beings taken individually and abstractly, as if they existed separately from each other and were soilless, and that animals did not count.

The starting point of civil association is the gourmet cogito, which is also an engendered cogito and a cogito concerned, as soon as it feeds itself, by the lot that it imposes on other human beings living far away from it, on present and future generations, and on other animals. When enjoying nourishment it is also connected with its ancestors, who left it an inheritance that it is not prohibited from transforming, but that the individual moral agent and communities cannot use to their discretion, as if it were their creation and their private property. Landscapes and culture are part of a common heritage that we cannot modify arbitrarily, without considering the criteria of justice mentioned above in the general formulation of the political problem.

In a way, each of us belongs to future generations, and we are connected to past generations as well, to all those lives within us, and, therefore, to all humanity. Animals considered individually also have interests to preserve and are able to communicate them to other members of their species, as well as to other species, and to human beings, as long as we allow them to express themselves by not imposing a mutilated life on them. Our political community, within its limits and with the cultural resources that allow it to interpret the public good, is not separated from other communities, past, present, or future, nor from other beings. It testifies, through its singularity, to their presence in its midst and indicates, through its laws, what it wishes to maintain, modify, and transmit.

In other words, the new social contract does not rely on the symmetry of individuals, even if it is defined as a pact of utility and its objective is to realize public good, which we redefine by integrating the protection of the environment and respect for the interests of other human beings, other cultures, and animals. Politics has a depth related to the philosophy of 'living from' that allows it to understand the human condition in a way that is richer than when human beings are considered as an empire within an empire, and as only seeking their own satisfaction. It is not limited to the art of managing individual passions to avoid a war of everyone against everyone, nor is it to achieve economic prosperity viewed in a purely quantitative manner, as when we calculate growth in terms of GDP, ignore the importance of happiness in the definition of interest, and encourage activities that generate growth, even if they are environmentally and socially disastrous.

Hannah Arendt's definition of the common world gives us an idea of this political depth, which overrides the individualistic foundation of the classical liberal state. In *The Human Condition*, she writes

> The common world is what we enter when we are born and what we leave behind when we die. It transcends our lifespan into past and future alike; it was there before we came and will outlast our brief sojourn in it. It is what we have in common not only with those who live with us, but also with those who were here before and with those who will come after us. … Without this transcendence into a potential earthly immortality, no politics, strictly speaking, no common world and no public realm, is possible.[76]

We are suggesting that animals should enter into the definition of the common world, and that we have to envisage, as we will do in the last chapter of this book, on a new cosmopolitanism, which is connected not only to nature, but also to the earth – to this planet that current technologies and the environmental crisis lead us to consider as a whole. However, the way in which Arendt suggested that our existence is overwhelmed by that of others who have lived, are currently living, or who are not yet born, is even more valuable because this aspect of the human condition is often absent from political programmes.

Another point is worth emphasizing. It involves the strengthening of political liberalism by relying on the idea of the sovereignty of the subject as its main axis. The protection of privacy, ensuring that everyone is out of the view of others, is a fundamental and enforceable right. This right derives from the dialectic between the inside and outside that we have described when speaking of the home that protects our privacy and allows us to receive visitors. The intrusion of people into the private lives of others is a violation of individuals whose secrets and privacy are exposed in the open.

As Kant demonstrated by imagining human beings whose thoughts, even in dreams, would immediately be translated into words, the ideal of transparency that leads individuals to say and publish everything that is related to privacy makes social life impossible.[77] According to Kant, this ideal would only make sense if we were as pure as angels. There is also nothing democratic about it, because it violates everyone's right to secrecy. The disclosure of words that are only addressed to an entourage contributes to the erosion of any sense of grandeur. Considering their neighbours as well as those entrusted with functions of authority, individuals adopt the point of view of valets for whom masters, discovered in slippers or in the bath, have nothing noble about them, as Hegel said. Finally, this ideal of transparency is opposed to the dignity of the person, as it hurts their modesty.

Not only is the first principle of justice as the sharing of nourishment the defence of individuals, on whom the state cannot impose any kind of life under the pretext that it would be morally more noble than another, but, in addition, the refusal of state paternalism goes together with the protection of privacy. When individuals do not cause damage to others, they should not be bothered by the law. This refusal of paternalism, which allows for a strict distinction between morality and right, is very important when dealing with issues of morality, because it avoids, as Ruwen Ogien says, the criminalization of victimless crimes. It is, however, counterbalanced, in the social contract we are proposing, by a eudaimonia that associates happiness with citizenship or the public good.

Admittedly, we may think that the role of the state and of public policies is to encourage a more restrained consumption of animal products. Similarly, its mission is to help farmers who are converting to organic or sustainable agriculture, as well as farmers aiming to improve the living and slaughtering conditions of their animals. However, considering that the objective of these measures is to educate citizens would be a misinterpretation. Rather, public policies must integrate the concern of improving the animal condition and the defence of the environment into all decisions, since animals and the environment are part of the public good and, as we will specify in the last chapter of this book, of the common world.

Similarly, representatives will ensure that the various economic activities are organized so that their meaning, as well as the value of human and non-human lives involved in these activities, is respected. The educational virtues of these measures are undeniable, but they are indirect. The elected have no moral message to pass on, but they aim to promote the public good, which is not limited to the defence of interests and freedoms of current human beings. A paternalistic state is a state that justifies its political decisions through morality and declares that certain laws are legitimate because they develop certain virtues in citizens. Not only is this manner of governing counterproductive, because adult individuals dislike being treated as minors, but, moreover, it is not fair, since politics is not morality, and changes in lifestyles, required by the ecological crisis and the improvement of the animal condition, can only derive from individual consent.

It is up to individuals to think and feel that their good and personal interests imply respect for other human beings and animals, as well as the protection of the environment. Yet they can only integrate this public good into their individual good by experiencing the world as a world of nourishment offering itself to their enjoyment, adorned, inhabited, and shared – as a common world that overwhelms their individual existence and of which, here and now, they are the guardians and the guarantors. The new social contract implies a certain eudaimonia, since there is a new alliance between happiness and virtue, but the key to ethics and justice is feeling, and not intellect alone.

On the other hand, unlike what we find in Aristotle, there is no well-defined sovereign good, conceived in terms of whatever the nature might be, that is to say the end or the *telos* of humans. Neither is it a simple hedonism, since individuals are neither the starting point nor the arrival point of ethics and justice as the sharing of nourishment. Not everything starts and ends with the ego, since the cogito is a gourmet and engendered cogito and we are in a radical phenomenology of sensing where, prior to representation, there is 'living from'. However, we mention the cogito because, unlike plants and animals, we can set out the principles of justice and deduce from them the laws that will constitute the frame of the social contract specific to a community.

Finally, we use the term 'eudaimonia' because consideration of the public good, other human beings, and animals, as well as concern for the beauty of the world, which constitute an alliance between

happiness and utility characteristic of the new social contract, is
connected to something profound in human beings – akin to a
disposition to good. However, it is important to develop this sense
of justice as the sharing of nourishment because, even if it is not
contrary to nature, it needs, like Aristotle's virtue, to be cultivated and
encouraged by institutions for it to have an effect, beyond a simple
power or disposition to good. The role of chance or the *daimon* is
not negligible either, insofar as certain emotional, social, and cultural
conditions, as well as the existence of people embodying this ideal
of justice and serving as models, may help individuals experience
the love of life and beauty that characterizes the phenomenology
of nourishment.

The principles of justice as the sharing of nourishment

What are, then, the principles of justice as the sharing of nourishment?
They are deduced from the existentials described in Part One of
this book. Their concise formulation should not make us forget
the methodology that allowed their foundation. Such an oversight
would only reveal injunctions akin to empty shells, or would seem
arbitrary. However, the process by which these principles are set out
to summarize the results or conclusions of the arguments developed
above has a pedagogical advantage, in that it provides reference points
that are easy to use.

The first principle, which shows the anchoring of the new social
contract in liberalism, organizes the separation between morality and
law, especially when it concerns human beings belonging to the same
generation and the same country. This principle that implies doing no
harm to others mainly applies to questions of mores and relationships

that anyone has with their own body or with that of others. The condition is, as in Mill, that the persons involved are consenting and competent adults, which excludes any abuse of weakness.[78]

One of the limitations of this line of liberal argument, which belongs to minimalist ethics, holds onto the fact that the legitimacy of practices and claims that go beyond the question of peaceful coexistence of individual freedoms and that have an impact on institutions and on the whole of society cannot be assessed. Yet this is the case for many bioethics issues, and also for any reflection on the consequences of consumption habits for the environment, future generations, and other living beings.[79] It is therefore necessary to depart from the strict framework of liberalism, as defined by Mill, to address these issues.

Minimalist ethics allows one to identify confusion, often present in the moral argument, that may exist between aesthetic values expressing taste or repulsion, moral intuitions, and normative judgements relative to the just and the unjust, the good and the bad.[80] To dispel false evidence specific to our moral intuitions, and to identify inconsistencies resulting from the application to different situations of our moral principles (whether they are ethical or consequentialist), a rigorous method, which involves considering the role of intuitions in the justification of moral theories, contributes to the shaping of minds often inclined to dogmatism. The development of a critical sense, which requires moral experimentation and confronting situations, of the sort facilitated by the moral puzzles considered by Ogien in *Human Kindness and the Smell of Warm Croissants*, allows for the recognition that nothing in the principles and methods of moral philosophy is immune to challenge and revision. This methodological approach, which owes much to analytical philosophy, teaches us moral scepticism, which has nothing to do with relativism but contributes to the quality of public deliberation in a pluralist democracy. Minimalist ethics can therefore be used as a criterion of legislation in a democracy when the challenge is to organize the peaceful coexistence of the freedoms of existing human adults. The separation between morality and law enables us to denounce the return to a repressive and reactionary moral order, which can disguise itself behind the reference to the common good and to uncriticized and intimidating principles.

The second principle therefore involves the search for a consensus or, rather, reasonable disagreement on questions that go beyond the problem of peaceful coexistence of freedoms, and that have an impact on the meaning of institutions, as well as on the different actors who have divergent interests and conflicting values. While formulating points upon which it is impossible to arrive at an agreement, as is the case with a number of undecidable issues linked to the power that everyone grants themselves regarding their lives and deaths, it is important to establish the common good by searching for an appropriate legislative solution that takes positive laws, existing practices, and different actors into account. The first thing to do is to narrow down the subject by determining the problems that arise and those for which no solution has yet been found.[81]

Narrowing down a subject by abandoning controversy and holding the different points of view at the same time allows us to move forward in a public deliberation. This essential point highlights both the fertility of Rawls's method and its limits when dealing with issues such as bioethical and ecological issues that require our examining the conceptions of the good or the ontologies that underlie our stances or moral judgements. We cannot place our moral or ontological conceptions behind a veil of ignorance, but we can confront them by identifying the points for which an agreement cannot be found by those who are capable of making a common, reasonable decision that may be recognized as valid by those who address the question through a consideration of the common good, and not only their personal interest.

The conditions for appropriate legislation on issues that go beyond the problem of peaceful coexistence of freedoms and the equitable allocation of resources will be examined in the next chapter, relating to deliberation. We will also see that it is important, when dealing with environmental issues for which expertise is essential, to reconsider the relationship between the sciences, society, and power, to appreciate the relevance of argumentation in public deliberation, and to insist on the training in meta-ethics of those who are represented and their representatives. It was however important, after having insisted on the liberal framework of the state, which requires the refusal of paternalism, to show that it is possible, by means of a rigorous methodology, to reach a consensus that has nothing to do with a 'neither-nor' policy, and which does not assume to confine itself to a principle that belongs to minimalist ethics.

The third principle concerns the relationship of human beings with humanity and with the world as a whole, including all living beings. Its main axis is the criterion of irreversibility. It commands us to refrain from using any techniques that can lead to an irreversible destruction of the planet, whether total or partial. Similarly, it requires that our consumption habits and development model do not lead to a point of no return that makes the restoration of a viable situation concerning air, ecosystems, global warming, and pollution impossible.

The fourth principle concerns the relationship of current human beings with future generations. It is consequentialist and enjoins the avoidance of anything that might impose a diminished life on future human beings, such as harmful sanitary conditions affecting their quality of life, a degraded environment – on the level of both resources and aesthetics – and the fact that they would have to spend fortunes to repair the damages caused by previous generations and to repay the debt contracted by the latter. These efforts would be real burdens and would prevent them from reaching a threshold of well-being beyond which enjoyment is possible. Moreover, the transmission of institutions allowing future generations to promote a just society and to develop their abilities to act would be jeopardized if they inherited an uninhabitable environment or excessive debt. The second criterion for defining this principle is relative to the obligation that is made to current human beings to leave to their descendants a cultural inheritance that gives them the possibility of experiencing beauty and of educating their senses and their taste.

The fifth principle enshrines the right of all human beings and animals to have access to food and drink in sufficient quantity and quality. In addition, the appropriateness of a diet is not limited to its nutritional value, it must also suit individual needs, according to age, culture, and species. It must have taste and it must be enjoyable.

The sixth principle refers to habitation, which is a structure of existence and implies that everyone has a home, in order to preserve their privacy and their way of life and to feel that their existence is attached to a place. Not only does this entail a prohibition on expropriation and on colonization, but, moreover, it means that we must not compel a population to practise a mode of agriculture foreign to its milieu (in its ecumenical dimension) and to the savoir-faire of the inhabitants. The emotional value that a landscape represents for its inhabitants must be considered: it cannot be demolished without their consent, whatever the alleged economic objective may be, such as the construction of a highway or an airport. With habitation being different from 'human garages' and always referring to a cohabitation with other human beings and other living beings, conviviality is among the objectives of urbanization projects. It is also unfair to destroy the habitat of other species and, if this destruction is justified by security reasons, animals must be given another home that suits them and that allows them to flourish according to their own norms.

The seventh principle demands respect for other cultures, especially those of peoples who have developed a way of life different from ours, such as the Native peoples living in the Amazon rain forest. Deforestation and the construction of dams that jeopardize their ways of life are unfair. It is also important to take account of the consequences that interactions or exchanges imposed on these peoples have for their culture, especially the youngest of them, who can break from their traditions and undermine the social link.

The eighth principle refers to the organization of work and of economic activities. Justice assumes that production is organized on the basis of the exploited entity. When dealing with living beings, their structure and dynamism must be respected, especially if they are animals. Animals, being holders of direct rights, cannot be detained in just any way, which means that human beings do not have the right to impose a life on them in which their ethological needs are frustrated and in which they experience pain and suffering, boredom, and depression. The death of an animal, whatever it may be, should be painless. No circumstances and no traditions justify animals being tortured, nor them experiencing anxiety before dying.

Moreover, the organization of the work of human beings depends on the goods produced and the services provided. Neither a priori norms nor the evaluation of performance, based on maximum productivity figure set in advance, is legitimate. Efficiency and the quality of the service depend on the type of good or service, which prohibits the assimilation of cattle rearing and agriculture to an industry, and subtracts care, research, and police investigations from the performance criteria that are meaningful in marketing. The same principle applies to commercial exchanges, which cannot be organized without considering the value of the food to be traded. This means, for example, that staple foods will be exempt from speculation and that the food trade will be regulated so that competition is fair.

The ninth principle involves our relationship with animals. We have specific duties towards domestic animals that are dependent on us. Anyone who abandons an animal, detains them in conditions incompatible with ethological norms, or abuses them must answer for their action before a court that recognizes the legal status of animals. Considered as sentient beings, animals are non-representational subjectivities whose interests enter into the definition of the common good. Their emotional and social needs must be respected.

Ideally, cattle should not be killed when they are very young. Certain practices to which too much suffering is attached and that meet futile needs must disappear, such as foie gras and fur. It is to be forbidden to kill wild animals for their skin. The latter have the right to live independently from us and the respect of this right implies that, through our activities, we avoid destroying their habitat. Safaris for hunting are forbidden, as well as the capture and detention of wild animals in circuses. Zoos are only acceptable if animals born in captivity benefit from living conditions that do not condemn them to boredom and frustration. Work involving animals is only legitimate if it brings compensation and rewards to the animals. Anyone using animals must be able to ensure that they are happy to work and that they do not suffer from their working conditions. Finally, we must be sure, in the development of cities, territories, and habitations, not to encourage the proliferation of liminal animals. The use of trapping, which causes intolerable suffering, is to be prohibited. Vivisection should be abolished and animal experiments should be avoided as much as possible, especially in the development of cosmetics and industrial products. The 'rule of the three R's' (Reduce, Refine, Replace) should be scrupulously applied, as well as the voluntary development of alternatives to animal testing, in order to do everything possible to get closer, in the short term, to the ideal of abolishing all testing on animals.[82]

All political decisions involve an environmental aspect and are assessed on the basis of their impact on the condition of animals. The protection of the environment and the improvement of the animal condition are new duties of the state and appear as such in the constitution. Thus, on the cultural and educational level, the promotion of environmentally friendly lifestyles that respect nature and animals in the domains of food, fashion, cattle rearing, and leisure activities, is encouraged. Similarly, everything that develops in childhood, the love for animals, which, as we have seen, goes together with the love for justice, should contribute to the transversal treatment of animal issues.

The will to significantly improve the animal condition is at the heart of the new social contract that sets out the principles of justice as the sharing of nourishment. If this objective is central, this is not only because of its own importance, but also because it assumes that human beings have reconciled with the pathic dimension of their existence and that this dimension promotes such reconciliation. Our relationship with animals therefore represents a decisive step towards the promotion of justice as the sharing of nourishment, and in the enlargement of the self that this theory implies.

For it is at the heart of individuals, in the manner in which they integrate their concern for other human beings and other living beings into their lives, that social ties are woven and a self is built that is capable of instituting the common good and responding to environmental, social, and spiritual challenges of the present in a democratic way. This integration of the interests of others into our own interest and the general interest can only occur if we are in harmony with ourselves in terms of emotions and feeling. This level is the one that we occupy when communicating with animals. The latter teach us how to reconnect with our emotions and feeling. Therefore, the improvement of our relationships with them makes us progress both individually and collectively. Thus, when we are working towards improving the condition of animals, we are also working for the progress of mankind, by celebrating a humanism in which the gourmet and engendered cogito, who feels that its happiness is not only relative to its individual self, positions itself as the guardian of creation.

5

Reconstructing democracy

'Democracy' refers to a government (*kratos*) with and by the people (*dêmos*) in a territory. The link between a people and a territory and the obligation of the state, 'which owes to every citizen a certain subsistence, a proper nourishment, convenient clothing, and a kind of life not incompatible with health', are explicit.[1] The preamble to the Environmental Charter, which has been integrated into the French Constitution since 2005, states that 'resources and natural balances have determined the emergence of humanity', and that its future and existence 'are inseparable from its natural milieu'.[2]

Several texts, both in France and internationally, testify to the existence of a right to the environment and even to the anchoring of this right within the scope of the other human rights that it determines.[3] Additionally, Article 13 of the treaty on the functioning of the European Union made consideration of the animal condition into an essential value. Finally, the Aarhus Convention, adopted on 25 June 1998, to implement the commitments made in 1992 at the Rio Earth Summit, and which concerns access to information, participation of the public in the decision-making process, and environmental justice, underlines the constitutional value of the 'right of citizens to personally contribute to the formation of laws' set out in Article VI of the Declaration of the Rights of Man and of Citizens of 1789.

We could multiply the references, either to laws and/or declarations, and add to this list an impressive number of articles and books that converge on a number of points. The latter relate to the assertion of the interdependence of human beings and the environment, the redefinition of justice and international relations in the light of environmental challenges, the evolution of the legal status of animals, and the need to amend the rules of decision making. All of these data illustrate a general awareness and willingness, shared by rulers and the ruled, to install at the heart of the social contract a respect for nature and for living beings, along with a concern for future generations. This progress is based on a conception of well-being that takes into account our corporeality, considered in its fragility, as well as the aesthetic dimension and the conviviality that we need in order to flourish. Yet despite this theoretical contribution and this evolution in terms of values, ecology has failed to change politics.

States, which are still conceived as defending the interests of one community against another, and the representative system, which is structured by electoral competition, are unable to integrate global, transversal, and often long-term environmental issues. They also experience many difficulties in learning from the local experiences of citizens in different places, in considering the power to propose and to mobilize that associations held, and in addressing the intelligence of individuals in order for them to take part in decision making. These inadequacies are connected. They do not spell the end of representative democracy, but they do require its modification at several levels.

Thus, the developments needed to bring ecology, concern for the long term, and improvement of the animal condition into the political agenda are institutional, but they must also go together with a rigorous interrogation of the changes required to train and select elected representatives, and with a review of the role of experts in a society faced by several major challenges. Finally, it is indispensable to address political culture, which involves at the same time the role of argument and the affects in political debate, rhetoric, and the deontology of the media.

This chapter is devoted to this work, which relates to the renewal of democracy: unlike the previous chapter, which dealt with the principles and purposes of the state and was concerned with the theory of justice, this one focuses on the how, on the manner in which we can organize not only the state, but also political life. The latter is not limited to the art of conquering and retaining the power, nor to strategic struggles. It rather implies the institution of the common good by citizens and requires their commitment, the exercise of their autonomy, and the assertion of their responsibility in a context marked by pluralism and by recognition of the moral equality of individuals. We are thus considering how the promise that has been attached to the definition of democracy since antiquity can be held, in demographic, ecological, cultural, and social conditions that make the representative system unavoidable as well as reveal that it needs to be perfected.

Supplementing the representative system

The paths that we are proposing do not require a return to direct democracy. Moreover, participation is not a magical principle. This word even seems worn out, because citizens, whose opinions often have no decisional value, feel that we are only pretending to associate them with political decisions. They view participation, often reduced to consultation, as an alibi used by officials who are convinced of being the only ones possessing the authority and skills essential to the management of the affairs of the city. It is nevertheless important to understand that additional elements brought to the representative system, which will be discussed first, have little relevance when we separate them from the entirety of the restructurings and changes that are needed.

These entail two essential components. The first makes use of the normative wealth related to the theories of deliberation that ideally require that all decisions should be preceded by an argument geared towards the common good, whereas the second one deepens the constituent link between culture and democracy. It is at the end of this investigation that the issue of the participation of citizens, which is very important for matters relating to diet and ecology, makes sense, since our objective is not to oppose deliberation to participation, but rather to assess both the institutional and cultural changes that are needed to repair and reconstruct democracy.

Representative democracy no longer constitutes an oxymoron as it did in the eighteenth century, and, if it is difficult in modern states composed of millions of people to return to the Athenian ideal of direct democracy, it is undeniable that the two ways of thinking about political representation are equally subject to criticism. Whether we adopt the mirror model, according to which our representatives must reflect the diversity of the people and resemble it, or we admit a certain superiority of representatives over ordinary citizen does not affect the situation. The faults of each model – the risk of populism in the first and the oligarchic abuses with the second – seem to weigh more than their respective advantages.

Moreover, representative democracy is going through a legitimacy crisis. It is as if citizens believed that their sovereignty had to be confiscated by elected officials who are unable to make appropriate decisions, because they do not understand the expectations of those they are supposed to represent, because it is difficult for them to see what the common good is, and because their power is diluted or contingent on a globalized economy that leaves them no flexibility.

In the current state of things, representative democracy seems powerless in resolving environmental challenges and in promoting more social justice. Similarly, there are hesitations on the part of legislators on a number of societal issues relating to the evolution of morality and bioethics, as well as to taxation, which yet would allow for the reduction of inequalities that today mostly involve heritage.[4] Many experts' reports are delivered to governments, but their influence on public decisions is not apparent. Finally, fear of the street and of the polls, along with pressure from lobbies, often dictates the conduct of representatives.

These shortcomings, for which representatives are held accountable, generate a loss of confidence among citizens towards politicians. This loss of confidence is widely exploited by those who despise democracy. There is an obvious crisis of representation, but the gap between the representatives and the represented cannot only be imputed to the personalities selected in the electoral races that characterize competitive democracy.

Furthermore, the deficiencies of representative democracy encourage the withdrawal of individuals into the private sphere. This behaviour comforts the political and intellectual elite in their authoritarian and vertical representations of power. To break this vicious circle, three levels must be considered: the institutional component, which adds to the representative system a non-representative system in charge of including the long-term, ecological, and animal issues at the heart of politics, and of thinking about the place of science in debates and decisions; the deliberative component, which requires departing from political passions and which is supportive of Habermas's ideal of the public sphere; and the cultural component, which revives Rousseau's concern about forming the public opinion and developing certain moral traits allowing this democratic reconstruction project to rest on solid and sustainable foundations.

Rather than rejecting the representative system straight away, we should first specify why, by nature, it is unable to effectively grasp environmental issues. Today, these are mostly problems related to the crossing of limits corresponding to thresholds of danger, whether it is climate change, the rate of erosion of biodiversity, disruption of the nitrogen and phosphorus cycles, the depletion of the stratospheric ozone layer, the acidification of the oceans, the use of freshwater and soil, chemical pollution, or the impact of atmospheric aerosols.[5]

This analysis, which highlights the specificity of environmental issues, serves as a starting point for proposing several reforms, which can supplement the representative system and swing competitive democracy towards a deliberative democracy that will more effectively take on all the issues that the phenomenology of nourishment has installed at the heart of the social contract. However, it is not enough to say that representative democracy is almost exclusively focused on the immediate interests of current human beings, and that it sacrifices the interests of other species and future generations. We must also understand that, if these environmental problems have a destructive potential and threaten the conditions of the existence of humanity, they also have the characteristic of escaping from the immediate perception of individuals.[6]

The representative system, which is based on the idea that electors are the judges of their own well-being and choose representatives who are most likely to defend their interests and their vision of a good life, is poorly adapted to environmental issues, which are not limited to the pollution or degradation of the resources of a territory. Not only are environmental issues global, extending beyond national and territorial boundaries represented by the parliament and the senate, but, moreover, environmental violations are largely invisible.[7] Whether we consider the state of the microfauna of the soil, the presence of micro-pollutants or sources of radioactivity, the chemical composition of the atmosphere and of food, or the acidity levels of oceans, without the mediation of scientific knowledge, it is difficult for citizens to have an adequate apprehension of these issues. Our senses do not provide us with any information about the measure of PPM (parts per million) of CO_2 in the ambient air, nor about the presence of endocrine disrupters. We are therefore not able to judge our own interests regarding our health and that of our loved ones. Thus, there is a contrast between the cognitive situation of electors and their sense of well-being. As a result, the spring of the representative mechanism, the one's own self-apprehension, no longer works.[8]

In addition to their ubiquity and invisibility, environmental issues are characterized by their unpredictability. It is only in retrospect that we discover the effects of the interaction of a molecule on the milieu. Dominique Bourg illustrated this phenomenon with the example of chlorofluorocarbons (or CFCs), which were discovered in 1928 and were massively used in the 1950s, and despite their chemical neutrality and stability were found in the 1970s and 1980s to build up formidable greenhouse gases (GHGs) that destroy the stratospheric ozone.[9] No government can truly foresee the consequences of our technologies in the middle and long terms, nor guarantee citizens a degree of absolute safety.

Finally, inertia and irreversibility are true obstacles to an appropriate ecological policy.[10] Indeed, the reaction of ecosystems to degradation is not immediate, and the consequences of the disturbances of the major mechanisms of the biosphere may remain undetected for several decades. Yet we irreversibly determine the evolution of climate. Moreover, the time during which it is still possible to react is short. If nations had reached an agreement at the Copenhagen Summit in 2009, it would have been possible to not go over 450 PPM of CO_2 and to have odds of three out of four of limiting the average warming to 2 degrees before the end of the century by reducing global emissions by 3 per cent per year. But it is too late. Even if this commitment has been made in Paris in 2015, it is necessary to reach the same objective to reduce our emissions by 6 per cent per year starting in 2021.[11] Thus Thomas F. Stocker writes that the window for action to limit global warming to 2 degrees is now shut.

The hypothesis of a third chamber, and the role of experts

Thus, the very nature of environmental issues compels us to imagine institutional innovations that meet two objectives. The first is to instigate concern for the long term and take into account the interests of other species in the representative system devoted to current human beings and to territories. The second must allow scientific data to enter into political debates by avoiding expertocracy which would introduce a confusion between the role of decision-makers and that of scientists, and might reflect a naive conception of science, a major characteristic of which being that it generates controversies and can in no way produce a unique and definitive truth in the face of a complex problem.

To respond to the first challenge, it might be appropriate to create a third chamber, as envisaged by Pierre Rosanvallon and Dominique

Bourg.[12] The two current chambers, the parliament and the senate, would be maintained; only the first would be allowed to engage the responsibility of the executive power, and the second, representing territories, would serve a decentralized state. Next to these two chambers would be a third one dedicated to environmental matters.

Strictly speaking, it is impossible to represent trees and ecosystems, or even to select spokespersons for future generations. Indeed, the representation that forms the basis of election is only legitimate if those who are represented have their say, can challenge the decisions made in their name, and can dismiss their representatives by ceasing to vote for them. Ecosystems, future human beings, and animals cannot show their displeasure by dismissing those who speak for them. Certainly, they have a response, since as soon as we affect their interests, they die or suffer, and animals communicate their emotions. However, this response is not articulated, and it has no political force if it is not relayed through the words and actions of human beings.

Thus, the third chamber would not be representative, in the sense that it would not be composed of elected representatives. However, its members would have the role of reminding individuals that politics is zoopolitics and cosmopolitics, that the interests of future generations and animals, even loosely apprehended, enter into the definition of the common good, and that the value of ecosystems is not only relative to the immediate benefit that we can receive from them. They would thus grant a political force to future generations, ecosystems, and other species.

These persons who are appointed to impose that long-term concerns are debated in the parliament and senate, and to ensure that the new duties of the state regarding the interests of future generations and animals are respected, would not pass laws. They would, however, intervene in the legislative process by having a right of veto over bills that have been adopted but not yet promulgated.

This assembly could then oppose the measures that would not take into account the principles of justice as the sharing of nourishment. It would exercise its vigilance so that territorial development, taxation, agricultural policies, as well as changes in the fields of transport and education, would not only be decided based on the immediate benefits of current human beings. In their bills, elected officials would thus have to consider the interests of future generations, other species, and the current state of resources, as well as the degradation of the biosphere, increase of the sea level, and so forth.

This third chamber could be referred to by the two others, as well as by the government, the president, and the citizens by means of petitions signed by a large number of people. Dominique Bourg considered that it would be used to enforce environmental rights, in order for them not to be eclipsed by immediate interests. In my view, it would also have the role of enforcing the principles mentioned in the previous chapter, such as the right to food and the promotion of justice towards animals. If an agreement between the two chambers is impossible, this third chamber could refer to the constitutional court, which would ensure that the fundamental rights of the environment are not jeopardized and that the principles of justice and the sharing of nourishment are respected. It could also turn towards the president, who would also be a holder of this constructive right of veto.

Rather than naming it the 'long-term Assembly', as Dominique Bourg did, we would designate it the 'Assembly of Nature and Living Beings'. Considering the characteristics of ecological issues previously mentioned, it is evident that the protection of nature requires mediations, especially scientific ones, so that individuals know what to do. Similarly, today, ecology and animal matters do not allow elections to be won, because they enter into competition with the immediate interests of individuals and with the current organization of the economy. However, the defence of the biosphere, the right of future generations to live a happy life, and respect for animals are not external to human beings, as we have demonstrated in Part One of this book.

It is by starting with human beings and by considering the conditions of their existence, which are material and also refer to enjoyment and conviviality, that nature can be protected, as we have attempted to demonstrate by speaking of nourishment instead of resources. We have also insisted on the place occupied by the relationship with animals in our relationship with ourselves and in the transformation of the subject that is at the heart of the new social contract. A third chamber called the Assembly of Nature and Living Beings is therefore useful for reminding governments and those governed that current human beings are not the only actors nor the only recipients of justice. Its role is to counteract the effects of a political game that only bears on immediate interests, or even on each person's representation of what they believe to be their immediate interest, that is, on profit.

If the legitimacy of this third chamber cannot be elective, it nevertheless assumes that the colleges that constitute it are composed of qualified persons, who are recognized for their skills in environmental matters, for their commitment to major environmental issues and the improvement of animal condition, for their ethological knowledge, and for their expertise regarding the biological dimension of the human condition and bioethics. Dominique Bourg suggested that, for this chamber's first college, a list of suitable candidates should be established with three times as many names as required, and that one out of three should be selected randomly. This process reduces the risk of instrumentalization or corruption of the proposed personalities. The designation of friends or relatives, which undermines credibility and effectiveness in a number of instances, commissions, or ethics committees, is also avoided. The second college of this assembly would assemble ordinary citizens using a procedure similar to the one used to organize panels during citizen conferences, especially by random selection from among volunteers.

However, the legitimacy of this third chamber would not only be ensured by the expertise of its members. Random selection, which guarantees a certain impartiality that the pressure of lobbies makes impossible when other procedures are followed, is also insufficient to confer a strong legitimacy to this assembly. In addition, its members must have a sense of the universal. Dominique Bourg focused on the institutional component of political ecology and, even though he insisted on participation, he failed to completely prevent his ecological democracy from becoming a democracy of experts.[13] On the contrary, we believe that the functioning of such an assembly, which is a sort of counter-power at the heart of power and which ensures the spirit of laws, is subordinate, if not to the acquisition of certain moral traits, at least to the acceptance of the defining principle of deliberation. It is required to look towards public interest and give assent to the best argument, by putting special interests and vanity aside.

No modification of institutions makes sense if we do not work at the same time on improving the quality of the debate that determines the vitality of democracy while also highlighting the importance of contemporary political theories dealing with deliberative democracy. Any democratic progress, whether in the form of improvements of the representative system, deliberation, participation, or even anything that has to do with the role of the media and culture, cannot survive on its own. It is indeed essential to take the measure of the changes required in our ethical representations, and to develop an ontology that goes beyond values and has a certain universality, recognized as such by those who accept the phenomenological method. This is why, if we had to compare this work to that of an architect, this part would build the roof and pillars of a political theory, of which the phenomenology of nourishment would be the foundation.

The relationship between science and power is the second problem that needs to be addressed if we want representative democracy to acquire the means of resolving environmental issues, elected representatives to make appropriate decisions concerning dilemmas related to bioethics, and animal issues to become politicized. The creation of a 'College of the Future' is an interesting possibility; this ad hoc institution would be devoted to scientific oversight and in charge of keeping elected officials informed.[14]

It is obvious that representatives cannot be scholars, philosophers, physicians, geologists, and ethologists at the same time, even if they must rule on all of these subjects. The hearing of specialists by parliamentarians and senators in the various committees on bioethics, animals, or GMOs is satisfactory in terms of neither methods nor results. Elected officials need to have international data on climate and specific reports related to the different topics covered. However, the time scale for research and even for expertise is long. It cannot be modelled on that of politics or opinion. The objective is therefore to ensure that elected officials and citizens can benefit from syntheses of scientific work.

Hopefully, these syntheses would be performed by competent persons, able to make this scientific research accessible without erasing its richness. Moreover, instead of entrusting environmental information to the media and lobbies and letting the doxa take hold of the subjects of bioethics, it is necessary to set up an impartial instrument to monitor and diagnose environmental issues and to present works reviewing problems related to medical practices and biotechnology, which can be used as benchmarks, even temporarily, for various legislative proposals and public policies.

Therefore, this college's mission would be to collect data on mineral and energy resources, on ecosystems, and on the biosphere, and its regulatory mechanisms. It could also present technical and scientific oversight on complex issues, especially regarding medicine or animal experiments. Rather than multiplying the redundant notes and opinions of learned societies and relying on agencies, experts should be professionalized.[15] The work required to characterize all specific bioethical problems cannot be properly carried out by individuals with busy professional lives who meet from time to time within an ethics committee.

The members of ethics committees, including the Comité Consultatif National d'Éthique (CCNE), often do not have enough time to thoroughly work on the topics submitted to them, but, moreover, the composition of ethics committees, which is supposed to represent the diversity of citizens, and sometimes also the lack of transparency of their designation, explains why the scientific quality of their reports and opinions is variable. Nonetheless, it would be preferable if the professionalization of experts were provisional. It is indeed essential to avoid the instrumentalization of the members of the College of the Future. The latter could have three branches, one dedicated to ecology, one to bioethics, and the last one to animal issues and ethology. It is also important that researchers, when becoming experts, not lose their independence of thought and their interest for fundamental research, without which their work would not have as much value. Moreover, recognized researchers could be mandated to rigorously investigate specific domains of interest. The results of their work would then be debated by ethics committees, for example the CCNE, whose mission is less to establish the scientific or philosophical truth on a subject than to wisely consider what should be done on the collective level in order to give an advisory opinion to legislators.[16]

The college's second task would be to inform the government, members of parliament (especially those from the third chamber), and citizens about the evolution of knowledge regarding the climate and the biosphere, and to present to them the work done by researchers who were mandated for a limited time to scrutinize a particular subject. We suggest that a team of people trained in scientific mediation should be added to this college: its task would be to translate the work of the researchers into a language accessible to everybody. Rather than merely delivering the results of their analyses, as parliamentary assistants often do, or even making a summary that only preserves the elements likely to conform to the power in place, they would clearly convey the approach that forms the basis of the argumentation and the methodology followed. These mediators would be trained in a scientific discipline related to at least one of the three fields studied (biology and medicine, environmental sciences, and ethology), as well as in the human and social sciences. They would also be holders of a master's degree in scientific mediation, or have skills in the field of communications, and could organize events at which scientists and members of the college would present their research on specific topics and benefit from the assistance of these specialists in communications with the general public.

Finally, on the regional level, it would be appropriate to establish alongside the regional council a chamber composed of consumers, farmers, breeders, or veterinarians selected at random and for a limited time. This chamber would ensure that the interests of future generations, other species, and individual animals are taken into consideration on the local level. As part of a territorial reform grouping regions together and reducing their number, the members of this regional chamber of the long term and of living beings would be connected at a national level. A document describing the specific geographic, demographic, economic, and socio-cultural aspects of each region would allow for the national and local levels to be articulated. This would facilitate the application of laws and the adaptation of general principles that derive from environmental protection and the consideration of the interests of future generations and animals in different contexts. This document would also be defended orally at a hearing before parliament, the senate, and the third chamber. This hearing, which could take place once a year, would also ensure that these regional assemblies are connected.

These proposals would supplement the current representative system and allow us to take charge of environmental issues that are likely to have a decisive impact on the future of society; they would also accompany changes in mores and a transformation in our relationship with animals, which could be the opportunity for a civilizational turn. However, to reconstruct democracy it will also be necessary to strengthen this representative system from within by restoring trust between citizens and their elected officials. This is essential, since the power of lobbies is one of the major obstacles to democracy and progress in the fields of social justice, environment, food, and animal welfare.

Trust cannot be imposed, nor can it exclusively be related to the personality of the actors. It could be beneficial to change the status of elected officials who, instead of necessarily being political professionals, could have a profession like other citizens. Their experience with the realities of this professional life, and certain commitments in favour of the public good, would give a supplementary legitimacy to the election. When someone has won a certain legitimacy in a field through their actions, knowledge, and constancy, their appointment as minister in a field in which they are competent is not arbitrary and does not give rise to mistrust. Moreover, citizens, who need to know that there is a captain on board and who are initially inclined to give credit to their representatives, would be reassured and would be willing to defer to their authority. If this person knows how to act at the right moment and to address citizens, we may believe that they will lead courageous and appropriate reforms.

The question of the training of elected officials deserves also to be considered, as it goes well beyond the specific skills of a representative. The latter should have had adequate training not only in a number of political, and scientific matters, but also in argumentation and ethics, especially meta-ethics. Communication and coaching are often more sought after by politicians, than dialogical virtues, which, as we will see when we discuss deliberation, go hand in hand with certain moral traits that allow us to listen to others. It seems difficult to ask citizens to respect representatives who stick to personal attacks, instead of trying to build a line of argumentation that could be used to identify a reasonable dissensus.[17]

In France, strengthening representative democracy would also imply exchanging a presidential regime based on the fifth constitution which was established in a particular context and associated with a head of state that has played a unique historical role, for a regime in which the parliament fully plays its role, as in other European countries. Rather than asking candidates in presidential elections to wear the costume of Charles de Gaulle, which does not fit anyone – both because the man had a solid stature, and also because the times and the people have changed and today most individuals would not support the paternalism of the state – it could be useful to redefine the president's mission.

It is possible that the presidential function retains more prestige when it stays away from the details of matters. This function goes together with a certain hauteur, since the president embodies the spirit of the republic. In other words, the prime minister could govern, being appointed by the parliament and not by the president, whereas the head of state would be the guarantor of the principles of justice, by ensuring that public policies are not contrary to the duties of the state that we have attempted to specify in the previous chapter in listing the principles of justice as the sharing of nourishment. The president would encourage the spirit of this new social contract, which requires ensuring safety and public peace, as well as developing the art of living together, a conviviality that requires the consideration of the interests of future generations, respect for ancestors and other cultures, and more justice towards animals. Detached from current affairs and therefore exempt from the criticism addressed to the government, he or she would be the one who brings the people together because in a democratic pluralistic and secular society, we can only assemble through ideas, through the general principles that reinvigorate politics and give a nation its specificity.

From competitive democracy to deliberative democracy

The theory of deliberative democracy that relies on Habermas's notion of the public sphere and Rawls's notion of public reason, and that has seen a dramatic growth in English-speaking countries since its appearance in 1980 and most of all in recent years, is unavoidable in the prospect of renovating democracy and improving public action.[18] The spirit of deliberative democracy is as important for us as the procedures that institutionalize it, by bringing together mini-publics consisting of informed citizens whom we ask to reflect on a subject and give an opinion, or by organizing adversarial debates among experts and elected officials. This spirit is understandable when we recall the meaning of the word 'deliberation' in English. Unlike in French, which associates this term with the making of a decision and its authority – often overshadowing its second meaning that refers to discussion – in English the same word designates the argumentative process that characterizes discussion conceived as a non-coercive communication.

Instead of aggregating individual preferences by vote and proceeding to bargaining and negotiations, as is the case in competitive democracy, the deliberative ideal requires that decisions be preceded by a discussion leading to the consideration of the pros and cons and aimed at the common good. James S. Fishkin, the inventor of the deliberative poll, clearly expressed this idea when he wrote that, unlike conventional polls, which only represent 'a statistical aggregation of vague impressions formed, most of the time, without really knowing the contradictory arguments in competition', deliberative polls reveal what the public would think if they really had the opportunity to study the topic discussed:

> Take a national random sample of the electorate and transport those people from all over the country to a single place. Immerse the sample in the issues, with carefully balanced briefing materials, with intensive discussions in small groups, and with the chance to question competing experts and politicians. At the end of several days of working through the issues face to face, poll the participants in detail. The resulting survey offers a representation of the considered judgment of the public.[19]

Beyond these procedures, deliberative democracy, which can supplement the non-deliberative democratic mechanisms such as elections, assumes that people who communicate address the reason of their interlocutor. Failing to be convinced solely by the strength of the best argument, as Habermas said, everyone will assess its pertinence and will modify the immediate point of view that they had on a topic beforehand. Arguments that establish a deliberative communication as such may relate to facts or values, but they have the characteristic of being proposals aimed at convincing auditors on the basis of their intrinsic validity.[20] Deliberation therefore goes hand in hand with non-plebiscitary rhetoric. In other words, the aim of discourses is not to get acceptance or win elections, and the relationship between the speaker and the audience is not structured by the promise of rewards or the uttering of threats.[21] The expression 'deliberative rhetoric' is used when the objective of debates is not to defend an ideological position, but to encourage questioning from everyone, by giving them the means to reflect on a subject and exercise their critical faculties.

Deliberation is therefore a communication that induces a reflection on preferences, values, and interests in a non-coercive manner.[22] To speak of deliberative democracy is not to imagine that, in practice, all decisions are based on prior argumentation addressed to the intelligence of free and equal people, seeking the common good and striving to reach a consensus. However, this ideal, which better accomplishes the democratic values of equality, responsibility, and political autonomy than electoral competition, must have the capacity to modify democracy from the inside.

Habermas quickly abandoned the expression 'communicative democracy' that he employed in *The Theory of Communicative Action*, replacing it with 'deliberative democracy'. Distancing himself from the idea of spontaneous exchanges, he thus held onto the manner in which deliberation institutionalizes itself in the procedures of the democratic rule of law. However, this does not mean that procedural legitimation is only formal. The materialization of deliberative principles has a very rich ethical content.[23] Moreover, its notion of a public space reconciled with reason is in keeping with the inspiration of Rousseau, for whom the law derives from the general will.

Habermas, so to speak, 'proceduralized' Rousseau's concept of general will.[24] The public no longer refers to what originates from the state; it is even conceived as being able to counteract the deleterious effects of a bureaucratic state. It is not identified as a specific sphere or social layer, but as private individuals making public use of their reason, such as the enlightened bourgeois who gathered in salons in the eighteenth century. By revisiting Kant's concept of the public sphere (Öffentlichkeit), Habermas operated a shift in the conception of the legitimacy of democracy.[25] It is not so much the source of authority that matters; it is the manner in which a decision is made that legitimizes it. The legitimacy of the state should not only be looked for, as in the classical theories of the contract, in the prior consent of individuals who will place their trust in representatives, but rather its action must be constantly evaluated.

Deliberation is therefore no longer the almost exclusive monopoly of representatives and it is not opposed to the masses. Unlike what is happening in competitive democracy, where the vertical model of power and the population's attitude of opposition go in parallel, deliberative democracy, whose founding moment is not the election but the formation of public opinion, is anchored in the exercise of citizens' political autonomy. This also means that, without merging public space with deliberation, we nevertheless remove the partition between public opinion and deliberation, thus suggesting that democratic will and practical reason can agree.[26]

Thus conceived, deliberative democracy, which assumes that citizens must also be the subjects of laws, does not revive the ideal of direct democracy. It is not certain that the civic ideal associated to the Greek model of the city, in which the citizens are those who participate in the polis, is necessarily the most relevant when considering the possibility to renovate democracy. This is what we see in Habermas, who conceived it on a communicative and dialogic basis and thus opposed to liberalism's atomistic vision, without however adopting a holistic representation, as in republican tradition. Its originality is precisely to show that there is a third path between political liberalism and republicanism.

As Benvéniste also pointed out in an article written in tribute to Claude Lévi-Strauss, the word 'citizen' that we mistakenly tend to use to refer to the city, as if *civitas* formed a real or symbolic entity given in advance, should rather be thought of in light of the word 'civis', which means 'fellow citizen' in Latin. If we are faithful to the Latin model of citizenship, then we must recognize that we are the cives of other cives before being those of a city.[27] Politics, which imply the existence of an irreducible plurality of fellow citizens, are firstly defined by the relationships that are formed between them. It is from these relationships and even from the conviviality between individuals that it is possible to think of democracy.

Public debate needs to be instituted, but its conditions must not be systematically decided from above. The deliberative imperative, whose spirit we have analysed, is the heart of the transformation of mass democracy, and may avoid an expertocratic drift, which is one of the risks attached to the modification of its institutions. However, this imperative must also go along with a larger participation of citizens. The objective of this participation is to reconcile, through a bottom–up approach, the top–down aspects that remain present in the representative and deliberative democracy. It is particularly important to make the voices of individuals heard, who experience on the local level the consequences of global transformations, such as those relating to climate change. It is also required to inform the governments in place about the challenges and possible solutions to environmental issues, especially those related to agriculture and food.

The public space, which is the constituent power, is therefore a critical counterweight to the state, as for Habermas. It presents itself as free, fair, and structured by the public confrontation of opinions, which allows for Kant's principle of publicness to be applied. State action must be justified in front of an external public space, which is a kind of court of opinion. Deliberative democracy requires that decision-makers be held accountable. This political responsibility of decision-makers before the public sphere is supportive of the ideal of the autonomy of citizens, whose abilities to act and reflection are encouraged.

Ideally, laws and political decisions are understood as the result of the process during which citizens had the possibility to defend solutions to common problems, on the basis of relevant reasons expressing widely shared democratic values, such as justice, freedom, equality of opportunity, or safety. Thus, they have the opportunity to present their personal interpretation of these principles, formulate the reasons for possible differences between these interpretations, and confront the interests that may be at the origin of their positions. This communicational effort, which allows everyone to abandon their confinement in doxa, enriches political debates. Not only are they no longer concentrated on the interests of some actors who represent a large electoral weight, as in electoral competition, but, moreover, the content of the electoral debates changes, which is essential when dealing with subjects that go beyond traditional divisions, as is the case with the majority of subjects related to the environment, food, and animal welfare.

Personalities willing to debate and to search for solutions establishing the common good, including abandoning traditional ideological divisions, may emerge, while competitive democracy tends to appoint to the higher functions of the state, and to elect as representatives, dominant politicians. In order to win an election that is considered a personal combat, the latter are inclined to manipulate the public by playing on their fears, threats, and the promise of compensatory measures. In other words, injecting a deliberative spirit into democracy gives back to politics all of its meaning, without reducing it to power struggles. Deliberative democracy is a challenge: it opens a field of possibilities that can feed the imagination of society, since it means that a public sphere can be organized differently than by abandoning it to the market, the struggles of influence among lobbies, and domination. However, this hope is sometimes dashed by the facts.

The heterogeneity of the public sphere and participation

Despite its theoretical interest, deliberative democracy raises a number of criticisms that point to two major difficulties. The first concerns the gap between, on one hand, the mini-publics composed of people placed, according to today's well-known procedures, in a situation that allows them to deliberate and, on the other hand, the transposition of this model to the wider public space. The multiplication of contradictory public debates and deliberative forums, even when they are well organized and produce interesting results, is not sufficient to spread the spirit of deliberation at the heart of the population, as the electoral successes of populist parties in Europe demonstrate.

Moreover, most of the opinions proposed by mini-publics are not necessarily accepted by the population when they are solicited by way of a referendum, as we have seen in British Columbia.[28] Finally, the deliberative instruments open to ordinary citizens are most often only consultative – which means that they remain, to speak with Nancy Fraser, 'weak publics'.[29] Moreover, they are not very inclusive.

This last point leads to the second reproach addressed to deliberative democracy, notably to Habermas's normative theory: the public space referred to is considered as homogeneous, meaning that it ignores the reality of social inequalities. Yet, public discussions cannot be limited to the common good, as if public reason were separated from social and economic life and the public space didn't have a social or historical dimension. Deliberative democracy must facilitate political and social transformation in a world subject to major environmental challenges, but where structural resistances of the dominant interests are enormous and where some people are excluded from deliberative processes and remain politically invisible because of the social and cultural dominations that they endure.

Furthermore, if the criterion of deliberation retained by Habermas honours reason, the role of emotions and passions in discussion must also be considered. This is particularly important when we are dealing with subjects related to life and death, the body, ecology, and animals. Indeed, conflicts that exist in these fields cannot solely be explained by conflicts of interest, nor by conflicts of value, as is still the case when it comes to taxation, the equitable redistribution of resources, and the fight against various forms of discrimination. Conflicts are also and mostly related to ontological positions, which require from everyone an explanation of how they consider and think their relationship with themselves, nature and other sentient beings, their biological traits, and the power that they can exert on their own life and death. Yet, it is not easy to clear the ontological foundation of the positions adopted on these questions. It is important to reach a consensus, which means finding an appropriate legislation that institutes the common good, on subjects related to ecology, animals, and bioethics; however, it is at the same time impossible to avoid the points of disagreement that sometimes occur with issues that are philosophically undecidable.

Most of the time, the ontological foundations of our opinions are implicit. However, they are expressed in emotions and aesthetic values, which can therefore be used by everyone as starting points to reveal the foundations of their ideological positions regarding ecological matters and most questions related to bioethics. This work requires us to be able to make public use of our reason, which means considering what could make sense collectively, and considering the interests of the different actors, without being prisoners of our history, nor blinded by our personal situations. In addition, it allows for a space of freedom to be conquered where we think with others while learning to better discern the reasons that explain why we adopt certain postures on some issues. It also helps in the development of self-knowledge, and confers both more depth, or universality, and more personality to one's thought. This assessment moves away from traditional ideological oppositions that lead to binary responses, which are as inadequate to resolve ecological challenges or to the problem of actively assisted death as the opposition between conservatism and progressivism.

The criticism of deliberative democracy underlines the need to associate deliberation and participation, and allows, at the same time, for the tensions existing between them to be assessed. Indeed, the first is focused on the quality of the argument, whereas the second aims to encourage a larger inclusion of citizens, so that the public space does not reflect the inequalities of power and of the relationships of economic, social, and cultural domination that exist in a society. Therefore, deliberation and participation, which appear as the principal approaches for reconstructing contemporary democracies, and which give rise to great creativity at the level of theory as well as in local experiences, do not address the same weaknesses of the representative system and do not mobilize the same tools to remedy their shortcomings.

Participatory democracy expects to reduce the gap between representatives and the represented, and to increase the knowledge and expertise of citizens who cannot be locked in passivity as if they were only consumers. In addition, the latter demonstrate a certain creativity, especially when it comes to subjects that affect their daily lives, as is the case with food and housing, but it is rare that they have the opportunity to bring their experiences up to the national and even the local political level. The idea is therefore to substitute a vertical conception of power with a more horizontal conception of government, and to embrace in some way the ideal of self-management, which is at the origin of the participatory theory of the 1960s and 1970s.

Thus, deliberation cannot renovate democracy by limiting itself to mini-publics and by abandoning mass democracy to its fate. It necessarily requires a greater involvement of citizens, which will not only consist in conferences of citizens and participatory procedures, even if these are the best way for people to learn how to reign, as Tocqueville said regarding juries.[30] Participation of citizens cannot be limited to consultation: the spirit of deliberation must also be present. The idea is to awaken a desire for quality argumentation in citizens by accustoming them to discussions in which everyone can justify their position, and to substitute plebiscitary rhetoric with deliberative rhetoric. This way, individuals will more easily agree to step aside to make discussion possible and, even, to achieve this distance from oneself that helps to apprehend the common good by being more open to others and which is one of the major contributions of philosophical education.

The achievement of this objective requires a number of mediations that are connected to the third component of our study, namely culture and the role of intellectuals and the media. However, to turn this into the aim of participation is to respect individuals and to open a dimension of hope without which we could never democratically deal with the problems that we face. The key to greater participation of citizens in the affairs of the city, and not only of issues relating to their neighbourhood, resides in the alteration of the political culture that is at the heart of the deliberative imperative. It requires a transformation of the political passions so that personalities less inclined to dominate, having a sense of public service, can be promoted. At the same time those who are governed must express an interest in public affairs, rather than retreating to the private sphere and developing an individualism that 'first dries up only the source of public virtues', and then attacks all others and absorbs them into a selfishness that 'shrivels the seed of all the virtues'.[31] The deliberative and participatory turn of democracy also aims to prevent the place of government from appearing, 'in a sense, empty' and social and political life from being degraded.[32]

In other words, it is important to multiply participatory experiences, as it occurred at the end of the 1980s in Porto Alegre, Brazil, and more recently in Europe,[33] when citizens came together to collectively define public investment priorities and to vote on a budget. Participation, which has a meaning locally, in community councils, and for everything that relates to the daily life of citizens, can also deal with matters that are relevant for the whole of society. Debates concerning our relationship with animals or the situation of farming in different regions can mobilize many individuals who worry about animals welfare, as in New York or Bogota, where men and women request that horse carriages transporting tourists all day long be banned. Participatory forums, illuminated by contradictory debates, organized here and there in order to provide information coming from various actors and improving conviviality, could slowly give shape to a richer public space, and make us more confident in the future and happier.

Thus, the political and non-political forces represented by users, citizens, workers, and the associative world are invited to invest in the public space apart from the main electoral events and to adopt a constructive approach that does not exclude protests, but is not reduced to them. It is by exercising our political autonomy that we demonstrate our vigilance. This may eventually result in procedures that relate to radical democracy, as was the case in 2003 in California, when a governor's recall was undertaken following the success of a petition demanding the dismissal of governor Gray Davis that collected enough signatures for a referendum to be organized.[34] However, the objective is, above all, to develop the critical sense of citizens at the same time as their ability to make proposals by raising the level of debates. Because they are the ones who will lead the elected to govern differently and move forward concretely on major projects that concern us, including social justice, equality between men and women, ecology, and the respect of human and living beings, notably animals.

Furthermore, as the improvement of the animal condition is a duty of the state, which is added to the tasks that are conventionally assigned to it and to the right to the environment, and animals being non-representational subjectivities that can be represented in trials, it would be normal for each political party to take a clear stand on this issue. Creating animals party, as in England, means that we acknowledge the inability of classical political formations – even the Green Party – to take account of this fundamental question, whose moral, ontological, and political importance we have stressed upon.

Similarly, the different associations should be organized into a network, as is the case in the Netherlands or in Austria, where there is a political force devoted to animal rights that has not taken the form of a federation, but which can pool the resources of different associations, such as media or legal tools, and make them available to the actors of the movement.[35] This structure could convene the decision-makers of the associations on a regular basis in order to review the activities of the various groups, and to envisage common strategies. It would advance the animal cause, which has progressed in the minds and hearts of citizens, but does not yet constitute a political force, because the actions are still too scattered and the militants, despite a dedication that commands admiration, are not yet able to propose solutions likely to create a consensus. It is important to also inject a deliberative spirit into organizations for animal protection that will allow us, by progressing step by step, to concretely improve the life of an increasing number of animals, and someday will make the improvement of the animal condition a duty imposed on all.

Culture and democracy: Intellectuals, media, and the schools

The passage from a competitive democracy to a deliberative democracy, where representatives and citizens grant an essential place to discussion and debate, assumes that we examine the role of the media and intellectuals in the formation of opinion. The latter, who may be writers, essayists, or academics, sometimes engage in certain social issues and express themselves in books and during conferences or debates with their peers, as well as in the mass media.

Intellectuals who take a position in the public space by publishing a newspaper article – as in the famous 'J'accuse!' by Émile Zola – by making a speech or even by taking part in a radio or television show, are non-negligible figures in a democracy. However, if writers still enjoy a certain prestige, especially in France, and if it is possible to spend entire days growing intellectually by listening to France Culture, it must also be recognized that the deliberative turn that is essential for the renewal of democracy requires certain moral traits that are related to cultural representations.

Many debates are organized in our countries, but as Habermas noted, discussion that 'seems to be carefully cultivated', and in which 'there seems to be no barrier to its proliferation', has in fact suffered from an essential transformation by becoming a 'consumer item'.[36]

The public sphere is invaded by commercialization. This is why the multiplication of debates and the success that they encounter do not necessarily translate into the reading of books, in which the thought of speakers is expressed with precision and nuance. We see an increasing number of newspapers and books, but our culture 'no longer trusts the power of the printed word', as the author of *The Public Sphere* believes.[37] Most of the time, it encourages the public and the stakeholders to only retain the results of the analyses. The different opinions are summarized, or even parodied, and debates are often binary. Moreover, the manner in which intellectuals defend their positions very often testifies to what the Italian political scientist Diego Gambetta called 'discursive machism'.[38]

These are stereotyped behaviours that are related to emblematic beliefs of a culture marked by discursive competition. The objective of an intellectual exchange is not to confront different points of view in order to assess their validity and improve knowledge of a subject, as in an 'analytical culture' (analytical knowledge), but to promote individuals (indexical knowledge).[39] While 'analytical culture' values argument and submits it to empirical testing and falsification, and the discussants sometimes have to acknowledge their ignorance, individuals belonging to an 'indexical culture' have strong opinions on all subjects. In addition, they defend them without imagining that they could learn anything from others. When a new idea appears, they declare that they had already thought of it, take ownership of it, or, to mitigate the merit of their interlocutor, argue that a past famous author had already expressed it. Diego Gambetta demonstrated this behaviour by referring to the Italian expression 'claro!'. Whatever you say, someone who behaves like a 'clarista' will not listen to your argument. They will deny its novelty and be unable to recognize the relevance of a statement or proposition that does not originate from themselves.[40]

While the 'analytical culture' that privileges discussion and thus encourages the deliberative turn of democracy goes hand in hand with the affirmation of the moral equality of individuals whose opinions must be listened to and respected, 'indexical culture" is associated to representations that equate discussion to a fight and is mainly structured by inequality. The claristas who feel able to enlighten the public on all subjects of society are unable to change their minds. They consider that doubt and ignorance on a subject represent weaknesses.[41] They also become *tuttologi*. This Italian term refers to individuals who have a definitive opinion on everything and who express it without taking the time to think, verify their sources, or support their understanding on that of Other persons.[42] In a 'culture of the claro', the word is an instrument that is used to crush others and the media is a springboard to establish one's reputation.

The concern for the common good, as demonstrated by Habermas, is not something that we can declare to possess a priori. It is essentially related to the public exercise of one's reason and to the acceptance of certain discursive rules. These guarantee the respect of others and require that we bother to debate, by thus giving ourselves the means to evolve and to arrive at a position that is both nuanced and constructive, likely to truly enlighten the debate and to be recognized as valid by others. Deliberation implies a certain generosity that requires that we make room for others and that we speak to the world, and not only about it. On the contrary, when intellectuals adopt the characteristic behaviours of 'the culture of the claro' and demonstrate 'discursive machism', they cannot enrich themselves mutually nor make a substantial contribution to the debates of society, which are reduced to personal clashes and often turn into pugilism.

This sterile behaviour that conveys, in addition, a negative image of the elites – of whom the public mainly perceives the vanity and bad faith – must therefore not only be analysed from a psychological perspective, as if 'discursive machism' were a character trait that is only encountered in male individuals from Latin countries. The interest of Gambetta's reflection is, on the contrary, to show that this behaviour, which encourages certain moral traits and selects certain personalities, refers to beliefs incompatible with the values of democracy embodied in the deliberative turn and Habermas's notion of the public sphere.[43]

If we want discussions to be constructive and the spirit of deliberation to enter society as a whole, to modify the attitude of representatives, and to urge citizens to exercise their political autonomy, it is important for intellectuals who play the role of mediators to behave differently than in an 'indexical culture'. In the meantime, discursive machism resembles the practices that everyone secretly disapproves of, but that no one dares to question for fear of being excluded. Gambetta illustrates this phenomenon by taking the example of the centuries-long custom requiring young Japanese women to bind their feet. One day, several isolated families decided to no longer impose this torture upon their daughters and allowed their sons to take a wife who had not bound her feet. These isolated initiatives spread and the practice has slowly disappeared.[44] We can therefore envisage that if, now, some intellectuals attempted to behave differently than the claristas every time they were on the public stage by defending an argument that addresses the intelligence of the listeners or viewers, then the media would gradually select fewer *tuttologi* and more scholars focusing on the common good.

This point leads us to address the issue of the role of the media in the formation of public opinion. If we want to go from a competitive democracy to a deliberative democracy, it is essential to consider the deontology of the media. The criticism that we can address to most of the mass media is not unrelated to what has been said above about 'indexical culture'.

Indeed, most of the time, the media organizes debates between representatives, intellectuals, and even scientists by asking them to present a readily identifiable opinion in record time. The format of television programmes and the manner in which the presenters intervene favour the claristas and, generally, the personalities likely to dominate and to make plebiscitary use of rhetoric. Those who seek to develop a line of reasoning must speak without trying to fill the space, focus on one important point, possibly leave the journalist's question unanswered, and orient the discussion towards a more complex reflection while remaining understandable and respectful. This amounts to introducing a dancer into a wrestling ring.

Currently, it is difficult for public men and women to avoid this double constraint, especially when they appear on television. The case of newspapers is slightly different. Their role is twofold. They must inform the public by presenting documented facts to them, which implies that the journalists must go through the trouble of checking their sources, whatever the importance of the subject. Their role is not to say what is important or not, because it is often difficult to predict the consequences of an event. However, the concern to reveal the truth to the audience by providing reliable information often prevails over the search for the scoop. Similarly, the task of journalists, which is also to express scientific discoveries in an accessible manner and to examine the state of social issues, requires that they associate the clarity of language to conceptual rigour. The quality of the articles published in the press is therefore essential to the information of the public and to the formation of opinion so as to allow better deliberation and greater participation of citizens in debates and collective decisions.

The second role of the media, especially of the press and the radio, is to constitute a counter-power. Journalists may reveal some information that the public ignores and, above all, their task is to disseminate knowledge that offers alternative interpretations to doxa and to exclusive thinking. They do not prevent corruption, but their action is still a deterrent. They also bring the influence of networks and the power of lobbies to light. To achieve this goal, newspapers need to be independent from power and industrial groups. Even if it is currently difficult to prevent the buying up of newspapers by big bosses or banks, these economic constraints must not lead journalists to falsify information. The fight against corruption and a monitoring role that is destined to evaluate the action of the state are among the essential purposes of the press.

In addition, one cannot write a newspaper article and intervene in a radio or television show without questioning themselves about the impact of their beliefs on the public and the different actors concerned with the subjects addressed. Rather than touting the ideal of transparency, which is incompatible with moral and political life and would only be pertinent for a population of angels, as we have already seen in Kant, it is important for intellectuals and journalists to assess the consequences of their words in the short and long terms, by asking themselves if they represent a democratic gain or not. Certain truths should not be told, not because they must be hidden, not even because they only represent an aspect of reality, but because they keep us away from the path that we must take to improve the quality of debates and operate the deliberative and participatory turn that is indispensable to the renewal of democracy.

This analysis of the relationship between culture and democracy includes a final component, which highlights the importance of education and research. Elementary school, high school, and university are places where education is provided. They require a specific location, away from the media and business, and a substantial amount of time, different from the requirements of information, allowing individuals to assimilate the knowledge that is provided to them, to develop their critical minds by pulling away from social determinism and the pressure of doxa, while at the same time strengthening their personalities by opening themselves up to the universal, as in the Cicero's ideal.

This objective assigned to elementary school and high school is particularly important in democratic societies, which are characterized by an egalitarian dynamic leading to the recognition of the value of personal decisions and the refusal of paternalism. In this context, which goes together with the erosion of the authority of parents and teachers, it is not enough to imagine new teaching approaches by making 'knowledge erotic', as Foucault used to say, by making it pleasant, and by ensuring that rather than being despised, knowledge honours those who feed from it.[45] It is also important to redefine the content of the programmes which would provide solid foundations and, at the same time, a more current scientific culture. In addition, it would be important that students in high school gain a good knowledge of the environment (considered as our oikos), ethology, technology, and biotechnology, as well as medical practices, since they will have to play a major role in the evolution of society as future citizens, and also as users and consumers.

This knowledge, far from being transmitted as simple data or facts, can be considered as the starting point of a critical interrogation on the dilemmas related to our uses of the earth and of other living beings, and the manner in which contemporary technology renews our questioning of the human condition. A real education on food and diet is required. This would not only concern nutrition and dietetics, but also the respect of food, which means learning how to cook, mix, and even how to produce it. We have pointed out the importance of the culinary arts in Part One of this book; this implies the education of taste not only through artistic activities, but also by learning how to cook and discover flavours. Finally, to accompany the deliberative turn of democracy, the mastery of language could be consolidated by teaching rhetoric, which could be implemented through scriptwriting and role-playing games.

These suggestions on a subject that would deserve its own book, do not mean that we turn a blind eye to the social realities that penetrate into schools and largely explain the failure of many students, especially those who come from disadvantaged backgrounds. However, rather than pointing out the social reasons for this failure, we are wondering what might make school both more effective and more attractive. Yet this can only be successful if culture becomes again the essential instrument of freedom and even happiness in the public mind.

Nourishment is both material and spiritual. Not only is culture not cut off from existence, but, in addition, it connects us to other human beings, past, present, and future, to those who live with us, close by or far away. Moreover, it should help us better understand other living beings. For all of these reasons, the Western literary or philosophical corpus cannot be the only one taught at school or high school. Similarly, history cannot be reduced to the history of human beings: the perspective of animals must also be considered. In other words, we cannot teach the humanities without considering the material and ecological conditions of our existence and our relationship with other living beings.

Finally, university, which is both the place of the transmission of knowledge and that of research and innovation, has the obligation to provide the means of carrying out rigorous research, which will also contribute to a country's influence and prosperity. The opening of the university to major contemporary issues, and respect for the criteria that guarantee the scientific quality of research and education, must be reconciled. Any initiative aiming to promote competitiveness of the university and to develop interdisciplinarity only makes sense if this balance is achieved.

However, none of the changes mentioned above is enough to create a public space if conviviality is not also present. For public space to be anything other than an abstraction, it is necessary to have meeting places. Cafés have long been this in-between that connects the home and the public sphere. It is in these cafés that autodidactic workers invented unionism and developed utopias.[46] It is important that they become privileged places of sociability and social mixing once again, so that individuals may come together.

This notion of encounter is central to a phenomenology of nourishment, as it supports the elaboration of a political theory associating justice with happiness and conviviality. Indeed, encounter requires the opening, or even the reopening of the possible and, as we have seen with the Maldineys's transpassibility, it assumes that we are able to welcome the new and unexpected, to hope for the unimaginable that is beyond all expectation. Yet many individuals have the feeling of being trapped in a life that leads them to withdraw into themselves, since apart from work and the exchange of services, there is no public space offering an opportunity to meet. These places of conviviality are missing as much as literary salons, which first appeared for the pleasure of games and had, in the eighteenth century, the role of attracting public opinion.

This term of Italian origin (salone) was first used in architecture to name the living room of an apartment; by metonymy it then designated the activity that took place there, the conversation among like-minded people invited by the owner.[47] These places, where individuals of different horizons once met, gave way to the clubs of the 1960s and 1970s that were at the periphery of political parties, and to think tanks. Literary dinners, such as those organized by the Andler brasserie in the nineteenth century, were not open to all. Salons favoured the expression of opposing points of view and thus delimited a democratic space, though they were not characterized by wide social diversity, even if they were attended by people of all ages and of both genders. However, the role that these salons played in the cultural, social, and political domains is undeniable.

As Count Roederer said in his *Mémoires pour servir à l'étude de la société polie*, it is in these salons that conversation was born, 'one of the greatest distinctions of the French nation', which has been 'the powerful vehicle of all perfections and all improvements of social life'.[48] One of the attractions of conversation (*conversatio*), which designates attendance, trade, and privacy, is to associate to the exchange of ideas the emulation and natural inclination that exists between men and women and that, as Montesquieu said, forms a natural prayer that both genders address to the Other.[49]

There are many cultural gatherings in our country, some of which celebrate both terrestrial and spiritual nourishment, but they often prove Habermas right, who deplored the fact that the public was split between a minority of specialists who made non-public use of their reason and a great mass of consumers receiving their culture from the media. To counter the effects of mass society, which destroys the public space and deprives human beings of their place in the world, while also depriving them of the possibility of building social and emotional relationships on bases other than interest or domination, it would be opportune to create places of conviviality in which utopias of today and tomorrow could be invented.

It is not only to fight indifference and stereotypes that it is important for different people to share places and moments. If we want thought to meet experience and philosophers or artists to speak to citizens, and not only in their place, it is necessary that they live with them. It is on this condition that they will contribute to the creation of an imagination revealing new meanings that will open up the possible and re-enchant democracy. By also placing themselves on the supranational level, where issues raised by the phenomenology of nourishment have a cosmopolitan meaning, they will provide the social contract with a powerful foundation in culture and allow for the establishment of a common world.

6

Beyond national boundaries

In the conclusion to *The Social Contract*, Rousseau briefly indicates that a reflection on the relations between states and on public rights should have completed this work that, at the origin, was part of a much vaster project and that constituted one part of a large treatise entitled *Political Institutions*.[1] It is not enough to consider the political body in itself, but it is necessary to analyse the relations of peoples among themselves and thus to examine 'the law of nations, commerce, the right of war and of conquest, public law, alliances, negotiations, treaties, etc.'[2] For if Rousseau, contemptuous of cosmopolitans, judges that we only begin to become human beings after having been citizens, and that it is at the heart of a particular society that we become conscious of our humanity, he nonetheless thinks that internal politics and external politics are intimately connected.[3]

The propensity of states to act aggressively towards other states is not unrelated to the place that is accorded to peoples in taking decisions that lead to war. Individuals, in contrast with kings, have everything to lose by going into combat.[4] The connection that exists most of the time between the republican form of a state and the rejection of offensive wars cannot be denied. Moreover, war places strain on peace and happiness, which are the ends of the social contract, which in turn is founded, particularly in Rousseau, on self-love and on the fact that life is our first good. Just as it is unsatisfactory to limit justice to the national level, as we have seen in speaking of eating and, in a general way, in insisting on the fact that in our uses of foods our behaviour has consequences for others, so too it is in vain to build a political theory that would limit itself to a society that is closed and cut off from the rest of the world.

Nonetheless this interdependence of internal politics and external politics takes a different form today than the one that Rousseau and Kant were able to conceive. These authors did not think that the relationship between states implied a calling into question of their sovereignty. This is explained by the fact that the wars of the eighteenth century were still limited wars. They conclude with the victory of one camp over another that shows signs of fatigue and is compelled to undergo a unilateral disarmament.[5] War is a decision by means of arms, and a sovereign state enjoys the right and the power to make war in the aim of defending its interests. For Kant, cosmopolitical rights frame the practices that prevail in conflicts and, if his ultimate objective is to ground an international order on rights rather than on violence, he is powerless to impose a durable peace, since for him respect for cosmopolitical rights rests on the effort of states to maintain a federation of free states and to renounce the politics of power to which they have always been accustomed.[6]

Moreover, for the cosmopolitanism that reappears in the Enlightenment by affirming itself as an ideal characteristic of this period's civilizational project, nature continues to play the role of a simple foundation. The idea that the planet and the earth themselves, and not only the part of the world constructed by human beings, can be threatened appears only in apocalyptic tales.[7] It inspires neither the external politics nor the internal politics of nations, which continue to ignore the place of nature in history and consider it as an object to conquer and exploit, as an ensemble of appropriable resources, and not as a source of life or as the nourishment that conditions our existence.

These two aspects of political thought — the fact of conceiving international relations as relations between sovereign nations and the idea according to which the cosmos to be preserved is only the human world, limiting politics to a game that essentially concerns rivalries and conflicts of power – are interdependent and mutually reinforcing. Yet they are entirely called into question by the nuclear threat. This threat directly underlines the transformations that are necessary in order to adequately appreciate environmental risks and to respond to them in an effective way, that is to say by finding the means to treat these problems at a scale that is local and global at once.

In the shadow of the bomb

The nuclear threat marks our arrival in an era in which extinction, that is to say the suppression of humanity and of all other species, present and future, can be envisaged. Here there would be no winner or loser, in contrast with what happens in conflicts that make use of conventional weapons. It is the possibility of life itself that would be destroyed in the case of a nuclear holocaust.[8] It would prevent human and non-human beings to come into existence, to reproduce, and to create. Moreover extinction, which makes birth impossible, is the suppression of the common world.[9] This common world, which we have seen, with Arendt, is what welcomes us at our birth and survives us, is constituted by institutions, works, and cities. We may add, in light of our earlier analyses, that it integrates the ecosphere into its totality. The nuclear danger compels us to be conscious of the ecosphere as a fundamental legacy, placing it, as well as other elements that had previously been neglected, such as biodiversity, at the heart of the common world.[10]

While death, including death in wars that make use of conventional weapons, terminates the lives of human and non-human beings, extinction prevents other human beings and other living beings from being born. It threatens the common world by causing cultural heritage and the possibility of memory to disappear, thus affecting the sense that we give to our existence. Confidence in life, which was immediate or tacit as long as humanity had not foreseen the eventuality of its annihilation, is shaken and, with it, the hope that we have of being able to transmit something. This is why the nuclear threat affects us in the most intimate parts of our life, as in our relationship to the body, to friendship, and to love. No longer having the feeling that our actions also take place on a plane that transcends our own individual existence, and living without a future and without a horizon of hope, we may have the tendency to curl up within ourselves, to seek distraction in activities that kill time, and to lose ourselves in a present without dimensions.

This is how things are because extinction is not only the irreversible destruction of a culture, but also the suppression of the biological heritage of the earth. It is a crisis of life that touches all the dimensions of our existence. It represents not only a danger for ourselves. In compromising the birth of our descendants, in casting all the beings that have not yet been born back into the nothingness that precedes life, it also does harm to us and has repercussions for us through the channels of the common world that we inhabit together, suggesting that all human beings to be born 'are we ourselves'.[11]

Extinction suppresses life and death, for if death belongs, in an ineluctable way, to the living beings that we are, and only has meaning for such beings, for each of them taken individually, life, as birth, belongs to the common world and goes beyond the strictly private plane of our existence. The very generosity of life is threatened, that is its exuberant fecundity, all the surplus that remains beyond what each generation can use for itself and that is passed on in a steadily growing accumulation, enabling all the generations to participate in a *life* of mankind which transcends individual life and is not undone by individual death.'[12]

To take the measure of the atomic threat is thus, as Karl Jaspers put it, to think 'in the shadow of the bomb'.[13] Nevertheless, we judge that it is less important to cultivate fear than it is to draw the ethical consequences from this thickness that the common world confers to our existence. This existence unfolds on two levels. As has been said throughout this book, in particular in the treatment of the question of eating, as well as when we introduced the thinking about the milieu that Watsuji Tetsurô holds dear, our existence not only has an individual sense. We are never totally alone when we eat, even when no one else physically shares our meal. Moreover, in each of us, there is the trouble of many existences, and future generations are already part of ourselves. What is more, the ecosphere in its totality and the biological heritage of the earth belong to the common world. To live is not only to live for oneself.

Of course, our acts have, first of all and immediately, a sense for us and for those close to us. We hope for successes that reinforce our desire to live, and that increase our prosperity as well as that of our descendants. The memory of our ancestors imposes on us the obligation to take decisions that do not dishonour them. We try to live well but, from the perspective that reduces ethics to the individual dimension of existence, our death is, for us, like the end of the world. This perception of ourselves, which subordinates the meaning of existence to what we accomplish for ourselves and for those near us, encourages a thought of being-towards-death, where the certainty that our time is limited triggers the resolution to do everything that we can to construct something that lifts us out of anonymity. However, such a conception of existence, which goes together with a belief in the originary character of thrownness, condemns us to live only on one plane, where everything begins and everything finishes with us, and where the private sphere is our only horizon.

On this approach, politics is reduced to management of the peaceful coexistence of freedoms. It will be said, citing Rawls, that this modesty in politics is healthy, since the spectre of ideologies pretending to ground collective decisions on a substantial vision of the good crashes into the fact of pluralism and contains the germ of all violence, private and public. However, this way of experiencing our existence and of defining the political by restraining it, as in the classical social contract, to security, freedom, the battle against discrimination, and the reduction of inequalities, leaves us blind to a dimension that provides substance to our ephemeral existence as well as to our collective life.

On the contrary, if we agree to welcome, in our daily acts, this collective dimension of existence, in which our life is overflown by that of other human beings, past, present, and future, and in which the common world is also a world inhabited by other living beings who share the *oikos* with us, our life thereby gains in depth. Our disappearance will not be the end of the world. Whatever we achieve, we will have, if not the desire to be useful, at least the concern to not destroy this common world.

The overflowing of our life by the lives of other human beings, past, present, and future, and even by other living beings, in particular animals, with which we are in a relationship of cousins, as Montaigne said, opens up a common world that is not only political, but also cosmopolitical. Our personal life may be happy or sad and, as the author of the *Essais* also writes, 'things … the beliefs, judgments, and opinions of men', have 'their revolution, their rationale, their birth, their death, as cabbages do'.[14] But how can we doubt about the meaning of existence when we also experience it in its collective dimension? God or ideology is not needed to realize that ethics and politics do not only concern relations between currently living humans. Nor is it necessary to consider oneself a genius or a saint in order to know that living is living-for.

It is particularly important today to be conscious of the fact that our existence has a double sense, both individual and collective. We need to not only transmit an inhabitable world to future generations, which permits them to breathe and to preserve or promote just institutions. Since the atomic bomb was created, we also have the unprecedented responsibility to do everything in order to avoid extinction. It is not a matter, as in nuclear deterrence, to ensure that survival, to adopt Churchill's famous phrase, be 'the sturdy child of terror'.[15]

In fact, in this strategy, which goes together with the recognition that nuclear holocaust would destroy both camps, we make avoidance of self-destruction depend on the threat of self-destruction which must be a certain outcome in order for deterrence to work. Such a policy testifies to the obstinacy of states in thinking that the world divides up into sovereign nations that have the right, as in the pre-nuclear world, to use violence in order to defend their interests. But in a nuclear world this policy is extremely dangerous, since it corresponds to a conception of politics grounded on fear, in which human beings as well as nations have not yet taken the full measure of the nuclear threat, which requires a divorce between politics and war.

What the threat of extinction changes in our lives, what it obliges us to understand, is precisely that love of life, which is love of what, in life, is connected to its generosity, to its surplus, must be the foundational principle of ethics and of politics at the national and international levels. This assertion has nothing angelic, for it derives from the most acute awareness of the possibility of absolute evil: to prevent the beginning of the life of all other beings, human and non-human.

Respect for life flows from the gratitude that is experienced by all generations towards their predecessors, who permitted them to exist. But our epoch is marked by the bomb, whatever we say and even though we do not have, in contrast with what happened during the Cold War, the feeling of constantly living under the threat of a nuclear conflict. Respect for life has the status of a principle, for the whole world was handed over as a hostage to nuclear arms. For the first time in the history of humanity, we have the means to prevent living beings from being born, which means that even if we do not have children, 'the nuclear peril makes all of us ... the parents of all future generations'.[16]

Nevertheless, it is not only or essentially this crushing and unprecedented responsibility that we wish to bring into relief in this work. We wish less to insist on the possible destruction of life than on its generosity, as well as on our capacity to recognize its nourishing character and to enjoy it. The principal tonality of this philosophy of nourishment is the love of life, whether it is a question of eating or of inhabiting, which is always a cohabiting. In this chapter devoted to cosmopolitanism, cohabitation acquires a new dimension connected to the common world, which is composed of all living beings, and which human beings, through their works and through language, pull out of forgetfulness and indifference. What is more, it is by repairing the damaged connection that we have with life (and with living beings) that we are again able to have confidence in it and to know, guided by an instinct for self-preservation that is more trustworthy than any reason, how to orient ourselves at the individual and collective levels.

The point of departure for this restoration of confidence in ourselves and in life, which is the only way to prevent the worst from happening and which leads us to instituting a common world at the individual, national, and cosmopolitical levels, is our body in its relationship to nourishment, at once biological and cultural, intimate and social. Through it, we are in contact with other living beings, human and non-human, and with past, present, and future generations. Our corporeal intimacy, that is to say our manner of eating, of inhabiting the world, of producing and consuming nourishment, of living love, and of making, in our existence and our daily acts, a place for others, is where we learn or relearn who we are.

Indeed, cosmopolitanism, as we will see, is a question of point of view, of scale, of optics, not a political reality that leads to the creation of a world state. It is founded on human rights, and thus on individual subjects. However, in our own work, it is a matter of substituting for the philosophy of the subject underlying human rights another philosophy of the subject, in which it is conceptualized in its relation to the Other. It is also a matter of substituting for the anthropology associated with human rights, and marked by a certain dualism of nature and culture, an ontology that takes seriously the corporeality of the subject and the materiality of its existence.

In other words, if the judicial and even the institutional aspect of cosmopolitanism is important, the ontological aspect, which is based on a phenomenology of nourishment, is no less so. It opens the way to an ethics and to a politics founded on an existence that always takes place on two levels, individual and collective, where none of our actions, even the most banal of them, has any strictly private meaning, and where the love of life, which is originary, as we see in human and animal babies, needs to be rediscovered. This love of life has nothing to do with sacralization of the living or with the refusal of any intervention in nature, of any artifice, but it implies that we know how to taste life in order to recognize its value, its creativity, and its plasticity. In the nuclear era, and at a moment in the history of humanity at which, although the idea of progress has not lost all of its meaning, we nonetheless know that evil exists and that anything, even the worst, can happen, this principle serves to ground ethics and politics on a new base.

No illusion is permitted, but hope is possible, for atomic weapons, Karl Barth maintains, have 'completed the self-revelation of war in its true nature', which is 'purely and simply murder'.[17] Indeed what the nuclear threat teaches us is that peace will not be 'the sturdy child of terror', and that, if 'survival remains the twin brother of annihilation', happiness is the best ally of justice in the task that consists in constructing an inhabitable world.[18] The desire to live and to live well is a compass that can orient us, for we cannot cultivate the love of life and wish, at the same time, for the annihilation of the world. The possibility of extinction marks the collapse of traditional wisdom and morality, but this situation, which enables us to understand the meaning of cosmopolitanism, is also the point of departure for a reconstruction of the foundations of ethics and of justice on the basis of a new understanding of the history of the world and even, as we will see, of a new Enlightenment, characterized not by the domination of nature but by the celebration of life.

Globalization, sovereignty, and methodological cosmopolitanism

The atomic threat brings about an 'extension of the planet' and brings to light the totalization of humanity and of the world. In this sense, it teaches us something essential, for this totalization of the world escapes our immediate experience. Certainly, the representation of a world divided into sovereign nations having the right to defend their interests through violence continues to dominate the imaginations of the majority of people. The idea of a common world to be preserved and even to be established, by working on the judiciary aspect of cosmopolitanism and by giving humanity the institutional means to prevent nuclear holocaust and the irreversible degradation of the planet, comes into conflict with the maintenance and even the reinforcement of the national paradigm, for which identity is connected to exclusive belonging to a particular community. However, the cosmopolitan perspective, which does not presuppose prior belonging to a global community, does not exclude the national perspective.[19]

Cosmopolitanism arises from awareness of the risks that we all run. It is thus connected to an involuntary community.[20] Judicial cosmopolitanism could not take the form of a global state, as we see in Kant. It is not rooted in the feeling of belonging to a single community sharing the same destiny, and does not require this as a presupposition. In the same way that the identity of a particular community is narrative and a posteriori, so too subjective cosmopolitanism, or the feeling of being a citizen of the world, is above all produced by the consciousness that individuals have of enduring the undesired consequences of risks that underline their interdependence. Thus, this feeling is above all connected to negative events, notably to risks and to the socially accepted construction of these global risks.

This cosmopolitanism is constrained, to the extent that these human beings are led to construct a common world on the basis of the 'negative solidarity' that derives, as Arendt said, from the risk of the self-destruction of humanity.[21] We do not have to feel that we are citizens of the world, or to think that we *belong* to one and the same community woven together by affective ties, in order to understand that we all *inhabit* a world on which our existence depends and whose unity is underlined by atomic weapons. Far from being opposed to the national perspective, cosmopolitanism, which may contain a judicial dimension but is not political in the sense that it is not connected to a world state, is above all a way of apprehending individual and collective history and of reinterpreting our being-in-the-world by taking note of the change in social and political grammar engendered by global risks.

Cosmopolitanism does not erase the differences and does not suppress the national scale to which the citizens of a particular community refer. Its significance is, on the contrary, the recognition of the alterity of others, affirmation of the moral equality of human beings and of cultures, and the will to contribute to the resolution of global problems.[22] In other words, it is a matter of articulating the levels of the citizen, the state, and the universe. Politics and society cannot have meaning only at the national level, which is not to say that the global is a superlative form of the national, as in the hypothesis of a political cosmopolitanism that would be, to adopt Kant's expression concerning the global state, a 'frightful despotism'. On the contrary, to consider that the nation is the only point of departure of politics is a form of blindness, the refusal to take into consideration the realities of the cosmopolitical era.

The situation in which we find ourselves since the twentieth century, in particular since the atomic bomb, as well as a consequence of a number of phenomena relating to climate change, to sanitary risks connected to the use of pesticides, to the global food crisis, and to social inequalities, is characterized by a cosmopolitanization of problems. We live in a globalized world, marked by planetary risks that do not stop at national borders, and by the fact that we are networked, with the mass media enabling us to know immediately what happens on the other side of the world.

Cosmopolitanization is a multidimensional and complex process, which is essentially accompanied by interdependencies that connect human beings with one another.[23] This phenomenon, which comes from below and is in itself neither good nor bad, is distinguished from globalization, which for its part is connected to the liberal economy and to the global market, that is to say to a certain way of organizing the common space by making it into a market space. Cosmopolitanism translates the point of view of men and women who, realizing the change in social and political grammar, accept that their existence unfolds at several levels. Their objective is to ensure that the world does not become a neutral space in which there are only clients, consumers, and private partners, and where the connections between human beings are fashioned exclusively by the market, but rather that it remain an inhabited space.

On the level of international relations, such a perspective implies calling into question the Westphalian model, which has dominated relations between states and which went together with the fact that war was the privilege of sovereign states.[24] It is not only atomic weapons that require us to modify the vision of international society that was born with the treaties of Westphalia in 1648. Mutations of the world economy and our fear that the world will become a vast market make necessary a new dialogue of states and an articulation of the global with the local and the national.

The objective is not to imagine a global citizenship, which, as we have already said, does not exist a priori, and which no group can legitimately represent, but on the contrary, to integrate, at the heart of national and transnational politics, the local level at which individuals pursue their struggles, whether it concerns the poor, women, or peasants suffering from hunger and malnutrition. It is indeed at the local level that human beings become conscious of the transnational dimensions, which is to say that there is no opposition between the local and the global, and that cosmopolitanism, far from being similar to a world order, presupposes the autonomy of individuals.

The misinterpretation, when speaking of cosmopolitanism, would be to imagine a set of global values that would be imposed everywhere in the world, or to dream of a worldwide identity of which one would hope to be the spokesperson. Such a fiction is not only dangerous; it is also contrary to the meaning of cosmopolitanism, which is inseparable from the recognition of the value of the plurality of the world, and of the diversity of values and cultures. Arendt showed in *The Human Condition* that birth, which is the possibility that someone new does something new and unpredictable, was the condition of possibility of the common world, which is anything but a homogeneous and closed space.

Structured by the possibility of novelty and the unexpected, the common world that is the horizon of contemporary cosmopolitanism gives access, more than Arendt admitted, to an existence that unfolds on several levels, which imply several identities and several loyalties. It is at the heart of a particular community that we become conscious of humanity, and that we acquire the *cultura animi*, the attitude that consists in knowing how to take care of the things of the world and to admire them. Moreover humanism, which depends so narrowly on the culture of the humanities, requires that people are educated and citizens of a *polis*. Cosmopolitanism therefore cannot require renunciation to the duties that are ours at the local and national scale.

As in Diogenes, the cosmopolitan is a citizen of the world.[25] However, one must add that they are also a citizen of the *polis*, that is to say that they have two loyalties.[26] Undoubtedly there is no cosmos when there is no *polis*, but the idea underlying the cosmopolitanism that in its philosophical dimension actualizes the Stoic ideal is that the perception of risk, lived at the local level by several individuals in different countries, institutes a public space beyond borders. It is this space that imposes, or should impose, a transnational opening on individuals as well as on national political representatives.

It is thus not a matter of stifling individual voices, but, on the contrary, of giving them the means to make themselves heard, precisely when states remain trapped in a politics of power that is, in reality, an illusion. It has often been said that cosmopolitanism presupposed renunciation to the model of the sovereignty of states. This assertion is both true and false. It is true because states are no longer autonomous and decisions made at the national scale imply that governments take the global and transnational dimensions into consideration. States are no longer like 'billiard balls' that can clash with each other while remaining independent from one another.[27] The Westphalian model, which rested on the equilibrium of sovereign powers limiting the confrontation between them by means of treaties, as well as maintaining an exclusive power over their own territory, is no longer suitable, since states are no longer the sole masters of their actions within their borders, and since the logic of external sovereignty implying that they are considered as the sole masters of their foreign policy decisions, is equivocal, and could not be sufficient for effectively regulating relations between states.

However, states do not abandon their sovereignty for the sake of the global order. They take into consideration global risks and cosmopolitanization, which imply that the problems with which we are confronted could not be solved by positioning ourselves exclusively in the point of view of the interests of a nation. Yet if this reality summons us to abandon the right to war that had been the privilege of states in the Westphalian scheme of sovereignty, this renunciation, which brings to its end a way of conceiving politics in terms of the possibility of war and of the domination of some by others, does not mean that states lose their identity, nor that they are deprived of all initiative. On the contrary, the legitimacy of the action of governments resides in their capacity to hear the voices of citizens, who exercise their citizenship not only in electoral meetings, but also in participating in public debates and in organizing themselves into associations that may be national or transnational, and deal with issues that go beyond the boundaries of their country.

Likewise, the sovereignty of states is not suppressed, but rather reconfigured. In this effort to recompose politics by articulating the different levels and the different scales, and by conceiving a common responsibility, however differentiated it may be, different governments are thus led to give greater attention to the individuals who endure, at a local level, the consequences of technologies, of economic activities, of multinationals, and of lobbies. The autonomy of individuals, their capacity to make their voices heard and to organize themselves, is the key to this cosmopolitanism that is rooted in the local (rooted cosmopolitanism).[28]

Cosmopolitanism is therefore nothing without the engagement of individuals who are conscious of inhabiting a finite world, from which they derive their subsistence and which is fragile. It is because human beings are mobile, and because the earth is not an infinite space in which human beings might spread out without ever encountering one another, that Kant imagines the conditions of an organized division of the common world. The idea is to conceive the juridical coexistence between human beings so that their relations may be ruled by something other than violence and domination, and so that they might exit the state of nature, which is a state of war. This need for a juridical organization and thus for a cosmopolitical right, whose content, for Kant, is limited to a universal hospitality that grounds the right of visitation (*Besuchsrecht*), removes nothing of the fact that cosmopolitanism is above all a question of perspective.[29]

One could say of cosmopolitanism what Jean Jaurès said of the republic, namely, that it is neither a dogma nor a doctrine, but a method for obtaining the highest efficiency from all human energies through the fullness of freedom. The question is now of knowing by what means it is possible to institute a common world that, in the cosmopolitical era that is also the era of the atomic threat, of the global food crisis, and of climate change, might take the path traced out by Kant, on the condition that we bring to the edifice that he conceived certain modifications or complements.

Cosmopolitical rights since Kant

Kant's decisive contribution to the reflection on cosmopolitanism stems from the way in which he makes it into a practical regulatory principle of politics. Not only do we have to abandon the illusion of a state cosmopolitanism, but, moreover, Kant affirms the necessity of a juridical organization of relations between states by considering its end or target, that is to say the hypothesis of a progress towards peace and towards the generalization of the republican form of government.[30]

There should not be war, and humans have the right to move across the surface of the globe (*Recht der Oberfläche der Erde*). History, according to Kant, testifies to the will of human beings to provide themselves with the political constitution they want, and to their disposition to avoid offensive wars. As Foucault writes, it is not the French Revolution that is in itself the sign of this end, but rather the enthusiasm that it inspired, in particular among those who did not participate in it, but who thus recognize a similar design in collective history.[31]

We may reproach Kant for not having gone so far as to imagine a supreme power, guaranteeing respect for our reciprocal rights and constraining the member states of the federation of peoples, by means of sanctions, to uphold their engagements. One could say, as Habermas does, that in the absence of a constitution that organizes it juridically, Kant, imprisoned by the dogma of the external sovereignty of states, is not able to remove the contradiction that is attached to this alliance of countries, of which we expect that they will subordinate, as needs be, their own *raison d'État* to the common end, which is to settle conflicts by a procedure, not by war. He does not conceive that cosmopolitical rights impose a revision of the external and internal sovereignty of states in order to transform international relations and to limit the politics of power of each country. Moreover, if they do not have their own armed forces, the United Nations, in spite of the resolutions of the Security Council, have only the voluntary cooperation of the member states, and thus are only a 'Permanent Congress of Nations'.[32] However, these critiques do not detract from the fact that the two principles on the basis of which Kant thinks about cosmopolitical rights, and even about his philosophy of history, trace out paths that are particularly valuable for understanding what cosmopolitical rights could be today.

In grounding himself on the right of each of us to move around the surface of the globe, he makes cosmopolitical rights depend on the rights of the individual subject. In other words, the key to cosmopolitanism, if we follow the Kantian path further than he himself imagined, does not reside so much in the fact that it would concern collective subjects of international rights, as in the fact that it is addressed to subjects of individual rights.[33] Individuals occupy an essential juridical place in this federation of cosmopolitans. Similarly, speaking in the third article of his *Perpetual Peace: A Philosophical Sketch* of a right to hospitality, Kant opens the path to an inscription or reinscription of duties and of human rights in a universal dimension of existence, connected to the roundness of the earth and to our reliance on the material conditions of our terrestrial inhabitation.

Of course, it is important to supplement these cosmopolitical rights not only by focusing on the finitude of the earth and on mobility, but also by drawing all the consequences of what the phenomenology of nourishment has uncovered. The right of each human being to food that is sufficient in quantity and in quality, as well as everything we said when we derived the principles of a theory of justice conceived as the sharing of nourishment, permits us to enrich the content of cosmopolitical rights. Moreover, the human rights that ground this cosmopolitanism subtract the autonomy of individuals from the sovereignty of states, which therefore must respect these fundamental rights that guarantee individual liberties, but are also essentially connected to a philosophy of corporeality. The latter underlines the dependency of human beings with respect to the material, social, economical, and ecological conditions of their existence, and it integrates, in addition to social rights, the dimension of enjoyment that is attached to the fact of being alive.

Thus it is a matter of taking up the Kantian frame, that is the concept of cosmopolitical rights that rest on human rights and presuppose that we consider these latter as a juridical tool, not as a moral criterion that helps us to assess the legitimacy of an action. However, these human rights are conceived in the light of existentials that are revealed by the phenomenology of nourishment, which is a philosophy of 'living from' in which ecology is centred on existence conceived in its materiality. Moreover the emphasis is not exclusively on what each one of us has a right for, but also on what the rights of other human beings require of me, of the states, and of the society as a whole. Finally, this subject of individual rights is, no matter what he does, in relation with other humans, past, present, and future, as well as with other living beings.

The metapolitical cosmopolitanism achieved by the phenomenology of nourishment relocates the individual at the heart of the common world. This world includes all living beings, underlining the particular responsibility that is incumbent on us in view of the power of our technology and of our discursive capacity, which maintains the common world and transmits its memory. It is no longer the individual moral agent, represented in a solipsistic and abstract way, which is the subject of human rights. On the contrary, through our relationship to nourishment, the relation that we establish with other human beings, past, present, and future, and with other living beings opens the path to a reinterpretation of human rights. A different usage of these rights, which constitute a reference point on the local and global levels with regard to justice towards human beings, between states and cultures, and towards animals, is at the horizon of this philosophy of 'living from'.

This philosophy not only renews humanism by placing responsibility at the heart of the subject and by expanding this responsibility to humanity as a whole, to other living beings, and to nature, as was the case in the ethics of vulnerability, which also emphasizes a humanism of alterity and diversity. By insisting on the pleasure attached to the fact of being alive, and by associating justice with conviviality, the philosophy of nourishment promotes a humanism of sharing, according to which my happiness does not depend only on what I possess and what I appropriate for myself, but also on the place that I accord to other human and non-human beings, as well as on the transmission of the common world.

The cosmology on which ancient cosmopolitanism rested is replaced by humanism: we are clearly in a modern schema. However, unlike modern cosmopolitanism, which conceives nature as a simple foundation and still subordinates peace and the resolution of environmental problems to the fragile accord of sovereign nations, the cosmopolitanism that we envisage presupposes a subject and a humanity convinced that the future of the common world, of which the ecosphere and the other living beings are a part, depends on their capacity to institute rules of justice that are not the reverse side of a politics of power, its alibi or its bad conscience.

Such a perspective permits us to better respond to environmental questions, underlining their anchoring in the rights of individuals who inhabit the world and cohabit with other species. It appears obvious that the failure of international negotiations on the climate and on the erosion of biodiversity is due in part to the fact that they take place between states that continue to think that the world is divided into sovereign nations, concerned above all to defend their economic interests and little inclined to abandon a politics of power that, in our time, consists as much if not more in competition for market shares as it does in arms.

Thus in international climate negotiations, as we saw in 2009 in Copenhagen, we are not dealing with cosmopolitical rights, but simply with international law. The equivocal character of this law explains the incapacity of states to agree on what would be required to reduce our ecological footprint, and to respect their engagements that they make. Moreover, in these negotiations, states, whose power is unequal and who do not adopt a democratic mode of interaction, are often the only actors, which is indeed the proof that it is not a matter here of cosmopolitical rights.

Environmental problems, whose effects are felt above all at the local level, as we see in climate change, are not treated at the global level, despite the importance of this level if we wish to find effective and durable solutions.[34] Moreover, individuals who should contribute to the debates and negotiations are rarely solicited, other than to give their opinion in a consultative way. This crucial point underlines the connection between cosmopolitanism and the capacity of individuals to organize themselves. It considers whether it is possible to speak of a global civil society, and what would be its role. In the same way, it raises the problem of the democratization of global governance, which relates to the concept of cosmopolitical democracy. However, before examining these notions of global civil society and of cosmopolitical democracy, we must return to a second feature of Kant's cosmopolitanism that is metapolitical and methodological or, more precisely, transcendental.

The major aspect of the Kantian perspective consists in that cosmopolitanism is a manner of projecting oneself towards the future. Because it is a regulative principle of political reason, it escapes from the accusation of irrealism or of utopianism. Kant does not say that the world in which he lives is a perfect world without conflicts, but in referring to a philosophy of universal history, he sets up an end, which is the idea of progress towards peace. It is on the basis of this hypothesis that he organizes the juridical construction that provides a place for cosmopolitical rights. The idea of a universal law governing the world is thus not a presupposition, as in Stoic cosmopolitanism, but it is rather a matter of constructing a juridical order that is external to states; in order to do this, we require a regulatory principle that orients our efforts.

One could say that Kantian cosmopolitanism reflects an optimistic vision of history. This is partly true. However, once we have understood that Kant's project of perpetual peace is a transcendental project, which entails a duty and a demand of reason, we cannot make the optimism of Kant an argument that deprives his constructivism of all of its contemporary relevance. Kant's construction needs to be complemented, but his method, which confers on cosmopolitanism a transcendental character and the status of a regulative principle, is particularly relevant today. We should act as if the desired end, namely peace and the preservation of a liveable world, were possible, by having as a project the construction of institutions that permit us to bring it about.

Philosophy, Kant writes, has its own chiliasm, but it is a chiliasm the idea of which alone could hasten its coming about. Giving a political content to the millenarian expectation, which no longer has any theological sense, the philosopher suggests that it is not immediate experience that provides the criterion establishing whether the goal of history is progress, or the apocalypse, or if one should stick to the neutralization of good and evil.[35] On the contrary, we know that *there is to be no war*, and that it is an 'irresistible veto of practical reason':

> So the question is no longer whether perpetual peace is something real or a fiction. ... Instead, we must act as if it is something real, though perhaps it is not; we must work toward establishing perpetual peace and the kind of constitution that seems to us most conducive to it (say, a republicanism of all states, together and separately) in order to bring about perpetual peace.[36]

While following Kant's approach, which declares that, 'even if the realization of our intention remained a pious wish, still we are certainly not deceiving ourselves in adopting the maxim of working incessantly towards it, because this maxim is our duty,'[37] we may indicate the new cosmopolitical ends that flow from the conception of justice as a sharing of nourishment. Thus the eradication of hunger from the world, the reduction of inequalities, the battle against climate change, and the improvement of animal conditions are the ends on the basis of which we can organize the rules of political life at the national and global scale.

Progress towards the realization of these ends is slow and in today's world, new conflicts occur every day showing that states and individuals are reluctant to abandon the scheme of power and domination to which they are accustomed and to adopt the cosmopolitical perspective that integrates other loyalties. However, this does not imply that our project loses any of its legitimacy, nor that we should renounce our efforts to institute a common world. The fact of bearing this ideal presupposes an acute awareness of the possibility of extinction and of the reality of evil. Moreover, its accomplishment requires efforts on several levels, which implies that progress, if there is any, cannot be represented one-dimensionally, and by the image of a ladder that one would climb.

In the end, in spite of all events that, even in liberal democracies, demonstrate an oversensitivity to identity, there are also forms of transnational solidarity and movements, like those motivated by food (e.g., the Sustainable Food Movement) or transition towns, that illustrate the capacity and desire of more and more individuals to exchange, and work for the common good, in inscribing these practices into their daily life.[38] This affirmation by citizens of their political autonomy outside of elections is what we will consider now, asking whether it is acceptable to speak of a global civil society, and what the emergence of transnational solidarities implies for global governance.

Global civil society and cosmopolitical democracy

Since Hegel, 'civil society' has designated a sphere of social life that is distinct from the state and in which individuals create relations and act publicly. This public space, which draws in a diverse ensemble of actors, enables individuals to exercise their autonomy and to have a responsibility that is independent of political authority. In 1990 a new expression 'global civil society' appeared, which refers to non-state organizations that structure the reality of the political world and are able to orient global governance in different domains of life that affect human beings as inhabitants of a world characterized by cosmopolitanization.[39]

The central idea of this notion of civil society is that political life is not limited to the functioning of state institutions. It is indeed also structured by other forms of organization, like associations, unions, or markets, which 'distil and transmit ... in amplified form to the public sphere' the problems that individuals encounter in their personal life, and which touches them not only as citizens of a country, but as inhabitants of the world. As a consequence, not only is the manner in which governments make decisions called to evolve towards more deliberation, but, moreover, this civil society cannot limit itself to a single nation.[40]

Do such remarks justify the extension of the notion of civil society to the global scale? The response depends on what is meant by civil society. It is not a matter of a global identity, which would amount to giving a political meaning, and not a metapolitical one, to cosmopolitanism. It is, moreover, difficult to imagine that the citizens of different countries speak with one voice. Their representation by a world parliament is often debated in the literature on this subject, but it is not certain that this manner of institutionalizing civil society is very relevant, for what is in play in the notion of a global civil society is not unity or homogeneity, but, rather, the diversity and heterogeneity of actors and their positions. To erase this diversity and this heterogeneity, considering that the duties of world citizens are better represented by certain actors than by others, would miss the type of innovations that are on the horizon of these movements that organize political life in a less vertical way than in the classical schema, in which representatives and states are the only actors in a decision.

In fact, associative movements create transnational connections and accustom the different parties involved to organizing themselves around problems that are relevant to them. This may concern individuals who endure the consequences of pollution or climate change, or who can no longer bear the violence inflicted on animals. These associations also bring together people who, becoming conscious of the political dimension attached to the act of eating, hold that the most important changes begin in our daily life and involve our body, in particular our way of eating. These non-governmental organizations profoundly modify the manner in which individuals consider themselves; the idea that we may exercise our responsibility on several scales is truly present for those who have this sort of engagement.

Thanks to these associations and their networking, individuals also develop a sense of cooperation. The feeling of belonging to a common world and of being an inhabitant of the planet does not necessarily precede the engagement of individuals in transnational associations dedicated to the protection of the environment, to the promotion of just and healthy food and of animal protection; however, this feeling develops or expands thanks to their adhesion to movements that engage these issues at the local, national, regional, and global levels, tracing out little by little the contours of a contributive democracy.

Such an exercise of citizenship both inside and outside the nation stimulates alertness in individuals, which is conducive to creating and reinforcing counter-powers. This vitality of civil society is likely to affect the democratization of power. Citizens who are more conscious of their responsibility and of their political force, accustomed to debating with other people who share common interests with them, but on the basis of political, religious, or moral foundations that are sometimes different, are more able to participate in the political life of their country and to help the competition-based democracy to evolve towards a deliberative democracy. They are also less easily manipulated, since they have sources of information that are often very precise, and they master the current means of communication with the larger public and with politicians. Finally, associations are laboratories of ideas. They propose paths whose innovative character is also related to the fact that their members interact with people in other countries, and that, while inscribing their actions at the local level, in particular as concerns agriculture and urbanization conceived in their ecumenical dimension, they are able to benefit from experiences conducted in other parts of the world.

Thus, we are dealing less with a global civil society than with a generalization of a tendency that consists for individuals in organizing themselves in networks in order to deal, in a local and global way, with questions arising from the transnational situation. It is because civil society manifests a great deal of creativity everywhere in the world that people have begun to speak of global civil society. Nevertheless, the key to this cosmopolitanism is very much the autonomy of persons. The will to take control of one's life, combined with the feeling that, paradoxically, in the era of cosmopolitanization and globalization, the individual maintains a certain power, motivates the desire to change the course of things and to orient public policies. This is done through debate, information, and communication, sometimes through contestation or by becoming a whistle-blower, as well as by inscribing one's political consciousness into one's life and into one's daily actions, notably by eating and consuming in a certain way.

Does the democratic and cultural gain from this creativity of civil society stop there, or does it also modify the rules of international negotiations, opening the path to what is called, since the 1980s, cosmopolitical democracy?[41] It is necessary to appreciate the fact that democratic nations, in which the freedom of expression and plurality are defended, are not always disposed in their relations with other states to apply democratic values. The latter include the refusal of violence and respect for the law, affirmation of the moral equality of individuals, and the resulting majoritarian principle, tolerance, recognition of cultural diversity, transparency, publicity, and participative management of problems. Nevertheless, one would be wrong to conclude that the democratization of global governance is a chimera, for democracy is a dynamic process, not a static reality. Moreover, it is related not only to institutions, but also to values, such as those that are elaborated above and that, applied in such a context, suggest that democracy possesses a certain plasticity, that it exists in different ways depending on circumstances.

Thus, the expression 'cosmopolitical democracy' designates the globalization of democracy as much as it does the democratization of society and, subsequently of the global governance which can no longer be entrusted only to political representatives, governments, and experts. The notion, valued by David Held, of a 'global social contract', does not give a sufficiently rich idea of the process that unfolds today at several levels with different actors and in various ways.[42] For what is essential depends less on the type of politics that would be generalized, such as social democracy, than it does on the manner in which citizens bring with them certain values on the local and global levels and are thus able to modify decision processes.

Cosmopolitanism, even when it is institutional, is not a political universalism, which does not mean that the cosmopolitical perspective and efforts to institute the common good, by organizing society according to democratic rules, are indifferent to the universalism that we have attempted to promote and that arises not from ethics or from politics, but from ontology or from the existentials described by the phenomenology of nourishment. However, the heart of these transformations of society and of institutions resides in individuals. Everything happens as if the most significant changes occurred in them first, at this contact point between theory and practice that refer to instituting imagination, thanks to which women and men unravel the future that they desire. In other words, one of the springs of this metapolitical cosmopolitanism, and of the individual changes that nourish it, is connected to creative imagination and to utopia.

Imaginary, utopia, and the heritage of the Enlightenment

The structure of action is symbolic.[43] We move around in the social, which we can never apprehend in a totally transparent manner. The institutions respond to the needs of individuals and thus have a functional sense, but they also have a symbolic component. Moreover, they have an effect only to the extent that they rely on the expectations and the illusions of individuals, which Castoriadis calls the 'imaginary', which is the source of alienation (or of heteronomy) and of creation, as a capacity of individuals to re-describe the real in order to discern other possibles.

The imaginary, which is the faculty of positing, in the mode of representation, a thing and a relation that are not given in perception, uses symbolism in order to express itself, to invent something from scratch, or to shift the symbols that are already available by investing them with other meanings than the normal or canonical ones.[44] Nonetheless, the opposite is also true: symbolism presupposes the capacity of the imaginary, for the institutions and even the needs to which they respond are connected to cultural elaborations, as we see with food, which does not include everything that is edible, but only what people accept to eat in a particular society. In the same way, the economy of modern capitalism only subsists to the extent that it proposes products that are adapted to the needs that it creates, which clearly means that the functional hangs on the imaginary.[45] Finally at a given moment, real problems become important challenges to address only in connection with the imaginary of a society, that is to say its ends and meanings. These imaginary social meanings connote the world that we perceive, whose capture is determined practically, affectively, and mentally.

We are thus always conditioned and can never completely move beyond the discourse that is imposed on us. It is important to denounce alienation, which is the fact of being trapped within a discourse that Castoriadis calls the 'discourse of the other', that is an ensemble of meanings in which we no longer recognize ourselves. However, we also have the possibility of recovering our autonomy. This is a collective enterprise,[46] and it does not have any sense if we think about it only for oneself; above all, it is essentially connected to creative projects. These projects propose other meanings that permit us to reconsider a number of fundamental questions anew, such as those concerning who we are, what we are for others, what we want, and what we are lacking. If the social world is articulated each time as a function of a system of meanings that make reference to the effective imaginary or to what is imagined, it is nevertheless possible to distance oneself from the latter and to envision another image of oneself and of life.

This gap between the instituting and the instituted social is one of the expressions of the creativity of history. It is, moreover, one of the functions of utopia as Ricœur analyses it, insisting on the fact that our identity is prospective, and that we are also what we are expecting.[47] Since it is an imaginative variation of power, an analogue to the Husserlian *epoche* that requires suspension of our assertions concerning reality, utopia helps us to take a critical distance from reality and to explore the lateral possibilities of the real. Not only by stepping aside and by 'coming from nowhere' do we experience the contingency of the order, but moreover, by looking forward, considering what we expect from the future, we acquire the possibility of realizing the impossible, for utopia is a dream that wants to be realized, and not only or essentially a phantasmagoria intended to distract us and to escape reality.[48]

Utopia is not only an alternative to the existing order, but rather it reveals the gap between established authority and the beliefs of citizens in a system of legitimacy. Ideology is a phenomenon that cannot be overcome, since we are unable to abstract away from social reality, which has a symbolic and imaginary constitution, associated with interpretations, images and representations of the social bond, of human beings and of life itself. It often has the role of preserving these institutions and of guaranteeing an identity. On the contrary, utopia helps us to no longer perceive this reality as natural and insurmountable. It enables us to glimpse new possible realities and new ways of living. This is why utopia, in its lack of congruence with ideology, has a creative function and represents a politically motivating force.[49] It goes hand in hand with the idea that reality is a dynamic process and that 'nowhere is humanity given'.[50] Drawing its force from the fact that it incarnates the human capacity of self-reflection, and that, in testing the limits of what is realizable, it represents a rational hope, it signifies that it is by the imagination, and not by violence, that we are able to achieve the necessary transformations.[51]

In a utopia, as we see, notably, in Charles Fourier, the passions play an essential role, since, if the good is neither a convention nor an essence, but the product of imaginative activity, it is essential to impassionate society, which reason alone is insufficient to bring about. Moreover, history cannot be comprehended only as the result of relations of production or of the struggle for power, and of the passions that this struggle exacerbates. Not only can individuals provide themselves with other meanings than those that are current in an imaginary that alienates them and maintains counterproductive institutions, but, moreover, they are not moved by their own interests alone, nor by the alliance between reason and the interests that grounded the expectations of the Enlightenment.

An imaginative redescription of the real, which reveals dimensions of life that are often eclipsed today by the organization of production and consumption, and which projects a future constructed on the basis of the alliance between justice and happiness or conviviality opens up a breach in the current system of power and in relations between people and between nations. Its action is not limited to challenging this system by emphasizing its unsatisfactory and ineffective aspects in the medium and long terms. The force of this dream, in which each person reconnects with the sensing and the emotions that truly represent our relationship to others and to nature, is that it also makes us wish to change our way of life.

Reflecting on what we want to be, we understand that domination is neither the only nor the best way of apprehending the real, nor is it the safest path for attaining happiness. The proof that more and more individuals are achieving this interior progress is furnished by the emergence of associations that aim to promote healthy eating and a habitat that is respectful of the environment and convivial. In the same way, the growing place that is occupied by debates focused on animals' condition and the recognition of the importance of animal mediation testify to a deep change in the way in which we think of ourselves as human beings, and in our relations with other species. Rationality, in particular instrumental rationality, is no longer the distinctive feature of our humanity, since we are not the only ones to possess intelligence, and since it is not the exclusive nor the privileged path leading to respect for alterity, whether it be our own or that of non-human living beings and of nature.

At this stage of the analysis, we have to envision two objections that will permit us to determine precisely the connection between the metapolitical cosmopolitanism that we have discussed, the philosophical universalism that is at the horizon of the phenomenology of nourishment, and utopia as the point of contact between theory and practice.

The first objection consists in asking whether it is legitimate to speak of social and global changes, while the key to these changes resides in individuals who, every time, have a solitary experience of their relationship to the world of nourishment. Can the aggregation of these individual experiences give rise to something other than scattered publics, which will have trouble constituting themselves in a common public and exerting influence on the international community? If individuals feel the need of associating with others, this is because they become aware that, at the national or international political level, the framework of domination, that is to say the representation of the Other as a rival or enemy, and of nature as a resource to conquer and to exploit, remains dominant. But do they constitute a political force that can change the way in which we conduct politics and make decisions at the global scale?

The second objection, which is also an interrogation, presupposes that, in deepening the political role of utopia and of imaginative fiction, we say whether we situate ourselves in a cultural and historical process similar to that of the *Aufklärung*, which identified itself by that name and which, as we see in Kant's text of 1784, in addition to its identity, had its maxim and its task. When proposing a phenomenology of nourishment, is it justified to place ourselves in the continuation of the heritage of the Enlightenment, which, notably in Kant, arises out of the philosophies of freedom for which nature is only a foundation? Do methodological cosmopolitanism and the universalizing dimension of 'living from', elaborated in this work, suffice for the legitimation of such a rapprochement?

In both cases, we must specify why we may speak of a metapolitical cosmopolitanism, returning to the intuition of Kant who, considering the Enlightenment, spoke of the profound change that was taking place and of which his own epoch displayed, in his view, certain anticipatory signs. As we have seen, what is significant in the French Revolution for Kant is not the revolutionary gesticulation, but rather the general sympathy it elicits. This way of interpreting Kant's work on the Enlightenment, in which the maxim of this period is the exit from minority and the conquest of an autonomy conceived as the capacity and the courage to make public use of reason, signifies that revolutions, when they occur, begin with individuals. What is significant in the most important social changes is not related to spectacular events, but to the depth and almost irreversible character of phenomena that are lived in several places in the world by several people. These phenomena arise from a realization or, more precisely, from a change at the level of the imaginary, of what gives meaning and orients the choices that we make in accordance with certain ends.

Indeed, it would seem today that with the emergence of associative movements working for environmental protection and the improvement of animals' condition, as well as with the demand of consumers who wish to buy products of quality and to obtain healthy foods whose provenance they know, we are witnessing a global movement that testifies to the desire to live better and in a more just way. The specificity of this desire for justice in relation to older political struggles is that it is expressed in daily life, meaning that street demonstrations and discussions in parliaments are not the only sites of political struggle.

Movements centred on nourishment are particularly indicative of this evolution, for they concern with daily actions, which thus have an impact on the economy, on production, and on distribution. People who belong to these movements do not need to gather together in a specific place, as one does in classical political demonstrations. They spread in an effective way because they have a certain ubiquity. Finally, the fact of inscribing one's ideal of justice in one's life and in one's body, which is the point of departure of the relationship to oneself, to others, and to nourishment, also explains that a political action, even if it contests the established order, can be radical and non-violent at once.

The generalization of this approach that consists in recovering the meaning of life and in re-appropriating the knowledge that relates to nourishment and to the manner in which we inhabit the earth does not exclude that resistances exist at the same time, and that numerous individuals are seeking consumer goods without considering the ethical and political implications attached to the act of eating. Moreover, it would be an illusion to think that this attitude, consisting in re-appropriating one's own needs, first and foremost an ethical attitude and thus an individual one, can, by being reproduced in diverse places throughout the world, give rise to a large public and to a global community.

As we have emphasized several times, the idea that a global community organized around values and even around shared imaginary meanings may exist is a dangerous fiction. However, the appearance of these movements and the fact that more and more people wish to eat well and discover the taste of life by associating savour with conviviality demonstrate that the obstacles to an evolution of individuals and of societies towards a justice conceived as the sharing of nourishment are disappearing gradually. In the same way, the access of more and more people to information makes impossible, in the medium term, the maintenance of an authoritarian and vertical form of power. In other words, a cultural process is under way. The question is to know whether this process can be connected to the Enlightenment.

What is remarkable in Kant's text of 1784 is that it deals with an epoch that identifies itself and formulates its own maxim, indicating what it should contribute to the history of thought and to the present. The *Aufklärung* designates a cultural process that is not intended to remain localized in a defined time and place, and that delivers a message whose universal dimension is undeniable. Another admirable aspect of this text is that its author is fully conscious of the role that he is led to play as a philosopher of his century, as well as in relation to the cultural process that he describes. He therefore presents himself as an element and also as an actor in this process. He is not pretending to invent something from scratch, but he is convinced of the necessity to express what is taking place, in order to guide those who will recognize themselves in the picture that he paints of his epoch.

It is also from this perspective that we must interpret the maxim of the Enlightenment: *Sapere aude*, 'Dare to think for yourself'. In order to understand its meaning, we must of course recall that human beings are responsible for the state of minority in which they sequester themselves, 'out of laziness or cowardice'. The emphasis placed on the public use of reason, which enables the redistribution of the relations between the government of the self and the government of others, explains the connection between autonomy and the political transformation of society and of the world. However, the fact of naming the cultural process to which we belong and the formulation of the task that we have to complete are also political acts, which give a meaning and a direction to the efforts of each person.

Not only is it said that something better and more constructive is possible, and that the future is open, but, moreover, this re-enchantment of political life, which has nothing to do with a blind optimism nor with an ignorance of the dangers that are incurred, comes as a result of giving a collective dimension, or rather a cosmopolitical dimension, to one's freedom.[52] This is not unconnected with what we said above concerning the thickness that belonging to the common world confers on our existence, which is both individual and collective. More precisely, this affirmation of the decisive importance of autonomy, in the context of a phenomenology of nourishment, illuminates the notion of freedom.

This notion gains in depth to the extent that we are intimately convinced that we inhabit a common world, the comprehension of which is separable from the uncovering of existentials that can be interpreted in diverse ways by different cultures in different epochs. Universalism, in the era of cosmopolitanization, is a universalism in context, and the Enlightenment is not only that of individuals conceived outside of the material conditions of their existence, but also goes together with a consideration of the corporeality of the subject and with the celebration of the nourishing essence of the world.

Such is the horizon of this philosophy of 'living from', for which nature cannot be a simple foundation and that articulates ecology and existence, going beyond the characteristics of the philosophies of freedom and, to a lesser extent, of deep ecology. The humanism of this phenomenology of nourishment, the universalizing dimension of the existentials that have been uncovered, the political constructivism, and the idea that the key to progress is to be sought in the capacity of individuals to place their confidence in life all together prove that we are indeed dealing with a philosophy that is in the tradition of the Enlightenment.

Certainly, the differences between the phenomenology of nourishment and the Enlightenment of the seventeenth and eighteenth centuries are important, as we have shown in recalling that, for the latter, nature plays the role of a simple foundation. Moreover, the transformations of our actions as a consequence of the power of our technology, and the dilemmas triggered by contemporary biotechnologies, enable us to measure what separates us from Kant. However, beyond these differences, it is important to be aware of the spirit that the phenomenology of nourishment shares with the Enlightenment, a constructive spirit that gives this philosophy a certain tone, connected to the confidence that we have in the capacity of human beings to take charge of their destiny.

Conclusion

On the final page of his work, *The Passing of an Illusion*, François Furet writes that the end of communism represented for human beings the 'shock of a closed future', compromising the very foundation of what had amounted to revolutionary messianism over the past two centuries. The idea of *another* society has become almost impossible to conceive, and nobody dared to advance on the subject or 'even [try] to formulate a new concept'.[1] Nonetheless, this situation is 'too austere and contrary to the spirit of modern societies'[2] to be able to last: 'Democracy, by virtue of its existence, creates the need for a world beyond the bourgeoisie and beyond Capital, in which a genuine human community can flourish'.[3]

This democratic demand for another society left the great historian of the French Revolution somewhat perplexed. Nevertheless, it is this demand that inspires this book, in which it appears that politics is inseparable from the hope for a better life, and that justice, which realizes the alliance between interest and happiness as conviviality, is indissociable from taste, that is to say from the capacity to recognize the beauty of the world, and of an unmutilated relationship to life. In fact, in its successes as in its failures, politics cannot be reduced to its economic results, nor to the technical prowess that it has made possible. As Bertrand Russell writes, it is 'in the matters that politicians usually ignore, science and art, human relations, and the joy of life' that a politics should be judged, and it is for the love of these things that we conceive theories or that we invent utopias that open up to the possible.[4]

The opening of the possible and conviviality

A philosophical essay cannot be a political programme. The phenomenological method, which has served to describe the structures of existence that are able to furnish the universalizable criteria for thinking about the human condition, and, from there, to draw out the principles of political rights, and to elaborate a theory of justice conceived as the sharing of nourishment, radically distinguishes this enterprise from any profession of faith. As we have underlined at several points, the existentials that flow from the phenomenology of nourishment, particularly from the analysis of eating, of the place and the milieu that are conceived in their ecumenical dimension, both geographical and social, of cohabitation, and of birth, have nothing to do with moral values that are the expression of normative judgements connected to subjective preferences. There is no question of founding a politics on a moral vision of the world, even supported by means of philosophical references, since we do not pass from morality to politics without imposing, by violence or domination, our own conception of the good. Pluralism, together with the affirmation of the moral equality of individuals, requires the recognition of Otherness and the respect of diversity, and even of the heterogeneity of the forms and styles of life.

Acceptance of the fact of pluralism does not however condemn us to relativism. On the contrary, in placing the emphasis on 'living from' and on the biological, ecological, and social conditions of our existence, in insisting on the corporeality of the subject who is born and who is hungry, we bring out structures that are meaningful for all societies and in all epochs. This universalism is however a universalism in context. The points of reference that it can offer are therefore interpreted each time anew by people who belong to a given culture and epoch and who evolve in a universe that has been fashioned by their history, their geography, their language, and their myths.

This work, which articulates ontology and politics, thus has an ambition that is theoretical and practical at once. The uncovering of dimensions of existence that are often hidden by Western philosophies, which are characterized by a certain dualism of nature and culture and are focused on freedom, as we have seen with the classical theorists of the social contract, changes the meaning ordinarily attributed to ethics and to justice. In the phenomenology of nourishment, these notions have a sense as soon as I eat; they designate positions in existence, for, in my manner of consuming and of inhabiting the earth, I reveal who I am and the place that I accord to other living beings, human and non-human.

What is more, the fact of being born, of eating, of living somewhere, and of using this or that technology, places me in a relationship with other human beings, past, present, or future, and with other living beings. My existence is not only outflanked by that of my ancestors and of the entire lineage of human beings who constitute me, but future generations as well are already part of me, because they will endure the consequences of my choices, and because, since the creation of the atomic bomb, we have the power to prevent them from being born.

Thus existence is not only individual, as if the horizon of our actions were purely private; it is also collective, for we belong to a common world that is composed by the works of our ancestors, by the ecosphere in its totality, and by biodiversity. This common world, which welcomes us at our birth, survives us, and our actions, even the most trivial of them, are also to be evaluated with respect to the manner in which we preserve this common world and offer to our descendants the possibility to draw nourishment from it and to nourish it. Moreover, our relations with other species, in particular with animals, which are non-representational subjectivities that experience their life in the first person and that share the *oikos* with us, confront us with problems of justice. They testify to our capacity to recognize in other living beings the right to exist, and they reflect, as in a mirror, our relationship to sensing, which is the mode by which we are able to encounter them, as well as to reconnect ourselves to our most archaic emotions, enabling us, prior to all thought and any identification with a species or with a social class, to make room for pity.

The consideration of this thickness of human existence which unfolds on two levels, the individual and the collective, and of its materiality, reveals that my relationship to nourishment is the originary site of ethics, and that justice cannot be limited to relations between human beings and between nations, nor can it amount to a distributive theory. This leads us also to modify the manner in which we conceive the ends of political organization at the national and global scales.

While the classical social contract is structured by reciprocity between symmetrical persons, and aims to guarantee security, the protection of individual freedoms, and the reduction of inequalities, the conceptual frame attached to the phenomenology of nourishment presupposes that the interests of future generations and of other species, even if these are apprehended in an approximate way, are integrated into the definition of the common good. Ecology and the animal question are placed at the heart of the social contract. The latter is always established between human beings, who are its only contracting members, but protection of the biosphere, its beauty, the possibility that present and future human beings are able to enjoy life, and the concern to not impose on animals a diminished life that condemns them to the non-expression of their senses are the new duties of the state.

It is also important to elaborate rules that would confer to social rights a greater effectiveness than in Rawls's ideal theory of justice, so that the right to eat is not only a right on paper. Such an approach presupposes that we are not only interested in formal freedoms, and that, in determining the content of certain first goods, we do not limit ourselves to conceiving justice in terms of the allocation or distribution of resources. The right to eat implies the reorganization of the global exchange of foodstuffs, seeking to promote food sovereignty in countries that experience hunger and malnutrition, and defending agricultural policies that are adapted to different geographical and social contexts.

The idea, when we speak of nourishment rather than of resources, is to insist on the dimension of enjoyment attached to the fact of being alive. Needs are not essentially thought of in the light of privation, as if to have something to eat in a sufficient quantity was enough to nourish us. It is indeed essential that individuals have access to enjoyment, to the pleasure of eating and of sharing a meal, savouring healthy and fair foods, of which they know the provenance and recognize the value. Justice thus no longer designates the alliance of interest and utility: a eudaimonistic motive, connected to enjoyment, illuminates it from within. The political problem to which the social contract responds is not only to ensure the security of individuals by limiting their greed and by preventing their passions from leading them to self-destruction; it is conviviality that becomes the horizon of social organization, whether it concerns recreational activities, urbanization, education, work, or public debates.

To exclude from the ends of politics the dimension of pleasure that reflects the fact of living together and to ignore the sense conferred by the beauty of things to our daily actions, as well as to our professional or collective accomplishments, is hardly surprising to people today. Yet, this manner of disconnecting politics from any reflection on happiness, or of limiting happiness to the obtaining of conditions that enable satisfaction, and this divorce between justice and conviviality are emblematic of a truncated conception of existence that affects political action. In addition, the elimination of the aesthetic dimension of existence, of the need to contemplate beautiful things and to nourish ourselves on them, testifies to a crisis of taste that has repercussions in all domains of life, and that also explains our difficulties in fighting against the degradation of the environment, the exploitation of human beings, and the objectification of living beings.

On the contrary, when we reconstruct our social and political organization, not on the basis of the individual conceived in an abstract and solipsistic way, but rather by taking seriously the relational dimension of the individual's existence – which the fact of being born and of being hungry makes manifest, as well as taste – we abandon the schema of symmetry and of give-and-take: we are led to recognize the dependence in which all human beings find themselves, in particular at certain ages of life. Such an approach implies that ethics and justice are essentially connected to self-limitation. The right of the contracting subject to make use of everything that is good for their preservation is bounded by the existence of other human beings who live far from them or come after them, as well as by other species. This limit is both external and internal, because the subject who founds the social contract is never alone, even when no one physically shares their meal. The right to life of others is in this sense at the heart of their *conatus*.

In fact, as soon as I eat, I am in a relationship with other human beings, past, present, and future, living here or there, and with other species, and the fact of being born means that there are many existences behind my own. In other words, the social contract that is founded on the engendered cogito and on the gourmet cogito illustrates a social and political organization whose objective is not only or essentially to guarantee the peaceful coexistence of individual freedoms, as if respect for the Others' freedom required from me that I limit my own freedom.

It is the existence of others in their materiality, their hunger, and their thirst, that calls me into question. In the same way, it is their status as engendered beings that obliges me to be attentive, in my relationship to nourishment, to not impose on them a degraded environment and conditions of life that force them to devote all their efforts and resources to repairing the world, or that denies them all joy and creativity.

Thus the phenomenology of nourishment leads us to formulate the political problem differently than in the classical social-contract theories, since, far from being external to us, ecology is articulated to our existence and animals are intimately mingled with our life. However, this does not mean either that individuals will be immediately inclined to modify their habits of consumption to respect the environment, or that they will promote more justice in their relationship to animals. It is not because the phenomenology of nourishment renews our conception of the subject that we are psychologically disposed to integrate concern for future generations, other species, and animals taken individually into the common good.

The existentials that have been uncovered by the phenomenology of nourishment are closely linked to a conception of the subject and of sociality that is radically distinct from the one proposed in the philosophies of the contract from Hobbes to Rawls. This foundation of political organization on the gourmet and engendered cogito also leads us to elaborate a conception of justice that is no longer only distributive. We thus challenge the philosophical presuppositions that found modern and contemporary political theories, and we propose another philosophy, which is not connected to the fiction of a state of nature, but to a phenomenology. This phenomenology does not rest on an analysis of the passions, as in the anthropology of Hobbes, Locke, or Rousseau. In fact, the ontology that flows from the phenomenology of 'living from' gives birth to a new philosophical anthropology. It uncovers meanings that are often eclipsed in the Western tradition, and in this sense it renews the way in which we apprehend the human condition. However, this passage from ontology to politics, which leads to a theory that arises from political phenomenology, does not presuppose that, in practice, human beings experience the common good as their own good. The problem is well known to contract theorists, since they resort to artificialism, suggesting that interest properly understood is not sufficient to guarantee peace and justice. This explains why the political theory that we are trying to elaborate is inscribed in the heritage of the contractualist tradition which goes back to Epicurus.

Before developing this point and dissipating the impression of a contradiction that might take hold of the reader at the moment they realize they are dealing at once with a phenomenology of sensing and of non-constitution, and with a political constructivism, it is important to return to the most distinctive trait of this philosophy of nourishment, its insistence on the dimension of enjoyment attached to the fact of being alive. It goes hand in hand with the affirmation of the originary character of the love of life and with the critique of Heidegger's ontology of care, which is inseparable from what he calls being-towards-death.

Love of life

Consideration of the collective character of human existence breaks with the philosophies of freedom, particularly those of Heidegger, for whom my death is like the end of the world. To live, when one situates one's action in relation to the common world, is to 'live for' and to affirm a being-towards-life, as we saw in the phenomenology of Watsuji Tetsurô. Moreover, to uncover the enjoyment in our relation to nourishment and to affirm the centrality of taste lead us to stress our immersion in the sensible world and our being-with-things-

and-with-others, and not only our being-in-the-world. Thrownness appears as a consequence of conditions of life that do not permit human beings to live well, to enjoy life, and to know joy. Privations, as well as the mutilation of our relationship to life, which is manifest in certain ways of eating, of making use of living beings, notably animals, of engaging in trade without concern for the sort of goods that are being exchanged, and of working without respecting the meaning of different activities, as we have seen with factory farming and with certain methods of agriculture, give individuals the sentiment of being thrown into a hostile world, in which fear and envy dominate.

Nevertheless, it is the love of life that is primary. The satisfaction with which we abandon ourselves to pleasure, which makes the elemental essence of things burst forth and underlines the agreement of the 'I' with the world through the sensing, and also our appetite, which expresses our desire to live, illustrate this precedence of love of life over worry and sadness. Moreover, the games, in which young animals and children engage spontaneously, testify to this generosity of life that goes beyond needs and danger. Life is not characterized by negativity, but by enjoyment, which is an insouciance regarding existence; it is a game in spite of the finality and of the tension of instinct. To live is to live from something without this something tending towards a goal, but rather because the activity itself that I live from pleases me and constitutes the grace of life.

Again, if the phenomenology of 'living from', which is a radical phenomenology of sensing whose emblem is less the stomach than the mouth, makes clear the happiness associated with the simple fact of living, this does not mean that it is easy to be happy. Not only does nourishment not fall from the sky in a world in which nearly three billion people suffer from hunger or malnutrition, but, in addition, we have also described in this book the suffering experienced by people who impose dietary restrictions on themselves and who have crises of bulimia. A serene relationship to eating seems to be the exception in our societies of abundance, in which individuals, subjected to contradictory injunctions, have trouble imagining foods in any other way than as enemies that can make them gain weight, or as fuels, energy products that they assimilate alone and without pleasure, reducing eating to food intake. Finally, the way in which foods are produced, in particular meat, which most often comes from animals that have endured the worst torments, and the transformation of foods by the agroalimentary industry show how little respect we have for ourselves and for those who nourish us.

In spite of this, we affirm that pleasure is the original mode of our relationship to the world. As we have seen, this is not because politics is concentrated most of the time on yield, on economic results, and on the power of financial exchange that the dimensions of individual and collective existence that give consistency to public action should be neglected. On the contrary, the phenomenology of nourishment suggests that conviviality is the horizon of a just social organization and, underlining the centrality of taste, it places aesthetics at the heart of ethics, while also rehabilitating the pathic dimension of feeling that is a being-with-things-and-with-the-world. However, it is important to construct a political and social organization that makes this joy of living possible and prevents the destruction of the common world. The love of life is primary; it contains freedom. Yet, without effort and without artifice, it is impossible to escape from violence at the national and international levels, whether it is a matter of the relationship between individuals, between nations, or between the human species and other living beings.

Our ambition is to accompany a cultural process, which will not necessarily be victorious, so powerful are the forces of destruction in the atomic era. Moreover, the liberalization of the market, which transforms living beings into manufactured products and merchandise, seems to pull humanity into an irreversible current. Nevertheless, the cultural process for which we have attempted to provide a conceptual basis that is ontological and political at once, is affecting more and more individuals, whatever their ethnic origin or their moral or religious beliefs. This cultural process, in which we are involved both as elements and as engaged actors, is expressed, notably, in the desire to live better by eating better, that is, by consuming foods that are more healthy and just, and by changing consumption habits in an effort to protect the environment, to encourage the types of agriculture that respect our relation to the living world and value human work, and to improve the condition of animals.

We intended to illuminate this anchoring of human beings in the materiality of their existence, by providing theoretical tools that may serve as a starting point for a philosophy of corporeality and of 'living from' that refers to our daily actions, but that at the same time, has meaning on the ethical, political, and cosmopolitical levels. In addition, we wished to propose a philosophy that places ecology and animal protection at the heart of the social contract. The idea was to show in what sense these questions, which lead to a renewal of humanism, also transform democracy, both in its institutions, and to the extent that it designates a type of society that is connected to cultural representations and to a way of thinking and of sharing power.

A constructive spirit thus animates this work, which places itself in the legacy of the Enlightenment, to the extent that it makes the promotion of justice as the sharing of nourishment, an objective around which political construction is organized. In the same way, autonomy is the key to progress, that is to say to the realization of this ideal of justice, of the passage from a competition-based democracy to a deliberative democracy, and of the institution of a common world. Nevertheless, it would be erroneous to think that this constructive spirit is the mark of a naive optimism.

To affirm that the love of life is originary, but that it needs to be rediscovered, and to say that it is necessary to have recourse to the artifice of the social contract and to a metapolitical or methodological cosmopolitanism, is assuredly to take a path that is not that of denouncing the faults of our epoch. Nor are nostalgia and the return to a retrograde order the paths taken in this book, in which we attempt to formulate the idea of another society that democracy, after the end of communism, is currently building. Yet, this aspiration to construct or to reconstruct presupposes a recognition that evil exists. Let us listen to the poet:

This murderous little world
Is aimed at the simple man
It snatches the bread from his mouth
And delivers his house to fire
Steals his coat and his shoes
Steals his time and his children

...

I have lived like a shadow
Yet I have known how to extol the sun
The whole sun which breathes
In every breast and in all eyes
The drop that of candour which shines after tears.[5]

A radical phenomenology of sensing and a political constructivism

It may seem strange to associate political constructivism with a radical phenomenology of sensing, which creates a crisis of representation and celebrates the reversal of the constituted into the constituent.

How can we praise our immersion in the sensible world, which emphasizes the nutritive essence of the world and the generosity of life, and at the same time advocate political voluntarism and the effort to repair democracy and institute a common world? How can a philosophy of corporeality, which extends an ethics of vulnerability whose key category is passivity, be reconciled with the social contract, of which many thinkers, from Spinoza to feminists, have said that it was a snare and a continuation of domination by other means?[6]

This contradiction evaporates once we understand that there is no opposition between sensing and intellect, the heart and the reason, force and fragility. The refusal of this dualism between nature and culture is one of the starting points for a phenomenology of nourishment, which articulates ecology and existence. This dualism is associated with many others. Taste, which involves the collaboration of all my senses and which brings out the savour of things, my being-with-them, which is both a sensing and a self-sensing, blurs the boundaries between the minor arts and the fine arts, between earthly nourishment and spiritual nourishment.

In the same way, it is not because I place within parentheses the preconceptions of the world, which lead me to represent things as objects perceived or conceived by subjects, that I turn away from knowledge. On the contrary, the phenomenology of 'living from', which invites us to get back into our bodies, to feel the ground beneath our feet, to experience the rhythm of a city, and to enjoy what we eat, makes us grasp a truth that is often neglected by philosophies of representation. By making eating into the paradigm of this phenomenology, and by analysing the transformations of this incorporation, in which the alterity of nourishment constitutes me, we see clearly that the world could not be a noeme. It is enjoyment, and not technology or science, that causes its elemental structure to burst forth.

This does not mean that we must disappear within sensing, as if we were to become our sensations. The world is neither what resists my effort, nor the decor of an existence whose main desire is to affirm itself against the existence of others. The secret of life is not revealed to a freedom that is jealous of its own authenticity, nor to a subject whose concern is to distinguish itself from others, but rather it appears in this contact between the 'I' and the world that is sensing, grasped in its pathic dimension. In art, in contemplation of the beautiful, in attention to others, and in communication with animals, we are not cut off from our intellect, but rather we are in the presence of things and of the world.

We abandon the posture of domination, which is that of a subject placed at a distance from what it is looking at, manipulates, and tries to control. This in no way deprives us of the privilege of being able, in speech or in writing, to rescue the things and the world from oblivion. What is more, by examining the words that we employ for apprehending the pain, the suffering, and the needs of others, we are even able to understand beings that are very different from us, as we saw with animals that do not have our language, and, in a general way, as we saw in the definition of empathy.

Sensing and intellect are thus not opposed to one another, and our capacity to know things does not necessarily depend on the control that we exercise over them from the outside. However, it remains for us to explain the union of the heart and of reason, and, above all, of instinct and the will. This question plunges us into the heart of the political problem as Rousseau formulated it.

In effect, the love of life is the principle on which the social contract is built. In order for the relations between human beings not to be founded on violence and domination, it is necessary to have recourse to a common convention, an artifice that will lead contracting members to submit to laws that make it possible to settle differences in an impartial way, removing human beings from slavery and guaranteeing to everyone a life that is free and exempt from fear. The love of life is originary; it gives to the social contract its reason for being, since the first end of the state is to ensure the security of individuals. However, it is threatened in the state of nature by the passions of human beings, which thrust them into collision with one another, and by the rivalries that the arts and culture exacerbate. Moreover, it needs to be rediscovered, since the worry that causes individuals to fear that they do not have a place in society buries it in the depths of the soul, from which it only comes out for brief moments of happiness that appear as exceptions or as respites.

Political constructivism is connected to the will to defend life, as we also saw with cosmopolitical rights. It is the effort by which human beings decide to institute a durable peace, by choosing institutions that will permit individuals to cultivate their talents. The social contract, like cosmopolitanism, is a method that allows the love of life, which is erected in principle, to be victorious, and all the destructive powers, which lead to war and could today lead to extinction, to be contained and combatted. The force of law at the national scale and the change of perspective indicated by cosmopolitanism, for which the world is no longer divided into sovereign nations, are the conditions of peace, of justice, and of the search for effective solutions to climate change and to the erosion of biodiversity.

Nevertheless, if we follow Rousseau, for whom the social contract, as for Locke, cannot be founded on subjection, we must admit that this artificialism does not only serve to thwart the forces that lead to destruction and to self-destruction. When he speaks of the legislator, Rousseau intends to show that the aim of the social contract is also to change human nature. In addition, human beings ought to be, prior to the laws, what they cannot be without them, since in a republican organization in which consent legitimizes political authority, individuals should conceive the common good as their own good.

The general will is not external to individuals, but it can be mute. In the same way, in the social contract that we are proposing, concern for future generations and justice towards other species are integrated into the definition of the common good. To the extent that ethics makes sense as soon as I am eating, and that we are never alone, since intersubjectivity is at the heart of the engendered subject which cohabits with others, the existence of other human beings, past, present, and future, and of other living beings, is a part of ourselves. Nevertheless, it is difficult for the majority of people to consent to changing their consumption habits in order to avoid imposing a diminished life on future generations, on human beings who live far from them, and on animals. It will thus be necessary to add another dimension to political constructivism, which will relate to the virtues that will help people to include among their preoccupations the protection of the environment, justice towards the poorest countries, and the improvement of animals' condition.

Thus instead of taking recourse, as Rousseau does, to a civil religion in order to give citizens the sense of obligation, the phenomenology of nourishment needs to be complemented by a virtue ethics, indicating which moral dispositions could sustain this philosophy of 'living from', and the theory of justice to which it leads. This task, to which we will turn in a future work, is indispensable if we wish to respond to the difficulties of environmental and animal ethics, which have not succeeded at placing ecology and the animal question at the centre of our lives, since these have been addressed to reason and not to the heart and to the affects.

In other words, this work calls for ethics of consideration, which will pursue in the field of moral philosophy, what we have attempted to elaborate here by presenting the ontological and political aspects of the phenomenology of 'living from'. This phenomenology extends what we have accomplished in earlier works, in which the ethics of vulnerability appeared as a philosophy of the subject affirming the centrality of responsibility and underlining, along with our fragility, our need to exist and to be recognized as persons, notwithstanding the physical and psychical conditions that can narrow our possibilities of life. In the present work, it is not vulnerability, conceived both as fragility and as a force, that is the fundamental inspiration, but rather pleasure. This does not mean that we disregard negativity. On the contrary, we may say with André Gide that the celebration of life in its immanence and its generosity is the gift of a 'convalescent':[7]

> Great fields washed in the whiteness of dawn, I have seen you; blue lakes, I have bathed in your waters – and to every caress of the laughing breeze I have smiled back an answer – this is what I shall never tire of telling you, Nathaniel. I will teach you fervor.[8]

Notes

Introduction

1 Maurice Merleau-Ponty, *The Structure of Behavior*, trans. A. Fisher, Boston, Beacon Press, 1967, pp. 126–7.

2 Cornelius Castoriadis, "Un monde à venir. Entretien avec O. Morel, 18/06/1993," published under the title, "La montée de l'insignifiance," in *Les carrefours du labyrinthe*, vol. 4, *La montée de l'insignifiance*, Paris, Seuil, 'Points Essais', 2007, p. 112; translation ours.

3 Capitalism is distinguished from liberalism, as we will recall in what follows, in particular in the first chapter of Part Two, where Locke, among others, is treated.

4 André Gorz, "Two Kinds of Ecology", in *Ecology and Politics*, trans. P. Vigderman and J. Cloud, Boston, South End Press, 1980, pp. 3–9. For Gorz, capitalism is connected to an anthropology that separates individuals and that functions thanks to marketing, which compels individuals to look for objects to which a certain prestige is attached and that not everybody is able to obtain, thus encouraging the purchase of private goods to the detriment of the utilization of public services that are less costly in energy, and favouring the production and consumption of sophisticated products.

5 Corine Pelluchon, *L'Autonomie brisée. Bioéthique et philosophie*, Paris, PUF, 'Quadrige', 2014; *Éléments pour une éthique de la vulnérabilité. Les hommes, les animaux, la nature*, Paris, Cerf, 'Humanités', 2011.

6 Recalling that 'economy' has the same etymological root as 'ecology' indicates that the former term, which concerns the management of the household and the domestic sphere – and which will be expanded to the city, to relations of production and exchanges and the national and

international scale – should in principle take into consideration our dependency with respect to the material conditions of our existence and of other living beings. Not only does an economy that deals with the latter as market goods bring about destructive effects at the ecological and social levels, it also betrays itself in misunderstanding the meaning of 'inhabiting the earth'.

7   Thierry Paquot, 'Habiter pour exister pleinement', *Habiter, le propre de l'humain. Villes, territoires et philosophie*, eds Thierry Paquot, Michel Lussault, and Chris Younès, Paris, La Découverte, 'Arimmaire', 2007, pp. 8–11.

8   Paquot, 'Habiter pour exister pleinement', p. 91. The author refers here to Max Sorre, *Les Fondements de la géographie humaine*, Paris, Armand Colin, 1948.

9   Hicham-Stéphane Afeissa, *Nouveaux fronts écologiques. Essais d'éthique environnementale et de philosophie animale*, Paris, Vrin, 'Pour demain', 2012, p. 24.

10   Aldo Leopold, *A Sand County Almanac & Other Writings*, New York, The Library of America, 2013, pp. 1–189, p. 97.

11   Cornelius Castoriadis, 'The Revolutionary Potency of Ecology', in *A Society Adrift. Interviews and Debates, 1974–1997*, eds E. Escobar, M. Gondicas and P. Vernay, trans. H Arnold, New York, Fordham University Press, 2010, p. 205.

12   Emmanuel Levinas, *Totality and Infinity*, trans. Alphonso Lingis, Pittsburgh, Duquesne University Press, 1969, p. 111.

13   Levinas, *Totality and Infinity.*, p. 156; Ibid., p. 145.

14   Ibid. See also Emmanuel Levinas, *Existence & Existents*, trans. Alphonso Lingis, Pittsburgh, Duquesne University Press, 2001, p. 37.

15   *Id.*, *Les Enseignements*, *Œuvres*, vol. II, Paris, Grasset, 2011, p. 192.

16   Ibid, pp. 183–4. On this subject see Corine Pelluchon, 'Le monde des nourritures chez Levinas: de la jouissance à la justice', in *Levinas: au-delà du visible. Études sur les inédits de Levinas, des* Carnets de captivité à Totalité et infini, eds Emmanuel Housset and Rodolphe Calin, Caen, Presses Universitaires de Caen, 2012, pp. 283–302.

17   'The material needs of my neighbour are my spiritual needs' (Emmanuel Levinas, , *Nine Talmudic Readings*, trans. A Aronowicz, Bloomington,

Indiana University Press, 1990, p. 99). Here Levinas cites the rabbi Israël Salanter, commenting on the obligations of Abraham towards the Other.

18 *Id.*, *Of God Who Comes to Mind*, trans. Bettina Bergo, Stanford, Stanford University Press, 1998, p. 175.

19 J. Baird Callicott, 'The Metaphysical Implications of Ecology', *Environmental Ethics* vol. 8, no. 2, 1986, 301–16, p. 315.

20 Levinas, *Totality and Infinity*, p. 129.

21 This hard-to-translate word cannot be synonymous with 'soul' or 'spirit'. It refers to the corporeal consciousness of sensation and of self-affection, and designates a disposition of the soul that is stable and that conditions the exercise of all of the faculties.

22 Id., *Difficult Freedom. Essays on Judaism*, trans. S. Hand, Baltimore, Johns Hopkins University Press, 1990, p. xiv, and *Nine Talmudic Writings*, p. 97.

23 Id., *Existence & Existents*, pp. 34–7, particularly, p. 36.

24 Id., *Totality and Infinity*, p. 134.

25 Fernand Braudel, *The Mediterranean and the Mediterranean World in the Age of Philip II*, trans. S. Reynolds, Berkeley, University of California Press, 1995, p. 20.

26 Levinas, *Totality and Infinity*, p. 134. See also 'Les Nourritures', *Oeuvres*, vol. II, p. 162.

27 Emmanuel Levinas, *Time and the Other*, trans. R. Cohen, Pittsburgh, Duquesne University Press, 1987, p. 56: 'To understand the body starting with its materiality – the concrete event of the relationship between Ego [*Moi*] and Self [*Soi*]', and not as a contingent falling of the spirit into the tomb of the body, 'is to reduce it to an ontological event'.

28 Id., *Totality and Infinity*, p. 131. The 'elemental' designates the 'non-possessable which envelops or contains, without being able to be contained or enveloped', like the sea, the earth, the city, light. It is at once the element in which I move and which is sufficient for me and which comes from nowhere and which I attempt to surmount or to domesticate – in building a house in order to organize my perception setting out from my at – home, and in working, in order to master that which is strange and to possess what I need in order to live. See, for a general account, the section entitled 'Interiority and Economy' in *Totality and Infinity*, pp. 107–83.

29 Jean-Jacques Rousseau, *The Social Contract*, in *The Social Contract and The First and Second Discourses*, ed. S. Dunn, New Haven, Yale University Press, 2002, pp. 149–254, 191–2.

30 Ibid., Book IV, ch. 1, pp. 127–8.

Part One

1 Levinas, *Totality and Infinity*, *op. cit.*, 110; 128–9.

Chapter 1

1 Erwin Straus, *The Primary World of Senses, a Vindication of Sensory Experience*, trans. J. Needleman, New York, Free Press of Glencoe, 1963, pp. 312–13, 317.

2 Straus, *The Primary World of Senses.*, ch. 9, p. 418; Ibid., pp. 351–52.

3 Emmanuel Levinas, 'The Ruin of Representation', in *Discovering Existence with Husserl*, trans. R. Cohen and M. Smith, Evanston, Northwestern University Press, 1998, pp. 111–21.

4 Id., *Totality and Infinity*, p. 134.

5 Ibid., pp. 130, 135. In Descartes, the sensible, which arises not from the true, but from the useful, has nothing to do with the Heideggerian tool, which is connected with a system of functionalities. The sensible qualities designate what is convenient to me and what I love: love, having only one essence, is an emotion that leads me to wilfully unite myself with what I think is fitting for me, with the result that foodstuffs are the object of our love, but also the bird, the tree, my children, and God. See René Descartes, *The Passions of the Soul*, in *The Philosophical Writings of Descartes Volume. 1*, ed. J. Cottingham, R. Stoothof, D. Murdoch, Cambridge, UK, Cambridge University Press, 1985, pp. 325–404, section 79, p. 356; René Descartes *The Philosophical Writings of Descartes, Volume 3: The Correspondence*, ed. J. Cottingham, R. Stoothof, D. Murdoch, Cambridge, U.K., Cambridge University Press, 1991, pp. 305–14.

6 Raoul Moati, *Levinas and the Night of Being: A Guide to Totality and Infinity*, trans. D. Wyche, New York, Fordham University Press, 2017, pp. 65–6.

7 Emmanuel Levinas, *Totality and Infinity*, p. 129.

8 Ibid., p. 111.

9 Ibid., pp. 111–12.

10 Ibid., pp. 140–2, 149.

11 Ibid., p. 145.

12 Ibid., 134.

13 Michel Onfray, *La Raison gourmande. Philosophie du goût*, Paris, LGF, 'Biblio Essais', 2005, p. 246.

14 Paul Ricœur, *Freedom and Nature: The Voluntary and the Involuntary*, trans. E. Kohák, Evanston, Illinois, Northwestern University Press, 1966, p. 118.

15 Levinas, *Totality and Infinity*, p. 134.

16 Ibid.

17 Ibid.

18 Id., 'The Ruin of Representation', p. 115. Moati, *Levinas and the Night of Being*, pp. 113–14.

19 Levinas, *Time and the Other*, p. 63.

20 Étienne Bonnot de Condillac, *Condillac's Treatise on the Sensations*, trans. M. G. S. Carr, Los Angeles, University of Southern California Press, 1930.

21 Ibid., de Condillac, *Condillac's Treatise on the Sensations*, Part 3, ch. 10.

22 Maine de Biran, *Mémoire sur la décomposition de la pensée*, in *Oeuvres*, vol. 3, Paris: Vrin, 'Bibliothèque des textes philosophiques', 1988, ch. 1, especially pp. 135–7, ch. 2, p. 147 sq., p. 154.

23 Michel Henry, *Auto-donation. Entretiens et conférences*, Saint-Mandé, Prétentaine, 2002, pp. 92–3. See also *The Essence of Manifestation*, trans. G. Etzkorn, The Hague, Nijhoff, 1973; and *Incarnation. A Philosophy of Flesh,* trans. K. Hefty, Evanston, Northwestern University Press, 2015, section 26, pp. 136–46.

24 *Incarnation*, section 27, pp. 144–6.

25 Ibid., section 31, pp. 159–65.

26 Straus, *The Primary World of the Senses*, p. 370.

27 Paul Ricœur, *Freedom and Nature*, pp. 335–6.

28 Straus, *The Primary World of the Senses*, pp. 17–19. See also Henri Maldiney, 'Le dévoilement de la dimension esthétique dans la phénoménologie d'Erwin Straus', *Regard, parole, espace*, Paris, Cerf, 'Bibliothèque du Cerf', 2012, pp. 188–90.

29 Maldiney, *Regard, Parole, Espace*, p. 191.

30 Ibid., p. 189.

31 Ibid., p. 176.

32 Maine de Biran, *Mémoire sur la décomposition de la pensée*, pp. 205–7.

33 Ibid., p. 205.

34 Michel Henry cites section 7 of *Sein und Zeit*, in which Heidegger says that *phainesthai*, 'to show oneself', is to place in the light (*Incarnation*, op. cit., section 1, pp. 22–5).

35 This is what leads Paul Ricœur to say (in *Freedom and Nature*, pp. 335–6), that Biran's philosophy and any thought that connects perception to a theory of action will bump up against its own limits. Following Erwin Straus, we have distinguished sensing from perception, the latter of which is connected to the object, but our analysis connects up with that of Ricœur, which we will encounter again at the end of this chapter, where we will treat the questions of birth, of filiation, and of the intersubjectivity that filiation places at the heart of our existence.

36 Roger Dadoun, 'La bouche d'Éros', in Catherine N'Diaye (dir.), *La Gourmandise. Délices d'un péché*, Paris, Autrement, 'Mutations', 1993, p. 54.

37 Jean Anthelme Brillat-Savarin, *The Physiology of Taste, or Transcendental Gastronomy*, trans. F. Robinson, Philadelphia, Lindsay & Blakiston, 1854, p. 56.

38 Ibid.

39 Ibid., p. 57.

40 Ibid.

41 Ibid., p. 83 and pp. 201–7.

42 Ibid.

43 Ibid., pp. 172–3, 309–10.

44 Ibid., p. 172.

45 Ibid. We also note that when they speak of someone who is a gourmet or of a dish that is appreciated after the fashion of the gourmets, the English and the Americans use the French word 'gourmet'.

46 Ibid.

47 Jacques Derrida, *Points ... Interviews, 1974-1994*, trans. P Kamuf et. al., Stanford, Stanford University Press, 1995, pp. 282–3.

48 Claude Lévi-Strauss, 'These Cooks did not Spoil the Broth', in *The Unesco Courier*, No. 5, 2008, pp. 35–8, 36.

49 Brillat-Savarin, *The Physiology of Taste*, p. 309.

50 Ibid., p. 207.

51 Ibid.

52 David Le Breton, *Anthropologie du corps et modernité*, Paris, PUF, 2008, 'Quadrige', p. 177.

53 Charles Fourier, 'Manuscrit', Cahier 54, cote 9, in René Scherer, *L'Écosophie de Charles Fourier. Deux textes inédits*, Paris, Anthropos, 'Anthropologie', 2001, p. 155: 'Cuisine among all arts is the most revered in Harmony: it is the pivot of all agricultural labor and the salon of education'.

54 Ibid. Fourier distinguishes 'the major saints or Gastrosophers from the parasitic class of civilized gastronomes'.

55 Pierre Bourdieu, *Distinction: A Social Critique of the Judgment of Taste*, trans. R. Nice Cambridge, MA, Harvard, 1984, pp. 177–83.

56 Bourdieu, *Distinction*, p. 193.

57 Ibid.

58 Brillat-Savarin, *The Physiology of Taste*, pp. 197–200.

59 Kakuzô Okakura, *The Book of Tea*, Rutland, VT, Tuttle, 1956, pp. 6–7.

60 Okakura, *The Book of Tea* p. 84.

61 Ibid., pp. 91–2.

62 Ibid., p. 147.

63 Claude Lévi-Strauss, 'These Cooks Did Not Spoil the Broth', p. 38. The author provides one of the recipes of the Tsimshian Indians, who live on the northwest Pacific coast: 'The fish are first dried in the open air. They are then boiled in vessels filled with water into which stones heated in the

fire are dropped, the fat being skimmed off as it rises to the surface. The remainder of the fish is afterwards spread on a sieve above some recipient, and an old woman presses it to her naked breast as hard as she can, to squeeze out the rest of the fat (men are strictly forbidden to perform this degreasing operation). The cakes of fish are then heaped up in a corner of the hut, where they lie rotting until they swarm with maggots. Despite the intolerable stench, they must not be thrown away. Moreover, none of the "cooks" concerned is allowed to wash; every one must remain covered with filth until the end of the proceedings, which may last for two or three weeks. Otherwise the fish would be "ashamed" and would never come back again.'

64 Bernard de Clairvaux, *Saint Bernard on Consideration*, Oxford, Clarendon Press, 1908, Book II, Ch. ix, p. 57.

65 Paul Ricœur, *Oneself as Another*, trans. K. Blamey, Chicago, Chicago, 1992, p. 150.

66 Edmund Husserl, 'Foundational Investigations of the Phenomenological Origin of the Spatiality of Nature: The Originary Ark, the Earth, Does Not Move', trans. F. Kersten and revised by L. Lawlor, in Maurice Merleau-Ponty, *Husserl at the Limits of Phenomenology. Including Texts by Edmund Husserl*, ed. L. Lawlor with B. Bergo, Evanston, Northwestern, 2001, pp. 117–31, 130.

67 Ibid., pp. 126–7.

68 Ibid., p. 130.

69 Ibid.

70 Ibid., p. 123.

71 Ibid., p. 130.

72 Ibid., p 123. and 130.

73 Levinas, *Totality and Infinity*, p. 138.

74 Id., *Discovering Existence with Husserl*, p. 85.

75 The 1954 text, 'Building, Dwelling, Thinking', testifies to a true thinking of dwelling, as we will see in the next chapter. See *Basic Writings*, trans. D. F. Krell, San Francisco, HarperCollins, 1993, pp. 343–63.

76 Levinas, *Totality and Infinity*, pp. 152–4.

77 Id., *Pouvoirs et origine, Oeuvres*, vol. III, pp. 109–50.

78 Ibid., pp. 109–10.

79 Ibid.

80 Straus, *The Primary World of the Senses*, p. 369.

81 Ibid.

82 Ibid., pp. 282–3.

83 Ibid.

84 Ibid., pp. 312–13.

85 Ibid.

86 Ibid.

87 Ibid.

88 Ibid., p. 319.

89 Henri Maldiney, *Aux déserts que l'histoire accable. L'art de Tal Coat*, Paris, Cerf, 'Bibliothèque du Cerf', 2013, p. 24.

90 Straus, *The Primary World of the Senses*, p. 319.

91 Ibid., p. 356.

92 Ibid., p. 360.

93 Ibid., pp. 357–8.

94 Ibid., p. 361.

95 Levinas, *Totality and Infinity*, pp. 156–9.

96 Ibid., pp. 154–5.

97 Ibid., pp. 267–9.

98 This passage will be completed in the next chapter, where we will oppose the conception of ethics in Watsuji Tetsurô to Heidegger's being-towards-death, but also in Part Two of this work, at the beginning of the third chapter, where we will treat the threat of extinction connected to the atomic bomb, and the definition of the shared world.

99 Ricœur, *Freedom and Nature*, p. 433.

100 Ibid.

101 Ibid., p. 442.

102 Ibid., p. 434.

103 Ibid.

104 Ibid., p.435.

105 Ibid.

106 Ibid.

107 Ibid., p. 439.

108 Ibid., pp. 442–3.

109 Ibid., p. 442.

Chapter 2

1 Éric Dardel, *L'Homme et la Terre*, Paris, CTHS, 'CTHS format', 1990, p. 2.

2 Heidegger, 'Building, Dwelling, Thinking', pp. 182–3; 355–6.

3 Augustin Berque, 'Entretien avec Stéphane Audege', *Nouvelle revue française*, No. 599–600, March 2012, 'Du Japon', pp. 33–5.

4 Ibid.

5 Augustin Berque, preface to Tetsurô Watsuji, *Fûdo. Le milieu humain*, trans. A. Berque, P. Couteau, and K. Akinobu, Paris, CNRS Éditions, 'Réseau Asie', 2011, p. 21; Tetsurô Watsuji, *A Climate. A Philosophical Study*, trans. G. Bownas, Japan, Ministry of Education, 1961.

6 Augustin Berque, *Écoumène. Introduction à l'étude des milieux humains*, Paris, Belin, 1987, p. 185.

7 Cited by Augustin Berque, ibid., pp. 155–9; p. 170.

8 Ibid., p. 281.

9 Ibid., pp. 30–5.

10 Jacques Derrida, 'Khôra', in *On the Name*, trans. D. Wood, Stanford, Stanford University Press, 1995, pp. 89–127, 111.

11 Derrida, 'Khôra', pp. 121–3.

12 Tetsurô Watsuji, *A Climate….*, pp. v–vi.

13 Ibid., p. v.

14 Ibid., p. 10.

15 Ibid., p. 9. See also Tetsurô Watsuji, 'The Significance of Ethics as the Study of Man', trans. D. A. Dilworth, *Monumenta Nipponica*, 26, no. 3/4 (1971), pp. 395–413.

16 Tetsurô Watsuji, *A Climate*...., p. 9.

17 Id., 'The Significance of Ethics as the Study of Man', p. 400.

18 Ibid.

19 Ibid., p. 401.

20 Ibid.

21 Ibid., p. 402.

22 Ibid., p. 403.

23 Ibid.

24 Ibid., p 404.

25 Ibid.

26 Ibid., p. 405.

27 Ibid., p. 407.

28 Ibid., p. 408.

29 Id., *A Climate*..., p. 13.

30 Ibid., p.14.

31 Ibid., p.13.

32 Ibid., p. 15.

33 Ibid., p. 16.

34 Ibid., p. 65.

35 Levinas, *Existence and Existents*, pp. 69–70.

36 Heidegger, 'Building, Dwelling, Thinking', 349.

37 Ibid., pp. 352, 360–61.

38 This American term refers to residential neighbourhoods, rich or poor, to which access is controlled and in which shared space is privatized. (In English in the original. *tr.*)

39 Jean-Marc Besse, 'Vues de ville et géographie au XVIe siècle: concepts, démarches cognitiv, fonctions', in Frédéric Poussin (ed.), *Figures de la ville et construction des savoirs. Architecture, urbanisme, géographie*, Paris, CNRS Éditions, 2005, p. 27.

40 Heidegger, 'Building, Dwelling, Thinking', pp. 191, 361–2.

41 Olivier Mongin, *The Urban Condition*, trans. G. Turner, Charles University, Karolinium Press, 2017.

42 'Art, architecture, urbain: rencontre avec Herni Maldiney', in Chris Younès (ed.), *Art et philosophie, ville et architecture*, Paris: La Découverte, 'Armillaire', 2003, p. 14. See also 'Rencontre avec Henri Maldiney: éthique et architecture', in Chris Younès and Thierry Paquot (eds.), *Éthique, architecture, urbain*, Paris: La Découverte, 'Armillaire', 2000, pp. 10–23.

43 Henri Maldiney, 'L'esthétique des rythmes', *Regard, parole, espace*, pp. 220–1.

44 Ibid., p. 208.

45 Ivan Illich, *Tools for Conviviality*, New York, Harper & Row, 1973, pp. 78–9.

46 Id., 'Dwelling', in *In the Mirror of the Past. Lectures and Addresses 1978-1990*, New York, Marion Boyars, 1992, pp. 55–64, 55.

47 Silvia Grünig Iribarren, *Ivan Illich. La ville conviviale*, doctoral thesis directed by Thierry Paquot, Université Paris-Est, 2013, p. 219.

48 Claude Lévi-Strauss, *Tristes tropiques*, trans. J. Weightman and D. Weightman, New York, Penguin, 2012, pp. 127–8. Cited by Mongin, *The Urban Condition*, p. 168 sq.

49 Mongin, *The Urban Condition*, pp. 133–4.

50 Ivan Illich, 'The Corruption of the Best is the Worst', in David Cayley (ed.), *The Rivers North of the Future: The Testament of Ivan Illich as Told to David Cayley*, Toronto, House of Anansi, 2005, pp. 161–2; Ivan Illich, *Toward a History of Needs*, New York, Pantheon, 1978, pp. 13–16.

51 Id., 'L'art d'habiter, p. 764; Id., 'Dwelling', pp. 62–3.

52 Silvia Grünig Iribarren, in her thesis, *Ivan Illich. La ville conviviale*, p. 23, cites Ildefons Cerdà i Sunyer (1815–76), who conceived the *Example* of Barcelona, and spoke for the first time of 'urbanization' in his *Teoría de la Construcción de Ciudades* (*Theory of the Construction of Cities*) not only to refer to any act that tends to concentrate that which is built and to regularize its functioning, but also to refer to the ensemble of principles and of rules that must be applied in order for that which is built to aid in increasing individual and collective well-being.

53 Illich, *La Convivialité*, p. 456. 'Beyond a certain threshold, the tool, the servant, becomes despotic. ... Society becomes a school, a hospital, a prison. Thus begins the great closing-in.'

54 Id., *Toward a History of Needs*, pp. 13–16.

55 Henri Maldiney, notably in his *Penser l'homme et la folie*, often cites fragment 18 of Heraclitus: 'If you do not expect the unexpected, you will not find it; for it is hard to be sought out and difficult' (trans. John Burnet).

56 To illustrate transpassibility, we can think of the passage in *Mélancolie et manie*, transl. J.-M. Azorin and Y. Totoyan, Paris, PUF, 'Psychiatrie ouverte', 1987, p. 59 sq. Ludwig Binswanger relates an episode in the life of one of his patients, Bruno Brandt. Intending to commit suicide, he goes into the forest and prepares to hang himself with his braces when all of a sudden there appears a weasel that has come out of nowhere: 'You've never seen a weasel before, give yourself some time', Brandt says to himself. He observes the animal and realizes that his suicidal intention is no longer so pressing. So he returns to the clinic. Something took up all his attention, giving him a point of anchorage that was different from those he could have expected, and which enabled him to experience his existence.

57 Illich, 'Dwelling', p. 60. See also *In the Mirror of the Past*, pp. 49–50.

58 Id., 'Guarding the Eye in the Age of Show', in *RES: Anthropology and Aesthetics*, No. 28 (Autumn, 1995), pp. 47–61.

59 Ivan, Sigmar Groeneveld, Lee Hoinacki, et al., *Declaration on Soil*, December 1990.

60 Iribarren, *Ivan Illich. La ville conviviale*, p. 373.

61 Ibid.

62 Such is the generic definition of 'care' proposed by Joan Tronto, *Un monde vulnérable. Pour une philosophie du* care, trans. H. Maury, Paris: La Découverte, 'Philosophie pratique', 2009, p. 143; Joan Tronto, *Moral Boundaries. A Political Argument for an Ethic of Care*, New York, Routledge, 1993, p. 103.

63 Michel Serres, *Les Cinq Sens*, Paris: Grasset, 1985, p. 260; Michel Serres, *The Five Senses. A Philosophy of Mingled Bodies*, trans. M. Sankey and P. Cowley, London, Continuum, 2008, pp. 244–5.

64 Jean-Marc Besse, 'Les cinq portes du paysage. Essai d'une cartographie des problématiques paysagères contemporaines', in *Le Goût du monde. Exercices de paysage*, Arles: Actes Sud, 'Paysage', 2009, pp. 15–70.

65 Ibid., p. 64.

66 Ibid., p. 65.

67 Ibid., p. 64.

68 Emmanuel Pezrès, 'La permaculture au sein de l'agriculture urbaine: du jardin au projet de société', in *VertigO - la revue électronique en sciences de l'environnement*, vol. 10, no. 2, September, 2010.

69 Masanobu Fukuoka, *The One-Straw Revolution: An Introduction to Natural Farming*, trans. L. Korn, New York, New York Review of Books, 2009; Masanobu Fukuoka, *Natural Way of Farming: The Theory and Practice of Green Philosophy*, trans. F. P. Metreaud, Tokyo and New York, Japan Productions, 1985.

70 Yvan Besson, 'Une histoire d'exigences: philosophie et agrobiologie. L'actualité de la pensée de l'agriculture biologique pour son développement contemporain', in *Innovations agronomiques*, No. 4, 2009, pp. 329–62.

71 Michel Serres, *Hermès III. La traduction*, Paris: Minuit, 'Critique', 1974, p. 246.

72 Straus, *Du sens des sens*, p. 234; Straus, *The Primary World of the Senses*, p. 194.

73 Edmund Husserl, in the fifth of his *Cartesian Meditations*, shows that this is the behaviour that makes the psychic present as an individual (*Cartesian Meditations. An Introduction to Phenomenology*, trans. D. Cairns, The Hague, Nijhoff, 1960).

74 Id., 'Welt und Wir. Menschliche und tierische Umwelt', in *Beilage X du Hua XV, Zur Phänomenologie der Intersubjektivität, Husserliana XV*, Dordrecht: M. Nijhoff, 1973: 'The beast posseses something of the structure of a self.'

75 Jacques Derrida, *The Animal That Therefore I Am*, trans. D. Wills, New York, Fordham, 2008, p. 13. Derrida says that many humans have never seen themselves being seen by an animal, that they have never taken into account the fact that an animal was able to look at them.

76 Georges Canguilhem, *Knowledge of Life*, trans. S. Geroulanos & D. Ginsburg, New York, Fordham, 2008, pp. 113–14.

77 Edmund Husserl, 'Zur Phänomenologie der Intersubjectivität', *Husserliana XV*, Ed. I. Kern, La Haye, M. Nijhoff, 1973, pp. 613–27.

78 Husserl, 'Zur Phänomenologie der Intersubjectivität'..

79 Jakob von Uexküll, *A Foray into the Worlds of Animals and Humans*, trans. J. O'Neil, Minneapolis, Minnesota, 2010. For an analysis of the surrounding world, see *L'Autonomie brisée*, op. cit., Part 2, ch. 4, pp. 389–401.

80 Merleau-Ponty, *The Structure of Behavior*, p. 125.

81 Ibid., pp. 126–7. On the importance of the category of signification in biology, see Maurice Merleau-Ponty, *Nature. Course Notes from the Collège de France*, trans. R. Vallier, Evanston, Northwestern, 2003.

82 Edmund Husserl, 'Normalité et espèces animales', in *Sur l'intersubjectivité*, trans. N. Depraz, vol. II, Paris: PUF, 'Épiméthée', 2001, pp. 249–63.

83 Jean-Claude Monod, 'Why I talk to My Dog: Extensions of Intersubjectivity', in *Environmental Philosophy*, vol. 11, no. 1, Spring, 2014, pp. 17–26.

84 It is in this sense that there are levels of empathy in animals that do not permit all of them to be able to respond to the distress of the Other by offering it targeted help. See Frans de Waal, *The Age of Empathy: Nature's Lessons for a Kinder Society*, New York, Three Rivers Press, 2009.

85 Ibid., p. 124.

86 Husserl, 'Normalité et espèces animales', p. 257.

87 *Id.*, *Cartesian Meditations*, V §55, p. 125.

88 Merleau-Ponty, *La structure du comportement*, p. 111. The conceptions of the animal in Husserl and Heidegger are analysed in more detail in Corine Pelluchon, *L'Autonomie brisée*, pp. 374–85.

89 This book is the object of analysis in the second part of Corine Pelluchon, *Éléments pour une éthique de la vulnérabilité*.

90 Max Scheler, *The Nature of Sympathy*, trans. P. Heath, London, Routledge & Kegan Paul, 1954.

91 Claude Lévi-Strauss, *Structural Anthropology, Vol. 2*, trans. Monique Layton, New York, Basic Books, 1976, pp. 37–43. Jean-Jacques Rousseau, *The Second Discourse: Discourse on the Origin and Foundations of Inequality Among Mankind*, pp. 69–148, 106–7.

92 Straus, *The Primary World of the Senses*, p. 201.

93 Ibid., p. 243; Ibid., p. 201.

94 Jocelyne Porcher, *Éleveurs et animaux, réinventer le lien*, Paris, PUF, 'Partage du savoir', 2002, p. 227.

95 Maurice Merleau-Ponty, *Phenomenology of Perception*, trans. C. Smith, London, Routledge, 2002, p. 296.

96 Porcher, *Éleveurs et animaux, réinventer le lien*, pp. 105–32.

97 See the film of Manuela Frésil, *Entrée du personnel*, 2013.

98 See the 'Loi de modernisation de l'agriculture et de la pêche' (LMAP) of 27 July 2010, voted by the French Parliament, particularly Article L230-5. This law authorizes the government to decree rules concerning the nutritional quality of meals served in schools and in other institutional dining services, as, for example Décret No. 2011-1227, and the order of 30 September 2011, pertaining to the nutritional quality of meals served in schools. The obligation to regularly serve meat and fish appears in Article 1 of this order.

99 Éric Baratay, *Le Point de vue animal. Une autre version de l'histoire*, Paris: Seuil, 'L'univers historique, 2012.

100 For a presentation and a refutation of this argument, defended notably by Baird Callicott, see Clare Palmer, 'The Idea of the Domesticated Animal Contract', *Environmental Values*, 1997, n°6, pp. 411–25.

101 The term 'zoopolis' was coined in 1998 by Jennifer Wolch, who by means of it described an urban environmental ethics that promotes an integrated vision of the mixed community that is formed by animals and humans. As in the book by Sue Donaldson and Will Kymlicka, *Zoopolis: A Political Theory of Animal Rights*, New York, Oxford University Press, 2011, our conception of the zoopolis implies a politicization of the animal question, that is to say that the interests of animals enter into the definition of the common good and that it is a matter of providing ourselves with the means of thinking about justice towards animals, determining their rights and our obligation towards them.

102 J. Baird Callicott, 'Genesis and John Muir', in *Beyond the Land Ethic: More Essays in Environmental Philosophy*, Albany, SUNY Press, 1999, pp. 187–221. The author reminds us that human beings are not the measure of all things, as God made human beings and cattle according to *their* species, thus representing 'an axiological reference that is external to human beings'. Moreover the second account of creation, from a Yahwist source, authorizes, according to him, an interpretation that goes further than the model of stewardship or of man as God's gardener, and is equivalent to the model of ecological citizenship, close to Aldo Leopold's ethics of the earth, which speaks of the 'biotic community'. See also Corine Pelluchon, *Élements pour une éthique de la vulnérabilité*, pp. 64–5.

103 Thierry Gontier, 'Descartes ou les raisons d'un refus', in Thierry Gontier (ed.), *Animal et animalité dans la philosophie de la Renaissance et de l'âge classique*, Louvain and Paris, Peeters, 'Bibliothèque philosophique de Louvain', 2005, pp. 107–28.

104 René Descartes, *The Philosophical Writings of Descartes: Volume 3, The Correspondence*, ed. John Cottingham, Robert Stoothoff, Dugald Murdoch, Anthony Kenny, Cambridge University Press, 1991, p. 266. See also the letter to Chanut of 6 June 1647, *The Philosophical Writings of Descartes: Volume 3*, p. 321; and *Principles of Philosophy*, in *The Philosophical Writings of Descartes: Volume 1*, p. 248.

105 Ronald Dworkin, *Taking Rights Seriously*, Cambridge, MA, Harvard University Press, 1977, p. xi.

106 Such is, for example the position of David De Grazia and, to a lesser extent, Martha C. Nussbaum, both of whom are also criticised in Donaldson and Kymlicka's book.

107 Robert Nozick, *Anarchy, State, and Utopia*, New York, Basic Books, 1974.

108 Donaldson and Kymlicka, *Zoopolis*, p. 48.

109 This refers to the set of conditions that make human cooperation at once both possible and necessary.

110 See Amandine Faynot's documentary, *Adak*, which shows sheep being ritually slaughtered in a specialized establishment in Turkey.

111 Donaldson and Kymlicka, in chapter 3 of their book, refer to Leslie P. Francis and Anita Silvers's 'Liberalism and Individuality Scripted Ideas of the Good: Meeting the Challenge of Dependent Agency', in *Social Theory and Practice* 33/2, 2007, pp. 311–34. In this paragraph we are instead drawing on Agnieszka Jaworska's 'Respecting the Margins of Agency: Alzheimer's Patients and the Capacity to Value', in *Philosophy and Public Affairs* 28/2, April 1999, pp. 105–38, already cited in Pelluchon, *L'Autonomie brisée*, pp. 67–9.

112 This practice is legal in Germany and Austria, including in the case of animals whose flesh will then be sold commercially, while killing on the farm is prohibited in France, except when the pig, for example is killed for personal consumption. The installation of a slaughterhouse at the farm and the possibility of calling for a butchering truck are however requested by a certain number of farmers who are concerned about the conditions of the animal's life and death.

113 Emmanuel Housset, *L'Intelligence de la pitié. Phénoménologie de la communauté*, Paris, Cerf, 'La nuit surveillée' 2003, pp. 43–53.

114 Ibid., p. 101.

115 Ibid.

116 Ibid., p. 109 and 111.

117 Émile Zola, 'L'amour des bêtes', in *Le Figaro*, 24 March 1896, republished in *Nouvelle campagne*, Paris, Bibliothèque-Charpenthier, 1987, pp. 87–97.

118 Ibid.

119 Literature testifies to this connection. See in particular the novels of Isaac Bashevis Singer, where we see former deportees or people suffering from Nazi persecution and racism, unable to bear that animals are being made to suffer, and adopting vegetarianism. See, among others, *Ennemis. Une histoire d'amour*, trans. G. Chahine, Paris, Stock, 1998, and the celebrated novella, 'The Letter Writer' (*The Collected Stories of Isaac Bashevis Singer*, New York, Farrar, Straus and Giroux, 1982), in which Hermann Gombiner, whose family was killed by the Nazis, develops affection for Huldah, a mouse that has moved into his home. After having been gravely ill, he becomes worried about Huldah, whom he could not feed. It is at this moment that, denouncing the complete asymmetry between human beings and animals, he pronounces this phrase that has become famous: 'For animals, it is an eternal Treblinka' (p. 271).

120 Emmanuel Levinas does not consider, in his writings, the animal as an 'Other'. The animal is not the object of our responsibility and neither is it responsible in the strong sense for us, even if, like the dog Bobby, 'the last Kantian in Nazi Germany', who barks when he sees the prisoners in the labour camp where Levinas was held coming back, it can be a witness to these beings who are still human. See 'Nom d'un chien ou le droit naturel', republished in *Difficult Freedom*, pp. 151–3. On the question of Levinas's relationship to the animal, see, among others, Tamra Wright, Peter Hughes, and Alison Ainley, 'The Paradox of Morality: An Interview with Emmanuel

Levinas', trans. A. Benjamin and T. Wright, in *The Provocation of Levinas*, ed R. Bernasconi and D. Wood, London, Routledge, 1988, p. 168–80.

121 Corine Pelluchon, *Tu ne tueras point. Réflexions sur l'actualité de l'interdit du meurtre*, Paris, Cerf, 'Passages', 2013, pp. 42–6, and 75–8.

122 Ibid., p. 85.

123 Here we distinguish the violence connected to industrial farming and slaughtering from homicide, without forgetting that there are certain human beings who rape animals and torture them in order to enjoy their domination over them.

124 Plutarch, 'The Eating of Flesh II', in *Moralia XII*, trans. H Cherniss and W. Helmbold, Cambridge, MA, Harvard, 1957, pp. 565–71.

125 Derrida, 'Eating Well', p. 280; *The Animal That Therefore I Am*, p. 104. See Patrick Llored, *Jacques Derrida. Politique et éthique de l'animalité*, Mons, Sils Maria, '5 concepts', 2013.

126 Leviticus 22, 43, commented by Moses Maimonides, *The Guide of the Perplexed*, trans. S. Pines, Chicago, Chicago, 1963, Book III, ch. 48, p. 599.

127 Gérard Charollois, *Pour en finir avec la chasse. La mort-loisir, un mal français*, Paris, Éditions IMHO, 'Essais', 2013, pp. 131–44.

128 The point is to revoke the paragraph 7 of Article 521 of the French Penal Code because this paragraph exonerates from penal responsibility the people who carry out these abuses on animals. In France, the *corrida* and cockfighting are considered exceptions, in certain places where an 'uninterrupted local tradition' is recognized, while the persons involved in these cruel games and those who torture their animals are considered as delinquents in 90 per cent of the territory.

129 Baratay, *Le Point de vue animal*, pp. 232–3.

130 Ibid.

131 These are the words of a person who practices ritual slaughter in Amandine Faynot's documentary, *Adak*.

Chapter 3

1 Aharon Appelfeld, *The Story of a Life*, trans. Aloma Halter, New York: Schocken Books, 2004, p. 104.

2 For an idea of the mental and physical disorders caused by hunger, see Knut Hamsun, *Hunger,* trans. Robert Bly, New York: Farrar, Straus and Giroux, 1998.

3 The FAO publishes this report, focused on *The State of Food Insecurity in the World,* with the International Fund for Agricultural Development and the World Food Program.

4 Jean Ziegler, *L'Empire de la honte,* Paris: Fayard, 2005, p. 127. The author refers to a survey in the Pela Porco neighbourhood of Salvador led by Mario do Soares de Freitas, a sociologist, and his associates at the Federal University of Bahia, in Brazil. It focused on understanding how starving individuals themselves feel about their situation. Shame, humiliation, and the feeling of being persecuted by hunger, sometimes called 'the thing' and conceptualized as separate from oneself, while it corrodes the body and obsesses the mind, stand out as defining elements of a situation in which individuals attempt to resist and escape, while rummaging through the trash and experiencing compensatory nocturnal visions, sometimes even hallucinations.

5 Kwashiorkor is a disease caused by an insufficient intake of calories and protein. It is characterized by the swelling of the abdomen and the extremities, hair and skin deterioration, and loss of teeth and muscles.

6 UNICEF and the World Bank, *Vitamin and Mineral Deficiency. A Global Assessment Report,* New York, Geneva, 2004.

7 It affects about 30 per cent of the world's population. Ziegler, *L'Empire de la honte,* pp. 128 and 118. Of the sixty-two million people who die each year in the world, thirty-six million die of hunger or diseases resulting from micronutrient deficiencies in 2003.

8 Jean Ziegler, *Droits économiques, sociaux et culturels. Le droit à l'alimentation,* United Nations Economic and Social Commission, 2001, p. 8 (http://www.droitshu-mains.org/alimentation/pdf/fev_01.pdf).

9 Amartya Sen and Jean Drèze, *Hunger and Public Action,* Oxford, Oxford University Press, 1989.

10 Amartya Sen, *Poverty and Famines. An Essay on Entitlement and Deprivation,* New York, Oxford University Press, 1981, chapter 6.

11 Thomas R. Malthus, *An Essay on the Principle of Population,* Oxford, Oxford University Press, 2008.

12 Amartya Sen, *Development as Freedom,* New York, Knopf, 1999, p 161.

13 In this context, we may take note of the change in recent years in how the United Nations approaches the global food crisis. See the reports by Olivier de Schutter, who has been the Special Rapporteur for the right to food at the United Nations Human Rights Council since May 2008, particularly the report of March 2014: (http://www.srfood.org/images/stories/pdf/officialreports/20140310_finalreport_fr.pdf; http://www.srfood.org/images/stories/pdf/officialreports/20140310_finalreport_en.pdf).

14 Ziegler, *L'Empire de la* honte, p. 245. We can add that hunger and debt benefit the 500 largest transcontinental capitalist corporations. These firms transfer stock profits to their headquarters. The currency reserves of a country's Central Bank, as in Brazil, are monitored by Nestlé. As for the other agrifood trusts, such as Aventis, Monsanto, Pioneer, or Syngenta, in 2004 they controlled a third of the global market in seeds. Each year they sell seeds to farmers, or the farmers must pay them a tax in order to have the right to collect the seeds that will be used the following year from the last harvest. This has led farmers indebted to local branches of these transcontinental corporations to suicide, as was the case in the state of Andhra Pradesh, in India, between 1998 and 2004.

15 Marcel Mazoyer, Laurence Roudart, *A History of World Agriculture: From the Neolithic Age to the Current Crisis,* trans. J. Membrez, New York, Monthly Review Press, 2006, pp. 492–4.

16 This is the case, for example in Mozambique.

17 Bruno Parmentier, *Nourrir l'humanité. Les grands problèmes de l'agriculture mondiale au XXIème siècle,* Paris: La Découverte, 'Cahiers libres', 2007, p. 185.

18 Marie-Anne Frison-Roche, *Les 100 mots de la régulation,* Paris: PUF, 'Que sais-je?', 2011.

19 Parmentier, *Nourrir l'humanité,* p. 201.

20 *Synhedrin 104 b,* Rabbi Yochanan, cited by Emmanuel Levinas in *Totality and Infinity,* p. 201.

21 This remark does not reduce the value of research assessing the malfunctions of certain neurotransmitters, which are molecules allowing the transfer of information between neurons, especially serotonin, which plays an important role in the control of feeding.

22 Michelle Le Barzic and Marianne Pouillon, *La Meilleure façon de manger. Les désarrois du mangeur moderne*, Paris: O. Jacob, 1998, pp. 172–3: 'The passage from incorporation to introjection is essential. Introjection takes place when the child experiments with the empty feeling in its mouth that is slow in filling itself with milk. The emptiness is then inhabited by cries that will make the mother appear: "Learn to fill the emptiness of your mouth with words, here is a first paradigm of introjection." With her ability to make her child wait without abandoning it, the "good enough" mother is the guarantor of this evolution. The waiting area is fed by its living presence and its vocal manifestations, and, "so the original emptiness will have found a remedy for all its lacks with the conversion to the relationship of language with the speaking community. Introjecting a desire, a pain, a situation, is making them pass through language to a communion of empty mouths"'. The quoted passages refer to the text by Nicolas Abraham and Maria Torok, 'Mourning *or* Melancholia: Introjection *versus* Incorporation', in *The Shell and the Kernel: Renewals of Psychoanalysis*, trans. N. Rand, Chicago: University of Chicago Press, 1994, pp. 125–38.

23 Jean-Daniel Lalau, *En finir avec les régimes: Vers une alliance du corps et de l'esprit,* Paris: Nouvelles François Bourin, 2012, pp. 9–10 and 114.

24 Ginette Raimbault and Caroline Eliacheff, *Les Indomptables. Figures de l'anorexie*, Paris: O. Jacob, 1980; Bernard Brusset, *Psychopathologie de l'anorexie mentale*, Paris: Dunod, 'Psychismes', 2008, p. 77; and *L'Assiette et le Miroir. L'anorexie mentale de l'enfant et de l'adolescent,* Toulouse: Privat SAS, 1991.

25 Le Barzic and Pouillon, *La Meilleure façon de manger.*, ch. 3, pp. 106–7, 111–17.

26 Ibid., pp. 34–5.

27 I would like to thank Jean-Daniel Lalau, physician and professor of nutrition at the Amiens Centre Hospitalier Universitaire, for allowing me to interview him on 24 January 2014.

28 Brusset, *Psychopathologie de l'anorexie mentale*, pp. 228–38.

29 Ibid., p. 52, Brusset writes that, during the war, there were still people with anorexia, but that when war was accompanied by food deprivation, anorexia disappeared.

30 Ibid., p. 179.

31 Similarly, surgery may help obese people who have failed to lose weight and who have diseases such as diabetes or hypertension but, without working on themselves and on their body image, without a change in their relationship with food and therefore with themselves, their bodies, the bodies of others, their impulses, the patient cannot succeed, and even when they have been operated and can no longer devour entire sandwiches, they may continue to eat baldly, absorbing sweet beverages and continuing to gain weight.

32 Ludwig Binswanger, *Introduction à l'analyse existentielle,* trans. J. Verdeaux and R. Kuhn, Paris: Minuit, 'Arguments', 1989. Some of the essays in *Introduction è l'analyse existentielle* may be found in English in Ludwig Binswanger, *Being-in-the-World. Selected Papers of Ludwig Binswanger,* trans. J. Needleman, New York, Basic, 1963.

33 Binswanger is discussed by Henri Maldiney in *Regard, parole, espace,* p. 137*sq.*

34 Ibid., p. 137. 'Behavior, conduct, words are a way of being in the world, a certain way of living. ... Their meaning is revealed in the *how.* ... Style responds to the how, like the meaning responds to the why'.

35 Lalau, *En finir avec les régimes,* pp. 251–7, 266–8.

36 Franz Kafka, *A Hunger Artist and Other Stories,* trans. Joyce Crick, Oxford; New York, Oxford University Press, 2012, pp. 56–65.

37 They can also be dependent on the effects of deprivation, which stimulates the secretion of hormones.

38 Evelyne Kestemberg, Jean Kestemberg, and Simone Decobert, *La Faim et le Corps. Une étude psychanalytique de l'anorexie mentale,* Paris: PUF, 1972.

39 Brusset, *Psychopathologie de l'anorexie mentale,* pp. 176–7. The author speaks of the organization of a 'false self'.

40 Jacques Maître, *Anorexies religieuses, anorexie mentale. Essai de psychanalyse sociohistorique (de Marie de l'Incarnation à Simone Weil),* Paris: Cerf, 'Sciences humaines et religions', 2000.

41 Kafka, '*A Hunger Artist*', p. 65.

42 These are the words of Laure, one of Professor Lalau's patients, citing pp. 229–30.

43 Lalau, *En finir avec les régimes,* pp. 228–9.

44 Ibid., p. 230.

45 Anorexic people, although very thin, always see themselves as too fat, even
if they can say of a woman walking down the street who is thin but 10
kilograms heavier than they are: 'She has a really nice figure.' Similarly, if we
take pictures of their arms, thighs, and waist, and we also photograph the
arms and thighs of another thin woman that fits the aesthetic criteria for an
anorexic (less than 50 kilograms for 1.65 metres), they would be surprised by
the difference between silhouettes. Anorexics do not see themselves as they
are and do not see at all the same image as we do in the mirror. Photography,
in this regard, is more instructional than the mirror and especially the
scale, since anorexics have a hard time with figures, a weight over 40 or 42
kilograms often being taboo.

46 Le Barzic and Pouillon, *La Meilleure façon de manger,* p. 103. We are not
talking about Roman practices that admittedly led to food orgies, but had
more to do with parties than with an illness.

47 Lalau stresses the contrast between, on the one hand, the facility of
expression of anorexic people, who often keep a journal during their
hospitalization and gladly volunteer for exercises allowing them to
describe what they feel, to work on their representations of themselves,
but also of food; and, on the other hand, the difficulties experienced
by bulimics and obese persons, whose expression is much less rich, as
if their relationship with themselves and others were buried under fat
deposits. We can add that nowadays, in industrialized countries, obesity
affects mainly the poor. Poor people with little access to education
necessarily have more difficulty expressing themselves orally or in writing
than others.

48 Charles Fourier, *Le Nouveau Monde amoureux*, Paris: Anthropos,
1967, pp. 126–7, 133; Charles Fourier, 'The New Amorous World', in
*The Utopian Vision of Charles Fourier. Selected Texts on Work, Love,
and Passionate Attraction*, trans. J. Beecher and R. Bienvenu, Boston,
Beacon Press, 1971. The opposition between harmonious wisdom,
which passes through fulfilment, and the culinary debauchery of Sade
is suggested by Noëlle Châtelet in *Le Corps à corps culinaire,* Paris:
Seuil, 1998, pp. 154–5.

Part Two

1 Rousseau, *The Social Contract, op. cit.*, p. 155.

Chapter 4

1 Hicham-Stéphane Afeissa, *La Fin du monde et de l'humanité. Essai de généalogie du discours écologique*, Paris: PUF, 'L'écologie en question', 2014, ch. 2. See Jonathan Schell, *The Fate of the Earth*, Stanford, CA, Stanford University Press, 2000, pp. 173, 116–18.

2 Michel Serres, *La Guerre mondiale*, Paris: Le Pommier, 'Essais et documents', 2008, pp. 137–9. It is about 'the war between everyone and the world ..., our whole kind to the global environment'.

3 Thomas Hobbes, *Leviathan: With Selected Variants from the Latin Edition of 1668*, Indianapolis, Hackett Pub. Co., 1994, ch. 17, pp. 106–10. Hobbes constantly opposes Aristotle by making a qualitative and not only quantitative distinction between the societies of gregarious animals and those of human communities, which can only be artificial or imposed. See Aristotle, *Politics*, I, 2, 1253 a-7-9, 18.

4 Epicurus, 'Principal Doctrines XXXIII', in *Principal Doctrines*, trans. R. Hicks, (http://classics.mit.edu/Epicurus/princdoc.html). 'There never was an absolute justice, but only an agreement made in reciprocal association in whatever localities now and again from time to time, providing against the infliction or suffering of harm'. See also Lucretius, *De natura rerum (On the Nature of Things)*, V, 925–1457, trans. A. Esolen, Baltimore, Johns Hopkins University Press, 1995.

5 Pelluchon, *Éléments pour une éthique de la vulnérabilité*, p. xx.

6 Virgil, *Aeneid*, XI, pp. 320–1. Cited by Rousseau, *The Social Contract*, p. 149.

7 Reduction, which is the phenomenological method implemented by Husserl, requires that we put our representations in parentheses, in order to describe the phenomena as they present to us. Those that we have described are not constituted by consciousness and refer to a phenomenology of non-constitution, as we have seen with food, habitation, and so forth.

8 David Hume, 'Of Civil Liberty', in *The Philosophical Works of David Hume*, vol. III, Edinburgh: Adam Black and William Tait, 1826, pp. 98–107.

9 Ibid.

10 Immanuel Kant, *On the Old Saw: That May Be Right in Theory, But It Won't Work in Practice*, trans. E. B. Ashton, Philadelphia, University of Pennsylvania Press, 1974, p. 65.

11 Jean Starobinski, *Jean-Jacques Rousseau. Transparency and Obstruction*, trans. A. Goldhammer, Chicago, University of Chicago Press, 1988, pp. 29–32. The following chapter will insist on the conditions of a transformation of democracy and will address the major problem of the social contract as posed by Rousseau: the circular argument that mores must change the laws and that the laws, at the same time, change the mores. This approach suggests that the second path (that of education), which also corresponds to the Kantian interpretation of Rousseau, is preferable to us. Note also that this circle assumes that we consider the moral dispositions needed in order to hold the promises attached to this political theory, and consequently that we introduce a virtue ethics. In any case, our purpose here is to reformulate the terms of the social contract, implying first of all that the use of this conceptual framework be justified.

12 Hobbes, *Leviathan*, ch. 13, pp. 74–9. See also *Human Nature and De Corpore Politico*, Oxford and New York, Oxford University Press, 1994, ch. 9, pp. 50–60 and ch. 14, pp. 77–81.

13 *Id.*, *Leviathan*, ch. 17, p. 106: 'And Covenants without the Sword, are but words, and of no strength to secure a man at all'.

14 As we already suggested in part one of *Éléments pour une éthique de la vulnérabilité*, our approach distinguishes itself from the solutions advocated by Hans Jonas, who speaks of 'benevolent tyranny' in *The Imperative of Responsibility: In Search of an Ethics for the Technological Age*, trans. H. Jonas and D. Herr, Chicago, University of Chicago Press, 1984.

15 Ibid., ch. 14, p. 83.

16 Ibid., ch. 13, p. 78.

17 Ibid., ch. 16, p. 101.

18 Ibid., ch. 17, p. 109.

19 Ibid., ch. 16, p. 104.

20 Ibid., ch. 17, p. 109.

21 Ibid., ch. 13, p. 76.

22 Ibid., ch. 21, pp. 138–9.

23 Rousseau, *The Social Contract*, Book II, p. 191.

24 Arne Næss, *Ecology, Community, and Lifestyle*, trans. D. Rothenberg, Cambridge and New York: Cambridge University Press, 1989, pp. 44–7.

25 John Locke, *Second Treatise of Government*, in *The Works of John Locke*, London: Thomas Tegg, W. Sharpe, and Son, 1823, ch. 2, § 6, pp. 9–10.

26 Ibid., ch. 11, § 137–138.

27 Ibid., ch. 2, § 5, § 12–13; ch. 9, § 123–127.

28 Ibid., ch. 8, § 95–99.

29 Ibid., ch. 13–14.

30 Ibid., ch. 19, § 211–217.

31 Ibid., ch. 19, § 218–222.

32 Ibid., ch. 19, § 224–225; § 230.

33 Ibid., ch. 15, § 171.

34 Ibid., ch. 5, § 25.

35 Ibid., ch. 5, § 28, § 44–46.

36 Ibid., ch. 5, § 30–31.

37 Ibid., ch. 5, § 34 and § 31.

38 Ibid., ch. 5, § 34.

39 Nozick, *Anarchy, State, and Utopia*.

40 Catherine Audard, *Qu'est-ce que le libéralisme? Éthique, politique, société*, Paris, Gallimard, 'Folio Essais', 2009, pp. 398–400. For Audard, ultraliberalism is a 'mystification' related to the 'construction of a "classical liberalism" that is a falsification of doctrines of Locke as well as of Adam Smith or John Stuart Mill'.

41 Rousseau, *The Social Contract*, Book I, ch. 6, pp. 163–4.

42 John Rawls, *Justice as Fairness: A Restatement*, ed. E. Kelly, Cambridge, MA, Belknap Press of Harvard University Press, 2001, p. 4.

43 The social contract assumes that laws are produced in such a way that they can be derived from the united will of the people, and this criterion measuring the legitimacy of a state gives a practical reality to this idea of reason, without the need to look for an event proving that this founding and inaugural act took place in the history of this people. See Kant, *On the Old Saw*, p. 65.

44 Rousseau, *The Social Contract*, Book II, ch. 8, pp. 183–85.

45 Ibid., Book II, ch. 12, pp. 191–2.

46 Ibid., Book IV, ch. 1, pp. 227–8.

47 Ibid., pp. 227–8.

48 Ibid., Book II, ch. 7, p. 182.

49 Ibid., Book IV, ch. 1, p. 228.

50 Ibid.

51 Ibid., Book I, ch. 6, p. 164.

52 John Dewey, *The Public and its Problems*, University Park, PA, Pennsylvania State University Press, 2012, pp. 74–5.

53 Ibid., ch. 4, pp. 101–19.

54 Rawls, *Justice as Fairness*, p. 34.

55 Gérald Hess, *Éthiques de la nature*, Paris, PUF, 'Éthique et philosophie morale', 2013, pp. 357–9. See Val Plumwood, *Environmental Culture: The Ecological Crisis of Reason*, London: Routledge, 2001.

56 In *Éléments pour une éthique de la vulnérabilité*, I attempted to build a rigorous concept of responsibility that can help us to respect other human beings, other living beings, and the environment, by showing that this responsibility is hyperbolic, not only as a consequence of the transformation of our capacities to act, including the power of our technique (Hans Jonas), but also because our responsibility exceeds our abilities of representation and identification, as when victims are too numerous to be represented (Günther Anders and the victims of Hiroshima) or they are not the object of our pity (ecosystems, trees, etc.).

57 In *Éthique de la consideration*, Paris, Seuil, L'Ordre philosophique, 2018, I developed a virtue ethics related to this philosophy of 'living from', allowing us to see how we can develop the sense of obligation linked to this new social contract.

58 Ricœur , *Soi-même comme un autre*, p. 236.

59 John Rawls, *A Theory of Justice*, Cambridge, MA, Belknap Press of Harvard University Press, 1971, p. 126.

60 Ibid., § 11–14.

61 Id., *Justice as Fairness*, pp. 42–3.

62 *Id.*, *A Theory of Justice*, pp. 136–42.

63 Ibid., p. 182.

64 Amartya Sen, *Rationality and Freedom*, Cambridge, MA, Belknap Press, 2002, p. 274.

65 Martha C. Nussbaum, *Frontiers of Justice. Disability, Nationality, Species Membership*, Cambridge, The Belknap Press of Harvard University Press, 2006.

66 Ibid., p. 205. See also Corine Pelluchon, *Éléments pour une éthique de la vulnérabilité*.

67 The Kantian version of the social contract, in contrast to Hobbes's version, implies that the just, even if instituted, corresponds to something objective or true in itself.

68 Mark Rowlands, *Animal Rights, Moral Theory and Practice*, New York, Palgrave Macmillan, 2009, pp. 131–62.

69 Rawls, *A Theory of Justice*, p. 505.

70 This statement goes further than Rawls and Kant would accept. The latter considers that we only have indirect duties towards animals, which means that cruelty towards animals is not bad in itself, but that it is unworthy of us and that it carries within it an extension to other human beings. See Immanuel Kant, *The Doctrine of Virtue*, in *The Metaphysics of Morals*, trans. M. Gregory, Cambridge, Cambridge University Press, 1991, pp. 237–8.

71 Rowlands, *Animal Rights*, pp. 155–8.

72 Levinas, *Of God Who Comes to Mind*, p. 172.

73 Rawls, *A Theory of Justice*, p. 568.

74 Ibid., § 44, pp. 287–8.

75 Axel Gosseries, 'Nations, Generations and Climate Justice', *Global Policy*, vol. 5, no. 1, February 2014, pp. 96–102.

76 Hannah Arendt, *The Human Condition*, Chicago, University of Chicago Press, 1998, p. 55.

77 Immanuel Kant, *Anthropology from a Pragmatic Point of View*, trans. R. Louden, Cambridge, Cambridge University Press, 2006, pp. 237–8.

78 This principle leads to not criminalizing prostitution between adults, for example. However, this argument has limitations, as seen with the example of prostitution. If some sex workers report having chosen to exchange sexual services for money, most of them were forced into prostitution and are struggling to get out of this system. Finally, this principle overrides induced preferences. Yet consent sometimes masks a sustained domination, the person wanting something or not wanting something else because they have internalized some representations of themselves which make them complexed or prevent them from having enough self-esteem.

79 Pelluchon, *L'Autonomie brisée*, Part I.

80 Ruwen Ogien, *Human Kindness and the Smell of Warm Croissants: An Introduction to Ethics,* New York, Columbia University Press, 2015.

81 Corine Pelluchon, 'Peut-on arriver à un consensus sur l'aide active à mourir?' published on 4 March 2014 on the *Terra Nova* website: http://tnova.fr/system/contents/files/000/000/232/original/03032014_-_Corine_Pelluchon.pdf?1432549176 The method for obtaining appropriate legislation for this problem, which goes beyond minimalist ethics and which refers to old oppositions that are explained in this text, is more important than the recommendations.

82 Compliance with directive 2010/63 of the European Parliament and of the Council of 22 September 2010, concerning the protection of animals used for scientific purposes, would already amount to a significant step.

Chapter 5

1 Montesquieu, *The Spirit of the Laws,* trans. T. Nugent, New York, Hafner, 1949, vol 2, Book 23, ch. 29, p. 25.

2 Quoted in Dominique Bourg (ed.), *Pour une 6e République écologique,* Paris: O. Jacob, 2011, p. 136.

3 See, for example, the Stockholm Declaration of 1972, adopted at the UN conference on the environment.

4 Thomas Piketty, *Capital in the Twenty-first Century,* Cambridge, MA, The Belknap Press of Harvard University Press, 2014.

5 Bourg (ed.), *Pour une 6e République écologique,* p. 61.

6 Ibid., p. 48.

7 Ibid., p. 53.

8 Ibid., p. 48.

9 CFCs are a subclass of fluorinated gases, which are among the halogenoalkanes. These are compound gases derived from alkanes where hydrogen atoms have been replaced by chlorine and fluorine atoms. First used in the 1930s as refrigerants, they were then exploited as a propellant for aerosols, as raw materials in the synthesis of organic compounds such as solvents, as extinguishers, and as expanding agents in plastic foams. They are responsible for the degradation of the ozone that protects the earth at high altitudes (the stratosphere) and absorb high-energy ultraviolet radiation, thus contributing to the greenhouse effect. In 1987 in Montreal, the main producers of CFCs and halons decided to stop production. Since October 2000, in Europe, CFCs are longer permitted to be placed on the market.

10 Bourg (ed.), *Pour une 6e République écologique*, pp. 57–60.

11 Thomas F. Stocker, 'The Closing Door of Climate Targets', *Science*, vol. 339, 18 January 2013, pp. 280–2.

12 Pierre Rosanvallon, 'Le souci du long terme', in Dominique Bourg and Alain Papaux, *Vers une société sobre et désirable*, Paris: PUF, 'Développement durable et innovation institutionelle', 2010. Bourg (ed.), *Pour une 6e République écologique*, pp. 165–74.

13 Yves Charles Zarka, *Inappropriability of the Earth*, Mimesis Edizioni, 2016.

14 Bourg (ed.), *Pour une 6e République écologique*, pp. 175–9.

15 Regarding the agencies to which certain bioethics issues are entrusted, we might think here of the Agency of Biomedicine, which decides on the possibility of removing organs from patients eligible for Maastricht III, meaning that they are not brain-dead but have been the subject of a decision to cease curative treatment.

16 Here, it is important to distinguish science from expertise in order to understand what the status of the members of this college, appointed on an interim basis, would be. Experts are scientists or individuals whose skills in a field are recognized by different academic or research institutions, national or international. If the objective of expertise is impartiality, it nonetheless requires that power relationships and political issues be more important than when it is only a matter of debate between scientists working on the same subject. This is even clearer when the report to be

delivered is based on works from different disciplines using different methodologies and tools of analysis, with the objective of highlighting various aspects of the same phenomenon. By becoming experts, scientists endorse other subjects than those that they deal with in their laboratories. Corine Pelluchon, 'Penser la place de l'expertise et de la délibération éthique dans la politique. Réflexions sur les conditions d'une plus grande innovation en matière d'action environnementale et en bioéthique', in Thierry Martin (ed.), *Éthique de la recherche et risques humains,* Besançon: Presses Universitaires de Franche-Comté, 'Les Cahiers de la MSH Ledoux', 2014, pp. 85–101. It is also essential to prohibit the plurality of offices and to sanction – with pay cuts, and with eviction – the absenteeism of elected officials, whether nationally, locally, or at the European level.

17 These remarks also assume that the head of state has a certain charisma, as democracy does not exclude all types of charisma, but may, on the contrary, need it, as explained by Jean-Claude Monod (see, *Qu'est-ce qu'un chef en démocratie? Politiques du charisme,* Paris: Seuil, 'L'Ordre philosophique', 2012).

18 The notion of deliberative democracy appeared for the first time in Joseph M. Bessette, 'Deliberative Democracy: The Majority Principle in Republican Government', in Robert A. Goddin and William A. Schambra (dir.), *How Democratic Is the Constitution?,* Washington, DC. AEIPPR, pp. 102–16. The major works include James Bohman, *Public Deliberation. Pluralism, Complexity, and Democracy,* Cambridge, MA, MIT Press, 1996; John S. Dryzek, *Deliberative Democracy and Beyond: Liberals, Critics, Contestations,* New York, Oxford University Press, 2000; Jon Elster (ed.), *Deliberative Democracy,* Cambridge, Cambridge University Press, 1998; James S. Fishkin, *Democracy and Deliberation,* New Haven, Yale University Press, 1995; *The Voice of the People: Public Opinion and Democracy,* New Haven, Yale University Press, 1995; *When the People Speak: Deliberative Democracy and Public Consultation,* Oxford, Oxford University Press, 2009; Amy Gutmann and Denis Thompson, *Democracy and Disagreement,* Cambridge, MA, Harvard University Press, 1999; *Why Deliberative Democracy?* Princeton, Princeton University Press, 2004. See also Bruce Ackerman, Simone Chambers, Joshua Cohen, Robert Goodin, Jane Mansbridge. In France, the works of Loïc Blondiaux, Yves Sintomer, and Marie-Hélène Bacqué that deal with participatory democracy are authoritative. The major texts of Habermas to which we refer are *The Structural Transformation of the Public Sphere: An Inquiry into a Category of Bourgeois Society,* trans. T. Burger, Cambridge, MA, MIT Press, 1989; and *Between Facts and Norms: Contributions to a Discourse Theory of Law and Democracy,* trans. W. Rehg, Cambridge, MA, MIT Press, 1996. See

also Rawls, *Theory of Justice,* and *Political Liberalism,* New York, Columbia University Press, 1993.

19 Fishkin, *The Voice of the People,* p. 89 and 162.

20 Jon Elster, 'Arguing and Bargaining in Two Constituent Assemblies', *University of Pennsylvania Journal of Constitutional Law,* vol. 2, no. 2, March 2000, pp. 345–421.

21 Simone Chambers, 'Rhetoric and the Public Sphere: Has Deliberative Democracy Abandoned Mass Democracy?', *Political Theory,* vol. 37, no. 3, June 2009, pp. 323–50.

22 'Vers un système délibératif mondial?' interview with John Dryzek conducted by C. Girard, J. Talpin, and S. Topçu, *Participations,* no. 2, 2012/1, pp. 168–80.

23 Yves Sintomer, 'Délibération et participation: affinité élective ou concepts en tension?' in *Participations,* no. 1, 2011/1, pp. 253–4.

24 Yves Sintomer, 'La démocratie délibérative, de Jürgen Habermas à la théorie politique anglo-saxonne', in Marie Frédérique Bacqué and Yves Sintomer (dir.), *La Démocratie participative. Histoire et généalogie,* Paris, La Découverte, 'Recherches', p. 124.

25 'Public sphere' (*Öffentlichkeit*) designates the public use of reason and the fact of making a debate public. As in Habermas, it refers to the public space and the public in the sense of *Publikum* in German or *public* in French.

26 Ibid.

27 Émile Benvéniste, 'Les deux modèles de la cité', in Jean Pouillon and Pierre Maranda *Échanges et communications. Mélanges offerts à Claude Lévi-Strauss,* Mouton, 1970, pp. 589–96.

28 In 2004, a citizens' assembly constituted of randomly chosen members was responsible for elaborating a reform proposal for the voting system, which was submitted the following year to a referendum, then rejected by the population. See Gordon Gibson, 'L'Assemblée citoyenne de Colombie Britannique', in Yves Sintomer (dir.), 'La Démocratie participative', *Problèmes politiques et sociaux,* Paris, Documentation française, no. 959, April 2009, pp. 62–3.

29 Nancy Fraser, 'Rethinking the Public Sphere: A Contribution to the Critique of Actually Existing Democracy', *Social Text,* no. 25/26, Duke University Press, 1990, pp. 56–80.

30 Alexis de Tocqueville, *Democracy in America*, trans. Arthur Goldhammer, New York, The Library of America, 2004, Book I, Part II, Ch 8 p. 316.

31 Ibid., Part II, ch. 2, p. 585.

32 Ibid., Part II, ch. 14, p. 630.

33 Carsten Herzberg, Anja Röcke, and Yves Sintomer. *Les Budgets participatifs en Europe. Des services publics au service du public*, Paris, La Découverte, 'Recherches', 2008. In France, in addition to district councils, there are other participatory bodies connected to the National Commission for Public Debate.

34 This has led to the departure of Gray Davis and the election of Arnold Schwarzenegger.

35 Dirk-Jan Verdonk, 'Mutualiser les ressources? La coalition pour les animaux: l'expérience des Pays-Bas', *Revue semestrielle de droit animalier*, pp. 411–25. In Austria, the VGT (*Verein Gegen Tierfabriken*), which is abolitionist, has managed to rally behind it the majority of abolitionist and welfare associations, although these two types of associations are aimed at different complementary objectives – the latter is able to dialogue with power, whereas the former ensures that compromises do not deform the struggle.

36 Habermas, *The Public Sphere*, p. 164.

37 Ibid., p. 164.

38 Diego Gambetta, '"Claro!": An Essay on Discursive Machism', in Jon Elster (ed.), *Deliberative Democracy*, pp. 19–43.

39 Ibid., p. 24.

40 Ibid.

41 Ibid., p. 29.

42 Ibid., p. 34.

43 Ibid., pp. 37–41.

44 Ibid., p. 41.

45 Michel Foucault, *Dits et écrits*, vol. I, Paris, Gallimard, 'Quarto', 2001, p. 1665.

46 Thierry Paquot, *L'Espace public*, Paris, La Découverte, 'Repères', 2009, pp. 41–5.

47 Ibid., pp. 37–41.

48 Count Roederer's quote is found in Roger Picard, *Les Salons littéraires et la société française. 1610-1789*, Paris, Brentanos, 1943, p. 39, given in an excerpt in Paquot, *L'Espace public*, p. 39.

49 Montesquieu, *The Spirit of the Laws*, vol. 1, Book 1, ch. 2 p. 4.

Chapter 6

1 Rousseau conceived it in 1743 and made an outline for it, but this treatise never appeared.

2 Rousseau, *The Social Contract*, p. 254.

3 Id., *Emile or On Education*, Introduction, Translation, and Notes by Allan Bloom, New York, Basic Books, 1979, Book I, p. 39: 'Distrust those cosmopolitans who go to great length in their books to discover duties they do not deign to fulfill around them. A philosopher loves the Tartars so as to be spared having to love his neighbors.'

4 Immanuel Kant, *Political Writings*, 2nd ed., trans. H. B. Nisbet, Cambridge, U.K, Cambridge University Press, 1991, p. 100.

5 Schell, *Le Destin de la terre*, p. 214; Schell, *The Fate of the Earth*, p. 191.

6 This will be at the heart of the Habermasian critique of Kant's project. Jürgen Habermas, 'Kant's Idea of Perpetual Peace: At Two Hundred Years' Historical Remove', in *The Inclusion of the Other: Studies in Political Theory*, trans. C. Cronin, Cambridge, MA, MIT Press, 1998, pp. 165–201.

7 For the distinction between earth, planet, and world, see Michel Lussault, *L'Avènement du monde. Essai sur l'habitation humaine de la terre*, Paris, Seuil, 'La couleur des idées', 2013. 'Planet' refers to the biological and physical systems that constitute nature in the sense of the sciences of life and of matter (ecosystems, biotic communities, and their abiotic milieus, living beings, and among these human beings), while the earth is the planet occupied by human beings and culturally invested by them. The world, finally, is the ensemble that is constructed by human activities, of which the earth and the planet are the conditions of possibility.

8 We are adopting from Jonathan Schell the expression 'nuclear holocaust' (*The Fate of the Earth*, p. 191), which signifies that to speak of 'nuclear war' is an abuse of language, as such war implies self-destruction, above all today, when the destructive power of existing bombs is infinitely superior to that of the bombs that were dropped on Hiroshima and Nagasaki.

9 Ibid., pp. 117–18.

10 Ibid., p. 122, 173.

11 Ibid., p. 154.

12 Ibid., p. 175.

13 Karl Jaspers, *The Atom Bomb and the Future of Man*, trans. E. B. Ashton, Chicago, University of Chicago Press, 1963, p. 10.

14 Michel de Montaigne, *Apology for Raymond Sebond*, trans. R. Ariew and M. Grene, Indianapolis, Hackett, 2003, p. 136.

15 Speech delivered to the House of Commons, 1 March 1955: 'Safety will be the sturdy child of terror, and survival the twin brother of annihilation'. Winston S. Churchill, *His Complete Speeches (1897-1963)*, ed. R. Rhodes James, New York, R. R. Broker, 1974, pp. 8629–30.

16 Schell, *Le Destin de la terre*, p. 175.

17 Jost Delbrück, 'Die Auseinandersetzungen über das ethische Problem der atomaren Kriegführung in den Vereinigten Staaten und der Bundesrepublik Deutschland', in *Abschreckung und Entspannung*, Veröffentlichungen des Instituts für Internationales Recht an der Universität Kiel, Berlin, Duncker & Humblot, 1977, pp. 95–147. See Karl Barth, *Les Cahiers du renouveau*, vol. V, *La Guerre et la Paix*, trans. J. de Senardens, Geneva, Labor et Fides, 1951, p. 11. Cited by Pierre Hassner, *Violence and Peace: From the Atomic Bomb to Ethnic Cleansing*, Budapest, Central European University Press, 1997, p. 120.

18 The expressions in quotation marks refer back to Winston Churchill's speech of 1 March 1955 (*His Complete Speeches*, pp. 8629–30).

19 Ulrich Beck, *The Cosmopolitan Vision*, Cambridge, U.K, Polity, 2006, pp. 24–33.

20 Ibid., p. 95.

21 Hannah Arendt, *Men in Dark Times*, New York, Harcourt, Brace & World, 1968, pp. 83–4.

22 Beck, *Power in the Global Age*, pp. 282–4.

23 Id., 'Le nouveau visage du cosmopolitisme', texts collected by C. Halpern, *Sciences humaines*, No. 176, November 2006.

24 Louis Lourme, *Le Nouvel Âge de la citoyenneté mondiale*, Paris, PUF, 2014, pp. 57–68.

25 Diogenes Laërtius, *Lives and Opinions of the Eminent Philosophers*, VI, 63.

26 Beck, *Power in the Global Age*, pp. 66–7.

27 Arnold Wolfers, 'The Actors in International Politics', in *Discord and Collaboration*, Baltimore, The Johns Hopkins University Press, 1962, p. 19, sq. Cited by Lourme, *Le Nouvel Âge de la citoyenneté mondiale*, p. 61.

28 Beck, *Power in the Global Age*, p. 67.

29 Kant, *The Doctrine of Right*, in *The Metaphysics of Morals, Power in the Global Age*, pp. 158–9; Kant, *Political Writings*, pp. 105–8.

30 Yves Charles Zarka, *Refonder le cosmopolitisme*, Paris, PUF, 'Intervention philosophique', 2014, p. 25.

31 Michel Foucault, *The Government of the Self and Others: Lectures at the Collège de France 1982-1983*, trans. G. Burchell, Palgrave Macmillan, 2010, pp. 18–19. See Kant, *Political Writings*, p. 184.

32 Habermas, 'Kant's Idea of Perpetual Peace', p. 169.

33 Ibid., p. 192.

34 John Dryzek, Richard B. Norgaard, David Schlosberg, *Climate-Challenged Society*, Oxford, Oxford University Press, 2013.

35 Kant, *Political Writings*, pp. 177–81.

36 Ibid., *The Metaphysics of Morals*, p. 160.

37 Ibid.

38 Since the first decade of the twenty-first century, transition towns are emerging that implicate individuals and the community, working together on their capacity to overcome the economic and ecological crises of towns confronted by the challenges represented by peak oil and climate disorder. The originality of this movement is that it also integrates an investigation of the psychological and existential consequences of these crises.

39 Lourme, *Le Nouvel Âge de la citoyenneté mondiale*, p. 110.

40 Habermas, *Between Facts and Norms*, p. 367.

41 Daniele Archibugi, *The Global Commonwealth of Citizens. Towards Cosmopolitan Democracy*, Princeton, Princeton University Press, 2008.

42 David Held, *Global Covenant: The Social Democratic Alternative to the Washington Consensus*, Cambridge, UK, Polity, 2004.

43 Cornelius Castoriadis, *The Imaginary Institution of Society*, trans. K. Blamey, Cambridge, UK, Polity, 1987, p. 117.

44 Ibid., 127.

45 Ibid., pp. 156–7.

46 Ibid., pp. 107–8.

47 Paul Ricœur, *Lectures on Ideology and Utopia*, ed. G. Taylor, New York, Columbia University Press, 1986, p. 311.

48 Ricœur, *Lectures on Ideology and Utopia*, pp. 299–300.

49 Ibid., pp. 312–14.

50 Ibid., p. 219.

51 Ibid., pp. 251–2.

52 Michaël Foessel, *Après la fin du monde*, Paris, Seuil, 'L'Ordre philosophique', 2012, pp. 65–71, 275–81.

Conclusion

1 François Furet, *The Passing of an Illusion: The Idea of Communism in the Twentieth Century*, trans. D. Furet, Chicago, University of Chicago Press, 1999, p. 502.

2 Furet, *The Passing of an Illusion*.

3 Ibid.

4 Bertrand Russell, 'The World as It Could Be Made', in *Proposed Roads to Freedom*, New York, Henry Holt, 1919, pp. 211–12.

5 Paul Éluard, 'The Last Night', in *Paul Éluard. Selected Poems*, trans. G. Bowen, New York, Riverrun Press, 1987, pp. 66–72.

6 For Spinoza, who disputes Hobbes's idea that a promise obtained under duress and threat could be valid, the pact is always concluded in a situation of duress or of terror and danger. This diminishes its relevance. See Baruch Spinoza, *Political Treatise*, the *Collected Works of Spinoza*, ed. E. Curley,

Princeton, Princeton University Press, 2016, pp. 503–604. See also Carole Pateman's book, *The Sexual Contract*, Stanford, Stanford University Press, 1988.

7   André Gide, *The Fruits of the Earth*, trans. D. Bussy, New York, Alfred A. Knopf, 1949, p. 3. '*The Fruits of the Earth* is the work of a man who, if not actually ill, was recovering, or had recently recovered, from illness, of a man, who had been ill. In its poetry there is the exuberance of someone to whom life is precious because he has been on the verge of losing it'.

8   Ibid., p. 16.

Index